A HISTORY OF NORTHERN IRELAND
1920–1996

A History of Northern Ireland

1920–1996

THOMAS HENNESSEY

GILL & MACMILLAN

Gill & Macmillan Ltd
Goldenbridge
Dublin 8
with associated companies throughout the world
© Thomas Hennessey 1997
0 7171 2623 4 hard cover
0 7171 2400 2 paperback
Index compiled by Helen Litton
Print origination by *Deirdre's Desktop*
Printed by ColourBooks Ltd, Dublin

A catalogue record for this book is
available from the British Library.

1 3 5 4 2

For my father,
Edward John Hennessey

Contents

Preface

The aim of this book is to provide the reader with a history of Northern Ireland that conveys this through the perceptions of the actors involved. If there is a central theme it is that many of the events chronicled, whatever the intended goal of a particular policy, were interpreted by unionists and nationalists according to their particular world views. This applied to economic, social, cultural or political policies and decisions. To illustrate this, much of the story that follows observes the reactions of unionists and nationalists to the same events and their differing interpretations of these.

No one participant in the Northern Ireland situation is solely responsible for the collapse of Northern Ireland into communal strife. All have made their own contributions, often oblivious to the ways in which their sincerely held perceptions have contributed to the instability of the province: successive British Governments in their neglect and inaction in the years of Stormont rule; successive Irish Governments and generations of nationalists for the denial of unionists' Britishness and the focusing on British Governments as the agents for ending partition; and unionists for their continuing perception of all of the Catholic minority as an 'enemy within', whose Irishness was to be subsumed within the Protestant and British part of the country.

Yet there have been changes, and movement within unionist and nationalist perceptions, although this is a long and slow process, given that, despite over a century of overt and subterranean conflict, there has rarely, apart from the 1991–92 talks process, been a substantial exchange of ideas and discussion of the nature of the problem, possibly since the Irish Convention of 1918. It is clear that throughout the history of Northern Ireland, unionists and nationalists have not respected the sense of belonging that the Other has seen as central to its own definition of its identity. Many of the myths that governed the perceptions of unionists and nationalists when the state was founded persist today.

Acknowledgments

Much of my research has been carried out in various archives and libraries, but I would especially like to thank the staff of the following institutions for assistance: the Public Record Office of Northern Ireland; the Main Library at Queen's University, Belfast; the Political Collection at the Linen Hall Library; and the Newspaper Library at the Central Library, Belfast. Over the years I have incurred many debts to a great many individuals. I wish to record my thanks to Professor Paul Bew, Dr Richard English, Professor David Harkness, Dr David Hayton, Dr Alvin Jackson, Dr Brian Walker, and Mr Robin Wilson. Any faults in the book are entirely my own.

Abbreviations

AOH	Ancient Order of Hibernians
APL	Anti-Partition League
ASU	active service unit
CCRU	Central Community Relations Unit
CDU	Campaign for Democracy in Ulster
CLMC	Combined Loyalist Military Command
CSJ	Campaign for Social Justice
DCAC	Derry Citizens' Action Committee
DUP	Ulster Democratic Unionist Party
EMU	Education for Mutual Understanding
FEC	Fair Employment Commission
HCL	Homeless Citizens' League
IDB	Industrial Development Board
INLA	Irish National Liberation Army
IRA	Irish Republican Army
IRSP	Irish Republican Socialist Party
LEDU	Local Enterprise Development Unit
NICRA	Northern Ireland Civil Rights Association
NICRC	Northern Ireland Community Relations Council
NICS	Northern Ireland Civil Service
NIDA	Northern Ireland Development Agency
NIFC	Northern Ireland Finance Corporation
NILP	Northern Ireland Labour Party
NIO	Northern Ireland Office
PD	People's Democracy
RIC	Royal Irish Constabulary
RIR	Royal Irish Regiment
RUC	Royal Ulster Constabulary
SAS	Special Air Service
SDLP	Social Democratic and Labour Party
SPA	Civil Authority (Special Powers) Act, 1922
UCDC	Ulster Constitution Defence Committee
UDA	Ulster Defence Association
UDR	Ulster Defence Regiment
UFF	Ulster Freedom Fighters
ULDP	Ulster Loyalist Democratic Party
UPNI	Unionist Party of Northern Ireland
UPV	Ulster Protestant Volunteers

USC   Ulster Special Constabulary
UUC   Ulster Unionist Council
UUP   Ulster Unionist Party
UUUC   United Ulster Unionist Council/Coalition
UVF   Ulster Volunteer Force
UWC   Ulster Workers' Council

A Note on Terminology

In the text the terms Unionist, Nationalist, Loyalist and Republican are capitalised to denote parties or organisations of these names and their members; without capitals they refer to supporters of these organisations or the wider community. Terms such as Ulster and Londonderry, used predominantly by unionists, and Six Counties and Derry, used mainly by nationalists, in referring to Northern Ireland and its second city reflect the differing political and cultural perceptions the two communities hold on the same geographical entities. Although not all Protestants are unionists and not all Catholics are nationalists, it is a commonly held perception, even in Northern Ireland, that religious belief corresponds to political allegiance. These terms are used in the text as they are employed by a particular individual or organisation whose perception, more often than not, merges political allegiance with group membership.

1

The Birth of Northern Ireland

1912–1928

The older and deeper roots of conflict in what was to become Northern
Ireland lie in the seventeenth-century plantation of the northern
province of Ulster. English and Scottish Protestants colonised land in
Ulster previously held by the Catholic 'Old English' and Irish natives.
As national and religious differences between Protestants and Roman
Catholics remained prominent in the following centuries, new political
philosophies crystallised among Ulster's inhabitants. By the late
nineteenth century there was a new divide, that between nationalists,
who wanted self-government for Ireland—which had been absorbed
into the United Kingdom of Great Britain and Ireland in 1801—and
unionists, who wished Ireland to remain part of the United Kingdom.
This division was widely considered by contemporaries to occur along
religious lines, with the former predominantly Catholic and the latter
Protestant. Numerically, by 1911 there were in Ulster 890,880
Protestants out of a population of 1,581,969; in the three other
provinces there were only 256,699 Protestants, scattered among
2,551,854 Catholics.[1]

The immediate origins of Northern Ireland lay in the upheavals of
the Home Rule crisis of 1912–14 and the First World War. In 1886 and
1893 two Home Rule Bills, to establish a devolved Irish parliament
within the United Kingdom, had been defeated in the Imperial
Parliament at London, which represented the whole of the United
Kingdom, and it was not until 1910 that the possibility of Home Rule
returned. Following the British general election of 1910 Herbert
Asquith's Liberal Government relied on the support of John Redmond's
Irish Party to secure a majority in the House of Commons. After the
passing of the Parliament Act, 1911, which restricted the power of the
House of Lords to reject legislation passed by the House of Commons,
a power previously used to block Home Rule, it appeared that the final
obstacle to Home Rule had been removed. It then became clear that
the 'Irish question' was in fact two questions: nationalist Ireland's

relationship with the rest of the United Kingdom, and Protestant Ulster's relationship with Catholic Ireland.

The nationalists of the Irish Party believed that the distinctiveness of the whole of Ireland meant that it was a 'homeland', a discrete national entity.[2] Nationalists argued that the political Irish nation was co-extensive with the geographical island of Ireland and rejected the argument that Irish Protestants might form a separate nation within Ireland.

In Ulster the Irish Party was led by Joseph Devlin. He was born in 1872 into a west Belfast working-class family and rose from humble beginnings as a potboy in a public house to become a Home Rule MP and finally, in 1903, holder of the key post of general secretary of the United Irish League, the main organisation of the Irish Party. From 1904 until 1916 Devlin dominated nationalist politics in Ulster. His political rise was closely associated with the revival of the Ancient Order of Hibernians, a Catholic secret society, which he converted into a personal power base within the Home Rule movement after 1905. The AOH saw its role as protecting the Catholic faith and population in Ireland. In 1905 Devlin established the Board of Erin as the controlling council of the AOH, with himself as president, a post he retained until his death in 1934. The attraction of the AOH was partly increased by the National Insurance Act, 1911, which registered the organisation as a friendly society, so that by 1915, with 122,000 members, it formed the grass roots of the Irish Party in Ulster.[3]

Unionists, and in particular those in Ulster, were violently opposed to Home Rule. The focus of opposition was the Irish Unionist Party, led by Sir Edward Carson. Carson, born in Dublin in 1854, was a member of the Church of Ireland and educated at Trinity College, Dublin, after which his main career was in law. From 1910 to 1921 he was leader of the Irish Unionist Party, when he spearheaded the anti-Home Rule campaign. In this he worked closely with James Craig. A Presbyterian, Craig had pursued a career in stockbroking, in the British army, serving as a captain in the Boer War, and finally as an MP, first entering Parliament for East Down in 1906 and ultimately becoming the first Prime Minister of Northern Ireland in 1921, which he remained until his death in 1940.[4]

Both Carson and Craig were members of the Orange Order, the largest mass Protestant organisation in Ulster. The order was formed in 1795 in County Armagh after a clash between Protestants and Catholics at the 'Battle of the Diamond'. Its annual Twelfth of July celebrations recall the victory of the Protestant King William III over the Catholic King James II at the Battle of the Boyne in 1690 as the point where religious and civil liberty was guaranteed under the British constitution. The effective founding of the Unionist Party was a meeting of seven Orangemen who were MPs at Westminster in 1886.

Unionists feared that a Home Rule parliament would preside over a confessional Catholic state. Catholicism and Presbyterianism, the largest Protestant denomination in Ulster, represented an ideological schism within Christianity of fundamental proportions. The sacramental role of the priest was seen by Presbyterians as hindering the right of individuals to approach God directly through his teachings in the Bible, and the institutional Catholic Church was perceived as wishing to control access to religious knowledge and exerting a powerful influence over political and social institutions within society.[5] The pronouncement in 1908 of the Papal decree *Ne Temere*, which declared that mixed Protestant-Catholic marriages not celebrated before a Catholic priest were invalid, added to these anxieties.

Ulster unionists also saw Home Rule as a threat to their Britishness and feared that the establishment of Irish self-government would lead ultimately to an Irish republic. Many unionists at that time thought of themselves as both Irish and British and, like the Scots or Welsh, saw no contradiction in this. They saw Home Rule as a dilution of their Britishness and of their part in a British nation that stretched throughout the globe in the form of the British Empire. For unionists it was the geographical unit of the 'British Isles', not Ireland, that constituted their political nation.[6]

Unionists believed that to preserve their membership of the British nation they had a right to threaten loyalist rebellion. In 1912 Carson had defined the unionist duty, as citizens, as to obey the law; but there was also a correlative government duty not to tamper with the rights of citizenship, for the subversion of political status was not government but revolution, as would be the case if a Home Rule parliament were established. Thus Carson declared that 'if it be treason to love your King, to try to save your Constitution, to preserve your birthright, and your civil and religious liberty, then I glory in being a traitor.' He argued that it was no answer to say to unionists, 'You are all Irishmen, go and live together with Nationalists': it was absurd, he said, because 'we consider that we are satisfied that we are one nationality with Great Britain, and we are satisfied to be.'[7] Unionists denied that nationalists had a right to even call Ireland a nation. Asking 'What constitutes a nation?' the Belfast *News Letter* argued that if Ireland were to be allowed to self-determine itself out of the United Kingdom, then why should Ulster not self-determine itself out of Ireland? Ireland, it was claimed, had not got the right to become independent, because it was not a nation but a part of a nation, the British nation.[8]

With these radically different interpretations of the Irish question, as the third Home Rule Bill made its passage through Parliament, Ulster Unionists formed themselves in 1911 into an armed militia, the Ulster Volunteer Force, whose membership was estimated by 1912 to be 100,000. The Ulster Unionist Council, which had been created in 1905 as a focus for a more effective voice for opposition to Home Rule, provided the central structures of unionist defiance and a quasi-democratic authority. Plans for a provisional government, should Home Rule come into force, were laid down and endorsed at a meeting of the UUC in September 1912; a more detailed scheme of resistance was approved in September 1913. From late 1910 and early 1911 the UUC helped import weapons into Ireland.[9]

Just as it appeared that Ireland might be sucked into civil war, the maelstrom of the Great War interrupted the domestic politics of the United Kingdom. The war radically altered the dimensions of the Irish question. At its beginning nationalism was represented by a political movement committed to securing self-government within the United Kingdom; by the end of the war the Irish Party had been swept away in the 1918 general election by Sinn Féin, which sought an Irish republic. The mood of nationalist Ireland had been altered by the Easter Rising of 1916 and by the belief that the Home Rule Act, 1914—which was passed into law at the beginning of the war but suspended for its duration—was not to be implemented. For Ulster unionists, on the other hand, the war confirmed their worst fears of nationalist disloyalty, in contrast to their own sacrifice for king and country, particularly in the slaughter of the 36th (Ulster) Division at the Battle of the Somme in July 1916.

The last realistic attempt to settle the Irish question during the war was the Irish Convention, which sat from July 1917 until March 1918 but failed to reach agreement on the questions of Ulster and the financial powers of the proposed Irish parliament.[10]

THE GOVERNMENT OF IRELAND ACT, 1920

In 1918, as the Great War drew to a close, the British Government once more attempted to settle the Irish question by framing a fourth Home Rule scheme for Ireland. The Government of Ireland Act, 1914, was due to come into operation automatically on the ratification of peace between the Great Powers. Politically it was deemed impossible for the British Government to repeal the Act, but now neither Nationalists nor Unionists found it acceptable. To find a solution to this problem the Government set up a committee, under the direction of a former leader of the Irish Unionist Party, Walter Long, to produce a new scheme of self-government for Ireland. Long's committee saw the proposed institutions of self-government in Ireland as part of a general scheme of devolved parliaments for England, Scotland, and Ireland, with an overall United Kingdom parliament concerned with imperial and foreign affairs. He found that Ulster Unionists would only accept a Home Rule scheme for Ireland if the country were partitioned and at least six of the nine counties of Ulster remained outside the jurisdiction of an Irish parliament. Long reasoned that a nine-county Ulster parliament should be established alongside a parliament for the remaining twenty-three counties, so that it would be more likely to produce a united Ireland and a federated United Kingdom.[11]

When he travelled to Ulster in 1920, Long found that Unionists were most interested in what the boundaries of any partitioned 'Ulster' would be. He recorded that Ulster Unionists held the view that the new 'province' should consist of the six counties of Armagh, Antrim, Londonderry, Down, Fermanagh, and Tyrone. The Unionist MP Captain Charles Craig explained to the House of Commons that Ulster Unionists, in accepting a six-county parliament of their own, had come to the conclusion that

> we have many enemies in this country [Britain] and we feel that an Ulster without a Parliament of its own would not be in nearly a strong position as one in which a Parliament which had been set up where the Executive had been appointed and where above all the paraphernalia of Government was already in existence. We believe that as long as we were without a Parliament of our own constant attacks would be made upon us ... to draw us into a Dublin Parliament, and that is the last thing in the world that we desire to see happen ... We see our safety ... in having a Parliament of our own, for we believe that once a Parliament is set up and working well ... we should fear no one, and we feel we would then be in a position of absolute security ...

Craig explained that Ulster Unionists had deliberately selected six counties, rather than the nine counties of the entire province of Ulster, to constitute the new jurisdiction because of their fear that if there were a nine-county Ulster parliament, with sixty-four MPs, the Unionist majority would be in the region of three or four, whereas in a six-county parliament, with fifty-two members, the projected Unionist majority would be ten. The three excluded counties—Cavan, Monaghan, and Donegal—contained some '70,000 Unionists' and '260,000 Nationalists', and the addition of such a large block of nationalist voters 'would reduce our majority to such a level that no sane man would undertake to carry on a Parliament with it.' The possibility of some Unionist MPs being ill or absent for some other reason 'might in one evening hand over the entire Ulster position, for which we have fought so hard and so long ... and that, of course, is a dreadful thing to contemplate ... We frankly admit that we cannot hold the nine counties.'[12] While Unionists freely accepted that they were carving out an arbitrary border within Ireland to protect their interests, they did not accept that this diluted their claim that there should be a border in Ireland, for if nationalists wished to secede from the rest of the British Isles, then Unionists believed that they had a right to secede from the rest of Ireland.

While the six counties were the maximum territory that Unionists could hold, almost a third of the population within the new boundary were non-unionist. Carson denied, as many nationalists claimed, that Unionists wished to establish a Protestant ascendancy over northern Catholics and believed that the establishment of a new parliament gave Unionists the greatest opportunity 'of showing there the reality of their profession of loyalty towards our Empire by displaying in their acts of government a tolerance, a fairness, and justice towards all classes and all religions of the community.'[13]

It has been said over and over again, 'You want to oppress the Catholic minority, you want to get a Protestant ascendancy over there.' We have never asked to govern any Roman Catholic. We are perfectly satisfied that all of them, Protestant and Catholic, should be governed from this Parliament [Westminster], and we have always said that it was the fact that this Parliament was aloof entirely from these racial distinctions and religious distinctions, which was the strongest foundation for the government of Ulster. Therefore, not only have we never asked to get an opportunity of dealing in a hostile way with the minority, but we have sought from beginning to end of this controversy to be left alone, and go hand in hand with Great Britain as one nation with Great Britain. It was only in the last resort that we were compelled to put forward proposals for the separate treatment of Ulster ...[14]

As the Government of Ireland Bill made its progress through the House of Commons, the position of nationalists in Ulster was hampered by divisions between the supporters of the Irish Party and Sinn Féin. Divisions had arisen over nationalist Ireland's attitude to the Great War. From the beginning of the war in 1914, Sinn Féin members had opposed the policy of John Redmond, who had advocated the enlistment of Irish nationalists in the British army to secure the implementation of the Home Rule Act, 1914, and its application to the whole of Ireland.

In Ulster, opposition to the Irish Party was further galvanised by the partition proposals of 1916, which witnessed Redmond agreeing to the temporary partition of Ireland, for the period of the war only; Unionists, on the other hand, had been promised that the partition would be permanent. The Irish Party withdrew from the scheme when the terms of the offer to the Unionists became public. Opposition to any form of partition, temporary or permanent, had crystallised among the Catholic Church's hierarchy in Ulster, which served as the focus for northern nationalist discontent with the Irish Party. The Catholic Bishop of Down and Connor, Joseph MacRory, had expressed opposition to the exclusion of Ulster, or any part of it, from a Home Rule parliament.[15] In July 1916 the Bishop of Derry, Charles McHugh, took the initiative in launching a loosely co-ordinated Anti-Partition League in Ulster, which became the Irish National League.[16] In basic philosophy, though, there was little to distinguish the INL from the Irish Party, and its influence never extended beyond its base in Tyrone, Fermanagh, and Derry.[17] Ultimately, in October 1917, it was absorbed by the new Sinn Féin movement, revitalised by the Easter Rising.[18]

In May 1918 Sinn Féin had its first electoral success in Ulster when Arthur Griffith, the party's founder, defeated the Irish Party candidate in the East Cavan by-election. As the Great War drew to a close and a post-war general election loomed, hopes faded of a pact between the Irish Party and Sinn Féin to defeat Unionist candidates in Ulster, which forced Archbishop McHugh to warn Sinn Féin that only a combined front could secure Ulster nationalists against the 'Orange ascendancy', reminding them that 'we cannot forget we are Catholics.' The prospect of the loss of six or eight seats to the Unionists through a triangular Nationalist-Sinn Féin-Unionist contest forced the Ulster Catholic bishops to call on the Lord Mayor of Dublin to convene a conference between Éamon de Valera, president of Sinn Féin, and John Dillon, who had succeeded the late John Redmond as leader of the Irish Party, to divide the Ulster seats between them. Faced with bleak electoral prospects outside west Belfast, Dillon was forced to accept. At a conference on 2 and 3 December 1918 the Irish Party and Sinn Féin agreed to an equal division of eight marginal seats, with Logue allocating them.[19]

In the event, when the general election was called for December 1918 the pact proved successful, with the adopted candidates returned in seven of the eight Ulster constituencies. West Belfast, North-East Tyrone, South Armagh, South Down and East Donegal returned Nationalists, and South Fermanagh and North-West Tyrone returned Sinn Féiners; only East Down failed to return an anti-unionist MP.[20] In total, throughout Ireland the general election of December 1918 saw Sinn Féin win seventy-three seats to the Irish Party's seven. Sinn Féin's MPs refused to take their seats in the British Parliament, instead constituting themselves in Dublin as the parliament of Ireland, Dáil Éireann, and issuing a Declaration of Independence, announcing an Irish Republic, in January 1919.

While the Irish Party had campaigned for a form of self-government within the British Empire, on the lines of Canada and Australia, Sinn Féin advanced the call for an Irish republic, separate from the British Crown and Empire. The ideological divisions between the two factions produced deep hostility between the parties. The *Irish News*, a supporter of the Irish Party, considering the might of the British Empire, asked, 'What do the Sinn Féiners intend to do? They may say—"We mean to establish an Irish Republic." Then the simple question presents itself—How can that be done?'

These divisions undermined the effectiveness of opposition to the Government of Ireland Bill. In effect, the abstention of the victorious Sinn Féin MPs from the British House of Commons left the debate about what the provisions of the Bill should be to the Ulster Unionists. The token Irish Party presence in the House of Commons had little impact. Joseph Devlin remained convinced that Sinn Féin could not obtain its objective of a republic and contended that it had miscalculated in abstaining from Westminster, arguing that if, for example, there had been an Irish Party composed of eighty members at Westminster after the general election, and with a post-war Peace Conference sitting, 'the Irish situation would be very different to what it is today. The House of Commons is the heart of the Commonwealth, and the best platform in the world ...'[21]

While Sinn Féin ignored the reality of the coming Northern regime, Devlin realised that its establishment would mean 'permanent partition'. 'Once they have their own Parliament, with all the machinery of government and administration, I am afraid that anything like subsequent union [with the rest of Ireland] will be impossible.'[22]

The Irish Party's final attitude to the Government of Ireland Bill in Parliament was made clear at a meeting on 24 April 1920, at which the party decided to abstain. Its MPs attacked the Bill as calculated to 'stereotype racial and religious differences' by creating an 'artificial area' under the 'ascendancy party'.[23]

The Government of Ireland Act became law on 23 December 1920, creating two new jurisdictions with their own parliaments. 'Northern Ireland' was to consist of the six counties of Antrim, Armagh, Down, Londonderry, Fermanagh, and Tyrone; 'Southern Ireland' was to consist of the remaining twenty-six counties. The Act provided for the establishment of a two-chamber Northern Ireland Parliament, consisting of a 52-member House of Commons, elected by proportional representation, and a Senate of 26 members, 24 of whom were elected by the House of Commons and two—the Lord Mayor of Belfast and Mayor of Londonderry—sitting *ex officio*. Section 75 of the Act provided that 'the supreme authority of the Parliament of the United Kingdom shall remain unaffected and undiminished over all persons, matters and things in Ireland and every part thereof.'

To represent the King, the post of Governor of Northern Ireland was created to replace the Lord Lieutenant, or Viceroy, of Ireland, in whom the executive powers of the Northern Parliament were invested. Northern Ireland was also represented in the United Kingdom Parliament by thirteen MPs. It was to make an 'Imperial Contribution' with regard to the relative taxable capacities of Northern Ireland and the United Kingdom as a whole. The Parliament itself was given a general power to make laws for the 'peace, order and good government' of Northern Ireland, subject to certain powers retained by Westminster relating to armed forces, the Crown, and imperial and foreign affairs. The Northern Parliament's fiscal powers were restricted, with Westminster reserving the power to levy income tax and customs and excise; and the Northern Parliament and Government were also prohibited from making laws and taking administrative action other than on the basis of religious equality.

The Act looked forward to the ultimate reunion of Ireland, by the consent of both Irish Parliaments, and made provision for a Council of Ireland to facilitate this. The preamble to the Government of Ireland Bill explained:

Although at the beginning there are to be two Parliaments and two

Governments in Ireland, the Act contemplates and affords every facility for union between North and South, and empowers the two Parliaments by mutual agreement and joint action to terminate partition and set up one Parliament and one Government for the whole of Ireland. With a view to the establishment of a single Parliament, and to bringing about harmonious actions between the two Parliaments and Governments, there is created a bond of union in the meantime by means of a Council of Ireland, which is to consist of 20 representatives elected by each Parliament, and a President nominated by the Lord Lieutenant. It will fall to the members of this body to initiate proposals for united action on the part of the two Parliaments and to bring forward these proposals in the respective Parliaments.

In November 1920 Carson, speaking in the British House of Commons, hoped

> that this Council, the liaison between North and South, is not going to be the impotent body that a number of people think it will be … I should have thought that the biggest advance towards unity in Ireland was this conception of the Council. The Council will be the representatives of the Parliament of the North and … of the representatives of the South, and they are to come together … to frame measures and suggestions for the benefit of the whole of Ireland … I am optimistic enough to hope that it is in this Council … that there is the germ of a united Ireland in future.[24]

However, the strict condition under which Unionists such as Carson were prepared to accept a united Ireland was one that would 'see Ireland one and undivided, loyal to this country [Britain] and loyal to the Empire.'[25] Carson told nationalists that

> you will have no unity in Ireland until the people of the South and West [of Ireland] give up their hatred and hostility to Great Britain. We feel that our interests are identical with those of Great Britain, and we will have no unity as long as this insane hatred is preached from the housetops in the South and the West of Ireland. Stop that to-morrow, and come and shake hands over a common friendship with Great Britain, and you will have unity in a very short time.[26]

The difference, for Unionists, between a new parliament in Southern Ireland and one in Northern Ireland was that Unionists believed themselves loyal to the British Crown and Empire, while nationalists were considered inherently disloyal.

COMMUNAL VIOLENCE

The birth of Northern Ireland was a bloody one, accompanied as it was by widespread communal violence. Between July 1920 and July 1922, 557 people were killed: 303 Catholics, 172 Protestants, and 82 members of the police and British army.[27] Of the 236 people killed between December 1921 and the end of May 1922, 147 were Catholics and 89 either Protestants or members of the security forces. Of those wounded in the same period, 166 were Catholics and 180 were Protestants or members of the security forces.[28] Although Catholics formed only a quarter of Belfast's population they had suffered 257 civilian deaths out of 416 in a two-year period. Catholic relief organisations estimated that between 8,700 and 11,000 Belfast Catholics had been driven out of their jobs and 23,000 forced out of their homes, with about 500 Catholic businesses destroyed.[29]

Against this the same period witnessed considerable activity by the IRA aimed at undermining the fledgling statelet. The two years between July 1920 and July 1922 witnessed a total of 254 Protestant and security force deaths. Ulster Unionists were angered by what they regarded as a deliberate campaign of sectarian assassination by the IRA in Southern Ireland, directed against Protestants as well as against members of the Crown forces in the RIC and the British army, which were regarded as 'their' loyal security forces. During what became known in the South as the Anglo-Irish War or War of Independence, the IRA carried out a campaign of ambushing, raiding police barracks and inflicting casualties that were estimated, between 1919 and 1921, at 600 killed and 1,200 wounded on the side of the Crown forces and 752 IRA men killed and 866 wounded.[30]

Carson warned that the continuing assassination campaign was alienating the North from the South and making a settlement between the two more difficult in the immediate future.[31] In July 1920 he stated: 'I tell the South and West [of Ireland], and I tell those who are always talking of unity … that every murder that is committed in the South and West drives a wedge between the North and the South which it will take years to pull out. I tell them that every policeman they kill is a nail in the coffin of unity …'[32]

Ulster unionists saw the violence in the South, and its spreading to Northern Ireland, as evidence of what they could expect in a united Ireland. For example, Ulster Protestants noted how in 1922 the Home Mission Report of the General Assembly of the Presbyterian Church stated that in almost every part of Southern Ireland the Protestant population had declined rapidly. Since 1915 there had been a 45 per cent decrease in the number of Protestant families in Cork presbytery (excluding the city of Cork), a 44 per cent decline in the Munster presbytery, a 36 per cent decline in Connacht, and a 30 per cent decline in Athlone. The decline in County Dublin (excluding the city) had been 16 per cent.[33] Ulster Unionists were alarmed by the IRA campaign in the South, which saw numbers of Protestants killed throughout the Anglo-Irish War and beyond. Throughout 1921 Ulster Protestants had followed the catalogue of killing of Southern Protestants that had accompanied the IRA campaign; the killing of twenty Protestants between January and April 1921 caused alarm and anger.[34]

In the North, Carson denied that the communal violence was motivated on the Protestant side by anti-Catholicism and asserted that it was directed against 'Sinn Féiners, who are engaged in a conspiracy in Ireland to overthrow the authority of the King and bring about secession from the British Government.'[35] However, the Unionist MP Major Hugh O'Neill, while accepting that Sinn Féin was not a religious organisation, recognised that a less sophisticated definition of what constituted a 'rebel' was used by many ordinary unionists when he argued that the 'ordinary working class Protestant' could not be blamed for thinking that Sinn Féin was a largely Catholic movement. The reason this perception was so strong among many Ulster Protestants was the belief that 'in so far as the Sinn Féiners profess any religion at all they are essentially people of the Roman Catholic faith,' and 'never on one occasion have the leaders of the Roman Catholic Church taken any steps to denounce the outrages and murders which the Sinn Féin organisation is carrying on.'[36] Many Protestants thus equated Sinn Féiners, and consequently supporters of the IRA, with the Catholic population of the North.

Nationalists, on the other hand, both north and south, saw the communal violence in Northern Ireland as evidence of a pogrom directed against the Catholic population. This view shaped Northern and Southern nationalist interpretations of Ulster unionism, which was interpreted as seeking a permanent Protestant ascendancy over the Catholic community. Aodh de Blácam summed up this perception of Orange bigotry when he wrote in *What Sinn Féin Stands For* (1921) that the horrors of sectarianism

> are not to be laid at the door of the Protestant religion ... They lie at the door of some anachronistic, totemistic, atavistic savage lust. There can be no doubt that the bigotry of North-East Ulster is a form

of mass insanity. Its accompaniment of hideous drums ... is confirmatory evidence. The savages' medicine-man is not wanting to complete the proof, for the infected masses are incited periodically by men who claim spiritual guidance—and who disgrace the faith ... by calling themselves Protestants.[37]

It was in Londonderry that the first intercommunal violence had flared, in April 1920. When 1,500 British troops arrived, on 23 June 1920, eight Catholics and four Protestants had been killed; eventually up to forty people were to be killed, many by the British army.[38] The news of the assassination of an Ulster-born police commissioner, Lieutenant-Colonel G. B. Smyth, in Cork on 18 July 1920 and the refusal of Southern rail workers to transport his remains back to Ulster incensed loyalist workers at the shipyard of Workman, Clark and Company, who, on 21 July 1920, under the guise of the Belfast Protestant Association, made their way to the Harland and Wolff yard and proceeded to expel Catholic workers. Many Protestant workers were armed with sticks, and a number of Catholic workers were severely beaten, while others were thrown into the water and had to swim for their lives.

After the resultant mass expulsion of Catholic and socialist workers from the shipyards, engineering works, and mills, Catholic crowds began to gather, and some Protestants were attacked. By the evening gunfire had erupted, and in three days eighteen people had been killed. Attacks followed on Catholic-owned businesses in Banbridge, Bangor, and Dromore.[39] Describing Colonel Smyth as a 'gallant Ulsterman' who 'had done his duty for King and country' in the war, Protestant workers at the Workman, Clark and Company yard passed a series of resolutions on 28 July 1920 stating 'that we, the Unionist and Protestant workers ... while deploring the wrecking and looting which have been going on in our city ... hereby declare that we will not work with disloyal workers ... and until Sinn Féin ceases its foul murder. Also, that in all future applications for employment we respectfully suggest that first consideration be given loyal ex-service men and Protestant Unionists.'[40]

Sir Ernest Clark, appointed as additional Assistant Under-Secretary in the Irish Office in London, with particular administrative responsibility for Northern Ireland, was instructed by the Chief Secretary—the British Cabinet minister responsible for Ireland—that it was a 'matter of paramount importance' that the Catholic workers be reinstated. Clark identified the chief causes of the expulsions as an emotional reaction, a desire for retaliation for an earlier expulsion of Protestant dock men from the Londonderry shipyards, and anger at the IRA murder campaign spreading into Ulster, although he found no evidence of a conspiracy on the part of the Unionist leadership to create a systematic pogrom. When he met a delegation of the Ulster Unionist Labour Association he was informed that while loyalist workers were prepared to accept Catholics back, the stumbling-block had been a proposed declaration of loyalty renouncing any association with Sinn Féin or the IRA. Clark negotiated an agreement whereby the expelled workers could be reinstated on the understanding that they were not, on their honour, associated with Sinn Féin. However, the murder of two Belfast policemen by the IRA caused further sectarian fighting and scuppered the agreement.[41]

As the violence continued, in August 1920 Bishop MacRory, a strong Sinn Féin supporter, Seán MacEntee, a senior Sinn Féin member of the Dáil, Denis McCullough, Frank Crummey, a teacher and IRA member, and Rev. John Hassan, a Belfast curate, launched the Belfast Boycott Committee, which petitioned Dáil Éireann to boycott Belfast goods and banks in retaliation for the 'war of extermination being waged against us.' MacRory for one saw the boycott as a weapon to prevent the establishment of Northern Ireland, believing that 'until this city [Belfast] is taught that it depends on Ireland, there will be recurring outbursts of bigotry ... and a standing obstacle to the settlement of the ... Irish Question.'[42]

Northern nationalists made use of the Belfast Boycott as retaliation against the violence that they saw as being orchestrated by the Ulster Unionist leadership. Joseph Devlin, unlike many unionists, drew a distinction between Sinn Féin and the IRA, and he believed that the communal violence from the Protestant side was motivated by bigotry directed against Catholics as Catholics. He argued that, though it might be said that the Catholic shipyard workers and other Catholics

> were attacked because they were Sinn Féiners ... even so, they had no right to be attacked. I am not a Sinn Féiner and never was, but every man has a right to his own opinion ... This is not a war against crime, but against opinion. Even if every one of these people are Sinn Féiners they have a right to their opinion provided they do not interfere with anyone else. I say they were not Sinn Féiners ... I say the attack in Belfast was made not because they were Sinn Féiners, but because they were Catholics, and that is why they were attacked.[43]

After fresh outbreaks of violence, Clark became convinced that an armed force of special constables should be formed immediately, because of the existence of a 'feeling of insecurity' in Belfast 'due to the recent developments of Sinn Féin activity.' By October 1920 the details of the Ulster Special Constabulary, comprising three categories, were published. Class A were to be paid and full-time but would only serve within the division where they were recruited, having the same arms and equipment as the RIC. Class B, or 'B Specials', as they would come to be called, were to be part-time and unpaid, apart from a small allowance for service and wear and tear of clothes. They were to do 'occasional' duty, usually one evening a week, day duties being required only in an emergency. Class C Specials were to be a reserve force and were to be called out in case of emergency.

By the end of 1920 the Special Constabulary totalled nearly 3,500 A constables, 16,000 B constables, and over 1,000 C constables. The force that emerged was based mainly on a reorganised UVF and therefore almost exclusively Protestant. It was to become a symbol of repression for many Catholics, with widespread allegations that its members were involved in the murder of Catholic civilians. From the Protestant perspective the Specials were seen as defenders of the statelet from an IRA terror campaign, and the killing of every policeman was seen not as the death of a member of the Crown forces but as the murder of another Protestant or loyalist by the IRA.

THE BIRTH OF NORTHERN IRELAND

As the first elections to the new Northern Ireland Parliament approached, Carson declined the offer to become Northern Ireland's first Prime Minister, with the honour then falling to Craig. Craig looked on the Northern Ireland election as a plebiscite on the single great issue before the voters: 'Who is for Empire and who is for a Republic?'[44] In his appeal to electors he ventured to speak for those who placed 'in the forefront of their ideals and aspirations, devotion to the Throne, close union with Great Britain, pride in the British Empire, and an earnest desire for peace throughout Ireland.' The new leader called on all loyalists to vote for the Unionist candidates, not only for a majority in the incoming Parliament but also because the responsibility of nominating the Northern quota in the Council of Ireland fell upon the Northern MPs. This was to prevent the Southern parliament encroaching on the Northern Parliament's rights and privileges, for 'to put it plainly, failure to secure an effective working majority would mean immediate submergence in a Dublin Parliament.'[45]

Sinn Féiners in the North sought guidance from the rebel government of the Republic, Dáil Éireann, on what their policy towards the election should be. The Sinn Féin MP Michael Collins, who was masterminding the IRA's campaign against Crown forces in the South, favoured participation in the election, with those Northern Nationalists elected forming part of the Dáil and ignoring the Northern Parliament. Éamon de Valera, the President of the Irish Republic, also favoured Collins's policy, which would preserve the 'unity of the Republic of Ireland', whereas boycotting the election would make it seem that they were accepting partition. De Valera hoped that the contesting of the elections would see the elimination of Devlin's Irish Party in the North, and he speculated that an abstention policy by the elected Northern Nationalists would allow intra-Unionist class tensions to arise within the new Parliament, so hastening its destruction, with the absence of Nationalist groupings putting 'the Labour and Capitalist sections of the Unionists struggling with each other for control in the parliament.' Collins argued that the elections should be contested on a strict abstention policy, the real importance of this course being the 'prevention of the idea and acceptance of the idea of partition entering into the minds and actions of the Irish people,' and he urged the necessity of making north-east Ulster realise that it was 'not a thing apart from the Irish nation.'[46]

By the end of March 1921 Seán MacEntee had completed an arrangement with Devlin's supporters allowing each party to field a maximum of twenty-one candidates in the election but binding the Devlinites to Sinn Féin's programme of self-determination and abstention from the Northern Ireland Parliament. There was opposition to any agreement with Sinn Féin from many of Devlin's supporters: Thomas O'Donnell, a former Irish Party MP for North Kerry, believed that Devlin ought to be devoting his energies to bringing about peace with the Ulster Unionists by working with them in the Northern Parliament. But Devlin was motivated by his hostility to the leaders of the Unionist Party, whom he blamed for much of the violence that had gripped Belfast. Furthermore, he remained convinced that without the pact the Irish Party would be unable to win a single seat outside Belfast.[47]

Appealing to the electors of the Six Counties, President de Valera announced that Dáil Éireann had given its sanction to the elections for the Southern and Northern Parliaments in order that the Irish people 'may have an opportunity of proving once more your loyalty to the principle of Irish independence.' The policy of Sinn Féin, he explained, remained unchanged:

It stands for the right of the people of this nation to determine freely for themselves how they shall be governed, and for the right of every citizen to an equal voice in the determination which stands for civil and religious equality ... It stands for an association of nations based upon self-determination ... It stands for Ireland undivided and a unit with regard to other nations and States ... You who vote for Sinn Féin candidates will cast your vote for nothing less than the legitimacy of the republic, for Ireland against England, for freedom against slavery, for right and justice against force and wrong here and everywhere.[48]

During the election campaign the Irish Party appealed to the electors of the Six Counties, describing the partition proposal as being 'as unnatural as it is unnational ... The insulting scheme is not an act of national peace and reconciliation, but a trick of English politicians.'[49] Devlin, at Ballycastle, County Antrim, put forward a view of partition that was common to all shades of nationalism in Ireland when he said:

Here in Ulster they were asked to start, not a Parliament for a nation, not a Parliament for a province: but a Parliament for a section of a province, of a section of a nation ... It might satisfy the hangers-on of the Unionist Party, but it would not satisfy the indestructible and undying national fervour of the Nationalist Ulstermen who were Irish first, Irish last, and Irish all the time. (Cheers). They declined to allow any English Government or any Ascendancy Party in Ulster to cut them off from their fellow-countrymen in the other twenty-six counties. They were proud to be Irish. (Cheers). Providence had fashioned this land to be one and indivisible. Ireland was one, not by direction of England, but fashioned out as one race, with a single purpose and an inspiring ideal, and they were going to make an earnest, a powerful, and a triumphant fight against this sacrilege upon their nation. (Cheers).[50]

On the eve of the election, in an effort to end the violence, a dramatic meeting took place in Dublin on 5 May 1921 between Craig and de Valera, engineered by Dublin Castle. The President of the Irish Republic recalled years later how Craig spoke of the union with Britain as a 'sacred thing', and de Valera interjected to explain to him how that union was corruptly engineered.[51] Such efforts to convince Unionists of the errors of their ways was lost on the Prime Minister of Northern Ireland, who regarded de Valera as a 'visionary, harping on about the grievances of Ireland for the last 700 years, instead of coming down to practical present day discussion.' After half an hour, recalled Craig, de Valera 'reached the era of Brian Boru.' Nothing more substantial emerged, and the two leaders, meeting for the first and only time, signed a note to acknowledge that 'Sir James Craig and Éamon de Valera held an informal conference at which their respective points of view were interchanged, and the future of Ireland was discussed.'[52]

The Northern Ireland general election, in May 1921, saw a turn-out of 89 per cent, with all forty Unionist candidates securing election, while the Irish Party and Sinn Féin won six seats each. Throughout the ten constituencies of Northern Ireland, Sinn Féin's twenty candidates dominated the Catholic vote and obtained 104,716 votes or 21 per cent of the poll, compared with the twelve Irish Party candidates' 60,577 votes or 19 per cent of the poll.[53]

The first Parliament of Northern Ireland was opened by King George V and assembled in the Council Chamber of the City Hall, Belfast, on 7 June 1921. The Lieutenant-General and Governor-General of Ireland, Viscount Fitzalan, swore in Craig and his Cabinet; thereafter the Speaker was elected and the members took the oath of allegiance, pledging: 'I swear by Almighty God that I will be faithful and bear true allegiance to His Majesty, King George, His Heirs and Successors according to the law. So Help me God.'[54]

The executive scheme adopted for the Northern Ireland Government consisted of seven departments. The Department of the Prime Minister was to be the channel of communication between the Lord Lieutenant of Ireland and the Northern Ireland Cabinet and between that Cabinet and the various Northern Ireland ministries. The Ministry of Finance administered the financial and tax business of the Government as well as having responsibility for public works and statistics. The Ministry of Home Affairs was to deal with law, justice, and prisons, while its Local Government Division took over the functions of the Local Government Board and the Inspector of Lunatics. The Ministry of Education was responsible for art, science, and education, covering primary and advanced schools. The Ministry of Agriculture looked after all aspects of agriculture and rural industries. The Ministry of Labour had two main divisions, Labour and National Health Insurance, and was responsible for industrial relations and working conditions. The smallest ministry, Commerce, was to administer services in connection with companies and commercial matters generally.[55]

TRUCE AND TREATY

In July 1921 attention in Northern Ireland became focused on the Truce signed in that month between Crown forces and the IRA. The purpose of the Truce was to allow negotiations to take place between representatives of the British Government and Sinn Féin. The position adopted by the Northern Ireland Government was that the negotiations should be confined to the relationship between the British Government and the rest of Ireland outside the jurisdiction of Northern Ireland. Craig told an Orange gathering in Belfast in July 1921 that he believed that the status of the Ulster unionist cause was enhanced by the Government of Ireland Act, that the Northern Ireland Parliament was now 'sacrosanct in the eyes of those who before never had an idea that we could have functioned it,' and that 'prior to the 7th of last month [June 1921] Mr de Valera or any of his party could look upon me as merely James Craig … I am no longer James Craig except to my friends … but to those who would tamper with Ulster's rights I am the Prime Minister of Northern Ireland.'[56]

After returning from consultations in London, Craig pronounced himself satisfied with the efforts being made towards peace. In answer to de Valera's claim that the Republic's President would base his claim for Irish independence on Ireland's right to self-determination, Northern Ireland's Prime Minister claimed that, by an overwhelming majority in the recent election, Northern Ireland had 'determined' its own Parliament. Craig claimed that de Valera and Sinn Féin had recognised the self-determination of Northern Ireland by selecting candidates for the election and submitting their policy of 'no partition' to the Northern electorate, which was rejected at the polls. It now remained for de Valera and the British Government alone to determine the settlement between Britain and Southern Ireland.[57] On behalf of the Northern Ireland Cabinet, he stated that having accepted the Northern Parliament as a final settlement, he felt bound to inform the British Prime Minister, David Lloyd George, that no meeting was possible between de Valera and himself until the former 'recognises that Northern Ireland will not submit to any authority other than his Majesty the King and the Parliament of the United Kingdom and admits the sanctity of the existing powers and privileges of Northern Ireland.'[58]

Face-to-face negotiations between the United Kingdom Government and representatives of Sinn Féin began in September 1921. As the negotiations approached, de Valera received nationalist deputations from Down, Derry, Armagh, and Belfast, but, while declaring his strength of feeling on Ireland's unity and self-determination, he offered the Northerners no undertakings, save an assurance that the deputations' views would be kept in mind in any Anglo-Irish negotiations. In fact it was not until September 1921 that the Dáil established an Ulster Committee to advise on the negotiations. The committee, with Professor Eoin MacNeill as its chairman and Seán Milroy its secretary, rejected the suggestion that Northern nationalists, such as the prominent Sinn Féiner and journalist Cahir Healy, should advise it on the partition issue, with Milroy regarding it as a slur on the delegates' integrity. The result was that Milroy became Griffith's principal adviser.[59] Discussions between W. T. Cosgrave, the Dáil Minister for Local Government, and the representatives of Northern locally elected bodies with a Nationalist majority saw Dublin advise that such bodies declare their allegiance to the Dáil, in the final weeks of the London negotiations, so as to emphasise the degree of opposition to the Northern Parliament. In response to this, Sir Richard Dawson Bates, the Northern Ireland Minister of Home Affairs, introduced the Local Government (Emergency Powers) Bill, empowering him, from 2 December 1921, to dissolve any refractory authority and replace it with a paid commissioner.[60]

Further negotiations in London between the representatives of Sinn Féin and the British Government took place in October 1921. Among those representing Sinn Féin were Arthur Griffith and Michael Collins. Griffith described for the British delegation the Sinn Féin attitude towards Northern Ireland thus: 'If you stand aside we will make them [Ulster Unionists] a fair proposal. If you do so, we can probably come to an agreement with them.' But as long as the British Government was behind the Ulster Unionists, they would be difficult.

The large minority within Northern Ireland was Michael Collins's immediate concern. On 14 October 1921 he told Lloyd George: 'You and Northern Ireland are faced with the coercion of one-third of its area.' The preference, he continued, of the majority in Tyrone and Fermanagh, more than half of Armagh, a great deal of Derry and a strip of Antrim should be under the jurisdiction of a Dublin parliament. Lloyd George conceded that if there were a plebiscite in Tyrone and Fermanagh there would be a Catholic majority but contended that there had to be a new unit and that the Six-County area had been acceptable to nationalists as preferable to a new delimitation of Ulster. More than once Lloyd George mentioned a Boundary Commission.[61]

As the terms of a settlement began to take shape, Lloyd George wrote to Craig on 10 November 1921, setting out the British Cabinet's terms for a settlement with Sinn Féin, proposing a united Ireland. Craig, however, refused to accept a united Ireland, and the break-up of the negotiations came not on the expected issue of Ulster but on the status of a self-governing Ireland. Sinn Féin, which had offered an Irish Republic associated with the British Commonwealth but outside, not inside, that Commonwealth, were told by Lloyd George that a self-governing Ireland must be part of and inside the British Commonwealth, accepting allegiance to the British king and therefore the status of British subjects; the alternative would be 'war, and war within three days.' The Sinn Féin delegates, including Griffith and Collins, were forced to accept these terms. The Articles of Agreement for a Treaty between Great Britain and Ireland established a partitioned 26-county Irish Free State. It was to have the same constitutional status in the community of nations known as the British Empire as the Dominions of Canada, Australia, New Zealand, and South Africa. As a Dominion, the Irish Free State was to have far greater powers than that of a devolved Parliament within the United Kingdom, as was the case with Northern Ireland. The Free State, for example, would no longer send MPs to Westminster and would have the right to set trading tariffs against British goods.

The Treaty also made the Irish Free State coterminous with the island of Ireland and therefore included Northern Ireland; article 11 of the Treaty, however, laid down that the 'powers of the Irish Free State shall not be exercisable as respects Northern Ireland until the expiration of one month from the passing of the Act of Parliament for the ratification of the Treaty.' Article 12 stated that if before the expiry of that said month an address was made to the King by both houses of the Northern Ireland Parliament to the effect that the powers of the Free State's Parliament and Government 'shall no longer extend to Northern Ireland,' the provisions of the Government of Ireland Act, 1920, so far as they related to Northern Ireland, would continue to have full force and effect. This allowed Northern Ireland to contract out of the Free State and resume its status as an integral part of the United Kingdom. Article 12 also stated that if such an address were made by the Northern Ireland Parliament then a Boundary Commission of three people, one each to be appointed by the Governments of the Free State and Northern Ireland and a chairman to be appointed by the British Government, would determine, 'in accordance with the wishes of the inhabitants, so far as they may be compatible with economic and geographic conditions, the boundaries between Northern Ireland and the rest of Ireland.'

From the perspective of the Ulster Unionists the Treaty drove a psychological wedge between themselves and the rest of Ireland. The Government of Ireland Act envisaged an eventual united Ireland within the United Kingdom; but the Treaty resulted in the secession of the Irish Free State from the United Kingdom and, from a Unionist perspective, in the artificial partition of the British Isles. As the Parliament of Northern Ireland duly contracted out of the jurisdiction of the Irish Free State, Craig told his Parliament:

The South have decided that they can do better separated from the great Mother of the Empire, that they can do better by isolating themselves and becoming what they call a Free State. We, on the other hand, say, No. We can do better for ourselves and for the Empire by maintaining the closest connection between Great Britain and ourselves—a connection which has served us in the past and has also served our colonies in the past, that has served the whole of the vast Dominions over which His Majesty rules ... and I pray God as long as I have anything to do with it we shall remain steadfast in the true faith.[62]

Generally, Northern nationalists welcomed the signing of the Treaty. Their representatives in Fermanagh and Tyrone were soon convinced by Griffith and Collins that article 12 of the Treaty, establishing the Boundary Commission, was intended to compel Craig to choose between entering an all-Ireland settlement and suffering a drastic reduction of up to a third of Northern Ireland's area. In Fermanagh and Tyrone nationalists were only too eager to see article 12 as the means by which the two counties would be absorbed into the Free State. In Belfast, however, the isolated nationalist minority feared that the Boundary Commission might leave them an even smaller minority within a separate 'Ulster' state.[63]

In the Free State the dominant issues in relation to the Treaty were the Free State's position within the Commonwealth and the taking of an oath of allegiance, which set in motion events leading to the splitting of Sinn Féin and a bloody Civil War. In Northern Ireland the majority of nationalists sided with the pro-Treatyites. For the Devlinite Irish News the Treaty offered Ireland its best chance of national freedom:

Not since 1172 have the Irish masses been supreme in their own country for a single year ... Ireland has not been a free nation since the first square mile of her territory was occupied by an English force

... Now a ... measure of national liberty has been placed at the disposal of the 75 per cent of the Irish people who live in the 26 counties; 25 per cent of the Irish nation are excluded from that measure of liberty; but 40 per cent of the 'excluded' people are at one in urging the 75 per cent of the nation to capture a great opportunity ... The national will has been made manifest. Those Deputies of Dáil Éireann who have deliberately resolved to defy it are withholding from the Irish people the right that British Governments and British military power had forcibly denied to all the generations of Irish men and women since Henry II left Dublin in 1172.[64]

The *Irish News* warned that the proposals of anti-Treatyites, such as de Valera's proposal for an Irish Republic, were an 'amateur political essay' to which no practical man in Ireland or Britain would give a serious minute's attention. It was an appeal to the Irish people to 'go back into the Wilderness. It has neither form nor substance.' It concluded: 'The Treaty is in danger; the nation's future is in deadly peril.'[65] The *Irish News* rejected the cry that an acceptance of the Treaty would mean that Northern nationalists would be sacrificed; this, it pointed out, had been done in 1918, not 1921, ever since the day it was made possible for the British Parliament to pass the Government of Ireland Act. Now, the paper claimed, Northern nationalists knew that their country's only hope rested on an immediate and unqualified acceptance of the Treaty. In the meantime Northern nationalists had to look to themselves and realise that their own security, and their very existence, depended on their own strength and solidarity. Whatever happened in Southern Ireland, Northern nationalists 'cannot hope for anything they cannot hold and win on their own account.'[66]

THE COLLINS-CRAIG PACT

With the advent of the Truce, a liaison system had been established whereby representatives of the British army, the RIC and the IRA could meet on equal terms to sort out local difficulties. Furthermore, the Ulster Special Constabulary was immobilised.[67] Eoin O'Duffy, a senior IRA staff officer, was sent north to become a Truce Liaison Officer for Ulster, and on 16 July 1921 he announced that all IRA sniping in the North would cease, except in the case of self-defence. No Belfast Division of the IRA had been constituted during the Anglo-Irish War until the establishment of the 3rd Northern Division in May 1921, under the command of Joe McKelvey, with an operational area of

Belfast, Antrim, and north Down. Before the Truce the IRA estimated that it had the support of only 25 per cent of the Catholic population of the divisional area, but with the ending of hostilities the Catholic population, believing that the IRA had been victorious over the Special Constabulary, 'practically all flocked to our standard.'[68] Following reorganisation and training during the Truce, the 3rd Northern Division had three brigades, of 1,222 members, with the Belfast Brigade comprising 632 men.[69]

The Unionist Government's relations with its own supporters were severely tested by its apparent ineffectiveness in dealing with the deteriorating security situation that arose after the Truce, for while violence ended in the rest of Ireland, in the North it continued. Services in relation to law enforcement and the administration of justice were not at first transferred to the Northern Ireland Government: from July 1921 to March 1922 the responsibility for security in Northern Ireland remained with Westminster, which in practice meant the British administration in Dublin Castle. This was deeply resented by the Northern Ireland Government, which felt that Dublin Castle was putting the political necessity of maintaining the Truce in the South before security considerations in the North. In addition, since the armed forces remained an excepted matter, control of the British army also lay outside the remit of the Belfast Government.

August 1921 saw increased activity by loyalist paramilitaries, including the Ulster Protestant Volunteers, which had originated as a vigilante force in east Belfast, eventually specialising in the random assassination of Catholics. Rioting in August and September 1921 saw the intervention of the British army, but the Northern Ireland Government complained of a lack of military willingness to quell civil disorder. Following an outbreak of serious rioting in late September 1921, the Special Constabulary was remobilised, under the control of the military. This brought a temporary lull in the disturbances, but there was more rioting in November.[70]

In an effort to end the continuing violence, Sir James Craig and Michael Collins, chairman of the newly established Provisional Government of the Free State, met in London on 24 January 1922. It was agreed that the boundary question would be dealt with not by the commission proposed in the Treaty but as a matter for mutual agreement between their Governments. Craig, however, rejected Collins's suggestion of a meeting of an all-Ireland body of MPs, proposing instead that the Council of Ireland be replaced by joint meetings of the two Irish Governments.[71] An agreement reached by the two Irish leaders decided:

(1) The Boundary Commission as outlined in the Treaty to be altered. The Governments of the Free State and of Northern Ireland to appoint one representative each to report to Mr Collins and Sir James Craig, who will mutually agree on behalf of their respective Governments on the future boundaries between the two.

(2) Without prejudice to the future consideration by his Government of the question of tariffs, Mr Collins undertakes that the Belfast boycott is to be discontinued immediately.

Craig undertook to facilitate 'in every possible way the return of Catholic workmen, without tests,' to the shipyards 'as and when trade revival enables the firms concerned to absorb the present unemployed.' In the meantime, relief on a 'large scale' was to be arranged to carry the unemployed over the period of distress. It was also agreed that a further meeting be held to discuss the question of political prisoners.[72]

Collins reassured his Northern supporters that his primary aim with regard to the Boundary Commission was to 'exclude English influence,' and it would be for nationalist Ireland to insist on its own interpretation of the commission. If it were handled properly, claimed Collins, 'we can make the whole agreement go towards unity.' Collins wished to fulfil his part of the pact, although he viewed the lifting of the boycott as a temporary step to give the Unionists a chance to demonstrate their good will; if they did not prove this, then Collins thought the Free State would be in a stronger position to impose tariffs 'in a definite way after this chance has been given.' With the Free State's Provisional Government having the allegiance of nationalists in south and east Down, Collins sought to reassure border nationalists that a great portion of Armagh and such places as Newry would not remain under the Northern Parliament's jurisdiction.[73] He thought it might be possible to reduce Northern Ireland 'to such limits [that] it cannot exist without us, and that it would be forced in,' although 'there might be much rancour in the train of this action. It would be far better to fix our minds for a united Ireland, for this course will not leave minorities which it will be impossible to govern.'[74]

Collins and Craig met again on 2 February 1922, this time in Dublin. The discussion was almost entirely confined to the subject of the Boundary Commission. Lloyd George had assured Craig that a settlement of the boundary question would involve only a rectification of the border, but at the meeting Collins produced maps showing Craig that he wanted half of Northern Ireland, saying that Lloyd George had told him that this was what he would get. Craig made it clear that Unionists would never abandon places such as Londonderry and Enniskillen, stressing their historic importance to Protestants, and declined to have any further discussions with Collins.[75] A statement from the two leaders announced that no agreement had been reached and warned that 'a very serious situation has consequently arisen.' Craig pronounced himself amazed by the Free State's proposal that almost half of Northern Ireland's territory was to be absorbed by the Free State. He proposed an adjournment of a week, which Collins refused, on the grounds that the difference between them was too wide. Collins took his stand on article 12 of the Treaty, which stated that Northern Ireland's boundaries were to be determined in accordance with the wishes of the inhabitants. He also suggested that the parliamentary representatives of the whole of Ireland should be called together to frame a constitution for 'our common country'.[76]

Following a meeting of the Northern Ireland Cabinet in London on 6 February 1922, Craig sent a letter to Lloyd George stating definitively the attitude of his Government to the boundary question. He quoted from an earlier letter from Lloyd George to de Valera that declared that an Anglo-Irish settlement 'must allow for full recognition of the existing powers and privileges of the Parliament and Government of Northern Ireland, which cannot be abrogated except by their own consent.' Craig wrote: 'We adhere throughout to this principle laid down by yourself, and cannot consent to any alteration of our boundary, except by mutual agreement,' failing which the boundary should stand as defined by the Government of Ireland Act, 1920.[77]

While Craig and Collins found themselves deadlocked, the violence continued. On 7 and 8 February 1922 the IRA made a series of cross-border raids in which they kidnapped forty-two local loyalists in Fermanagh and Tyrone, including the High Sheriff of Fermanagh. This caused uproar among unionists. Additional troops were sent into Fermanagh, and the Special Constabulary was mobilised. As reinforcements of A Specials moved into Clones, County Monaghan, in order to change trains, a detachment of the Specials became involved in a gun battle with IRA forces, in disputed circumstances, leaving five killed and nine wounded among the Specials and the IRA commandant dead. Loyalists referred to the incident as a massacre, and in reprisal Fermanagh loyalists drove Catholics suspected of Sinn Féin sympathies from their homes. In Belfast from 12 to 16 February 1922 there was renewed violence, with thirty-one people killed. The

Northern Ireland Cabinet, however, refused to introduce martial law, regarding that as a panic measure.

On 29 March 1922 a further meeting took place between Craig and Collins, this time at the Colonial Office in London. A second Collins-Craig Pact was announced. Clause 1 announced: 'Peace is to-day declared'; clause 2 committed both Irish Governments to co-operating to restore peaceful conditions; clause 3 suggested a mixed special police force and the establishment of a Police Advisory Committee, to be composed of Catholics who would recommend suitable Catholic recruits. Clause 4 advocated the establishment of non-jury courts, and clause 5 proposed a joint Catholic-Protestant Conciliation Committee to investigate outrages and their validity. Clause 6 stated that IRA activity in Northern Ireland was to cease; clause 7 stated that representatives of both Governments should meet before the 'Ulster month' of July began, to consider the issues of Irish unity and the Boundary Commission. Clause 8 called for the return to their homes of people who had been expelled in Northern Ireland and the Free State; while clause 9 dealt with unemployment and the issue of the expelled workers, with the British Colonial Secretary, Winston Churchill, promising £500,000 for relief work, one-third of this sum going to Catholics. The Northern Ireland Government agreed to use every effort to secure the restoration of the expelled Catholic workers and wherever this proved impossible because of the economic depression to ensure that they were provided with relief work. In Clause 10 it was finally agreed that political prisoners imprisoned before the date of the pact might be released if the two Irish Governments could reach agreement.[78]

The mood among many Northern nationalists was for a respite from the communal violence. At a meeting between Collins and Northern Nationalist representatives, where Collins admitted that 'for a good many months we did as much as we could to get property destroyed' in Northern Ireland, a section of the Belfast representatives urged restraint. Bishop MacRory declared that 'our people at the present time are more dispirited, discouraged, and cowed than they have been in the memory of anybody,' and he warned that a 'war policy' by the IRA would bring a 'terrible punishment' upon innocent Catholics. He remarked that a 'burning policy' would see the unionists 'repay you by destroying your lives.' Séamus Woods, commander of the local IRA, believed that nationalists were 'striving for existence' in Belfast, while the local IRA volunteers were demoralised by the prospect of long prison sentences and the 'unequal' nature of the struggle.

Among the border nationalists, Dr Gillespie, the east Tyrone delegate, offered resistance to MacRory's proposal, on the grounds that 'the best thing we can do is fight them out. There is no reason why we should go outside the Irish nation.' This view was shared by Cahir Healy, who argued that the pact should only apply to Belfast. The representatives from Northern Ireland were opposed to recognising the Northern political entity, despite the fact that, as the Free State minister Kevin O'Higgins pointed out, that the logic of the Treaty required 'reasonable co-operation' and recognition pending the outcome of the Boundary Commission. The Free State members were critical of the ambivalent attitude of the Northern Nationalist councils in declaring their allegiance to the Dáil. In the end a compromise, suggested by Healy, was reached, whereby the Dáil would convene a meeting of Nationalists of the various councils to discuss the matter, although it was felt that recognition should only be sought if a council could be sure of retaining its Nationalist majority.[79]

As part of Collins's non-recognition policy, Northern school managers and teachers were told that if they refused to accept school grants and salaries from the Northern Government, these would be paid by Dublin. On 17 February 1922 many schools joined the campaign, and the Free State Government agreed to pay the teachers' salaries from January 1922. This policy was ultimately reversed, and school managers were told to negotiate with the Northern Government, but it was not until November 1922 that the Free State Government ended the payment of teachers.[80]

THE COLLAPSE OF THE COLLINS-CRAIG PACT

From the beginning the chances of the pact succeeding were undermined by distrust between the two Irish Governments and the continuing violence. Since March 1922 there had been regular sorties across the border by the IRA, with pro and anti-Treaty units co-operating in these operations. Collins supplied guns to anti-Treaty IRA units on the understanding that they be sent to the Northern divisions of the IRA.[81] In this atmosphere the Police Advisory Committee met three times, its Catholic members chosen at a meeting of Northern Nationalists and the Free State Government, which MacRory and Collins attended. The Northern Ireland Government members of the committee felt that the Catholic members chosen were attempting to extract secret details of police organisation and numbers, to break down the RUC's machinery and, by demanding the abolition of the Specials and martial law, to prove to the world that the Northern Government could not govern. Ill-feeling within the committee increased when two of its Catholic members were arrested and attempts were made to arrest two others, while Catholic members were also disillusioned by the lack of movement on the question of Catholics expelled from their homes. On the Government side, Samuel Watt, Permanent Secretary to the Ministry of Home Affairs, believed that Collins's choice of 'extremist' members for the committee had indicated little desire to help the Northern authorities.

The Conciliation Committee set up under clause 5 of the pact met six times but, similarly, achieved little, as disagreements arose about its precise nature and powers. A Northern Cabinet meeting on 7 April 1922 clarified the situation by the statement that the 'Committee of Enquiry had no administrative power to summon witnesses, nor to call for official reports—it was merely to act as an Advisory Committee to the Ministry of Home Affairs and to exercise powers of moral suasion over the inhabitants.' Watt feared that if official recognition were given to the investigations and to reports of the committee it might 'interfere very seriously with the operations of the police and the general administration of justice ... The reports of the Committee will probably be used not for the purpose of assisting in stamping out crime, but for propaganda purposes.'

As with the Police Advisory Committee, the selection of Catholics for the committee, based on names mentioned when MacRory and Northern Nationalists met Collins on 5 April 1922, was criticised. Winston Churchill told Craig and Lord Londonderry, the Northern Minister of Education, at a meeting in Downing Street, that Raymond Burke, a Catholic unionist, and his associates had told him that the men Collins had put on the committee had tried to break up the committee and use it for belligerent purposes; this was confirmed by Joseph Devlin.[82]

In March 1922 Collins accused Craig and the Northern Ireland Government of failing to keep the undertakings made with the Free State Government and of having done nothing to restore the expelled Catholic and nationalist shipyard workers, while he (Collins) claimed to have undertaken to discontinue the Belfast Boycott. Collins denied a statement by Craig that the Free State sought to coerce Northern Ireland and stir up strife there by 'bombing and sniping her citizens,' describing this as an absolute fabrication. On the contrary, he claimed that the Free State's policy was to meet the objections and differences of Craig's party as far as they could. He could see no way out of the impasse until Craig 'radically alters his present inimical attitude towards the Government of Ireland and towards the helpless minority in Belfast.'[83] In a letter to Craig, Collins accused the Northern Ireland Government of being 'an authority in whose territory the members of the greatest Church in Christendom, which enjoys the protection of all civilised Governments, are harassed and persecuted in the most appalling fashion by armed mobs, who are apparently not interfered with in any way by your police and military.'[84]

In reply, Craig argued that securing the return of Catholic workers to the shipyards was a matter no government could undertake, because 'there is no law, as far as I know, whereby a workman can be compelled to work alongside somebody else whom he desires not to work alongside.' The Northern Ireland Government was prepared to give safe conduct to men to reach their work, and to help keep the peace when large bodies of men were marching to work in the morning, but no government could compel workmen to allow hands into their midst unless it be by the general approval of the workmen themselves. Craig had got the Belfast Loyalist Workers' Committee to discuss the matter with him, and they had agreed to the principle that the Catholic shipyard workers should be allowed to return, as the Craig-Collins Pact stated. However, it was felt that this could only be done if the fortunes of the shipyard industry revived and the yards were able to absorb the expelled workers; and with 67,000 people out of work, 8,000 of them ex-servicemen, Craig made it clear to Collins that before there could be any talk of 'returning any class whatsoever' of workers to employment in Belfast the case of the ex-servicemen had to be dealt with, for 'no one outside a lunatic asylum would suggest that, in order to make way for any persons, whatever their class or whatever their creed, there should be driven out of the yards other Loyalists.' Only if trade revived would Craig make a similar appeal to the shipyard workers.

On the question of the large-scale system of relief agreed in the pact, Craig argued that the agreement had been abrogated by an attempt to subvert the Boundary Commission with a large-scale 'predatory attack on our Ulster area' by the IRA, and it was not possible therefore for him to have gone on with the terms of the agreement. Collins, claimed Craig, was 'not big enough to stick to his signature.'

In attempting to find a more suitable system than the Council of Ireland for dealing with problems affecting all Ireland, Craig argued that the best method of achieving this was to have no such council, which he thought would be a constant source of friction. Peace in Ireland would be more easily obtained by each Government meeting the other as equals to discuss outstanding issues. Craig also denied Collins's claims that Ulster Protestants were engaged in a pogrom against Catholics.

> There are ... direct instances of attack upon us here in Ulster ... In the South, they were sending up their men, their bombs, and their arms for the very purpose of creating in this city and in the Six Counties a ... state of unrest and nervousness, and if possible of surrender amongst the inhabitants ... Underlying the thought behind certain leaders in the South ... we have the charge ... that there is a desire amongst the Protestants in the North and especially in Belfast, to carry out a pogrom against Catholics as Catholics ... I repudiate that with all the language at my command ... No such thing has ever been the policy of the Protestants here ... Outside the city of Belfast you have places like Portadown ... Lurgan ... Lisburn ... and Ballymoney ... where the Catholic population is in such a minority that if anything like a pogrom had ever entered the heads of the people those Catholics would have been swept into the Bann or swept out of Ireland ... I do hope ... that people will realise that the Ulstermen are up against, not Catholics, but that they are up against rebels, that they are up against murder ... Bolshevism, and up against those enemies not only of Ulster, but of the Empire ...[85]

Within the Northern Ireland Government there was resistance to the terms of the pact, which it was felt would undermine the effectiveness of the police and British army in combating unrest. Craig was advised by the Minister of Home Affairs, Sir Richard Dawson Bates, in April 1922 that to have released prisoners following the pact would have greatly affected the confidence of the regular police, the Special Constabulary, prison warders, and resident magistrates. The Northern Ireland Cabinet held the view, as Lord Londonderry told the British Home Secretary in December 1922, that the restoration of comparative peace by the summer of 1922 'has been attained through the firm, impartial and consistent administration of justice.'

Following the first Craig-Collins Pact, the Northern Ireland Minister of Finance had warned his Cabinet that any amnesty shown towards Sinn Féin political prisoners had to be extended to all unionist prisoners who could plead political extenuating circumstances, while Bates was of the opinion that it would be extremely inadvisable to release unionist looters and others who were convicted. Persuaded by these arguments, Craig wrote to Collins on 15 April 1922 pointing out that it could not be forgotten 'that there are many prisoners other than those of the Roman Catholic Faith who have been convicted of similar crimes and the efforts of our Government to restore law and order would be gravely handicapped if all those dangerous characters were released.[86]

In May 1922 IRA attacks continued, with the launch of an incendiary campaign aimed at the homes and businesses of prominent Unionists. Claims for compensation arising from malicious injuries totalled £794,678 in May and £760,018 in June 1922, compared with £252,578 for April. There was also an increase in intimidation and murder, with ninety murders in Belfast alone during May—although not all by the IRA—including that of the Unionist MP W. J. Twaddell, with no offenders caught.

Following the final transfer of security powers to Belfast on 22 May 1922, the Northern Ireland Government proscribed the IRA and related organisations and introduced internment of terrorist suspects. The police were given the power to close any road, lane, alley or bridge at a moment's notice to restrict IRA sniping. The opening hours of public houses were also curbed. Since 13 May 1922 Belfast had been under curfew between 9 p.m. and 7 a.m., and this was extended to the rest of Northern Ireland from 1 June for the hours of 11 p.m. to 5 a.m. In Belfast, 778 B Specials were mobilised for full-time duty; in County Down and County Fermanagh the figures were 820 and 1,060, respectively.

Many of the new security measures were carried out under the Civil Authority (Special Powers) Act, 1922, which extended the use of flogging and the use of armed guards on official and commercial buildings.[87] The Special Powers Act (as it is generally called) and the transfer of Field-Marshal Sir Henry Wilson—soon to be assassinated by the IRA in London—from his post as Chief of the Imperial General Staff to advise the Northern Ireland Government on security matters signalled the introduction of the new security policy. The Special Powers Act gave the Minister of Home Affairs the power to introduce regulations 'for making further provision for the preservation of the peace and maintenance of order.' The 'civil authority'—that is, the Minister of Home Affairs—was to have 'power, in respect of persons, matters and things within the jurisdiction of the Government of Northern Ireland, to take all such steps and issue all such orders as may be necessary for preserving the peace and maintaining order, according to and in the execution of the Act and the regulations.' The civil authority might 'delegate, either unconditionally or subject to such conditions as he thinks fit, all or any of his powers under this Act to any officer of police, and any such officer of police shall, to the extent of such delegation, be the civil authority as respects any part of Northern Ireland specified in such delegation.' The Act amounted to the civil equivalent of the statutory imposition of martial law.[88]

Even before the opening of the Civil War and Michael Collins's death during it, which distracted the Free State Government from the North, the IRA had in effect been defeated in Northern Ireland. From November 1921, when it accepted responsibility for law and order, the Northern Ireland Government had to rely on the Special Constabulary as its main counter-insurgency force. It was to form an integral part of a new police force, the Royal Ulster Constabulary, which was to replace the RIC but had still to become operational by the middle of 1922. Its target strength was to be three thousand, with a thousand places reserved for Catholics.[89] The effectiveness of the Special Constabulary in quelling IRA activity was acknowledged by the officer commanding the IRA's 3rd Northern Division, who admitted that its deployment had forced him to abandon flying columns in Antrim and Down within two weeks of a planned offensive in the summer of 1922. In the western part of Northern Ireland the IRA's 2nd Northern Division, and in Armagh the 4th Northern Division, suffered a similar fate.

On 9 July 1922 Northern IRA officers met Michael Collins and other members of the GHQ Staff in Dublin and agreed to call off the Northern campaign. On 1 August 1922 Eoin O'Duffy, the Chief of Staff, set up a separate command for Northern Ireland, with a military policy of avoiding conflict with the Special Constabulary and the British army; in this way the IRA offensive in the North was officially halted.[90]

The intensifying Civil War was to be confined to the Twenty-Six Counties. Only one complete division, the 4th Northern Division under Frank Aiken, took the anti-Treaty side; apart from individuals, the other divisions continued to take their orders from GHQ in Dublin. Northern pro-Treaty forces faced isolation, as all resources were concentrated in the South. Séamus Woods, commandant of the 3rd Northern Division, informed GHQ in July 1922 that there was now a feeling of abandonment by the Dáil among the Northern civilian population that had supported the IRA during the past months. 'Today,' he wrote, 'the people feel that all their suffering has been in vain and cannot see any hope for the future.' He warned that the divisional staff felt they could not carry on in such circumstances nor ask the IRA volunteers and people to support them any longer when there was no definite policy for the Six Counties.[91] By this time most of the pro-

Treaty IRA forces had joined the Free State army, leaving only a skeleton staff in the North. By January 1923 the Free State Government had decided to disband the pro-Treaty IRA organisation in the North.[92]

THE BOUNDARY COMMISSION

Following the ending of the physical force threat to Northern Ireland, the attention of unionists and nationalists switched to the Boundary Commission. The commission hung over the future of Northern Ireland, offering hope to Northern nationalists and the Free State Government that the province would be so repartitioned as to make it unviable, while for Ulster unionists it remained a continuing contribution to their sense of siege from Catholic, nationalist Ireland. From the beginning the Northern Ireland Cabinet saw its policy alternatives regarding the Boundary Commission as either stating that the Northern Ireland Government would not be a party to any agreement and refusing to be bound by any decision that might be arrived at or taking part in the commission and getting such terms of reference as were possible to act as safeguards for their interests.

At first Craig was inclined to accept the offer of Carson (now Lord Carson) to represent Northern Ireland within the commission and considered the possibility of compensation for loyalists forced to sell their properties on transfer to the Free State. In May 1922, however, following an electoral pact in the South between Collins and de Valera to prevent civil war over the Treaty, Craig came out openly against article 12 of the Treaty, calling the Boundary Commission the 'root of all evil' and picturing border loyalists 'being asked by us to hang on with their teeth for the safety of the province.' Craig felt he could 'picture their unspoken cry to us: if we sacrifice our lives and our property for the sake of the province are you going to assent to a commission which may subsequently by a stroke of the pen take away the very area you now ask us to defend?'[93]

Craig noted how Collins had recently stated that 'I have always said that the Treaty is a step towards a Republic. I do not withdraw one atom from any statement I have made about the Treaty.' Craig argued that the whole situation had been changed by the Collins-de Valera Pact, because when the British Government entered into the Treaty it was expected that when elections were held Collins would be returned by a majority in the Free State to a parliament within the ambit of the British Empire. This pact changed things, Craig claimed, because he was prepared to treat with a Free State Government within the ambit of the Empire but was not prepared to treat with a 'composite Government, one half of which is practically Republican in sentiment, while the head of the other half says that he does not go back upon a statement that he made that the Treaty is a step towards a Republic.' Before the Pact, if the Boundary Commission were to be set up, 'some of our most loyal people ... might have been lifted ... from territory in the British Empire and placed over the Border ... but still only putting them into another part of the British Empire.' But now the Northern Ireland Government declared that 'we will not have any Boundary Commission under any circumstances whatsoever ... What we have now we hold, and we will hold against all combinations.'[94]

In considering the Unionist Government's opposition to the Boundary Commission, the cultural and psychological importance of places in the west of the province, such as Londonderry and Enniskillen, dating from their significance in repelling the forces of the Catholic King James II in the Williamite Wars of the seventeenth century, cannot be underestimated. In opposing the Boundary Commission, Craig told how

> I said to Mr Lloyd George: 'Do you know that there is not an Orange standard throughout the world which has not got inscribed on it Derry, Enniskillen and the Boyne?' I said that it was unthinkable that the fixing of the boundary should rest in the hands of one man—one man who probably did not understand Ireland or Irish history, one who might by the stroke of a pen hand over the home, the cottages of those gallant men who spilt their blood for the safety of their own country, and one who might also sacrifice those historic emblems which every Protestant banner bore throughout Canada, Australia and America as well as here at home.[95]

On the nationalist side, the death of both Collins and Griffith in 1922 had begun a reassessment of the Free State's policy towards the North. Ernest Blythe had prepared a memorandum criticising the Provisional Government's policy of supporting IRA action and the economic boycott, emphasising that Ulster unionists could not be forced into a united Ireland.[96] Now it was Free State policy to make use of the Boundary Commission to achieve a united Ireland.

In October 1922 the Free State Government announced the establishment of a North-Eastern Boundary Bureau, headed by Kevin O'Shiel, a solicitor from Omagh, to compile Dublin's case for the Boundary Commission. O'Shiel established a Research Division, a

Publicity Division, and a North-Eastern Local Division, and legal agents were appointed to various districts within Northern Ireland. Because of the Civil War the Boundary Commission was not activated until hostilities ended. O'Shiel advised against an early formation of the commission, because of the impact of the contrast between the violence in the South and the 'law-abiding conditions' in the North. Furthermore, he felt that Bonar Law's new Conservative and Unionist Government at Westminster would lend its sympathies to the Northern Government because of the Civil War. W. T. Cosgrave, who had succeeded Griffith as the head of the Free State government, believed it a good tactical ploy to delay the appointment of the Boundary Commission until a new North-South customs barrier was in place, while O'Shiel argued that economic hardship would soon force traders in Northern Ireland to seek an end to partition.[97]

Among Northern nationalists the main division appeared to be less the old Sinn Féin-Home Rule controversy and more the geographical division between west Ulster nationalists, who expected the Boundary Commission to transfer Fermanagh and Tyrone to the Free State, and east Ulster nationalists, closely identified with Joseph Devlin, who were concerned at their plight if such a transfer were made.[98] The Irish News in 1923, with the Boundary Commission in mind, agreed with Cosgrave, who warned that some nationalists were not 'facing facts' with regard to partition but were waiting on the 'will of a Providence Who helps those who help themselves.' It warned that the average Northern nationalist 'cannot tell you what he expects: if he is of an exceedingly imaginative disposition he may, perhaps, look forward to the achievement of impossibilities through the agency of forces like the Lamp of Aladdin.' What nationalists needed, argued the Irish News, was a settlement, and such a settlement could not be framed until the question of the Boundary Commission had been disposed of.[99]

The Irish News was concerned because Northern nationalists were to have no control, no influence, over the movement of events. Yet nationalists were only really interested in one article of the Treaty, and until they knew what their position was it was impossible for them to frame a stable policy and course of action; but, warned the Irish News, days, weeks and months passed and nothing was done to relieve their suspense or enable them to face the future with a glimmer of knowledge about how they were to be placed.[100]

On the other hand, west Ulster nationalists, such as Cahir Healy, the Sinn Féin leader and journalist from Fermanagh, looked favourably towards the expected transfer of the two western counties to the Free

State. This expectation appears, given his later utterances on how to end partition, to have allowed Healy to comment favourably on the Northern Ireland Parliament contracting out of the Free State. He even argued that the Treaty gave effect to the principle of self-determination, not only for Ireland as a whole but also in relation to north-east Ulster. The Treaty, he believed, recognised and asserted the essential organic unity of the Irish nation: article 12 recognised the existence in north-east Ulster of a 'special problem demanding special treatment.' When article 12 permitted Northern Ireland to contract out of the Free State, the Boundary Commission was set up to determine Northern boundaries 'in accordance with the wishes of the inhabitants.' This meant, he claimed, that the principle of non-coercion was applied both to those who might not wish to remain under the Free State Parliament and to those who ardently desired to give it their allegiance. Healy argued that if the Belfast Parliament contracted out then the 'Nationalist majorities in the border areas must be given an opportunity of being restored to the Free State.' The principle of self-determination would thus be applied all round.

While Healy regretted that the north-east had contracted out, he accepted that it was entitled to do so, although he felt that 'if the common people of the north-east, who have so many traditions associated with the ideal of a united Irish nation, had been made aware of the issues involved in that decision, they would have insisted on remaining with the vast majority of their countrymen,' and he believed that 'even to this day the people of the Six Counties are ignorant of the privileges guaranteed to them by the Treaty.' Nevertheless he concluded that by contracting out of the Free State the Northern Ireland Parliament had tacitly admitted that it was bound by the whole of article 12 and that the principle of non-coercion, applied to the Six Counties as a whole, had now to be applied to those areas in the Six Counties where large majorities wished to be restored to the parliament of their choice.[101] Border nationalists, however, were to be disappointed.

In April 1924 Ramsay Macdonald, the new British Labour Prime Minister, requested that Craig appoint Northern Ireland's representative to the Boundary Commission. Craig formally refused on 10 May. On 5 June Mr Justice Feetham of the South African Supreme Court was appointed chairman of the Commission. However, the Judicial Committee of the Privy Council confirmed that it was beyond the powers of the United Kingdom Government to make an appointment on behalf of the Northern Ireland Government and that legislation would be required to enable it to do so. In September 1924 a supplementary agreement between Dublin and London allowed the latter to announce the appointment of J. R. Fischer, a former editor of the Ulster Unionist *Northern Whig*, as Northern Ireland's representative.[102] In October 1924 Craig had warned that if the British Government nominated a third member of the commission unacceptable to the Northern Ireland Parliament he would resign and 'place myself at the disposal of the people, no longer as Prime Minister but as their chosen leader, to defend any territory which we may consider has been unfairly transferred from under Ulster, Great Britain, and the flag of our Empire.'[103]

In the following year the Boundary Commission carried out its investigations, touring Northern Ireland's border areas, taking evidence and considering submissions. In response, in the spring of 1925 Craig called a Northern Ireland general election on the issue of the border to demonstrate unionist hostility to the commission.

In the end, however, the Boundary Commission was to secure Northern Ireland's boundaries, disappoint border nationalists, and produce a political crisis in the Free State. The chairman, Mr Justice Feetham, did not see that it was the duty of the commission, as many nationalists hoped, to reduce the viability of Northern Ireland by substantially reducing its territory. Although the wishes of the inhabitants were to be a determining factor, and the scope of the commission's work was not to be limited to a mere correction of irregularities in the existing boundary, Feetham also believed that it was not the commission's duty to reconstitute the Northern and Southern territories but to settle the boundary between them. Northern Ireland, he concluded, 'must, when the boundaries have been determined, still be recognised as the same provincial entity,' and the changes made should not be so drastic as to destroy its identity or make it impossible for it to continue as a separate province of the United Kingdom with its own parliament and government. The commission's findings recommended that the border be shortened by 51 miles and that 183,290 acres and 31,319 people be transferred to the Free State and 49,242 acres and 7,594 people be transferred to Northern Ireland.

The proposed redrawing of the border was never implemented. On 7 November 1925 the London *Morning Post* leaked the details of the settlement, together with a map of the boundary changes, causing a political crisis in Dublin[104] and forcing the Free State's representative on the Boundary Commission, Professor Eoin MacNeill, to resign in protest. MacNeill's resignation produced alarm among the border nationalists and a fear of abandonment. Healy complained to the editor of the *Irish Independent* that a suggestion by that paper that article 12 of the Treaty be scrapped in return for some financial concessions to the people of the Free State was 'a proposal so callous [that it] will not even be thought of by the Executive Council [the Free State government].' Healy pointed out that Northern nationalists had made as many sacrifices for the Treaty as the people of any other part of Ireland, and he found it amazing that, to free the people of the Free State from the legal obligations they had incurred under the Treaty, the liberties and rights guaranteed to the Northern nationalists should be scrapped and 'the people sold into political servitude for all time.'[105]

Border nationalists were shocked when a new agreement, negotiated by the British, Irish and Northern Ireland governments and signed by Baldwin, the British Prime Minister, Cosgrave for the Free State Government and Craig for the Northern Ireland Government declared that 'the British Government and the Government of the Irish Free State, being united in amity in this undertaking with the Government of Northern Ireland, and being resolved mutually to aid one another in a spirit of neighbourly comradeship,' agreed that article 12 of the Treaty, relating to the Boundary Commission, would be revoked and that the territory of Northern Ireland would be that set out in the Government of Ireland Act, 1920. Furthermore, it was agreed that the Irish Free State was to be released from its Treaty obligation to the British national debt; that the Free State government would assume liability for malicious damage to property in its area since 21 January 1919; that the Free State government would agree to promote legislation increasing the compensation in respect of malicious injury to property in its territory occurring between 11 July 1921 and 12 May 1923; and that the powers of the Council of Ireland would be transferred to the Parliament and Government of Northern Ireland, with a commitment by the Free State and Northern Ireland governments to meet together, as and when necessary, for the purpose of considering matters of common interest arising out of, or connected with, the exercise and administration of these powers.[106] The agreement was confirmed by the Free State and British parliaments, and the report of the Boundary Commission was suppressed for decades to come.

Defending the agreement, Cosgrave told the Dáil that he believed there was only one real security for minorities, on both sides of the border, and 'that is the good will and neighbourly feeling of the people among whom they live.' He felt that the meeting of Northern and Free State governments 'must inevitably tend to remove prejudice and allay anxieties, and to promote a better understanding.' Every step in this direction between North and South would react, Cosgrave claimed, through the development of a better spirit, in a favourable manner on the position of Northern nationalists, who themselves 'can assist in this development by becoming a connecting link instead of a wall of partition between Dublin and Belfast.'[107]

When the compromise agreement was revealed, in December 1925, Healy and the other nationalist MPs for Fermanagh and Tyrone claimed that the border nationalists had been 'callously betrayed' and that they were neither morally nor legally bound by the new agreement, as the Free State representatives had no authority to alter the Treaty.[108] Not all Northern nationalists, however, were dismayed by the outcome. Representing the views of the nationalists of east Ulster, the *Irish News* stated:

> We are glad this Settlement has been made and signed. Nothing but suffering and misery, unrest, ill-feeling, and the possibility of frenzied action on the part of political intriguers leading to disaster for the masses of the people could have resulted from an indefinite prolongation of the conditions that prevailed since 1921 ... We have gained one advantage—and it is neither small nor mean: we have passed out of a period of uncertainty, deceit, false pretence and humbug, and we find ourselves face to face at last with the stern realities of the situation which so many amongst us declined to consider during the past three or four years ... The Nationalists of the Six Counties must look ahead, examine their political resources and resolve to utilise them, resist the tendency to indulge in recriminations ... and realise, once and for all, that their fate in Ulster rests with themselves.[109]

A SECTARIAN SOCIETY: EDUCATION IN NORTHERN IRELAND

The sectarian nature of Northern Ireland society, coupled with the bitter legacy of the communal violence accompanying the birth of the new statelet, meant that reactions to the Northern Ireland Government's policies and initiatives, whatever the Government's intentions, were almost inevitably judged on sectarian cleavages. This was particularly so in the field of education.

The Education Act (Northern Ireland), 1923, which sought to transform education by establishing a non-sectarian, secular system, instead heightened sectarian tensions and grievances. The Catholic Church's educational demands were that Catholic children were to be educated in Catholic schools with a Catholic ethos; teachers were to be trained in Catholic teacher training colleges and appointed by Catholic clerical managers, who would also supervise their textbooks. This long-standing demand for separate schooling for Catholics was reiterated by the new Code of Canon Law that came into effect in 1918. This was the de facto education system in operation in Ireland in the early part of the twentieth century.[110] This policy produced opposition among Ulster unionists, who feared the Catholic Church's power; the *Northern Whig* in 1918 interpreted the Catholic Church's opposition to a British education measure as proof that

> the Hierarchy are more interested in ... Education ... than they are in Home Rule. They see ... a threat to their monopolies ... Ireland is to be educated according to the decision of Pope Leo XIII, and the aim of Irish education is to be, not the training of young Irishmen to play their part in life as self-respecting, honest, loyal citizens, but to be docile and submissive slaves of Mother Church and her Bishops.[111]

These underlying perceptions shaped Protestant and Catholic attitudes to the Education Act.

The Act created three categories of school. The first category consisted of 'provided' schools, which were built by newly established local education authorities, and 'transferred' schools, which were schools transferred to civic management by their former managers; both categories had their teachers' salaries paid by the Ministry of Education and all heating, cleaning, maintenance and capital expenditure covered by central and local government funds. The second category, 'four and two' schools, whose managers accepted the establishment of a special management committee, received complete payment of teachers' salaries and half the expenses of heating, lighting, cleaning and equipment, repair and general upkeep from the local rates, with a discretionary capital expenditure grant from the local authority. The third category consisted of those schools whose managers chose to remain completely independent of local control, receiving the full payment of teachers' salaries from central funds but no money whatever for capital expenditure, although they usually received half their heating, lighting and cleaning costs from the local rates. This third category, with its distinct financial disadvantages, became the norm for Catholic schools, because of the Catholic Church's demands that Catholic children be educated in Catholic schools with a Catholic ethos.

The Catholic bishops' anxieties regarding the new local education authorities established by the Education Act centred on two issues: the probable non-Catholic composition of education committees, and their discretionary powers in allocating funds. The 'provided' and 'transferred' schools were unacceptable to Catholics because they were controlled by local authorities rather than by individual Catholic clerical managers and because religion was at first excluded from the timetable for compulsory attendance. In practice few Catholics were nominated to education committees, and Cahir Healy protested that there was not a single regional education committee that was not under Unionist control.[112] The unacceptability of such schools meant that the Catholic bishops lost the opportunity to build new schools at public expense. The reluctance to adopt such committees arose from an unwillingness to have any dealings with local government bodies, first as part of the general boycott of the Northern Ireland Government and later pending the outcome of the Boundary Commission. The Catholic Church deeply resented the poor financial provisions for voluntary schools, and in their statement on Catholic grievances in October 1923 the Bishops protested that 'Catholic schools are starved, unless ... they go under a control that is animated by the dominant spirit towards Catholics.'[113]

Education in Northern Ireland, however, proved to be a highly contentious political issue for Protestants also. The Catholic hierarchy, opposed to partition, had refused to nominate representatives to a committee of inquiry into education, the Lynn Committee, appointed in 1921, with the result that the committee contained only one Catholic, a senior Southern civil servant. Lord Londonderry, the Minister of Education, saw this as a direct challenge to the Northern Ireland Government, a view compounded when a third of all Catholic elementary schools and a considerable number of secondary schools refused to recognise the authority of the Ministry of Education. The Lynn Committee, dominated and influenced by Protestants, suggested that what was wanted was compulsory Bible teaching, which would mean in effect the endowment of Protestantism by the state. Lord Londonderry in turn refused to accept the Lynn Committee's recommendations regarding religious instruction.

In December 1924 the United Education Committee of the Protestant Churches was formed among Presbyterian, Anglican and Methodist school managers. On 27 February 1925 the UEC met leaders of the Belfast Grand Orange Lodge and prominent Unionist politicians and decided to hold a Six Counties educational conference, in early March, to pressure the Government into amending the Education Act.

Under the rallying cry of 'Protestants awake!' the UEC's propaganda warned that the Act allowed 'a Bolshevist or an Atheist or a Roman Catholic to become a teacher in a Protestant school.' Joint agitation by the UEC and the Orange Order forced Lord Londonderry to concede that in future local educational authorities would be empowered to require that a programme of simple Bible instruction be given in provided or transferred schools in the period set aside in the timetable for religious instruction. This Bible instruction was not to include denominational or catechetical points: it was to be Protestant in nature but not distinctive of any Protestant denomination. Teachers were also to be compelled to give such Bible instruction as part of their required educational duties.[114]

THE ABOLITION OF PR

The Unionist Government's decision to abolish proportional representation in local and then in parliamentary elections also aroused bitter controversy between nationalists and unionists. The system of PR in local government elections was established under the Local Government (Ireland) Act, 1919. For the purposes of electing county councillors, each county was divided into county electoral divisions, each of which sent forward one councillor, with the two exceptions of Lurgan and Portadown. Similarly, for the election of rural district councillors and guardians the counties were divided into district electoral divisions, each of which was allotted two councillors. In the case of urban districts and county boroughs (cities) the electoral unit was the ward.

In the event of the abolition of PR, provision would have to be made for reversion to the pre-1919 system of electoral wards.[115] Section 14 (5) of the Government of Ireland Act, 1920, permitted this and allowed the Northern Ireland Parliament, three years after its establishment, to alter the qualification and registration of electors, the law relating to elections, the constituencies, and the distribution of the members among the constituencies, provided the number of members was not altered, with due regard being given to the population of the constituency.

On 16 April 1922 the Northern Ireland Parliament passed the Method of Voting and Redistribution of Seats Act (Northern Ireland), which abolished PR for local government elections, making necessary a revision of constituency boundaries. The Act had two main purposes: (a) to revert to the system of local elections that obtained before the

Local Government (Ireland) Act, 1919, and (b) to impose a declaration of allegiance on the officials of local bodies.[116]

On the question of PR, Craig wanted its abolition, not because he wanted to reduce Nationalist representation in the Northern Ireland Parliament but to reduce the representation of the Labour Party and independent Unionists, which he feared could undermine Northern Ireland's position within the United Kingdom through a combination of Nationalist and Labour members taking political power. He feared that Protestants might be seduced into supporting an anti-partitionist Labour Party, and he sought a strong government with a 'strong solid majority'. He wanted what he saw as the fundamental issue of Northern Ireland's politics—unionism versus nationalism—laid clearly before the voters. 'The real question at the bottom of the heart of every person in Ulster' was 'whether we are going to remain part and parcel of Great Britain and the Empire or whether we are going to submerge ourselves in a Dublin Parliament.' The only sure way to achieve these related ends, Craig argued, was by the encouragement of a stable two-party system in which Unionists and Nationalists, the 'two active, alert, vigorous parties in Ulster,' were opposing each other in a straight fight. General elections would then become what Craig thought they should be, a 'referendum on the question which of two Governments shall be returned to power.'[117]

The initiative for the abolition of PR in local elections came from rank-and-file Unionists, especially those in the western part of Northern Ireland. A special meeting of the General Committee of the West Down Unionist Association on 13 April 1922 passed a resolution proclaiming that PR was 'unsuited to Ireland and detrimental to the interests of the Unionist and Loyalist section of the Community,'[118] while Mrs Dehra Chichester MP summed up the anger of many Unionists when she told the Northern Ireland House of Commons: 'I come from an area where ... we have had to sit and listen to our King being insulted, to our Government being derided. We have been told that killing was no murder unless committed by the foreign invader.'[119]

Only one set of local elections, in 1920, and two general elections, in 1921 and 1925, were held under PR. In Belfast the overrepresentation of Unionists, traditional under the simple-majority voting system, was dramatically ended. Belfast City Council had usually consisted of 52 Unionists and 8 Nationalists, but after the 1920 local election it comprised only 35 official (that is, Government-supporting) Unionists, 2 independent Unionists, 13 Labour, and 10 assorted Nationalists. In the 1925 parliamentary election official Unionist representation was reduced from 15 to 8, with the loss of 3 seats to Labour and 4 to independent Unionists. In Belfast, Nationalists remained under-represented despite PR, partly because of the split between the Irish Party and Sinn Féin and partly because the city's constituencies were too small to give adequate representation to a minority whose votes were largely concentrated in one constituency, West Belfast.

Labour Party candidates, particularly in Belfast, objected to the equating of the religious composition of constituencies with Nationalist and Unionist votes cast. Outside Belfast, however, there was indeed a close correlation between parliamentary representation and the relative sizes of the Protestant and Catholic population. Comprising roughly one-third of the population, Catholics felt entitled to 16 or even 17 of the 48 non-university seats and 11 of the 32 seats outside Belfast and Queen's University. The former target was never achieved, but the latter was, in both general elections under PR. In County Antrim, for example, the nationalist vote of 16 per cent was so distributed that under the majoritarian system nationalists were unable to return a single representative to the Northern Ireland Parliament, while under PR they were able to return one out of the seven MPs for the county.

PR was abolished in parliamentary elections by the House of Commons (Method of Voting and Redistribution of Seats) Act, 1929 (Northern Ireland), which created a reversion to single-member electoral areas and constituencies. The effect of this was that Unionist representation on elected public bodies increased at the expense of all other parties. In Belfast, official Unionist representation increased from 8 in 1925 to 11 in 1929, at the expense of Labour and independent Unionist candidates. Under PR, Nationalists secured 33 per cent of the parliamentary representation outside Belfast and Queen's University; after 1929 they secured at most 28 per cent. On balance, however, in parliamentary elections Nationalists lost only one MP through the abolition of PR. However, Unionist representation on, and control of, local bodies was increased by the abolition of PR in local elections. After the 1920 local elections, held under PR, the Irish Party, Sinn Féin and the Labour Party controlled 24 of the 75 local public bodies, or 32 per cent; by 1927 Nationalists and Labour controlled only 12 councils, or 16 per cent. In Fermanagh, Nationalists had returned 63 members to the Unionists' 57 under PR: that is, they secured 53 per cent of all representation. This fell to 43 after the abolition of PR, while Unionist representation increased to 74. Catholics in Fermanagh, comprising 56 per cent of the population, obtained only 37 per cent of the representation on public bodies.[120]

ELECTORAL REDISTRIBUTION

What made the abolition of PR so controversial was the consequent redrawing of electoral boundaries. A commission, under Judge John Leech, the Deputy Recorder of Belfast, was appointed to hold inquiries in areas where distribution was likely to be a controversial issue. A series of public inquiries, to which ratepayers were invited to submit suggestions, was held at the beginning of 1923, with the object of arriving at equitable schemes of representation, largely on the basis of population but also taking into consideration the rateable valuation of property where the population could not be equalised, as was the norm in the local government franchise in Britain and in the Free State. Nationalists, however, boycotted the commission, mainly because they feared jeopardising their claims for transfer to the South under the Boundary Commission.

As a result, in all but five instances Unionists were represented at Leech's inquires, while in only two instances—at Irvinestown and Ballycastle—did Nationalists fully co-operate and help shape the new arrangements. At Irvinestown the only scheme presented to Leech was drawn up by a committee on which both Nationalists and Unionists were represented, while at Ballycastle the Nationalist case for equal representation was accepted in a scheme jointly submitted by Nationalists and Unionists. At the Dungannon inquiry the Nationalist delegation attended but offered no comment on the scheme submitted by Unionists and generally took no part in the proceedings; at Omagh the rural district council's Nationalist solicitor intervened only to condemn the proceedings and withdrew after his call for an adjournment had been rejected as obstruction. At Downpatrick a scheme was submitted by two Nationalist ratepayers, but they withdrew from the inquiry when Leech ruled, in commenting on the Unionist scheme, that suggestions need not be confined to changes within existing boundaries but could recommend the transfer of districts from one union to another. Usually, however, only a handful of Unionists attended the inquiries, and only one scheme, well worked out in advance, was submitted. These, in the main, were accepted by Leech with minor alterations. The non-participation of Nationalists allowed Unionists to dispute Nationalist claims of gerrymandering. Leech's recommendations were accepted by the Minister of Home Affairs, and Leech, at Lisnaskea, argued that nationalists had an opportunity to present their case and it was their own fault if they did not present schemes.[121]

Nationalists had boycotted Leech's commission, believing that the Unionist Government's aim was to gerrymander the new constituencies, regardless of Nationalist views. The *Irish News* claimed that Leech's duty was to do nothing 'but look wise, accept the schemes, and maps, and boundaries prepared in advance by the local political agents of Toryism.' But the *Irish News* also complained that all these preparations were proceeding without advertisement or opposition from Nationalists, who left themselves open to Unionist accusations that they had only themselves to blame. Nationalists of the Cookstown District, the *Irish News* pointed out in 1923, registered a formal complaint 'and did nothing more.' The Nationalists of the Cookstown District had no district organisation, it complained, and the situation was the same in the province as a whole, and Nationalists were therefore hapless 'in the face of the Government's determination to gerrymander.' The paper commented: 'It is this all over the Six Counties: one third of the population act—or rather do not act at all—as if they have abandoned all hope of ever asserting themselves again.'[122]

Nationalists were convinced that the Unionist Government had deliberately decided to gerrymander all constituencies to its advantage. Cahir Healy and his fellow-Nationalist representatives accused the Unionist Government of employing all its resources to thwart the Treaty settlement while the Free State had made good its obligations 'at very great cost in blood and treasure.' It was claimed that, not content with 'injuring the healing power of the Treaty by partition,' the Unionist Government 'inaugurated a policy whose declared purpose was to reduce the great Nationalist minority of 450,000 people to the status of helots in their own land.'

Nationalists claimed that they had 'none of the rights and powers enjoyed by citizens of modern democratic communities.' The first major grievance was the 'complete abolition of Nationalist representation on the public boards.' The principal steps identified as having realised this were (a) the abolition of PR, (b) the 'systematic gerrymandering of electoral areas,' and (c) the alteration of the franchise to the disadvantage of the nationalist minority. In the case of urban district councils, Nationalists claimed that the Unionist object referred to was achieved by the abolition of PR and a return to the old ward system, 'which had been drawn in the interests of the Unionists many years before.' They also claimed that the appointment of a Commissioner to revise the district electoral divisions on the basis of equality of population and valuation made it 'impossible for districts containing overwhelming Nationalist majorities to return a majority of the representatives.'

In the example of Omagh Rural District, Nationalists accused the Commissioner and the Unionist Government of accepting a scheme put forward by local Unionists that reduced the electoral value of the nationalist vote and exalted the value of the unionist vote. The electoral units were so arranged that large nationalist majorities were lumped together and given the same representation as the smaller unionist majorities. In this way, it was claimed, 5,381 unionist electors were assured of 21 seats at the next election, compared with 18 seats for 8,459 nationalists.[123]

The question of the local government franchise was employed by both Nationalists and Unionists to bolster their case. In local government elections in Northern Ireland, as in Britain, there was a property qualification. A man (women had yet to be given the vote in local elections) had the franchise where, on the last day of a qualifying period, he occupied, as owner or tenant, any land or premises in a local government electoral area and had so occupied it during the whole qualifying period. The valuation of the premises was immaterial as far as his voting rights were concerned.

The Unionist Government had to respond to repeated deputations to the Ministry of Home Affairs regarding the necessity for legislation to remedy abuses in connection with the local government franchise. For example, in Enniskillen Urban District the council let potato patches to a considerable number of people, and these were all admitted to the local government franchise; in the same district a set of stalls in a fairground was let to various people, which qualified them for a vote. Similarly, over fifty votes were obtained out of small bog plots of no value, the owners of these plots living in and having votes in a different electoral area. Thirty votes were also given in respect of a stable at the rear of a Catholic church used only on a Sunday.[124]

The Unionist MPs for Fermanagh and Tyrone were much concerned with what they called the 'faggot vote', which saw any land or premises occupied by a man entitling him to the local government franchise, creating 'bogus votes to an extent that creates a scandal.'[125] The Ministry of Home Affairs therefore recommended that legislation be introduced whereby no person would be entitled to the local government franchise who was not the owner or occupier of (a) a dwelling-house or (b) land or premises of a yearly valuation of not less than £5.[126] The Unionist Government and its supporters rejected Nationalist claims that the redistribution of electoral areas amounted to the 'usual jerrymandering [sic] tactics,' as there had been no revision of these areas 'since they were originally formed at some remote date.'

Unionists claimed that the redistribution was fair and impartial, arguing that, far from Fermanagh having previously been gerrymandered, Nationalists had a representation 'far in excess of that which they were entitled [to].'

Taking the valuation of electoral districts cited by the Nationalist *Fermanagh Herald* as evidence of Unionist gerrymandering, it was argued that the electoral districts that were described as Unionist had an average Poor Law valuation of £3,711 8s 9d, while the Nationalist districts had an average valuation of £2,765 6s 8d, so that each Unionist division under the redistribution scheme had, in this district, on average nearly £1,000 greater valuation than the average of each Nationalist district. Moreover, argued the Unionists, the total valuation of Unionist electoral divisions was nearly £40,000 more than the valuation of the Nationalist divisions. Notwithstanding the preponderance of valuation in favour of the Unionist electoral divisions, each Unionist division had an average of 258 voters, while each Nationalist division had 263 voters, or five more than the Unionist divisions. Thus, Unionists claimed that Nationalists had not suffered in respect of the low valuation of their areas. With this pattern repeated throughout the county, Unionists argued that, contrary to Nationalist claims, and based on the standard British qualification for the local government franchise on the basis of property, not population, 'Fermanagh is a Unionist and Protestant County,' because Protestants paid 75 per cent of the rates, and consequently nearly all Fermanagh was preponderantly Unionist, while Nationalist areas were principally in remote mountain districts of low rateable valuation. Therefore, argued Unionists, Nationalists had been given full representation, and 'it is rather difficult to understand the Nationalist case.'[127]

In this way, in reply to Nationalists, Unionists claimed that Omagh Rural District Council had been gerrymandered for twenty-five years by Nationalists. Local Unionists argued that before redistribution there were seven electoral districts in the Fintona Dispensary District— Carryglass, Derrabrad, Draughton, Fallaghearn, Fintona, Seskinore, and Tattymoyle. Fintona, which had sent a Unionist to Omagh District Council, had for many years had a population of 1,611, while Carryglass, Derrabrad, Draughton and Tattymoyle had populations of 324, 325, 534, and 565, respectively. Unionists pointed out that four Nationalist divisions thus returned eight representatives, while Fintona, with almost the same population as the other four, returned only two.[128]

The results did produce some startling advantages for Unionists. The following councils, which were Nationalist under PR, were captured by Unionists under the post-1922 electoral arrangements:

Londonderry County Borough (i.e. City) Council
Fermanagh County Council
Cookstown Rural District Council
Lisnaskea Rural District Council
Omagh Rural District Council
Omagh Urban District Council (from 1935)
Tyrone County Council
Enniskillen Urban District Council
Dungannon Rural District Council
Magherafelt Rural District Council
Strabane Rural District Council
Armagh Urban District Council (from 1946)

In addition, Belleek Rural District (County Fermanagh) was captured by amalgamating it with the Unionist-controlled Irvinestown Rural District; and Castlederg and Downpatrick Rural Districts, which divided fifty-fifty under PR, became safely Unionist under the post-1922 arrangement. This gave a total of thirteen councils formerly under Nationalist control and two evenly divided that the Unionists won. The Nationalists were left with the following councils, which they had won under PR and retained after 1922:

Ballycastle Urban District Council
Keady Urban District Council
Strabane Urban District Council
Ballycastle Rural District Council
Newry No. 1 Rural District Council
Downpatrick Urban District Council
Newry Urban District Council
Warrenpoint Urban District Council
Kilkeel Rural District Council
Newry No. 2 Rural District Council

To these were added Limavady Rural District after the Second World War, making a total of eleven authorities in Nationalist hands out of seventy-three. Not only was this a smaller number than the Unionists won from them after the abolition of PR but they were less substantial. The post-1922 electoral changes cost the Nationalists control of a city and two counties; the largest local authority district left in their hands was Newry Urban District, with a population of 12,000.[129]

Whether or not Unionists intended to gerrymander is not the essential point here. Nationalist and Unionist interpretations of discrimination were coloured by their perceptions of the other community's motives. Property valuation was the established qualification for local government voting throughout Britain and Ireland; but it also gave a political advantage to Unionists. Nationalists believed that Unionists wished to established a Protestant supremacy by gerrymandering the state, but Nationalists also were guilty of failing to test the reality of this proposition by boycotting any participation in the redistribution scheme.

In the redistribution of seats following the abolition of PR for parliamentary elections—in contrast to the consultation process begun when the local government boundaries were redistributed—the Unionist Government took on itself full responsibility for producing the scheme. It attempted to cause the minimum of disturbance to existing electoral areas and administrative boundaries and to produce accessible constituencies. Craig (now Viscount Craigavon) told the Northern Ireland House of Commons in March 1929 that the Government hoped to 'secure to this House when it meets again after the next election that it will be composed as nearly as possible of the balance of power which exists today.'

The Government presented its various conclusions in schedules to the House of Commons (Method of Voting and Redistribution of Seats) Bill (Northern Ireland). The only opportunity the opposition members had of commenting on the proposed new constituencies was during the passage of the Bill through Parliament. The Unionist Government alone decided which of the schemes were to be applied and in fact resisted the partisan schemes suggested by local Unionist associations. For example, the scheme suggested by the County Down Unionist Association would have given Unionists seven of the county's eight parliamentary seats, instead of the six they had won in the 1921 and 1925 elections under PR, while Londonderry Unionists put forward a scheme that would have given them all five, instead of just three, of the city's and county's seats and 'put an end to Nationalist aggression for all time.'

The impression of partisan government was reinforced by the results of redistribution. The Parliamentary Draftsman reckoned that the new seats had been so arranged as to maintain Nationalist representation at twelve, giving Nationalists the same number of seats they had obtained in the PR elections of 1921 and 1925. He calculated that the number of Nationalist MPs was likely to be reduced from two to one in County

Armagh; and although one Nationalist member for County Antrim would certainly disappear, these losses would, he thought, be offset by an increase in Nationalist representation in Belfast from one to three.

The results of the 1929 general election bore out the general accuracy of this forecast, except that Nationalists won only two Belfast seats, thus reducing their total representation to eleven, a result that contrasted markedly with the figure of sixteen or seventeen MPs that all those voters described as 'nationalist'—that is, Catholics—should theoretically have returned.

The difficulties in devising a scheme to maintain the balance of parties in Parliament were complicated by the distribution of religious denominations throughout Northern Ireland. For example, the 38,619 Catholics of Antrim, some 20 per cent of the county's population, were scattered throughout the county, while the 49,990 Catholics in Armagh and 32,455 Catholics in Fermanagh were largely concentrated in particular parts of the two counties, and the 95,682 Belfast Catholics—some 23 per cent of the city's population—were similarly concentrated in particular parts of the West Belfast parliamentary division. However, wherever areas of doubt existed in fixing electoral boundaries they were resolved in favour of the Unionist Party. While it was difficult to find fault with the redistribution in Counties Down, Tyrone, and most of Londonderry, elsewhere questions were resolved so as to maximise Unionist representation. The Government tolerated inequalities in Belfast, where Unionist constituencies with populations of eighteen to twenty thousand contrasted with a Nationalist constituency of over thirty thousand. The small Unionist majority in Antrim, less than 56 per cent of the county's population, was given 75 per cent of the county's representation, while the 56 per cent Catholic population of County Fermanagh was allotted only 33 per cent of the county's seats.[130]

The question of discrimination was coloured as much by the preconceived notions of Nationalists as by the actions of Unionists. Nationalists refused to participate in the decision-making process that set the new boundaries. This confirmed the Unionist view that they were unwilling to participate in the political life of Northern Ireland. Nationalists were convinced that the Unionist Government had intended to gerrymander the process from the beginning; the abolition of PR and the Unionist Government's failure to consult Nationalists about the redistribution of parliamentary seats merely confirmed for Nationalists what they had known all along: that the Unionist Government was out to discriminate against the minority. A vicious circle of distrust was created by the communal perceptions that Unionists and Nationalists had of each other.

THE NATIONALIST PARTY AND ABSTENTION

Nationalist perceptions of Unionists were reinforced by the treatment they felt was reserved for them after they took their place in the Northern Ireland House of Commons. After initially boycotting the Parliament, Devlin and County Antrim Nationalists took advantage of the statement by the Catholic bishops in October 1923 that 'the time has come for our people to organise openly on constitutional lines' and protest against various aspects of the Unionist Government's policy, notably in education. The division among Nationalists remained, however, and in Fermanagh and Tyrone they continued to place their faith in article 12 of the Treaty until 1925.[130] Cahir Healy, elected to the Imperial Parliament, had gone some way to ending his abstentionist stance by taking his seat there, a decision that struck at a fundamental tenet of Sinn Féin philosophy. Séamus McManus, a friend of Healy's from Mountcharles, County Donegal, expressed his disappointment at Healy's decision, writing to him to express how

> I got a mighty rude jolt when I read recently … that Cahir Healy, Sinn Féin advocate, had, amid the rapturous cheers of the English members, taken his seat in Britain's Parliament House!
>
> For twenty years they strove in vain to either break or sweep away the master-plank of the Sinn Féin platform. And after they had given up their efforts as a vain task, unable ever to break, bribe or intrigue even the weakest advocate of the policy … [that] a man of thought, culture and ability, voluntarily gives them their victory … is the poignant part of the shame to me.[132]

When Healy attempted to raise Nationalist grievances at Westminster he found that he was prevented from doing so by the Speaker's ruling that such matters could not be discussed at Westminster—as was the situation with domestic issues falling within the remit of the Canadian or Australian Parliaments—these having been transferred to the purview of the Northern Ireland Parliament. *Éire*, the official organ of the IRA, summed up the abstentionist response to this, arguing that even if Healy had been able to make his case it would be no more than an empty demonstration, for 'a minority in a foreign assembly, be its numbers three or eighty, is literally the voice of one crying in the wilderness.'[133]

Despite this setback, the mood of Northern Nationalists was shifting towards ending abstentionism. In 1925 a Northern Ireland general election fought on the border issue saw their seats increase from six to ten, and while their share of the vote increased from 12 to 24 per cent, that of the Republicans fell from 20 to 5 per cent. Devlin interpreted the results as a vindication of his policy of attendance at the Northern Ireland Parliament. In April 1925 Devlin and T. S. McAllister, MP for County Antrim, took their seats. Following the failure of the Boundary Commission to fulfil the hopes of border Nationalists, a County Down Nationalist convention in February 1926 asked its MP, Patrick O'Neill, to take his seat. On 10 March 1926 O'Neill and the two Nationalist MPs for Derry took their seats, with O'Neill explaining that 'they had now decided to accept the situation as it is, and to endeavour to make the best of it.' The remaining five Nationalist MPs, led by Cahir Healy and Alex Donnelly, finally relented in October 1927 and took their seats.[134]

In entering the Northern Ireland Parliament, Healy claimed that Nationalists did so not to 'throw complaints across the floor' but to criticise and draw public attention to injustice and to suggest ways and means of administering the Six-County area more efficiently and cheaply. Since the Nationalist minority in the Six Counties comprised nearly a third of the population, Healy believed they should become a 'great force in all legislative matters,' and he was sure, 'when the old bitterness simmers down,' that there would be a 'balance of power, between the crusted Tories of the Unionist Association and the other opposition groups that are developing.'[135]

However, any hopes that a Nationalist-Labour alliance might develop were dashed by the abolition of PR for parliamentary elections. Devlin, in 1927, called the decision to abolish PR in parliamentary elections a 'mean and contemptible thing ... when you have a majority and it is done deliberately in my opinion for the purpose of robbing the minority which I represent.' He believed, correctly, that the abolition of PR sought to destroy any other parliamentary opinion beyond that of the Unionist and Nationalist parties, and he accused the Unionist Government of wanting no independent opinion to 'tamper with the pure and undefiled Toryism they represent.' The consequence of this, Devlin argued, was that

when there are too many workers out of employment and you come along to this House and say 'What are you doing for the unemployed,' the reply will be 'We are doing what we can for the unemployed, but if you listen to this man it may be that the Pope will be again supreme in Ulster.' Some other social or economic or industrial grievance has to be redressed, and we raise it here. 'Oh,' we are told, 'you are not animated by true and lofty motives at all; this is not the reason why you are raising it. It is because you want to put us under a Dublin Parliament.' And so long as it is pure Protestantism and Toryism on that side, and Nationalism and Catholicism on this side we will go on and on discussing the most vital and sacred things that concern the domestic welfare of our people and the happiness of their lives and the prosperity of the State, but not as these matters should be adjusted for the welfare of the vast mass of the people; we are only anxious to discuss them from the point of view as to whether you will be put into the Dublin Parliament or whether, as I said, the Pope will reign supreme in Ulster.[136]

Devlin became more and more frustrated by what he saw as the Unionist Government's refusal to make concessions to the minority. By the beginning of 1927 he felt deflated by the failure of any of his amendments to be accepted, the negative response of the Government to his programme for unemployment relief, and the failed attempt to attain minority representation in the Senate. Despairing, he asked: 'What are we here for? Up to the present the Government have overridden on every occasion the views of the minority. They have trampled upon every right of the Opposition ... The Opposition are treated with contempt ...'[137]

2

Cold War

1928–1962

ECONOMIC AND FINANCIAL RELATIONS, 1928–1950

Northern Ireland's economy was heavily dependent on the markets of the British Empire. Many of its most important industries, particularly shipbuilding and linen, were to suffer from the worldwide depression that engulfed the industrialised countries following the Great War. In shipbuilding the work force had shrunk by 1933 to a tenth of its 1924 total of 20,000, with Workman, Clark and Company—the 'wee yard'— closing in 1934.[1] To help shipbuilding, Northern Ireland copied, and then made more generous, a British scheme for guaranteeing loans raised by ship owners ordering ships from Belfast yards. However, the Loans Guarantees Acts, 1922–1936, probably only slowed down the rate of decline. In the inter-war years unemployment in shipbuilding never fell below 13 per cent and at one time was as high as 65 per cent.

In the linen industry, unemployment ranged between 6 per cent, in 1927, and 56 per cent, in 1938. By the late nineteen-thirties Northern Ireland, with 30 per cent unemployment, outstripped Wales, with 24 per cent, and Britain as a whole, with 13 per cent. Northern Ireland had become the poorest part of the United Kingdom, with its people earning far less than those in Britain: in 1939 the average income per head in Northern Ireland was 58 per cent of the United Kingdom average, or £64.70 as against £111.

In an attempt to encourage new industrial growth the Northern Ireland Parliament passed the New Industries (Development) Acts, 1932 and 1937, offering limited incentives to bring industries to Northern Ireland: at first rent-free sites and relief of rates and later interest-free loans. However, the only large industry attracted in the inter-war period was an aircraft factory outside Belfast, Short Brothers and Harland, which the Government assisted with an annual grant of £2,709. Ultimately the number of firms taking advantage of the policy was only fifty-four, and even by 1955 they were providing work for only six thousand workers, mostly in Short Brothers and Harland.[2]

During this period Northern Ireland's most successful economic sector was agriculture. It was Northern Ireland's largest industry, and within it small mixed farms predominated; even at the end of the thirties half the population lived in rural areas. Before 1928 the Ministry of Agriculture's main work involved improved breeding and marketing methods, as well as education, research, and the extension of credit and co-operation. In 1928 a new phase was ushered in with the Miscellaneous Provisions Act (Northern Ireland), permitting legislation in the area of livestock and produce marketing. A series of Acts followed that ensured that by the time British protectionist economic policies were adopted in 1932, Northern Ireland eggs, potatoes, meat, dairy and orchard products were among the best available. The derating of land, on the British model, relieved a £14 million industry of a £1 million burden, while regulatory powers were introduced to alter farming practice, bringing significant results in the post-1932 period. The redirection of pig breeding, for example, increased the numbers involved from 219,767 in 1932 to 457,873 three years later. At this time also the Milk and Milk Products Act (Northern Ireland), 1934, graded milk, fixed prices, encouraged herd health, improved hygiene, and increased the production of subsidised school milk.[3]

Northern Ireland's economic and social conditions were determined by its relationship with the rest of the United Kingdom. Its financial and expenditure relations were the subject of negotiation between the British Treasury and the Northern Ireland Ministry of Finance. The underlying principle was that Westminster retained control of finance but expenditure was a matter for Stormont. The bulk of taxation was a matter reserved to the British Government; Northern Ireland was to receive a proportion of the revenue raised from taxes, after the 'Imperial Contribution' (for defence, foreign service and the like) was deducted. The amount of this was to be fixed by a Joint Exchequer Board, which consisted of members selected equally from the Treasury and the devolved administration, with an independent chairman appointed by the Crown. As a result of these measures four-fifths of the Northern Government's revenue came from London; in contrast, four-fifths of expenditure was left for decision in Belfast.[4]

In 1930 a step-by-step policy, matching improvements in the provision of welfare in Britain, brought health insurance into line, which had included, as in Britain, cash payments during sickness but not, unlike Britain, medical care. The conditions and level of unemployment benefit followed those in Britain, and in the thirties national assistance was added to unemployment insurance. Old age pensions, out of step for a few months in 1924–25, were brought into line in 1925, after which all pensions were on a par with Britain.[5]

Within the Northern Ireland Government this created a division between those who advocated the extension of social policy along the lines in which it was evolving in Britain and those who considered such a path unsuitable for Northern Ireland. One group centred around Sir James Craig, John Andrews, the Minister of Labour, and Sir Richard Dawson Bates, the Minister of Home Affairs. Broadly speaking, this relationship was characterised by a combination of sectarian and democratic policies and a high consumption of public funds. Another group, centred on two Ministers of Finance, Hugh Pollock and John Milne Barbour, and the head of the Northern Ireland civil service, Sir Wilfred Spender, strove to keep policy in line with pre-Keynesian financial policies in Britain.

Many fundamental financial decisions were taken at Whitehall and Westminster, but in Belfast the Ministry of Finance was not always able to impose agreements made in London on the Northern Ireland Cabinet. The Northern Ireland Ministers of Finance, as well as sharing orthodox British views of economic thinking, were also aware of growing economies in Britain. Craig and his politically sensitive colleagues held a different view. Pollock saw no shame in receiving hand-outs from London, pointing out that Northern Ireland's was a subordinate parliament, and its financial position as well as its social conditions were, he argued, from time to time fixed in practice by the attitudes of the British Government. He argued that the people of Northern Ireland had not asked for a devolved parliament, and as they paid the same taxes as the rest of the United Kingdom they were entitled to the same social services as other British subjects. For example, the Government of Ireland Act made no financial provision for unemployment benefit. Andrews argued that Ulster workers should not suffer worse benefits than those in the rest of the United Kingdom and that Northern Ireland should not be required, any more than Glasgow or Sheffield, to bear the cost of its own unemployed.

The plea for an amalgamation of the Northern Ireland unemployment fund with that of Britain was met by a Belfast-London agreement that in effect recognised Northern Ireland's disproportionate unemployment burden, which stood at 25 per cent in 1925, compared with 11 per cent in Britain, and saw the British exchequer defer three-quarters of its excess costs.[6]

Sir Wilfred Spender saw Craig as the epitome of 'little Ulsterism', overresponsive to any non-Catholic pressure group while remaining indifferent to wider British and imperial interests. For example, Craig literally asked to be bribed with armaments contracts by the British Government in return for his acquiescence in a London-Dublin deal in 1938.[7] Although by 1931 Northern Ireland's Imperial Contribution had dwindled to almost nothing, so also by 1932 had London's unemployment support payments. The Belfast administration was forced to keep itself afloat by a series of fudges, such as using reserve and road funds to prevent a budget deficit. It had to give way to Treasury pressure, and the province was submitted to revaluation, which had an impact on income tax assessment, improving the yield, and the levying by local authorities of an education rate.[8]

The step-by-step policy was maintained, however. In 1938 the principle of parity in the provision of services for Northern Ireland was conceded by London, and in 1942 it was recognised that Northern Ireland had 'leeway' to make up in order to attain British standards. By 1950 an expenditure system was being operated based on an assessment of local needs. The British Treasury was perfectly content with this arrangement, in that the Northern Ireland Department of Finance had a Treasury-type relationship with the other departments. Once the total sums had been agreed, the Treasury could then leave matters in the hands of the Department of Finance, secure in the knowledge that expenditure would be properly scrutinised.[9]

THE 1932 RIOTS

1932 saw one of the few instances of inter-community action, based on working-class opposition in Belfast to cuts in 'outdoor relief' during a period of high unemployment. A programme of cuts implemented by the coalition Government in Britain led to a campaign of protest in many cities, which took the form of riots in Birkenhead, Bristol, and London. These measures cut unemployment benefit by 10 per cent and increased insurance contributions. They also subjected transitional benefit (which had been introduced as uncovenanted insurance benefit) to a family means test and transferred its administration to the Poor Law machinery. This brought many people—in Northern Ireland as well as the rest of the United Kingdom—into direct contact with the Poor Law for the first time.

By British standards those in Northern Ireland were badly off. Belfast's outdoor relief rates were the lowest in the United Kingdom. In Manchester a married couple with one child received £1.05 a week, in Liverpool £1.15, in Glasgow £1.26, and in Bradford £1.30. The rate in Belfast was twelve shillings (60p) a week.[10]

The recorded unemployment figure for Northern Ireland in 1932 was 76,000, a 27 per cent annual average, compared with 22 per cent for Britain. Distress was uneven but was acute in Belfast, where the shipbuilding industry had run down to a work force of 1,900, less than a tenth of its total a decade earlier. The number of relief cases mounted steadily during 1932, with the Belfast Board of Guardians recording 884 cases in early January, involving 4,008 people, 1,985 in mid-June, involving 9,144 people, and 2,612 by September, involving 11,983 people. Many workers remained outside the unemployment insurance provisions, while for those insured the full payment of benefit lasted only for twenty-six weeks. After this there was sometimes a brief delay before transitional benefits were paid, so that for such people, as for the uninsured, the only source of livelihood available was the workhouse or outdoor relief, involving a strict means test and the obligation to undertake task-work, such as road-mending.

Disquiet had been growing about the condition of the city's poor, and it was noted that the children of the unemployed were more stunted and underweight than those of the middle class. In April 1932 Bates had lamented the lack of money for maternity and child welfare services, preventing him from attempting to reduce the mortality of women and children, which he described as a 'reproach to our state.'[11]

An outdoor relief workers' movement was established, with the aim of bringing Northern Ireland's outdoor relief rates into line with the rest of the United Kingdom and changing the administration of the relief, which, it was felt, was aimed at saving money for ratepayers and blaming the poor for their condition. Although the Unionist Government paid out an extra £300,000 on relief schemes, this was not in time to prevent trouble in the streets. The outdoor relief workers went on strike on 3 October 1932, their protests going in tandem with those of single people who were not entitled to any relief at all. Mass meetings and demonstrations were held, and later in that week there were minor outbreaks of disorder in Belfast's poorer areas. The workers were organised by a committee heavily influenced by the Revolutionary Workers' Groups,[12] a communist group opposed to the Northern Ireland Labour Party's programme of reformism and constitutionalism. The RWG sought from 1931 to inspire a strong revolutionary working-class movement that crossed sectarian lines by capitalising on working-class anger over unemployment, cuts in unemployment benefit, and the hardships of the Poor Law system.[13]

A 'monster' meeting was prohibited by the Government, but the RWG urged workers to defy the ban, and on 11 October 1932 the RUC attempted to prevent the march getting under way, with the result that intense rioting ensued in both Protestant and Catholic areas. While the police had concentrated their forces in the Catholic Falls Road, rioting became general in Protestant streets in support of the Catholic workers. The result was that two workers were shot dead and scores of workers and policemen were wounded and injured. In the Cabinet, Bates expressed the view, rejected by Pollock, that unless adequate measures were taken to relieve unemployment and poverty there was 'grave danger that the peace of the province will be endangered.'[14] As the trouble subsided the Poor Law Guardians announced an increase in the rates to £1 per week for a married couple, £1.20 for a couple with one or two children, £1.40 for a couple with three or four children, and £1.60 for a couple with five or more children. These terms were accepted by the workers at a mass meeting on 14 October.[15] Tommy Graham of the Revolutionary Workers' Groups commented:

> What we have achieved is in direct contradiction to those who said that the workers could not unite and could not fight, and the past fortnight will be recorded as a glorious two weeks in the history of the working class struggle. We saw Roman Catholic and Protestant workers marching together and ... fighting together. As a result poverty and destitution have been swept away and homes will be made brighter for many of the unfortunate workers.[16]

LOYALTY AND THE STATE

Non-sectarian class unity was short-lived, however, and the aftermath of the 1932 riots saw a resurgence of sectarianism. The 1932 riots have been interpreted by many socialists as evidence of the potential for working-class solidarity; however, they might also be interpreted as an aberration in a highly sectarian society.

Among the political representatives of nationalists, frustration had reached breaking point in May 1932, when, following a bitter parliamentary exchange on the reserved services, Joseph Devlin had led his supporters out of the House of Commons, complaining: 'We did not seek office. We sought service. We were willing to help. But you rejected all friendly offers. You refused to accept co-operation ...'

Following their withdrawal from Parliament, Northern Nationalists turned their attentions towards the Free State for support. In February 1932 Éamon de Valera's Fianna Fáil party was victorious in the Free State election. In February 1933 Devlin and Cahir Healy met de Valera and Seán T. O'Kelly in Dublin, with a request that they be admitted to Dáil Éireann as an alternative to the Northern Ireland Parliament. De Valera refused to consider this, and further declined to tender any advice to the Nationalists with regard to attendance at Stormont.[17] In November 1933 de Valera stated that Fianna Fáil's policy on the North was to see the first step towards national unity as getting substantial agreement and a common policy among those in the North opposed to partition. Once that was achieved Fianna Fáil would do its utmost to co-operate in making this policy effective. Fianna Fáil's aim was to consolidate Northern Nationalist forces, not divide them.[18]

De Valera's election victory produced a different reaction among Unionists. The Unionist Government feared there would be a repeat of Southern incursions into Northern Ireland, as in 1920–22. In 1932 Bates feared there would be 'tip-and-run' raids, and he was worried that if large bodies of men crossed the border 'we have no means of dealing with the situation except by means of troops.' Enniskillen was considered the most vulnerable point, and Bates feared there was nothing to prevent an armed mob of two or three thousand sacking the town before any forces could deal with the invasion. The Minister of Home Affairs was alarmed by the intense sectarian feeling that was abroad in Belfast and the unemployment levels there, which could see any outrage, however small, producing disastrous results, preventing the movement of either police or troops to oppose Southern incursions.[19]

The Unionist sense of siege focused on the threat to Northern Ireland from within and without. The Ulster Protestant League, an extremist organisation set up in 1931, condemned the 1932 riots and those Protestants who had been 'misled'. During the next four years the league, at first small and insignificant, grew in numbers and influence, receiving support from leading figures in the Unionist Party.[20] Major Henry McCormack, the Unionist MP for St Anne's in Belfast, was a leading figure, while the league used the Unionist Party head office in Glengall Street in Belfast for their meetings.

At the core of this agitation was a debate whether or not Catholics could be considered loyal to the Northern Ireland state. Of particular concern to the Northern Ireland Government was the employment of 'disloyalists' within the Northern Ireland administration. The Nationalist Party attacked the employment practices of the Unionist administration as sectarian, claiming that it refused to employ Catholics within the state apparatus on religious grounds, despite the fact that Catholics made up a third of the population. Such statements by Craigavon in 1932 that 'ours is a Protestant Government' were regarded as testament to this. Yet these statements have to be understood in the context of the perceptions Ulster Unionists had of the Irish Free State.

Ulster Unionists believed that nationalists had always been disloyal to the Crown and in pursuit of an Irish Republic. During a parliamentary debate on the state employment of Catholics in 1934, Craigavon moved an amendment to state that the employment of 'disloyalists' entering Northern Ireland from the Free State was prejudicial not only to the interests of law and order and the safety of the Northern state but also to the prior claims of 'loyal Ulster-born citizens' seeking employment. Although he claimed to have laid down the principle that he was the Prime Minister not of one section of the community but of all of it, he also admitted that he was an Orangeman first and a politician and a member of the Northern Ireland Parliament afterwards. In reply to a Nationalist MP who raised the matter of Catholics employed by the state, Craigavon asked him to 'remember that in the South they boasted of a Catholic State. They still boast of Southern Ireland being a Catholic State. All I boast of is that we are a Protestant Parliament and a Protestant State.' Were memories so short, enquired Craigavon, that Nationalists had forgotten those who came into Northern Ireland and attempted to prevent its government from being established? Unionists would 'never forget all the turmoil, murder, and bloodshed,' he said. He pointed out that in the Dominions—in Canada, New Zealand, and South Africa—people likely to endanger the safety of the state—the people he referred to in his amendment—were not admitted to its territory. He therefore thought it right to give a warning to the people that they should not employ anyone coming over the border who might be drifting into Northern Ireland to 'destroy the constitution and to start over the trouble which we overcame in 1920, 21, 22.' Further, he did not see why the 'loyal Ulster artisan', at a time when there were 63,000 people unemployed, should pay contributions in order to maintain people who came from the other side of the border, and he took the opportunity to 'urge the public to employ only loyalists—I say only loyalists. I do not care what their religion may be. I say that as long as they are loyal people we will engage them and give them every chance.'[21]

From the formation of the state itself the Unionist Government had attempted to secure itself from penetration by 'disloyalists'. A person engaged in public employment was required to take an oath of allegiance to the Government of Northern Ireland. This was resented by nationalists, while unionists saw it as an essential test of loyalty to the new state. In 1922 the Parliamentary and Financial Secretary to the Ministry of Finance argued that the Promissory Oaths Bill should be extended to school teachers, given that oaths of allegiance to the King and the Government of Northern Ireland were required of anybody serving in either a local government capacity or the RUC.[22] Craig thought the oath a precaution on the Unionist Government's part in leaving no loophole for people who were not in favour of British rule to creep into Government departments, as had happened in the past, particularly in the penetration of Dublin Castle during the Anglo-Irish War, and using their civil service positions to undermine the loyalty of those departments towards the Crown and the Government. Thus the Government was determined that every man, be he civil servant or teacher, in the pay of the Government should take the oath to the King and Government.[23]

However, the sense of siege felt by Unionists meant that the state employment of 'loyalists', for many members of the Northern Ireland Government, came to mean the employment of Protestants only. Bates refused to allow Catholic appointments to the Ministry of Home Affairs. In 1926 John Andrews, the Minister of Labour and later Prime Minister, found two 'Free Staters' in his ministry and instituted a tightening of regulations to disqualify such candidates automatically. In 1927 Edward Archdale, the Minister of Agriculture, boasted that there were only four Catholics in his Ministry.

In 1932 a storm of controversy was begun by Sir Basil Brooke, a parliamentary secretary in the Unionist administration, when he told an Orange audience:

There was a great number of Protestants and Orangemen who employed Roman Catholics. He felt he could speak freely on this subject as he had not a Roman Catholic about his own place. He appreciated the great difficulty experienced by some of them in procuring suitable Protestant labour but he would point out that Roman Catholics were endeavouring to get in everywhere. He would appeal to Loyalists therefore, wherever possible, to employ good Protestant lads and lassies.[24]

In his defence, Brooke claimed that he had never approached the employment question from a religious point of view. He denied that his remarks were an attack on the Catholic Church, asking, 'What ... has the difference in the principles of the Christian faith or in the various methods of worship got to do with the status of Ulster?' 'Absolutely nothing,' was Brooke's answer, arguing that his comments were an attack on the Nationalist Party, which he accused of defining all Catholics as nationalists, and pointing out that it was the Nationalist Party that used the words 'Roman Catholic' in a political as well as a religious sense. He quoted an example from a previous election, where Nationalist voters were instructed to vote for Irish unity and for their Catholic co-religionists, a definite example of the use of the words 'Roman Catholic' in a political sense.

Brooke told the Northern Ireland House of Commons of how, when in the Ulster Special Constabulary, he was informed of a plot to kidnap his eldest son. Therefore, taking every precaution, he 'got rid of every man in the place who I thought might betray me.' By inference this meant every Catholic or nationalist. He explained:

> There is, in fact, a Catholic political party, which ranges from what I might call benevolent nationalism to the extreme of the extreme. That is true, but the one plank in their platform is the destruction of Ulster as a unit and as a constitution. That is the policy, and it simply varies in method. Directly the hon. Gentlemen [Nationalist Party MPs] are attacked politically they play the old familiar game ... and hang on to religion and say 'You are treating us in a tyrannical manner; you are bigots' ... May I explain what I mean by the word 'disloyalist' ... A disloyal man is a man who is scheming and plotting to destroy the country in which he lives. It does not mean a man who lives in that country and lives under the constitution but is opposed to the Government ... but any man who is out to break up that constitution, which has been established by Great Britain, is to my mind disloyal. That is what I mean by disloyal ... These gentlemen have been questioning ... my urging that Roman Catholics— political Roman Catholics—should not be employed ... What they [Nationalists] like to do is to employ all their own people of the same political faith, and leave our people to employ those they cannot employ themselves. There are three reasons to my mind why disloyalists should not be employed. Those who support the constitution, whether they agree with the policy of the present Government or not, should have the benefit of that constitution. Secondly every disloyalist allowed to come in is a potential voter for the destruction of this country. And, further, there is a grave danger in employing men who at the first opportunity will betray those who employ them ... I shall use all my energies and whatever powers I possess to defeat the aims of those who are out to destroy the

constitution of Ulster be they Protestants or be they Roman Catholics.[25]

Nationalists reacted angrily to such charges and pronouncements and instead saw Unionist pronouncements of loyalty as an elaborate fabrication. Joseph Devlin rejected the charge that Nationalists were enemies of the British Empire and argued in Parliament that the worst thing that had happened to the empire was to 'inoculate it with revolutionary ideas,' and 'the first time we ever heard of rebellion or revolution we heard it here in Ulster, and it was not against the Nationalists, but against the authority of Parliament which you now regard as so sacrosanct.' When in 1912 the British Parliament, 'about whose glory we have heard much, and whose prestige is so essential to the stability of our institutions,' attempted to pass the Home Rule Bill, 'you [Ulster Unionists] threatened to rebel. You organised rebellion, and you have no right to charge me, who never threatened to rebel, and, what is more, never did rebel, and, what is further, never will rebel.'[26]

Cahir Healy, answering the accusation that Catholics were not loyal, asked:

> Loyal to what? ... When they [the Government] speak of loyalty they mean loyalty to His Majesty the Prime Minister. The King governs through his Ministers, and the Administration here does not know when a Socialist Government [in Britain] may replace the National one, so they stipulate for a conditional loyalty to the Throne, just so long as it suits. We have not forgotten 1914 and the [Unionist] Provisional Government set up here. We may live to see the praters about loyalty to the Constitution take their guns again and go out to attack the King's troops ... Nationalists are described as disloyal because they would change the Government by constitutional means ... If Nationalists are not permitted to work for a united Ireland by the vote, I ask what other means are left to them? You are coming to the time when Nationalist exercise of the franchise anywhere will almost seem a wasted effort.

Quoting the Prime Minister's brother, Captain Craig, in 1911, that 'Germany and the German Emperor would be preferred to the rule of John Redmond,' Healy and his fellow-Nationalists expressed the belief that Unionist attachment to the empire was a fraud. Nationalists, he pointed out, were accused of disloyalty yet 'never said they would prefer the Kaiser to the King ... No, instead, they sent out their sons to die for an ideal ... When someone said it was a war to make the world safe for democracy, he was merely telling a lie.' Referring to the proverb 'Treason never does prosper,' Healy told Unionists: 'When treason prospers men do not call it treason. Treason has prospered with you. You have achieved place and power by treason. There can be no better authority upon disloyalty than the Prime Minister.'[27]

These remarks reflected the view, as Jack Beattie, the Labour MP for East Belfast, stated, that Unionists 'have always been the most disloyal element in the Ulster Province, because they are only conditional Loyalists.'[28]

Referring to Brooke's statement that he had not a single Catholic in his employment, James McCarroll, MP for Foyle, did not admit that 'any man born in Ireland is a disloyalist. I do not admit that any man born in Cork, Kerry, or anywhere else in this country, is disloyal if he is loyal to his native land.' McCarroll believed that Brooke's statements were directed 'not against ... mythical disloyalists ... from the Free State, but ... against the Catholic Irishmen bred and born in the Six Counties.' Quoting the Grand Master of the Orange Order, Sir Joseph Davison, who stated, 'Whenever a Roman Catholic is brought into Protestant employment it means one vote less,' McCarroll concluded 'that this question is not one as between loyalist and disloyalist, but as between Catholic and Protestant.' As proof, opposition MPs quoted numerous occasions of alleged discrimination against Catholics; McCarroll claimed to know of an example of a Catholic veterinary surgeon who had served in the Great War, obtaining the rank of captain, but who lost out to a Protestant who had stayed at home during the war, when both applied for the same post.[29]

THE 1935 RIOTS

While Unionists in Government may have claimed that they made a distinction between 'political' and 'religious' Catholics, the practical impact of such pronouncements had a negative effect on community relations. Besides anti-Catholic pronouncements, the Unionists and the Ulster Protestant League carried out extensive anti-communist propaganda. A 'United Front' by the Labour movement and the Communist Party of Ireland on certain issues during 1934 and 1935 enabled the Unionists and the UPL to brand the whole labour movement as communist. The offices of both the NILP and the Communist Party in Belfast were attacked by Protestant mobs in June 1935. Labour was also tainted with Irish republicanism, as a result of the Republican Congress of April 1934, in which left-wing members of the

NILP, the left wing of the IRA and the Communist Party had participated.

Reflecting the deteriorating community relations was the fierce communal rioting that erupted in Belfast in the summer of 1935. There had been isolated outbreaks of sectarian disorder in 1933 and 1934, but the real trouble started around the time of the silver jubilee celebrations of King George V in May 1935. T. J. McCoubrie, election agent for the NILP, complained that it had been impossible to hold meetings or distribute literature since the beginning of May, when Protestant bands had played party tunes in a Catholic area and started trouble. McCoubrie specifically blamed the UPL for breaking up Labour Party meetings. On 12 July 1935 the Orange parade, originally banned by Bates, who revoked the ban under pressure from the Orange Order, was fired on near Belfast city centre, triggering off the worst wave of sectarian rioting the city had seen since 1920–22. Rioting continued on and off for three weeks, during which thirteen people were killed, scores were injured, and hundreds of families—mainly Catholic—were driven from their homes.[30]

Cahir Healy, in a letter to Sir Thomas Inskip, the British Solicitor-General, charged Northern Ireland ministers with responsibility for the disturbances, claiming that 'the identification of certain Northern Ministers with the Ulster Protestant League, whose watch word is "Protestants employ Protestants," indicates that they have been ... the moving spirits in a most intolerant and reactionary effort to stir up old animosities amongst the most ignorant and excitable classes in the community.' Healy complained that Sir Basil Brooke, now a Cabinet minister, was the principal speaker at a UPL meeting at the Ulster Hall.[31] The Irish News believed that 'during the past few weeks the lives of Catholics have been menaced in Belfast because of their religion. Catholics have been made to flee their homes because of their religion. This week Catholic workers have been intimidated because of their religion.'[32]

In August 1935 Brooke made a speech in which he insisted that Unionists 'had no quarrel with Roman Catholics as such, but with their members who strive to tear them from the Empire. It was a political and not a religious quarrel.' The News Letter commented that in the past Unionists, including Brooke and the Prime Minister, had been 'careless' in their remarks. This earned the rebuke from the Irish News that

even if we agree with the News-Letter that 'neither the Prime Minister nor Sir Basil Brooke had in mind any other distinction than the political one,' it is not enough to dismiss their anti-Catholic speeches as mere carelessness. What might be forgiven as carelessness from a speaker in a street-corner argument cannot be excused coming from the mouths of Cabinet Ministers, who are supposed to consider carefully their public utterances, and who in this case have allowed two years and a period of bloody rioting to elapse before discovering the 'error' of using sectarian nomenclature ... We do not dispute that the political goal of the Catholics of the North is a United Ireland; but the great majority of them favour working for that end by constitutional means, and, while they abide by the laws, no one is entitled to reproach them with disloyalty, even to 'Ulster' ... As to the conditions on which the Catholics of Northern Ireland wish Northern Ireland to be joined to the Free State there has never been any authoritative utterance whether it should be as a Dominion or a Republic.

There is a minority among Northern Catholics attached to a body which is definitely committed to an Irish Republic, and which admits the use of force to be justifiable. But this is a small minority, and would be smaller still if the Northern Government had made a bold attempt to treat the Catholics of Northern Ireland as subjects with rights equal to those of their Protestant fellow-citizens.[33]

The *Irish News* argued that by every test Catholic citizens in Northern Ireland were as loyal as any government could desire. They obeyed the laws, paid their taxes, and lived in friendship with their neighbours. In semi-public organisations, such as trade unions and chambers of commerce, they played their part in advancing the interests of their brethren of every religion. Their public representatives, argued the *Irish News,* in numerous local government bodies gave freely of their time and ability in helping to maintain and improve the amenities of the towns or rural districts in which they lived. Their representatives in Parliament performed the duties of an official opposition, and, with the exception of the IRA, the 'Catholics of Northern Ireland have for a long time recognised that the Northern parliament has come to stay for a long time, and have abandoned any connection they had with unconstitutional or secret political movements.' The truth for Catholics who posed as rebels and who 'abstract themselves into the world of sunbursts and round towers' was that 'however uncongenial it may sound to them ... they are not rebels; they are loyal citizens.'[34]

The *Irish News* attacked those anti-Catholic orators who, when charged with bigotry, replied that they did not object to the Catholic religion but to the activities of those Catholics who tried to upset the constitution. Referring to a charge in the *News Letter* that in Northern Ireland, and the Free State, the Catholic Church was disloyal to the Crown, it answered, 'It draws no fine distinction between religion and politics.'[35]

NORTHERN NATIONALIST POLITICS

Despite the communal trauma of the 1935 riots, the Nationalist Party remained deeply divided about the best course for furthering their cause. James McCarroll informed Cahir Healy that 'I have no desire to open my mouth in the place [Stormont] unless it is to expose some grievance.'

Abstention was undermining a tenuous Nationalist unity, and the 1935 Westminster elections presented Nationalists with a difficult problem.[36] Healy, the most senior Northern Nationalist following Devlin's death in 1934, explained to de Valera that he feared that Republicans were threatening to put up candidates in Fermanagh and Tyrone, in opposition to Nationalist candidates, at a general convention for Northern Nationalists. This, he pointed out, would lead to the withdrawal of the Nationalists and a repetition of 1924, when Republicans caused the seats to be lost to the Unionists by majorities of 38,000.[37]

As an alternative, George Gilmore of the Republican Congress, joint secretary of the Republican-Labour Committee, suggested to Healy that he convene a broadly based conference of Republican and Labour workers, based on the call 'Break with the Empire: build the Republic,' with the intention of ensuring unity of action at the elections and with a view to returning Nationalist representatives to an all-Ireland parliament in Dublin, which he believed de Valera could not refuse, on the two planks of 'Out of the British Parliament: into the all-Ireland parliament of an independent Ireland.'

The possibility of Nationalists attending the Southern parliament was to become a recurring theme in the search for an alternative to their inability to end partition. In practice, however, Gilmore conceded that the laws of such an all-Ireland Parliament would not function in the north-east of Ireland 'on account of the British occupation ... [but] it would be the beginning of the end of the Imperial rule there.' The north-east, he argued, would no longer be a foreign country, to be suddenly remembered in the South for a few weeks when an election was occurring, but as an ever-present problem. The IRA, Gilmore felt, were heading for the 'old Sinn Féin wilderness, and are aiming at using the Northern Elections to give an artificial backing to a policy of sheer abstention.'[38]

In reply, Healy explained that he lacked the authority to call a Republican and Labour convention but was responsible for convening a Nationalist convention in Omagh. Healy's main concern was that 'if the IRA persist in their course here, they will reduce the former strong anti-Partition vote here to an insignificant figure. We can poll a 90 per cent poll; they will not get a 25 per cent one. We have the election machinery for a vast area like this one with almost 400 polling stations, they have none.' In these circumstances, Healy could not see what could be achieved by way of such a conference.[39]

The Republican candidates issued a manifesto in which they declared that the election was a plebiscite against British rule and domination and against the claims of the 'English Parliament' to legislate for the Irish people. The election, it said, was also a plebiscite against the partition of the Irish nation and against any attempt by England and its agents to conscript Irishmen for service in an imperial war and the use of Ireland as a war base. 'It is particularly deplorable that citizens styling themselves "Irish Nationalists", should sit, in defiance of the wishes of the Irish nation, in the Parliament of the conqueror. Representation in the Parliament is a symbol of Ireland's slavery and subjection." The manifesto continued:

> The Proclamation of the Republic guarantees religious liberty to all citizens. Republicans uphold that principle and we plead for religious toleration and for the ending of sectarian strife. We condemn religious persecution and pogroms incited by the Imperial leaders to serve the Imperial object of keeping Ireland at enmity. England and her agents foment sectarianism to keep the mass of the people divided, so that they will be a more easy prey to economic exploitation ... People of North-east Ulster, regardless of religious creeds, which in the past have kept you apart, you now have an opportunity to declare for national freedom and unity ...[40]

In the event, the Tyrone-Fermanagh Nationalist convention adopted an abstention policy in an effort to effect a compromise with the IRA candidates to save the seats. An agreement between the Republicans and Nationalists was reached when the former agreed to drop the nomination of their two candidates if the Nationalist candidates going forward for nomination would make a written declaration that if elected they would not enter the British Parliament. A settlement was reached on this point, and the Nationalist candidates, Mulvey and Cunningham, signed the declaration, stating: 'I publicly declare that if elected to membership of the British Parliament I will not under any circumstances enter that Parliament or any partition Parliament in Ireland.'[41]

By 1936 Northern Nationalists had lost all semblance of unity, and the urgent need for a new, clear-sighted policy exercised the minds of its more perceptive members. In July 1936 negotiations were opened by the various elements with a view to organising a new Nationalist structure. Conventions were organised for Tyrone, Derry, and Armagh; at Armagh the delegates resolved 'that an association be established to have the partition of the country abolished as quickly as possible, to look after the interests of the minority ... and have all victimisation ... exposed ...' A Belfast Nationalist convention the previous month had proved abortive, but an 'extreme wing' associated with Harry Diamond proceeded in July to form a National Unity Organising Committee, pledging itself to a Republican stance, determined 'to repudiate the British-imposed Treaty of 1921 ... and to ensure that no representative of the organisation will take part in the proceedings of any partition Parliament, or any Parliament other than the sovereign independent legislature of all Ireland ...'[42]

Another Nationalist association, centred around Healy's supporters, emerged in September 1936. The Irish Union Association was launched with the hope of uniting all aspects of Nationalist opinion on a common basis of agreement within the organisation. Its constitution declared that its objects would be:

1. The National Unity and Independence of Ireland.

2. To foster a spirit of co-operation and national ideals.

3. To seek the co-operation and support of all our fellow Irishmen for the reunion of the country and to ensure that no final settlement with Britain is made by the Irish people which will permit the present system of a partitioned Ireland to be continued.

4. To promote a national outlook upon all public matters.

5. To assist in securing social services for all citizens; to assist the workers in procuring proper housing and living conditions, and to co-operate with any movement which has [as its aim] the betterment of the people.

6. To attend the work of Registration.[43]

From the South, Éamon Donnelly, TD for Laois-Offaly and later a

Stormont MP for Falls, Belfast, urged Healy in September 1936 that the time was ripe for Northern Nationalists to do something positive about ending partition. Donnelly was critical of the lack of progress on this issue, warning that since partition had been in operation for the previous fifteen years, 'if the present position lasts for another ten years we may chuck [it] in. No one will mind us except as a lot of weaklings who saw what to do and didn't do it.' As a solution, Donnelly suggested: '1st Leave Stormont' and '2nd Demand admission to the Dáil.' He was convinced that this would pull together nationalists, north and south, and would make the question of reunification practical politics again.[44]

Healy thought that Donnelly's proposal was blighted by new legislation in Northern Ireland that compelled candidates to sign a nomination form declaring that if they were elected they would take their seats: otherwise, within three months the seat would be declared vacant and a new election held. Arthur Griffith, argued Healy, had only intended that abstention would be used for a definite period and to meet a certain situation. Healy felt that it soon led to an aggressive policy of non-recognition, which no people could carry on for any length of time. He argued that for an abstention policy to work a united people was required, but 'nowhere can such a people be found today.'

As a compromise, Healy suggested that those elected could take their seats, make a considered protest, and then leave, which he believed would be just as effective as any total abstentionist policy. He was also conscious that a member of the Northern Government had warned that if the Dáil made provision for Northern MPs, or senators, to sit in the Dáil, those people would be interned or given the option of going to the Free State permanently. Healy pointed out that 'our abstention from the Imperial Parliament has not made one particle of difference here or elsewhere. Already the Irish people have forgotten whether our members are at Westminster or not. They hardly know their names. The British people are not aware of it.'[45]

Donnelly, in reply, called Healy's attitude 'purely provincialism and partitionist,' arguing that the issue was not a matter for either North or South but for all of Ireland, claiming that Healy was wrong about abstention from Westminster and concluding that 'our quarrel is not with deluded, ignorant Orangemen. The responsible people are in Downing Street ...'[46] Abstensionism, however, continued to divide Northern Nationalists, and by October 1937 the Irish Union Association was declared defunct.[47]

NORTH-SOUTH RELATIONS

The Gaelicisation of the Free State began a process of alienation by Ulster Unionists from their sense of Irishness and a greater reliance on their sense of Britishness. The Sinn Féin philosophy had been that to de-Anglicise Ireland they had to de-Anglicise themselves first. The pro-Treaty party, Cumann na nGaedheal, decided that all instruction in the first two years of national schools be in Irish, a policy that Fianna Fáil expanded to permit even greater emphasis on Irish.[48] Ulster Unionists, not surprisingly, saw 'Pro-Gaelic' as 'Anti-British'.[49] However, for many Northern Nationalists the opposite was the case. Cahir Healy argued that

> nationality is not politics; it is greater than politics; and superior to all vicissitudes of parties. A man may think for instance, because he is a Republican, a Free Stater, an Hibernian, or some other school of politics that he is thereby a Nationalist in the real and true sense. He may or he may not. He may shout 'Up the Republic,' or something else or vote for this policy or that policy, and have scarcely any nationality in his system. Such a man may care very little about the language, traditions, history, literature, music, games or amusements of his ancestors. In his outlook on life, he may be a mere imitator of English ways, an anglicised and denationalised Irishman—an Irishman merely in name, and yet call himself a Republican, Free Stater, or an Hibernian ... Nationality is that living spirit that makes a man love, respect and reverence the land of his birth, and her people, and all her various features and distinctive characteristics, her scenery, her language, her traditions, her music, her games and amusements ... Hence the true national ideal means far more than an Ireland governing herself without interference from any outside source. It means an Ireland true to herself, true to her past, therefore living her own life, thinking her own thoughts, preserving and proud of her own distinctive characteristics that have come down through the centuries. This is the Ireland that the true Nationalist loves, honours, and is prepared to defend with his life. In a word, it means an Irish-Ireland—not an anglicised Ireland.[50]

Ulster Unionists, on the other hand, were further alienated by the Catholic nature of the Free State. The power of the Catholic Church in the South was obvious and public, and a religiously homogeneous Irish state was assumed and legislated for. Developments included legislation prohibiting divorce; de Valera's publicly expressed view that, while there would be no religious discrimination against the Protestant minority, the Irish people were 'ever firm in their allegiance to our ancestral faith and unswerving even to death' in their devotion to the Holy See; and the recognition, in article 44 of the Constitution of Ireland, drawn up by de Valera and enacted in 1937, of the 'special position' of the Catholic Church 'as the guardian of the Faith professed by the great majority of the citizens.' All these served to confirm the Ulster Protestant fear of domination by the Catholic Church in a united Ireland.[51]

Ulster Unionists were also alienated by the increasing republicanism of the Southern state, the removing, for example, of all references to the King from the Constitution and an increasing separation from the British Commonwealth. In 1937, after the Pope's envoy in England said that the Pope urged on his followers the solemn duty of 'honouring the name of Catholic' by being the best of citizens and being loyal to the authority vested in the British King and all civil power, since it took its authority from God, the *News Letter* drew a distinction between Catholics in England and Catholics in Ireland.

> If to be 'a good Catholic' is to be a good subject of the King and a good and loyal citizen, serving country and Empire, the vast majority of Irish Roman Catholics fall far short of such a standard. They are not loyal to King and Empire. In the Free State large numbers of them are not even loyal to constituted authority, and in Northern Ireland they are, for the most part, hostile to constituted authority ... In Northern Ireland Roman Catholic school children were not encouraged to show loyalty to the authority vested in the King or respect for civil power. Objection was taken, in many instances, to a display of the flag of Empire ... In both the Free State and Northern Ireland Roman Catholics as a whole denounce any sign or symbol of the British Crown as 'Imperial propaganda.'[52]

Ulster Unionists were angered by the South's territorial claim, in the Constitution of Ireland, to the territory of the whole of Ireland. Article 2 of the Constitution, defining the Irish nation, declares:

> The national territory consists of the whole island of Ireland, its islands and the territorial seas.

Article 3 states:

> Pending the re-integration of the national territory, and without prejudice to the right of the Parliament and Government established

by this Constitution to exercise jurisdiction over the whole of that territory, the laws enacted by that Parliament shall have the like area and extent of application as the laws of Saorstát Éireann and the like extra-territorial effect.[53]

The reaction among Northern nationalists was, naturally, far more favourable. The Irish News welcomed the new Constitution as providing, at some future date, the inclusion of Northern Ireland in 'Éire'.[54] Cahir Healy felt that the Constitution had taken notice of partition for the first time, and although it did not mean the immediate release of Northern nationalists, 'it is, at least, comforting to know that they have not been forgotten.'[55] Cardinal MacRory welcomed the Constitution as a 'great Christian document full of faith in God as the Creator, Supreme Lawgiver and Ruler, and full also of wise and carefully thought out provisions for the upbuilding and guidance of a Christian State.'[56] The Irish News also welcomed article 44 of the Constitution, stating that the chief point in its favour was that it was the recognition of a 'plain fact'. In contrast, it pointed out that the statement that Stormont was a 'Protestant Parliament for a Protestant people' was refuted by its own inaccuracy, and that if there were a united Ireland in the morning the Roman Catholic Church would still be the faith of a great majority of its citizens. No attempt, said the Irish News, had been made to ignore the Protestant minority in the South, and fear of religious persecution 'is not a real obstacle to Irish unity, but the fear will always be played upon by those whose own ideas of religious tolerance are summed up in their "Protestant Parliament" slogan.'[57]

Craigavon's response to the new Constitution was to declare that 'it makes not a pin of difference what takes place in Southern Ireland as far as our position in the United Kingdom and the Empire is concerned.' He felt that the man was not born who could produce the 'miracle union' of North and South, and he warned that if attempted, a situation would develop similar to the violence of the civil war then enveloping Spain, only that in Ireland it would be a hundred years' war. Therefore, Craigavon considered it better for the North and South to carry on as they were, with the latter governing their country, obtaining law and order and peace, while the former would be left 'absolutely free to be able to shake hands' with those who were 'English-born, Scottish-born, Welsh-born, or born of that stock in other parts of the world in all equality under British citizenship, saying to each other: "How can we help to develop the Empire?"'[58]

At Stormont the Minister of Finance reassured Unionists that, with regard to articles 2 and 3, the Southern Government had no jurisdiction over Northern Ireland and that Northern Ireland's constitutional position within the United Kingdom was fully protected by the Government of Ireland Act and other statutes of the Imperial Parliament. No special steps, therefore, were considered necessary to safeguard the maintenance of Unionist citizenship within the United Kingdom.[59] Such claims to Northern Ireland reinforced the Unionist sense of siege and, as Lord Londonderry had explained some years before, unlike any community in England, Scotland, or Wales, for years the Ulster unionist community was, in varying degrees, a threatened community; and 'a threatened community presents many additional difficulties to those who try to govern that community. Suspicion runs like wildfire, and any misunderstanding is liable to widen into a chasm of doubt and uncertainty.'[60] Bates told the Victoria Women's Unionist Association in 1938:

> So long as we live there will always be the danger of Home Rule or merging into the Free State. We will never get rid of it. One has only to go to England to see the extraordinary apathy towards us by people who should be our friends. We do not understand this apathy in England towards us ... All we want is to live our lives as God has placed us here. Yet, we have this continual menace at our doors—a menace which will last as long as we live.[61]

The announcement in 1938 that British and Irish ministers were to meet in an attempt to settle prolonged Anglo-Irish difficulties, including the so-called 'Economic War' between Ireland and Britain over the repayment of land annuities dating from the Union, raised Northern Nationalist hopes that an end to partition was at hand while at the same time heightening Ulster Unionist fears. The *Irish News* described the announcement as 'sensational' and claimed that the negotiations were not going to be concerned with defence and commerce alone. Looming large was the issue of partition, and Northern nationalists would 'rejoice' at this news. The removal of partition was, said the *Irish News*, essential if negotiations between England and Éire were to lead to a better understanding.[62]

A meeting of Nationalist members at Stormont welcomed de Valera's announcement in the Dáil that partition was to be one of the several questions to be raised in the negotiations and assured him that Northern Nationalists 'shall be most anxious to co-operate with [their] Unionist fellow-countrymen here upon all matters of mutual interest, once the unity of the country is established.' Alderman Richard Byrne

MP said that he would be delighted if the discussions resulted in the border being abolished; Senator T. McLaughlin called on all lovers of peace in Ireland to sink any difference of opinion, come together and decide on united action under the banner of a united Éire; while H. K. McAleer, MP for Mid-Tyrone, trusted that the Irish delegates would not allow themselves to be 'dodged', for any settlement that did not include the abolition of partition would be 'fruitless'.[63]

Setting forth their implacable opposition to partition, Northern Nationalists forwarded a memorial to de Valera outlining the grievances against partition but adding: 'Even were its [Northern Ireland's] regime one of justice and equality, of liberty and fair play, we should still oppose the dismemberment of our Fatherland, for we are Irish, and until we are united with our brethren of the rest of Ireland not only are we deprived of our rights as Irishmen but the historic Irish nation, unnaturally divisioned, is robbed of its glory and greatness.'[64]

In response to the announcement of talks, Craigavon felt it necessary to 'put the position of Ulster beyond doubt' and allow the people to pronounce on the issue, and a general election was set for January 1938.[65] 'We yield nothing to any opponent either without or within,' he declared in response to a loyalty resolution from an Enniskillen Orange lodge, while his reply to another was, 'Not an inch.'[66] Sir Basil Brooke summed up the attitude of Unionists to de Valera's proposal to raise the issue of partition during the talks by drawing an analogy with the United States and imagining that in Anglo-American trade talks Canada's territory should be part of the bargain. It was intolerable, said Brooke, that a part of the British Empire should have the impertinence to come along and say that Ulster should be deprived of the constitution given it by King George V.[67]

For Northern Nationalists the solution for partition lay with the British Government. Cahir Healy accepted that overtures to the Unionist Government to end partition were 'absolutely wasted'. He believed that 'the only hope, therefore, there can be of making an end of Partition was England, who had made Partition and would unmake it when it suited her.' How soon that occasion might be was difficult to tell, Healy conceded, but he added:

When that time comes I have no doubt, remembering English history, and knowing it as a country which has always compromised, that England will be perfectly willing, for the sake of having at her doorstep a friendly neighbour in her hour of crisis, to put the question of ending Partition as a moral necessity to the Northern junta, and in that way the Irish question will be settled and Irish unity restored.[68]

At a Fianna Fáil meeting in Donegal, Healy called on de Valera to use the dispute over the payment of land annuities between Ireland and Britain to drive home to the British that there could be no final solution until they conceded the right of the whole Irish people to choose the government they wanted. There was, said Healy, 'no money advantage which would ever compensate the people for the right of being masters in their own land.'[69]

Healy, together with the Nationalist MPs Joseph Stewart and Patrick Maxwell and Senator T. McLaughlin, travelled to London, where they met de Valera. After the meeting Healy issued a statement declaring that 'however strong we have been behind Mr de Valera in the North in the past, we would regard it as a betrayal of all our interests if he ignored the problem of partition by getting a trade and defence agreement only, although we think that he has no intention of doing such a thing.'[70] Northern Nationalists hoped that 'Dev will let the ground be prepared for trade ... and get as many cards as he can, put on the table by the British, and work up to a point, and then stand on [the] solution of partition.'[71]

The National Council for Unity, supported by the abstentionist MPs A. J. Mulvey and Patrick Cunningham, argued that the people of the Six Counties had never been allowed to express their mind on the single issue of partition. They called for a straight referendum on the question of unity and were confident that if the whole people of the Six Counties were freely allowed to vote 'yes' or 'no' on partition, the great bulk would declare against it. Such a referendum, they argued, would have to be held separately from a general election, so that all citizens would be free to be asked, 'Are you in favour of the Unification of Ireland on a just and equitable basis?'[72] The National Council for Unity aimed to demonstrate that the 'partitionists' of the Unionist Government were a 'faction subsidised by a foreign power and residing in a small district not having a single county solidly behind them.' While approving of any equitable trade agreement between Britain and Ireland, they reminded negotiators on both sides, with regard to the prominent question of the defence of Britain and Ireland, that 'the only country against which Ireland at present needs to be defended is the Power which upholds with arms and money, the outrageous partition of our land and people ... We affirm, therefore, that we are opposed to any agreement with Britain for co-operation in the defence of these islands against other Powers until the supreme grievance of Partition is rectified.'[73]

During the negotiations, de Valera had wanted the pressure for the ending of partition to come from within Northern Ireland, and he desired a series of anti-partition meetings for this purpose.[74] Healy agreed and took the *Irish Press* to task in January 1938 for its suggestion that Northern Nationalists should ignore the forthcoming Northern Ireland elections, arguing that 'this means, in practice, handing over the seats to Lord Craigavon ... How could such a result strengthen the national position here or elsewhere? Lord Craigavon could boast that we were now so content with his rule that we did not dare to contest the elections, fearing that there had arisen a considerable body of Nationalist opinion who believed no longer in separation from England.'[75]

The Northern Ireland Government, on the other hand, had decided that it did not wish to be directly represented in the Anglo-Irish negotiations and instead asked that the British Government, in concluding any agreement, take into account the Unionist Government's concerns. In January 1938 Craigavon forwarded to Samuel Hoare, the British Home Secretary, details of how grievously the economic war between the South and Britain had affected Northern Ireland. Craigavon 'most earnestly' urged the British Government to secure concessions from Éire that would 'help to revitalise certain features of our industrial life,' as well as the adoption of measures to 'safeguard our industrialists against the influx of goods across the land boundary from a highly protected market.'

Éire, however, was unwilling to concede a free trade agreement with the United Kingdom as a whole or Northern Ireland in particular. The Northern Ireland Government warned the British Government that it wanted free trade between Éire and Northern Ireland within a year and that any other arrangement would further weaken the ailing Northern economy by placing 'in the hands of the Government of Éire the means of bringing further economic pressure on Northern Ireland.' Such an arrangement, Craigavon told the British Prime Minister, Neville Chamberlain, would present the Northern Ireland Government with serious difficulties, for it 'will be argued that the disloyal part of Ireland is getting a substantial advantage at the expense of the loyal portion.'

Stormont considered two options in the face of continued opposition from Éire to their demands: the acceptance of an agreement with compensation from the British Government as 'some tangible advantages for undertaking a risk which is bound to have a very disturbing effect both politically and economically,' or publicly opposing any agreement. From the beginning of March 1938, in the Northern Ireland Cabinet, John Andrews and Sir Basil Brooke considered resignation and public opposition. Such an action followed by a Northern general election could, the British Cabinet were told, create a political crisis in Britain.

Craigavon, however, unaided even by officials, took charge personally of the negotiations with the British Government and in an interview with Chamberlain promised to support any agreement, provided adequate compensation was offered to Northern Ireland. Brooke and Andrews were dumbfounded to find that Craigavon had pledged his support to the proposed agreement, despite warnings of the possible consequences at home. Andrews considered resigning but was persuaded to stay on by Sir Wilfred Spender, who felt that 'in regard to Éire the damage was beyond repair & the best course open to him was to do what he could do for Ulster.'

Chamberlain had appealed to Craigavon to support the proposed agreement to reduce his 'anxieties over the international situation [because] it has become almost essential for me to show some evidence that the policy of peace by negotiation can be successful ... An Anglo-Irish agreement ... would greatly add to the impression made upon the world. And it is very necessary that an impression of solidarity here should be made, and not least in Berlin.'[76]

From the viewpoint of the Belfast-London axis, the Anglo-Irish Agreement in its final form was threefold: some agricultural subsidies applying to Northern Ireland would in future be borne by the British Treasury; arrangements were devised to relive possible future budget deficits in the province; and Belfast was assured that London's contributions under the Unemployment Insurance Agreement of 1935 would not be re-examined should they exceed the agreed limit of £1 million, with the prospective deficit for 1938 standing at £1.7 million.[77]

The disappointment among Northern Nationalists was immense. The Irish Government had been unable to move the British Government on the question of partition, which was regarded by the British as a matter for the Northern Ireland Government and Parliament. Controversially, the British Government did concede the return of the Southern naval ports that it had retained under the terms of the Treaty.

Following a meeting in Belfast, the Northern Nationalist representatives issued a statement that, while welcoming the financial settlement, placed on record 'our profound disappointment that the agreement between the Governments of Éire and Great Britain did not include any reference to Partition, the main matter of interest to our people here,' and expressed the hope that all parties in Éire would unite in making known abroad the conditions under which nationalists existed in the north-east. One of the statement's signatories, Senator John McHugh, was more forthright in his views, complaining to the *Irish News* that he believed de Valera 'has no policy about the North. He is only using us for his own purposes.' Referring to de Valera's call in the Dáil in October 1937 that 'the time is now ripe for a united national move forward for the security of our unity,' McHugh replied that he considered de Valera's statement as having 'nothing behind it' and of being 'more harmful than helpful … Such statements hinder rather than help the members of the minority in the Six Counties.'[78]

WORLD WAR, 1939–1945

Following the disappointment of the Anglo-Irish Agreement, Northern Nationalists turned their attention to the possibilities another world war between Britain and Germany might create for the ending of partition. In 1938 the Nationalist MPs and senators had observed how the British Government was so troubled by the affairs of Czechoslovakia that 'she has strongly recommended that the grievances of the German minority should be removed, and that they should have full national autonomy in administrative affairs.' Their disabilities, it was claimed, were very similar to those of Northern nationalists, and the Nationalist representatives regretted that, so far, the British Government had not made any recommendation to the Unionist Government in its 'penal treatment' of the Northern minority and expressed no disapproval of the 'policy of sectarianism' engaged in by the Northern Ireland Government.[79]

Healy, in September 1938, thought it an opportune moment for Northern Nationalists to take counsel on what their immediate course of action ought to be should war become a reality. He thought it was the intention of Britain to try to influence the United States, in the event of war, to join with Britain and France. He proposed that the most influential Irish, Italian and German people in the United States should be organised to make an Anglo-American 'union of hearts' impossible. Northern Nationalists, he argued, should be in a position to put the facts of their case before Irish America and to invite their aid. Healy thought it significant that President Roosevelt should at that point have sent a Catholic, Joseph Kennedy, as American ambassador to London and another as minister to Dublin. He suggested the calling of a convention that would invite delegates from every party opposed to partition and that from such a conference a number of delegates should be selected who would be empowered to put their case to the world.[80]

Peadar Murney, secretary of the National Council for Unity, concurred, regarding the consolidation of nationalists and 'anti-partitionists' in one solid block demanding the sovereign unity of the nation as a 'first-class national and political achievement.'[81] However, the question of abstention again raised problems, with Murney claiming that the majority of nationalists endorsed the Council's abstentionist policy and that 'in view of that, we feel that we would be weakening the effect of our own efforts ... if we co-operate publicly with ... active members of the Belfast Parliament.'[82]

Healy, in reply, stressed that his proposal did not seek to debate the issue of abstention but concentrated on agreement between all those opposed to partition. He believed the nationalist people would welcome a united front at this time and that all parties would be willing to make some concessions to achieve such a desirable end.[83] Where all Northern Nationalists were united, however, was on the attitude that they would adopt in the event of the United Kingdom, and consequently Northern Ireland, becoming involved in hostilities. Looking to a future conflict, the National Council for Unity declared:

> The fact that part of our country is occupied by the armed forces of Great Britain ... may make our land a target for Britain's enemies. Moreover it is just possible that conscription ... may be threatened in the six severed counties ... We are as much opposed to conscription as All-Ireland was in 1918. Ireland is a moral unit in spite of the British law dividing it, and a time of crisis, we trust, will prove that the natural consequences of that fact will outweigh any efforts of man-made partition.
>
> There doesn't seem any reason to doubt that ... all-Ireland is united in the desire to live at peace with all nations and ... we recognise that the only sensible course for us in a world war is one of neutrality.[84]

When war did break out between Nazi Germany and the British Empire, in September 1939, Ireland was the only Dominion that remained neutral. This policy was wholeheartedly supported by Northern Nationalists. In December 1939 a special conference of members of the National Council for Unity and Nationalist parliamentary representatives, noting how Britain had declared war in defence of the principle of democracy and the rights of small nations to decide their own destiny, free from aggression and the fear of aggression, demanded that Britain apply these principles to the Irish nation, one of the oldest and smallest European nations and one regarding whose natural boundaries there could be no possible dispute. Their statement declared that British aggression was responsible for dividing Ireland and that that division had been perpetuated by British subsidies to the Northern Ireland Government. The statement concluded by saying that if Britain's declared aims and policy in the war were not to be exposed to the world as cant and humbug, Britain had to apply those principles to Ireland and to see that control of the Irish nation's destiny was vested in the Irish people, 'without hindrance or interference from any other power.'[85]

As the Second World War progressed, the Unionist Government sought Nationalist participation in a scheme for home defence. Joseph Stewart, a Nationalist from Dungannon, summed up the feelings of many ordinary nationalists when he said that 'it would be disastrous for any one of us to be a party to asking our people to join ... any force under the administration of the Northern Government ... The Irish Party got their lesson in 1914 and I can never forget the treachery of England ...'[86]

As rumours began to circulate in mid-1940 that the British and Irish Governments were involved in talks that might lead to the ending of Irish neutrality in exchange for a British declaration that they were in favour of Irish unity, a conference of the Northern Nationalist representatives in Armagh in June 1940 passed a resolution stating:

They would remind their fellow-Nationalists across the Border that declarations ... were made in the years 1914 to 1918 by Irish political leaders, with disastrous results to themselves and the national cause ... The leaders of that day ... trusted the British Government's promise of Home Rule for all of Ireland. We know how that promise was implemented when peace was established ... There is no issue which ought to take precedence of Partition. If it is not settled now, it may drift along for half-a-century. At all events, we believe the Government of the Twenty-Six Counties ought to proceed cautiously with schemes fraught with menace to the peace and manhood of this divided country until they get an undertaking that the democratic principles for which Britain went to war abroad are to be put into practice at home.

We have been placed in such a position that it might be said that we have no country to defend; one of the belligerents is still in possession of part of the Irish nation. There is nothing to arouse the enthusiasm of the young people or to inspire them to acts of patriotism and sacrifice ...[87]

One of the signatories, Peadar Murney, told the *Irish Press* that all Six-County Nationalists approved of the Irish Government's policy of neutrality and that they were anxious that it should be respected by all the belligerents, and for the whole country. 'We in the North regard Partition as Ireland's supreme grievance.' Nationalists believed that partition took precedence over all other issues in the present crisis, because Ireland would be easier to defend if it was a unit, and unity was the national objective. Murney argued that partition endangered neutrality, because it left a 'vital part of the country occupied by one belligerent and a standing temptation to the other.' If the Six Counties were actively involved in the conflict, Murney feared that the whole country would be drawn in, and all the nation's gains would be thrown into the melting-pot. Partition, he argued, prevented Ireland being defended as a strategic unit, 'which it is by nature,' and the Irish Government's defensive plans were thus crippled. An immediate solution would for the British Government to open discussions with the Irish Government and to transfer all its reserve powers, which included defence, to the Irish Government. 'Once these were restored to the national authority,' concluded Murney, 'local adjustments could be made between Irishmen.'[88]

The extent to which Northern Nationalists saw partition, rather than the war, as the fundamental issue for their community was illustrated in August 1940 when three Nationalist politicians—Senator T. McLaughlin from Armagh and John Southwell and Peadar Murney from Newry—decided at a meeting in Dublin with Dr Edouard Hempel, Nazi Germany's representative in Ireland, to place the Catholic minority in the North under the protection of the Axis powers. Soon afterwards an unnamed Nationalist delegation from Lurgan raised the issue of partition with the German and Italian ministers in Dublin, who both promised support and indicated that the matter would be raised in broadcasts by German and Italian radio stations.[89]

Other nationalists, however, were less content with such passive alliance-building with the Axis powers. A potentially greater danger to the Northern Ireland statelet was provided by the efforts of the IRA to build alliances with Nazi Germany. Since 1938 the IRA, under its Chief of Staff, Seán Russell, had conducted a bombing campaign in England. The IRA refused to recognise the legitimacy of either the Northern or Southern Irish parliaments but instead recognised the remaining handful of Republican members of the second Dáil Éireann, elected in 1921—that is, those Republicans who rejected the Treaty but did not join de Valera's Fianna Fáil—as the sole legitimate government of

Ireland. On 8 December 1938 Russell announced that these members of the second Dáil had signed over their authority to the Army Council of the IRA, making it the *de jure* government of the Irish Republic and thereby giving the IRA the right to use force and levy war. On 12 January 1939 the IRA sent an ultimatum to the British and Northern Ireland Governments, declaring

> that the government of the Irish Republic, having as its first duty towards the people, the establishment and maintenance of peace and order, herewith demand the withdrawal of all British armed forces stationed in Ireland ... The government of the Irish Republic believe that a period of four days is sufficient for your government to signify its intention in the matter of the military evacuation and for the issue of your declaration of abdication in respect of our country. Our government reserve the right of appropriate action without further notice if, on the expiration of the period of grace these conditions remain unfulfilled.

When the four days had elapsed the IRA issued a manifesto declaring war on Britain. By July 1939 there had been 127 explosions in British cities, and by August these had resulted in the death of seven civilians. In general, the bombings had little effect on British policy towards Ireland.

With the advent of the Second World War, Russell made contact with an agent of German military intelligence who visited Ireland in 1940. Later that year Russell arrived in Nazi Germany for training in espionage, and it was agreed that he should return to Ireland. Unfortunately for the IRA, Russell died *en route* on board a German submarine; after this a number of German spies sent to Ireland were quickly captured, and the IRA's attempt to build an alliance with Nazi Germany came to nothing.[90]

For Nationalists the supreme question remained partition; and sympathy for the IRA's aims, if not its methods, was ever present. The execution of IRA members convicted of participation in the bombing campaign elicited latent sympathies. Cahir Healy, Joseph Stewart MP, Patrick Maxwell MP, Alex Donnelly MP, Senator John McHugh and Senator T. McLaughlin wrote to Sir John Anderson, the British Home Secretary, accusing the British Government of an 'inherent antipathy to the Irish race' following the execution of two IRA men.

> The men never intended to take life. However misguided their policy might have been and however regrettable its effects, it is certain that

the vast majority of the Irish people, knowing their motives, combined to ask your Government to spare their lives ... The British Government cannot appreciate the motive which actuated the two Irishmen whose actions were designed primarily to draw attention to the hypocritical action of the British Government in making war in Europe for principles which it so shamelessly outrages at home ... If the result be to establish here a united front amongst all classes against British Imperial aggression, the lives of the two Irishmen will not have been given in vain.[91]

Not surprisingly, the attitude of Ulster Unionists to Nationalist reactions to the war created further political tensions. On the evening that war was declared on Germany the Northern Ireland Government had interned forty-five IRA men, adding them to those already in confinement under 'grave suspicion'. In Parliament, Craigavon justified the action, declaring that the Government was not there for citizens to have their lives and property destroyed by 'cowardly assassins, men who never hesitate to do what they can to destroy the State,' especially at the moment when the empire was at war and when every assistance was wanted; therefore 'nothing should be done to put sand in the wheels of our defence here at home.' 'They are the King's enemies,' Craigavon said. 'Can any punishment be too great for them?'[92]

From the Unionist Government's perspective, a far greater threat to Northern Ireland's position within the Union than any that could be offered by the IRA began to appear in June 1940, when the British Government opened discussions with the Irish Government on the possibility of abandoning its neutrality in return for a British declaration in principle in favour of Irish unity. May and June 1940 had witnessed severe British defeats in the Battle of France, and Britain's position appeared desperate. Neutral Ireland exposed a serious strategic risk to the security of Britain. The Prime Minister, Neville Chamberlain, sent Malcolm MacDonald to Dublin as an emissary to meet the Taoiseach, Éamon de Valera, to negotiate a possible solution. When he heard of this, Craigavon urgently telegraphed Chamberlain: 'Profoundly shocked and disgusted by your letter making suggestions so far reaching behind my back and without any pre-consultation with me. To such treachery to loyal Ulster I will never be a party.'[93]

When asked to join with Éire in facilitating the defence of Ireland as a whole, Craigavon laid down three conditions. The German and Italian ambassadors, who continued to be officially resident in Dublin, should be asked to leave. Éire should abandon neutrality, a term the

Prime Minster found 'nauseating', declaring: 'We have either to fight for Britain in every way we can or we are against her along that horrible, dirty path of neutrality.' The third condition was that constitutional questions not be raised until after the war. Was it unfair, Craigavon asked, for all political questions of this kind to be laid aside so as not to hamper their efforts to defeat the enemy? 'We have only one enemy that Ulster looks to,' he argued,

> and that is the one that we, along with the rest of the United Kingdom, are hopeful of being able to beat in the end. Would it strengthen and help the defences of Great Britain if the whole of Ulster were neutral like the South? If all the Army and the Navy and the Air Force were told that this being a neutral part of Ireland they must retire and go back to their own country in England, Scotland and Wales, would that help the British people? Would it help if our people were compelled to pull down the Union Jack and to stand neutral under a flag whose colours—even at the moment I could not tell you what they are? Would that help in any way?[94]

Craigavon's privately preferred solution, which he called on the British Government to implement, was as follows:

1. A Military Governor should be appointed over *all Ireland*, for the period of the war, without any consideration of the political border ...

2. Subject to supreme control by the Military Governor civil administration to be carried on through the two Parliamentary institutions as at present.

3. To meet the susceptibilities of the South, the Defence Force might be composed chiefly of Scottish and Welsh Divisions, all ranks to be especially warned of the strength of the IRA ...

4. A few carefully selected Irish-speaking Officers should be attached to the Dublin headquarters of the Military Governor.

5. There should be disseminated throughout Éire ... pamphlets in English, and Irish, explaining that the military were there to defend the interests of the Irish people—no question of 're-conquering Ireland' ...

6. The American Ambassador should make the necessary representations to render impossible the export of munitions of war from the United States to *any* section of the Southern Irish.[95]

Craigavon's hysterical pronouncements demonstrated the fear he felt for Northern Ireland's position within the United Kingdom. Sir Basil

Brooke later disclosed that his main worry in this period, apart from security, was the prospect of de Valera reaching an agreement with the British Government, whereby he traded neutrality for the ending of partition. Brooke wrote that 'at a moment of crisis in the death struggle Northern Ireland could have been sacrificed. I had an awful feeling that had we refused, we would have been blamed for whatever disaster had ensued.'[96]

In June 1940, when Brooke met the Southern senator Frank MacDermot he told him that 'the south had to give some proof of its pro-British, pro-Ulster tendencies ... namely declare war before any discussions could take place.' MacDermot added that Brooke 'admitted privately that if the south were to join the war on Britain's side in return for post-war unification, Craig's Cabinet would be split with his [Brooke's] own vote favouring a new relationship with the south.'[97] Brooke's son recalled how at that time

> my father told me that ... there were pressures on the Northern Ireland Government. He said that if he were faced with the choice of losing our civilisation or accepting the unification of Ireland, he would find a very difficult decision. He regarded western civilisation as of greater worth than anything else, being absolutely convinced of the menace of Nazi Germany. It was my impression ... that in those circumstances, he would have to do his best to ensure Irish unity.[98]

The crisis passed, however, when de Valera formally refused the British advances, mindful of the bitter experience of John Redmond's involvement in supporting Britain in the Great War.

Thereafter, Northern Ireland was primarily concerned with its role in the British war effort. Its main contribution came in the areas of food production and munitions. Between 1939 and 1945 farmers almost doubled their acreage under the plough and provided Britain with an average of £3 million worth of cattle and sheep a year and 20 per cent of its supplies of home-produced eggs. In four of the six wartime winters 25,000 gallons of liquid milk were despatched daily to Scotland from Northern Ireland ports. In industry, between 1940 and 1944 Belfast's shipyards produced 140 warships, including six aircraft carriers. In addition, 123 merchant ships were launched—10 per cent of the total output of the United Kingdom—and 3,000 ships were repaired or converted. Harland and Wolff also diversified its production, which included 500 tanks and over 13 million aircraft parts. The Short and Harland aircraft factory completed 1,200 Stirling bombers and 125 Sunderland flying-boats, sufficient for over a hundred squadrons, and carried out repairs to roughly three thousand aircraft. In the Belfast area, munitions producers manufactured 75 million shells, 180 million incendiary bullets, 50,000 bayonets, and a variety of other military material.[99]

In total, over 38,000 men and women from Northern Ireland enlisted and saw combat in every theatre of war. Northern Ireland's only Victoria Cross was won by James Megennis, a Belfast Catholic in the Royal Navy, in July 1945. The final known casualty figures for men born in Northern Ireland exceeded 4,700, including 2,256 in the army, 1,112 RAF, 843 Royal Navy, and 524 merchant navy.[100]

At home, the horrors of the war were demonstrated to the people of Belfast when, in the course of four nights in 1941—7/8 April, 15/16 April, 4/5 May, and 5/6 May—a total of ten hours of bombing by the Luftwaffe killed 1,100 people, damaging over 56,000 houses, or 53 per cent of the city's housing stock, and making 100,000 people temporarily homeless. Belfast came twelfth in a league table of urban areas attacked in the United Kingdom in terms of weight of bombs dropped.[101] It was estimated that no city apart from Liverpool had more people killed in one night of bombing than Belfast.[102]

The strategic position of Northern Ireland was perhaps the most significant contribution by the province to the British war effort, and it earned Westminster's gratitude. This was made doubly so by Ireland's continued neutrality throughout the conflict. In the Battle of the Atlantic—the Allied campaign to supply and maintain the United Kingdom with food and materials for the British population and military—Ireland's denial to Allied shipping of the ports returned by Britain in the 1938 Anglo-Irish Agreement meant that Northern Ireland's ports, anchorages and airfields became vital to Britain's survival. By 1943 the port of Londonderry had become the most important escort base in the north-western approaches. In 1943, 21 per cent of submarines destroyed by the RAF Coastal Command were by aircraft based in Northern Ireland. During the war an estimated 1,900 survivors of German submarine attacks in the North Atlantic were rescued and brought to Londonderry. Churchill referred to Northern Ireland's role in the provision of a safe conduct for food and munitions, observing: 'We were alone and had to face single-handed the full fury of the German attacks ... seeking to strangle our life by cutting off the entry to our ports ... Only one great channel of entry remained open. That channel remained open because loyal Ulster gave us full use of the North Irish ports and waters ... But for its loyalty ... we should have been confronted with slavery and death.'[103]

Domestically, political tensions between the two communities were never far beneath the surface of Northern Ireland society. Nationalists were mobilised by Unionist efforts to extend conscription to Northern Ireland, proposed in April 1939 by Craigavon. Cardinal MacRory issued a statement making clear the Catholic Church's opposition to conscription, declaring how Ireland was 'an ancient land, made one by God ... partitioned by a foreign power, against the vehement protests of its people. Conscription would now seek to compel those who writhe under this grievous wrong to fight on the side of the perpetrators.'[104] He described the proposal as the 'greatest tyranny' and claimed that resistance would be morally justified. De Valera said that if conscription were imposed it would be an 'act of war against our nation.'

Given this hostility, Craigavon was asked by Neville Chamberlain if Ulster was out to help in Britain's war effort; when Craigavon replied in the affirmative, he was told by Chamberlain: 'If you really want to help us, don't press for conscription. It will only be an embarrassment.' Sir Basil Brooke reflected on the mood of the Unionist Party, which felt 'resentment, anger and hurt pride at the feeling of having been snubbed.' Brooke attributed the decision to the existence 'in their midst [of] a minority who whilst prepared to share in the benefits of Empire ... were either afraid or too despicable to take a hand in the defence of the country who defended them and were prepared to go to any length to prevent the loyal and brave men ... from doing their duty.'

During the opening phase of the war, recruits were coming forward at the rate of 2,500 a month, but by the spring of 1940 this had fallen to 1,000 a month; by December 1940 it had fallen to 600 a month.[105] When, in May 1941, the British Government began to reconsider whether conscription should be extended to Northern Ireland, the Unionist Government welcomed the opportunity to participate more fully in the war. The British Government, however, was advised that a substantial proportion of those who would be conscripted would be Catholics rather than Protestants, who worked in key industries. This, it was suggested, would lead to opposition from the Catholic hierarchy and raised the possibility of arrests, hunger strikes, gun battles, and a boost for the IRA. A province-wide anti-conscription campaign was orchestrated by Nationalist representatives and the Catholic hierarchy, culminating in a mass rally in Belfast attended by ten thousand people. This so impressed the Northern Ireland Prime Minister, John Andrews (Craigavon had died suddenly in November 1940), that he contacted the British Home Office on his own initiative to concede that the level of opposition would be greater than he had thought and that though his

Government favoured its application, 'the real test ... must be whether it would be good for the Empire.' The next day the British Government agreed a statement that concluded that conscription in Northern Ireland 'would be more trouble than it was worth.'[106]

Ultimately, the Second World War reinforced the psychological gap between Ulster unionism and Irish nationalism. While there may be debate about how much or how little Northern Ireland contributed materially to the British war effort, the very fact of Ireland's neutrality reinforced the divergent definitions of nationality in Ireland. While the war years saw the reinforcement of claims to Southern Ireland's separate nationhood, for Ulster Unionists the strategic and material role of Northern Ireland reinforced their sense of Britishness and difference from nationalists. Sir Basil Brooke, Northern Ireland's Prime Minister from 1943, argued at the end of the war:

> We have gone through five to six years of war. We have taken our part—it may not have been in the aggregate a great part; but it was the greatest part we could play—in the maintenance of the freedom of the world, and so far as we could assist we helped the freedom of Éire, which, had it not been for the victory of the Allies, would have suffered the same fate as Holland and Denmark ... I have heard it said in a boasting manner that Éire men went forward to the war. Of course they did, but they were our men; they were our people who thought as we did ... What these gentlemen [Nationalists] emphasise is the physical boundary, the physical border, whereas it is the ideological border that really counts. In Éire you have a Government which calls itself Republican, says it has not a King ... There has been throughout history an anti-British feeling in Southern Ireland ... Here there is a pro-British feeling ... That is the boundary of the mind which exists between us and the South ... Strategically Northern Ireland played an immensely important part in the last war. The bridgehead, the Rock of Gibraltar, as it was called, was the mainstay in the Battle of the Atlantic. Is it not better for England and the Empire to make sure of that rock rather than the shifting sands of disloyalty and hostility? I am convinced that our different outlooks and our different loyalties cannot go on together. Our ideals and feelings are so different that I can see bloodshed and riot if that were to happen ...[107]

WELFARISM

The legacy of the short-lived premiership of John Andrews, Northern Ireland's Prime Minister from 1940 to 1943, was the raising aloft of the standard of post-war reconstruction in Ulster, following the British Government's commitment in 1941 to extensive social reform. Andrews found that the minds of many people in Northern Ireland had been directed towards the 'new order' and the 'fair deal' that would emerge after the war. He feared the emergence of political difficulties if the Unionist Government appeared to be prepared to do less than the British Government.

> Our people frequently chafe at their feeling of inability to exercise any sort of initiative in their desire for reform. For a very considerable time a very definite and sustained demand has been pressed upon me that I should give a real lead as regards the government's intentions on social problems in future years. We cannot maintain the necessary interest in our parliamentary institutions if we are not allowed to exercise some initiative.

A post-war Planning Committee was established under the chairmanship of Sir Basil Brooke. Andrews proceeded to commit the Unionist Government to its own post-war programme of social reform in a speech at Stormont in July 1941, promising slum clearances, a housing programme, expansion in the provision of education, and large-scale extension of water mains, sewerage and electricity to rural areas. Andrews emphasised that the programme was his own Government's concern, though it would be related to British plans.[108] When Brooke became Prime Minister—following internal Unionist Party dissension with Andrews's performance—he and his colleagues committed the Unionist Government to following Westminster in implementing the Beveridge Report, the basis of the new National Health Service in Britain.

With the arrival of a Labour Government in Britain, the Unionist Government was confronted with a party in power that the Unionist political elite had traditionally regarded as hostile to Northern Ireland's position within the Union but that was introducing significant social reforms that would be welcomed by working-class Unionist voters. The Northern Ireland Cabinet was concerned with both the socialist nature of the Labour Government's programme and the implications of this legislation for the division of power between Stormont and Westminster. In November 1945 Brooke warned that while the adoption of some of the measures being passed at Westminster could be justified on the grounds that they were an unavoidable part of the war's aftermath, as time went on 'more extreme socialistic measures' might have to be introduced into Northern Ireland because of the financial relationship between Stormont and Westminster, which would be unacceptable to members of the Unionist Party, on whose support the Government had to rely. Brooke suggested that possible alternatives should be explored to see whether such a situation could be averted, such as the possibility of Northern Ireland accepting Dominion status as a separate state within the Commonwealth, like Canada or Australia, or a return to Westminster and total integration within the United Kingdom, like Scotland or Wales.

Within the Cabinet, Brian Maginess and Sir Ronald Nugent argued that Northern Ireland should become a Dominion, warning that Britain appeared to have shifted sufficiently 'leftwards' and that Governments, whether Labour or Conservative, would thereafter assume a much tighter policy of planning and control, 'irksome to Ulstermen used to "independence".' They both stressed that the new status should not militate against the introduction of welfare legislation, with Maginess emphasising that 'our industrial, though not our social legislation can no longer run on parallel lines.' In asking for Dominion status and a greater degree of responsibility it would also be necessary to request continued financial assistance from Britain. But Dominion status would have to be rejected, admitted Maginess, if it meant Northern Ireland living within its own resources, for 'it might mean that our present standards might have to be lowered, [which] would tend to lessen the difference to the worker between Northern Ireland and Éire and therefore ... would weaken one of our most telling arguments against Union with [Éire] ... On the political side it would present the Labour Party here with the best election platform they could ever hope to have ...'

In a series of agreements with the British Treasury from 1946 onwards, the Unionist Government was able to obtain the financial guarantees that would underwrite the reforms Andrews had promised in 1942. These agreements fully integrated Northern Ireland into the British welfare state and enabled the Northern Ireland exchequer to put financial resources into local services rather than going to Whitehall. For example, from 1947 the Treasury allowed the Northern Ireland Ministry of Finance to divert revenue from the Imperial Contribution to a Capital Purposes Fund for industrial development and other projects. At the same time Westminster made it clear that these concessions were incompatible with an increase in devolution.

Given these changes, the Unionist Government resisted backbench opposition to the introduction of a Health Services Bill, a Northern Ireland Housing Trust, and a Northern Ireland Transport Board, which involved the nationalisation of the almost bankrupt local railway system. While opposition from within the Unionist Party forced the Government to dilute certain legislation, Brooke and his ministers committed Northern Ireland to the 'step-by-step' policy of introducing welfare legislation. In late 1947 Brooke claimed that a modern democratic government must assume responsibility for a wide range of activities in the interests of the community, and he rejected the 'indiscriminate charge' of socialism as 'unjustified and absurd,' arguing that there was a need for a middle course between the 'extreme philosophy of *laissez-faire* and the fetish of socialisation.' He rejected outright the demand for Dominion status when he told a Unionist rally in Larne:

> To attempt a fundamental change in our constitutional position is to reopen the whole Irish question. The government is strongly supported by the votes of the working class who cherish their heritage in the Union and to whom any tendency towards separation from Britain is anathema ... The backbone of Unionism is the Unionist Labour party. Are those men going to be satisfied if we reject the social services and other benefits we have had by going step by step with Britain?[109]

With the Unionist Government firmly committed to the economic benefits of the United Kingdom, the financial provisions that underpinned the relationship of parity between Stormont and Westminster evolved in three stages between 1946 and 1951. The first stage, in 1946, accepting the parity of services and taxes between Britain and Northern Ireland, required Stormont's Ministry of Finance to liaise very closely with the Treasury and to have the Northern Ireland budget approved in advance. In the second stage, national insurance was all but amalgamated into the separate insurance funds of the administrations. In July 1948 comprehensive national insurance legislation in Britain became operative throughout the United Kingdom and was anticipated in the National Insurance Act (Northern Ireland), 1946, which provided for the same benefits for the unemployed, the sick, the retired, widows and orphans, women during maternity, and those incurring the cost of funerals. The third stage was reached in 1949 and dealt with national assistance, family allowances, non-contributory pensions, and the health service. This ensured that if the cost of these services should prove to be disproportionately higher in Northern Ireland than in Britain, Westminster would pay 80 per cent of the excess.

In education, the Education Act (Northern Ireland), 1947, introduced a new structure of primary schooling (now ending between the ages of eleven and twelve and not fourteen, as before), secondary and further education; a commitment to raise the school leaving age to fifteen; and the establishment of single, reconstituted education committees for each county and city. The Act required county schools to hold collective worship and religious instruction but released teachers from the previous requirement to teach religious education if called upon to do so. The Act raised the grants given to voluntary schools for new building and reconstruction, maintenance, lighting, heating and cleaning from 50 to 65 per cent. Finally, it laid obligations on education authorities to provide extensive free services to all schools, relating to medical treatment, transport, school meals and milk, books, and stationery.[110]

As the extension of the welfare state continued, a new Ministry of Health and Local Government was created through the Public Health and Local Government (Administrative Provisions) Act (Northern Ireland), 1946, the Public Health (Tuberculosis) Act (Northern Ireland), 1946, and the Health Service Act (Northern Ireland), 1948. The Ministry of Home Affairs in 1943 had found that 70 per cent of existing houses needed repairs and that the minimum number of new houses required was 100,000—twice that figure if slums were to be cleared and overcrowding eliminated. The new Minister of Health and Local Government, William Grant, undertook this with the Housing Act (Northern Ireland), 1945. Following the establishment of the National Health Service in Britain, general medical, dental, pharmaceutical and ophthalmic services were administered by the Northern Ireland General Health Service Board, which was appointed by the Minister. The distinction between rural and urban housing was abolished and the administration rationalised, and local councils became housing authorities. A new Northern Ireland Housing Authority was established to build houses at the British Exchequer's expense.

Northern Ireland benefited disproportionately from state aid in housing compared with the English regions and Wales. The annual rate of construction more than doubled from the passing of the Act.[111]

THE IRELAND ACT

Any fears the Unionist Government had regarding the intentions of the British Labour Government towards Northern Ireland were dispelled when the Irish Government announced in September 1948 that it was severing all ties with the British Commonwealth. Brooke's main fear focused on the Irish Government's policy of ending partition. He feared that nationalist Catholics might cross the border to take up temporary residence in Northern Ireland in order to outvote unionists in elections for Westminster. Technically, since no residence qualification was needed to vote in Westminster elections, other than an address in Northern Ireland, the use of an overnight address could qualify citizens of Ireland to exercise the franchise in Northern Ireland. Brooke asked the British Prime Minister, Clement Attlee, to impose a residential requirement for Irish citizens in the United Kingdom similar to the one that applied to Irish citizens who wanted to qualify for the franchise to vote for the Northern Ireland Parliament. Attlee was against having different qualifications for voting in Britain and Northern Ireland for Westminster elections and explained the administrative difficulties in differentiating between Irish citizens and British subjects at elections in Britain. He reassured Brooke by telling him that he could state publicly that he had received an assurance on behalf of the United Kingdom Government that 'the constitutional position of Northern Ireland would be safeguarded.'

In December 1948 the Northern Ireland Cabinet asked that Attlee's constitutional assurance be put into statutory form, guaranteeing the constitutional position of Northern Ireland and its position as a part of the United Kingdom. A committee established under Norman Brook, the British Cabinet Secretary, recommended that all British political parties should make a pledge reaffirming Attlee's assurances on the constitutional position of Northern Ireland but that if this did not satisfy the Northern Ireland Government then it should be proposed that a new Act of Parliament would include a formal affirmation that Northern Ireland would in no event cease to be part of the United Kingdom, except at the request and with the consent of the Northern Ireland Parliament. Brooke told Attlee that in order to prevent the reorganisation of the Ulster Volunteers he required a public assurance from the British Government that they would use troops to defend Northern Ireland against aggression as readily as they would use them to defend any other part of the United Kingdom.[112]

To demonstrate Northern Ireland's determination to remain within the United Kingdom, Brooke called a general election for 10 February 1949, announcing: 'We are going to the country on one question and one question only: whether this country is as determined as it was in the past to remain part of the United Kingdom.' In his manifesto, on 23 January 1949, he declared: 'Our country is in danger ... Today we fight to defend our very existence and the heritage of our Ulster children. The British government have agreed to abide by the decision of the Ulster people. It is therefore imperative that our determination to remain under the Union Jack should be immediately and overwhelmingly re-affirmed ... No Surrender, We are King's Men.'[113]

The British Government's Ireland Bill, when it emerged, recognised that from 18 August 1949 'Éire' ceased to be part of His Majesty's Dominions, declared that in future it would be known as the 'Republic of Ireland', but confirmed that although the Republic of Ireland was not part of His Majesty's Dominions it was not to be regarded as a foreign country, nor were its citizens to be aliens for the purposes of any law in force in the United Kingdom or its colonial territories.

With reference to Northern Ireland, the Ireland Bill introduced a residence qualification for electors in Westminster elections. The key clause of the Bill, clause 1 (1) B, reads: 'Parliament hereby declares that Northern Ireland remains part of His Majesty's Dominions and of the United Kingdom and affirms that in no event will Northern Ireland or any part thereof cease to be part of His Majesty's Dominions and of the United Kingdom without the consent of the Parliament of Northern Ireland.'[114]

In a parliamentary debate on the Republic's secession from the Commonwealth, Brooke (now Viscount Brookeborough) pointed out that the Irish Government's action in declaring a republic illustrated that 'we are two separate communities,' arguing that 'our outlook is different; our politics are different; our religion is different.' He claimed that 'what the Free State are after is the rape of Ulster; it is not marriage. It is the rape of Ulster they want, and when they have done that dreadful deed they would throw the wretched girl on one side and rob her of means.' For Brookeborough, the Republic's and Ulster's traditions and loyalties were growing further and further apart. Turning to what he considered the 'crucial question', he argued: 'That is our allegiance to the Crown; that is our sentimental side. The sentimental side of the Opposition is an Irish Republic, but we differ entirely. Here we look upon the Crown as a symbol of freedom; in the Free State the Crown is said to be a symbol of aggression.'[115]

Dehra Parker, Stormont MP for South Londonderry, explained to

Nationalists that since the twelfth century the 'people of Ireland have been subject to the British Crown and have been part of the British nation' and that she believed that when the majority of the inhabitants of the Twenty-Six Counties chose to repudiate those ties to the British Crown 'they were, in fact, establishing Partition … They … were the actual secessionists … It is you [Nationalists] who have seceded from the British nation.'[116]

THE ANTI-PARTITION LEAGUE

The end of the Second World War had seen Northern Nationalists raise the question of partition once again. A Nationalist Convention in Cahir Healy's constituency, South Fermanagh, decided in favour of attendance at Stormont. The Tyrone county convention deferred the abstention question to a general post-election Nationalist convention. The Nationalists put up eleven candidates, winning ten seats, losing Falls to a former Nationalist, Harry Diamond, who stood as a Socialist Republican, but winning South Armagh from a Labour candidate. In July 1945 the Westminster election saw Mulvey and Cunningham re-elected for Fermanagh and Tyrone, joined by Beattie in West Belfast. The election of a Labour Government in Britain, which they believed would be sympathetic to the nationalist cause, convinced the Northern Nationalists that they should take their seats at Stormont and Westminster.

An extra-parliamentary pressure point was established in November 1945 when two Stormont MPs, Eddie McAteer (a brother of the former IRA Chief of Staff Hugh McAteer), and Malachy Conlon, invited all 'nationally minded' groups and public representatives to a conference in Dungannon on 15 November 1945. The conference was attended by all Nationalist Party MPs and about five hundred delegates and local councillors. The Catholic dimension was emphasised by the presence of a large number of priests and by messages of support from the Bishops of Derry and Dromore. The convention decided to set up a new organisation, the Anti-Partition League, with the object of uniting all those opposed to partition. James McSparran, a prominent Catholic barrister and MP, was elected chairman and Malachy Conlon MP full-time secretary. An executive was elected consisting of all the Nationalist MPs and senators and three representatives of each county and city. The league represented the Catholic small businessman, farmer and professional class, with a predominantly rural support.[117]

The APL was encouraged by the formation in 1945 of the Friends of

Ireland, a group of thirty or so British Labour MPs, mostly of Irish extraction, who were committed to drawing attention to the minority's grievances and supporting Irish unity. One of the most prominent was Geoffrey Bing, a Protestant lawyer from Northern Ireland, who was MP for Hornchurch. The APL was also encouraged by the rise of a new political party in the Republic, Clann na Poblachta, led by Seán MacBride, a former IRA Chief of Staff and the son of Major John MacBride, executed after the Easter Rising. In the 1948 general election Clann na Poblachta won ten seats, mostly from Fianna Fáil, and formed a new coalition Government with the Labour Party and Fine Gael. John A. Costello, leader of Fine Gael, became Taoiseach and MacBride Minister for External Affairs. Denis Ireland of the Ulster Union Club and Dr Eileen Hickey, an Independent Nationalist MP for Queen's University, were appointed to the Seanad and the National Health Council, respectively.[118]

The APL's greatest success was in reconciling the divergent views of the different sections of nationalist politics: the old Redmondites, the more militant Fianna Fáil supporters, and Republicans. A widespread publicity and propaganda campaign generated a sense of euphoria among rank-and-file nationalists. Following the declaration of the Republic of Ireland, Northern Nationalists renewed pressure on the Southern parties for 'some National Council in Dublin which would take partition out of the political cockpit, [in] which [the] two parties in Dublin seem inclined to keep it.' The result of this call was the establishment of the All-Party Anti-Partition Committee in Dublin in January 1949. Some of the more militant APL members, such as Eddie McAteer and Malachy Conlon, appealed to Costello to admit them to Dáil Éireann but were informed that the Republic's Government foresaw constitutional, legal and other difficulties.

By February 1950, discontent among militant Nationalists saw conventions in Fermanagh-South Tyrone and Mid-Ulster endorse an abstention policy once again. In May 1950 the Anti-Partition League passed a resolution urging the admission of its elected representatives to the Dáil. They were informed, however, that this was not possible, because there 'was not general agreement amongst TDs' for the necessary legislation to be introduced. Northern Nationalists were disappointed once more, although Cahir Healy admitted that he had supported the call reluctantly, doing so only because he had been asked to do so by the APL convention. By 1951 the APL was visibly fragmenting and did not seem able to produce, let alone enforce, a policy, with individual MPs determining their own policies and tactics.[119]

The vacuum left by the demise of the APL created an opening for militant nationalism. The IRA was reorganising, although it was not moving fast enough for some of its members. In October 1951 the IRA expelled Liam Kelly of Pomeroy for taking unauthorised action. Kelly took most of the Tyrone IRA with him and established a new paramilitary organisation, called Saor-Ulaidh (Free Ulster). On Easter Monday 1952 armed members of Saor-Ulaidh occupied Pomeroy in the early hours of the morning, cut telephone wires, set up road blocks, and read the Proclamation of the Republic in the village centre. Kelly stood in the 1953 Stormont election as an abstentionist candidate for the Mid-Tyrone constituency, defeating the outgoing Nationalist by 4,178 votes to 3,376. Before the election he had let it be known that

> I will not take the Oath of Allegiance to a foreign Queen of a bastard nation. I took an Oath of Allegiance to the Irish Republic when I was sixteen. I have kept that oath and I intend to keep it. I do not believe in constitutional methods. I believe in the use of force; the more the better, the sooner the better. That may be treason or sedition, call it whatever the hell you like.

A month after his election Kelly was arrested and charged with making a seditious speech. During his trial, in December 1952, he outlined Saor-Ulaidh's policy, which was very close to Clann na Poblachta's. Saor-Ulaidh accepted the 1937 Constitution, which laid claim to Northern Ireland as part of the national territory, and its aim was to put that claim into effect. It also accepted the legitimacy of the Dáil and the Southern Government but rejected the authority of Stormont or Westminster.

Kelly was convicted and bound over to keep the peace for five years, but on refusing to give such an undertaking he was jailed for twelve months. This caused widespread indignation in the Republic, and Seán MacBride put down a Dáil motion condemning his incarceration. Some days later six hundred people attended a convention in Pomeroy and established a new political party, called Fianna Uladh, whose aim was 'to develop an organisation of Republicans in occupied Ireland into a disciplined political movement and to use every legitimate means to bring about the re-unification of the territory of the Republic of Ireland.' An executive committee was elected, and Kelly was appointed chairman.

In May 1954 a new coalition Government was formed in the Republic, dependent on Clann na Poblachta support in the Dáil. Kelly, still in jail, was elected to the Seanad on MacBride's nomination. His early release in August 1954 saw a crowd of ten thousand, including MacBride, meet him in Pomeroy, and a pitched battle ensued with the RUC, leaving twelve policemen and forty civilians injured.[120]

The IRA decided to follow Kelly's example and to contest the Westminster election of 1955 in order to get a popular mandate for a renewed military campaign. Alarmed by this, Cahir Healy argued with Costello that the admittance of Northern Nationalists to the Dáil would give them hope and show that the new Irish Government was working for the reintegration of the Irish nation.[121] In a memorandum to Costello he attempted to undermine the Republican revival by setting forth the Nationalist reasons for requesting representation in the Dáil, stressing that a refusal could result in the loss of the Nationalist-held border seats.

(1) If the border seats are lost, the entire Six Counties can be shown in British propaganda abroad to have become wholly pro-partition.

(2) Our people are in the front-line trenches of the struggle for reunity, daily victims of active and passive discrimination. The enactment of the Republic of Ireland Act was seen as the first positive step ... which (as we see it) is suspended until it is given realistic effect by the admission of two [Northern] elected representatives [to] Dáil Éireann.

(3) British willingness to accept our representatives at Westminster, when contrasted with our own Government's refusal to accept them, has an adverse effect on world opinion and is a continual source of disillusionment and frustration ...

(4) Their admission by the Irish Government would be an assertion of our Government's right to the whole of Ireland.

(5) The joint conventions of the two constituencies decided unanimously that the members should seek admission to Dáil Éireann. Only in the event of their request being refused were they to seek seats at Westminster.

(6) The problem of attendance or abstention ... arises at each general election for the Imperial Parliament. This issue causes widespread dissension in our ranks. At present, the only alternative to attendance at Westminster is abstention ... and it is not viewed as a satisfactory solution by many of the Nationalist people. Abstention leads to neglect of registration, and creates a general condition of apathy regarding elections in general. This issue can only be resolved by admitting the two elected representatives to Dáil Éireann.

(7) Distinction must be drawn between our relation to Stormont and our connections with Westminster. Stormont legislates for local services, and might well [continue to] function for the greater part of its existing area ... in a United Ireland.

(8) Attendance at Westminster ... may show some sanction for the occupation of the Six Counties by an outside power.

(9) Representation of the two constituencies in Dáil Éireann ... will give practical effect to the idea of an Irish Republic, and will open a new chapter in the ... history of our country.

(10) Until now, our people have, little by little, been drawing apart, because of the lack of regular contact, and exchange of ... ideas. Our representatives would re-establish, for the first time since partition, official contact with Dublin. As members of [the] Irish Parliament, their prestige would be great, North, South, and abroad; they would be of constant service ... to the Nationalists of the Six counties, and to the Irish Government. They would form a direct, personal, official link between the Irish government and its foreign-occupied territory.[122]

This request did not produce a favourable response, and by November 1954 Patrick McGill told Healy that the situation in the border counties was 'beyond remedy.' He suggested non-recognition of the Unionist minority candidates, who were almost certain to be returned as MPs. All Nationalists could do was (1) deny the title of MP to the Unionists elected who had received a minority of the votes; (2) refer to them always as the 'defeated candidate' for the particular constituency; (3) remind the public that in twenty-five years the Nationalist Party had never put these seats in jeopardy, or lost them; and (4) give prominence to the parliamentary representation of 'our people's views by the quasi-MPs.'[123]

In desperation, the Unionist Government's Attorney-General was approached by several Nationalist MPs, who suggested that the Northern Ireland Government should introduce legislation requiring candidates to take the oath of allegiance at the time of their nomination. Their object was to prevent Sinn Féin candidates going forward for election who had no intention of sitting in Parliament if elected, and they contended that if a number of Sinn Féiners were elected it would destroy the Nationalist Party. The members who spoke to the Attorney-General assured him that if the Government introduced such a measure they would not criticise it.[124]

By 1955 Healy was forced to admit that the Nationalist Party was no nearer achieving its goal of ending partition.

I cannot say … that we have progressed much towards freedom. Our success … depends on world factors … Our efforts are to keep the national spirit and ideal alive and active under adverse conditions … Our population in the Six Counties continues to increase despite all efforts of the Government … I try to use the Parliament as a sounding board for our grievances … We keep every circumstance before the public and the world which either contribute to … the morale of the man in the street, or show injustice, to which he is subject, to the wider public …[125]

The IRA border campaign

The dissolution of the Imperial Parliament in 1955 saw Sinn Féin name candidates for all twelve Westminster seats, half of whom were in prison for the Omagh raid, all standing on an abstentionist platform. At the Nationalist convention for the Fermanagh-South Tyrone constituency Very Rev. John Nolan of Fivemiletown opposed the nomination of the Republican candidate, Phil Clarke, on the grounds that if the convention selected Clarke it would be claimed that it had sanctioned the policy of physical force, which Nolan considered to be morally wrong. The Republic's leadership, he pointed out, had declared that a policy of force used against unionists would be fatal for Ireland and would not be successful, either from a political or a military point of view.

In proposing his candidate, Healy said that two issues stood before the convention: whether they were to approve of 'outsiders' coming in and 'telling them what to do,' and whether they were ready to change to a physical force policy. To adopt such a policy would, he warned, have the effect of putting young people in peril of their lives, for Sinn Féin and the IRA were 'stable-companions'. Nobody, he argued, could see any consequence of the use of force except defeat and imprisonment for those engaged in violence. He also warned that abstention could only lead to the nationalist people being forgotten, as they had been in the ten years between 1935 and 1945. The Northern Nationalists, Healy argued, would not have the approval or support of any of the two parties in the Republic, so they would be left standing without aid or sympathy.[126]

Despite these pleas, the convention proceeded to nominate Republican candidates for the general election, including Phil Clarke, selected by 114 votes to 71.[127]

As polling day approached, Republicans were clear about what support for their candidates would entail. At a public meeting in Belfast a Sinn Féin spokesman, S. O'Sorahan, warned: 'If our constitutional campaign fails then inevitably there will be nothing for it but the use of physical force—the gun, rifle and hand grenade in an effort to take back by force what was taken from us by force.' He told his audience that it was an open secret that there were men ready and trained with the 'ideals of past generations who will fight and who will win.'[128]

No Nationalist Party candidates stood against the Republicans on polling day, with the result that they received a total of 152,310 votes and won the two Nationalist seats of Mid-Ulster and Fermanagh-South Tyrone, by 260 and 261 votes, respectively. It was the biggest anti-partition vote since 1921 and nearly fifty thousand more than the total anti-partition vote in 1949.

Phil Clarke and Tom Mitchell, the Republican elected for Mid-Ulster, were both serving ten-year sentences, and it was doubtful if either was legally eligible to be elected. The Unionists were successful in petitioning to have Clarke unseated and their candidate declared elected instead, while the British Attorney-General proposed that the Mid-Ulster seat be declared vacant and a by-election held. The by-election saw Mitchell increase his majority by 806 votes; but the Unionist candidate was declared elected on a subsequent petition.[129]

Following its electoral success, the IRA proceeded to prepare for a military offensive against the Northern state. The plan, 'Operation Harvest', devised for the IRA by Seán Cronin, had to be reduced in ambition but essentially formed the IRA's military strategy. After a period of training in the North, four mobile attack columns from the South of twenty-five men each would open the operation. The Dublin column would move into south Armagh and on to Fermanagh; the Cork-Limerick column would move into Fermanagh and then operate in Fermanagh-Tyrone; the Connacht column was to move into Fermanagh; and another was to be ready to move in after the first three in the Monaghan-Fermanagh-Tyrone area. During the first three months of the campaign, these four columns would hit priority targets, with the co-operation of local units, who would also raise new units. As the campaign intensified, the direction of operations would move from west to east as the IRA's control of the terrain grew. The mission of each force in these areas was to cut off all communications—telephone, road, and rail; destroy all petrol stations and enemy vehicles found; and hit strategic strongpoints, where supplies or the administration of the enemy could be found. The IRA's mission was to maintain and strengthen our resistance centres throughout the occupied areas and also to break down the enemy's administration in the occupied area until he is forced to withdraw his forces. Our method of doing this is use of guerrilla warfare ... and propaganda aimed at inhabitants. In time ... we hope to be in a position to liberate large areas and tie these in with other liberated areas—that is areas where the enemy's writ no longer runs.[130]

The IRA's secret training manual asserted:

A small nation fighting for freedom can only hope to defeat an oppressor or occupying power by means of guerrilla warfare. The enemy's superiority in manpower, resources, materials and everything else that goes into the waging of a successful war can be overcome by guerrilla methods ... In regular warfare the tactical objective is to destroy the enemy in battle by concentrating superior numbers at a decisive time and place. The guerrilla strikes not one large blow but many little ones; he hits suddenly, gnaws at the enemy's strength, achieves surprise, disengages himself, withdraws, disperses and hits again.[131]

On the night of 11/12 December about 150 IRA men attacked ten targets in Northern Ireland. A BBC transmitter was destroyed in Derry and a Territorial Army building in Enniskillen, while a courthouse in Magherafelt, a B Specials hut in Newry and a number of bridges in Fermanagh were damaged.

Sinn Féin issued a statement declaring: 'Irishmen have again risen in revolt against British aggression in Ireland. The Sinn Féin organisation say to the Irish people that they are proud of the risen nation and appeal to the people of Ireland to assist in every way they can the soldiers of the Irish Republican Army.'[132] The IRA campaign proclamation predicted: 'Out of this national liberation struggle a new Ireland will emerge, upright and free. In that Ireland we shall build a country fit for all our people to live in. That then is our aim: an independent, united, democratic Irish Republic. For this we shall fight until the invader is driven from our soil and victory is ours.' The following night the RUC barracks in Lisnaskea and Derrylin, County Fermanagh, were attacked. An additional communiqué noted that the RUC and Special Constabulary had co-operated in actions against the IRA, despite the warning in the IRA's proclamation that if they did not stand aside 'they will be adjudged renegades by the Irish people and treated accordingly by the Resistance Movement.'[133] Thus began a six-year campaign involving attacks on military and police barracks and personnel, primarily RUC men and special constables.

In the Republic the IRA's campaign contributed to the fall of the Government. After the death of two IRA men in Fermanagh, an estimated fifty thousand people attended one of the funerals in Limerick. The Taoiseach, John A. Costello, had most of the IRA Army Council arrested for a short period, which led Seán MacBride to table a motion of censure against the coalition, bringing down the Government. In the ensuing general election Sinn Féin polled 65,640 votes, its highest in the South since 1927. This success, however, was a double-edged sword, for a Fianna Fáil majority was returned, and de Valera introduced internment against the IRA.

In 1958, internment in the Republic and the extensive use of the RUC Reserve in the North, including the full-time mobilisation of the B Specials with their intimate local knowledge, restricted the IRA's capacity to conduct an effective campaign. By September nearly all the IRA Army Council were interned in the South, and their planned winter campaign had to be called off. The decisive factor in the defeat of the campaign was the leadership's realisation that nationalist support had dwindled considerably. In October 1959 the Westminster general election saw Sinn Féin receive 73,415 votes, less than half their 1955 total. In October 1961 a general election in the Republic saw their vote reduced from 65,640 to 36,393 votes, or 3 per cent of the poll, with the loss by Sinn Féin of all four seats it had won in the 1957 election. Although it still received a substantial vote in Northern Ireland, it was now clear that the Northern nationalist community's support for violence had waned.

After ordering their volunteers to dump arms, on 26 February 1962 the IRA announced that it was to end its campaign. Eight IRA men and one sympathiser, two Saor-Ulaidh members and six RUC constables had been killed. The damage was estimated at £1 million and the cost of security in the North at £10 million. The IRA statement declared: 'The decision to end the resistance campaign has been taken in view of the general situation. Foremost among the factors motivating this course of action has been the attitude of the general public whose minds have been deliberately distracted from the supreme issue facing the Irish people—the unity and freedom of Ireland.'[134]

THE ECONOMY, 1950–1962

In 1950 the principal features of Northern Ireland's economic structure were the continued dominance of the two traditional staple industries and the high proportion of the work force engaged in agriculture. Of the total number of workers in manufacturing, 30 per cent were in textiles and linen and 20 per cent in shipbuilding, engineering, and vehicle repair. Agriculture accounted for one-sixth of the gainfully employed and almost a quarter of gainfully employed males. 1951 was the last year of the post-war boom in demand for manufactured products. By the summer of 1952 production had declined in a number of industries; in the three years to June 1954, linen employment had fallen by 15 per cent.

With Government assistance, a programme of re-equipment and modernisation introduced a large-scale reduction in employment in a productivity drive. But between 1954 and 1964 the number of jobs in plants employing twenty-five people or more—the great majority—fell from 56,414 to 33,957. The number of plants fell from 298 to 200.

In 1950 more than a tenth of Northern Ireland's manufacturing jobs, and about a fifth of those in Belfast, were to be found in the Harland and Wolff shipyards. Employing 21,000 in four yards, it was the largest localised shipbuilding complex in the world. By the late nineteen-fifties increased competition from Continental and Japanese companies saw the number of ships afloat exceed requirements. In Belfast the main decline occurred between 1961 and 1964, when employment in shipbuilding and marine engineering dropped by 11,500 or 40 per cent. In agriculture a declining work force produced an increase in output of 80 per cent between 1938 and 1960; between 1950 and 1960 total agricultural employment fell by 28,000 or nearly one-third. There was an increase in employment in the service sector of 18,500, because of Government investment in education and personal and public health; but the contraction in agriculture and the relatively high birth rate meant that throughout the period 1950–1960 unemployment never fell below 5 per cent and averaged 7 per cent, remaining the highest of any region in the United Kingdom.[135]

Some of the reasons for Northern Ireland's economic decline were identified in a report, *Economic Survey of Northern Ireland*, by two Queen's University academics, K. S. Isles and N. Cuthbert, commissioned by the Northern Ireland Government in 1947. Presented to the Minister of Commerce, Lord Glentoran, in 1955, the report was not published until two years later. It pointed out that while the Industrial Development Act (Northern Ireland) aimed at attracting large enterprises by providing factory premises and equipment with the necessary infrastructure, and the Capital Grants to Industry Act (Northern Ireland) provided for grants of up to a quarter of the cost of any investment in plant, machinery, and buildings, the total employment potential introduced to Northern Ireland was 26,000, representing a yearly average of 2,500, which compared unfavourably with the losses in the staple industries.

The report also took a critical view of Northern Ireland's local industries. The linen industry was dominated by small family-owned units, unsympathetic to rationalisation and changes in the world markets, while the number of private companies—60 per cent of all companies, compared with 35 per cent in the United Kingdom as a whole—prevented the investment of domestic savings in local industry. Principal shareholders were reluctant to seek an increase of capital for fear of losing control of decision-making, while most private firms had no intention of expanding, preferring to invest their profits in Government securities or divesting them by paying out high dividends and directors' salaries. There was a widespread habit of concentrating on profit margins rather than volume of sales.

The report also drew attention to the monopolist tendencies that had built up in the inter-war period, when trade associations had been formed to maintain prices. There was a general ignorance of 'modern business methods', with private firms lacking any breadth of experience in management, production or marketing and therefore lacking the ability to modernise.[136]

A crisis for Belfast's economy set in at the close of 1960, when the building programme at Harland and Wolff came to an end at a time of worldwide recession in the industry. Early in 1961 the yard announced that 8,000 of its 21,000 workers would have to be made redundant. The future of 8,000 aircraft workers at Short's was also in doubt, as orders for its main aircraft were insufficient. Over the next twelve months another 2,000 workers at Harland and Wolff were laid off. In 1961 there were 20 per cent fewer aircraft workers than three years earlier, while in the rest of the United Kingdom the contraction had been only 5 per cent.

In the Stormont election of 1962, while the NILP did not gain any extra seats its average share of the vote increased by 15 per cent. Under party and backbench pressure, in March 1961 Brookeborough and his principal ministers went to London for the first 'summit' since 1954 but could only extract a pledge from the Conservative Government to continue support for the existing measures of industrial promotion, together with an agreement to begin a joint study of the unemployment problem and how it might be dealt with. Any positive results that might have arisen from the agreement were erased by the introduction of a

United Kingdom payroll tax and a mini-budget that increased the bank rate and imposed credit restrictions. The payroll tax enraged linen manufacturers, who claimed it would destroy their export competitiveness. The Minster of Finance, Terence O'Neill, managed to win the concession that local government would have a free hand with revenue from the tax, and Brookeborough announced further concessions from Westminster, including no slowing down in the industrial programme; local authorities were also told they could carry on with their work programmes, and building subsidies were to be increased.

This did not mollify the Unionist Government's critics. In August 1962 twelve thousand workers marched to Belfast City Hall for a meeting addressed by NILP, independent and Nationalist MPs and Irish Labour Party TDs, at which a resolution, also supported by Belfast Chamber of Trade and Unionist city councillors, was passed calling on the British Prime Minister, Harold Macmillan, to take immediate steps to provide contracts and financial assistance to Short's. An NILP petition to recall Stormont gathered 100,000 signatures in four weeks, while October saw an announcement that a further 620 shipyard workers would be made redundant by November, to be followed by two or three thousand more by the end of the year.[137] The political consequence of these economic crises were to hasten Brookeborough's departure as Prime Minister.

COMMUNITY RELATIONS AND PERCEPTIONS, 1930–1962

Beneath the surface of an outwardly stable society, Northern Ireland's communal divisions persisted in a form of cold war. Much of the antagonism between the two communities was based on preconceived notions of the other. The existence of truth in some of the charges was taken as evidence that all charges against the other community were justified. For example, in the nineteen-thirties, from the perspective of the Unionist Government there was a strong case against many of the Nationalist charges of discrimination. The Government denied that there had been any gerrymandering of constituency boundaries on political or religious grounds. The thirteen parliamentary constituencies for the Westminster Parliament were mapped out by the Imperial Government before the passing of the Government of Ireland Act, 1920. With regard to the constituencies that returned members to the Northern Ireland Parliament, the Unionist Government claimed that the minority retained eleven of the twelve seats it won under PR.

On the question of electoral boundaries for local government it was argued that the commission established to examine them invited both Nationalists and Unionists to attend but 'the Nationalists rigidly abstained from taking part and left the Tribunal with the onerous duty of deciding how the boundaries should be drawn. If the Nationalists suffered as a result, it certainly appears to be their own fault, inasmuch as they refused to give the Tribunal the assistance to which they were entitled.'

With regard to Nationalist charges against the RUC, the Unionist Government pointed out that of the three thousand allocated places, two thousand were reserved for Protestants and one thousand for Catholics. However, 'the minority flatly refused to join the Force, and their places had necessarily to be filled up by others. Consequently, if there is a disproportion, it is due to the refusal of the minority to join in the first instance in organising the force and generally in making the new Government a success.'

On the question of judicial appointments, the Government 'absolutely denied that there has been any discrimination on religious or political grounds.' The first Lord Chief Justice was a Catholic, and since the original appointments there had been only two vacancies. These, it was claimed, had been filled irrespective of religious considerations, and it would be impossible to consider judicial appointments on the basis of religious or political opinion. However, in the County Court judiciary and the resident and other magistracy there were a number of office-holders who belonged to the minority.

The Nationalist grievance regarding education was also challenged by the Unionist Government. As in England and Wales, there were in Northern Ireland two classes of elementary school, the voluntary or denominational schools, which were Catholic, and the provided and transferred schools, which were under the management of the local education authorities and predominantly comprised Protestant schoolchildren. The direct grants from the Government to both classes of schools were distributed under identical regulations, the whole set of teachers' salaries being defrayed by the Ministry of Education. This expenditure, shared equally by the voluntary and the provided transferred schools, accounted for over 93 per cent of the total amounts spent on elementary education from public grants. The only difference in the distribution of the 7 per cent expenditure falling on the rates was that while the cost of building, maintenance and upkeep of transferred and provided schools was wholly defrayed by the local authorities, grants towards the maintenance of voluntary schools were limited to 50 per cent; on the other hand it was permissible for these authorities under the Education Act, 1923, to make grants in any proportion that might be agreed on towards the building of voluntary schools. As these building grants were not available unless the trustees set up a body of managers, as in England and Wales, for the control of the voluntary schools, Catholic clergy had declined such assistance, and to meet this objection the Government introduced legislation in the Education Act, 1930, enabling them to pay 50 per cent of the cost of any building or improvement schemes promulgated by those individual managers who had objected to transferring their schools outright or to setting up management committees.

Except for this one difference in the proportion of the grants towards building and maintenance, Catholic schools 'share in every privilege given to the others,' and such schools were recognised and received state assistance wherever at least twenty-five or thirty Catholic pupils were available for attendance. The Unionist Government pointed out that provision was made, with Government assistance, for Catholic male students to attend a Catholic teacher training college, St Mary's College, Strawberry Hill, near London.

In every other sphere of social life the Unionist Government denied there was any discrimination on grounds of religious belief. On the contrary, it was claimed that in all schemes for alleviating distress, in the application of health and unemployment insurance, widows', orphans' and old age pensions, 'absolute impartiality is observed.' On the question of the alleged abuse of the Union Jack, the Government concluded that 'the logical remedy would appear to lie with the minority themselves. There is nothing to prevent them from flying the Union Jack and breaking down any monopoly of its use.'[138]

All this, however, does not mean that discrimination did not occur. The case of Londonderry illustrates how some of the minority's grievances were justified. In the 1929 parliamentary redistribution the Unionist Government felt unable to accept the Londonderry Unionist Association's scheme to secure the city from Nationalist control. The Unionist Government contravened its own rule that redistribution should conform to existing administrative divisions. The city had a nationalist majority of 2,000 on the parliamentary register; Nationalist domination of the city council was prevented by combining the city with parts of the surrounding countryside, thus creating two constituencies, with the city a safe Unionist seat and the Foyle division a safe Nationalist seat. Under PR, Nationalists had controlled the city council, with 6,868 nationalist electors returning 21 councillors and

6,340 Unionists returning 19. The abolition of PR returned the city council to Unionist hands. Control was achieved by dividing the city into five wards, three of the wards having Unionist majorities and the other two Nationalist majorities, the Nationalist wards being significantly larger than the Unionist.

By the nineteen-thirties, however, Londonderry Unionists were becoming insecure. Although majorities in two of the Unionist wards were substantial, in the third, the North ward, Unionists feared that Nationalists would be able to reverse the Unionist dominance. In 1936 Londonderry Unionists approached the Government with a view to the alteration of wards and a reduction in the size of the council. The Government was sympathetic, with Sir Richard Dawson Bates telling Craig in July 1934 that 'unless something is done now, it is only a matter of time until Derry passes into the hands of the Nationalist and Sinn Féin parties for all time. On the other hand, if proper steps are taken now, I believe Derry can be saved for years to come.'

The Ministry's scheme reduced the number of councillors to twenty and secured a Unionist majority of four on the smaller council by carefully arranging the electorate into three wards, into one of which the majority of Nationalist electors were placed; two wards contained safe Unionist majorities. Now 9,961 Nationalist electors returned 8 councillors, while 7,444 Unionist electors returned 12 councillors.[139]

Two social anthropologists, Barritt and Carter, found that both Catholics and Protestants accepted that discrimination in employment was natural and that 'a man should look after his own.' Many members of both communities considered that preference on grounds of religion or politics was right, Protestants regarding this as the best way of maintaining their supremacy and the all-important safeguards of the constitution, Catholics considering that, since they suffered most from poverty and unemployment, it was only reasonable that their co-religionists should have preference.[140] Newry Nationalists, for example, did not challenge Unionist accusations that they discriminated against Protestants in local government appointments. In 1958 Unionists pointed out that Newry Urban District Council had twenty full-time clerical staff, all of whom were Catholics; it had seventy full-time members on the outdoor staff, all of them Catholics. Newry Gas Works, owned by the council, had eight full-time staff, all Catholics; the council also employed seven plumbers, of whom six were Catholics, and six stokers, nine labourers and one temporary labourer, all of whom were Catholics. Unionists also pointed out that Newry Technical School, also under council control, had twenty full-time teachers, only two of whom were Protestants, while the two employees of the town library and the three full-time clerical staff and fifteen outdoor staff of the Newry Port and Harbour Trust were all Catholics.[141]

Unionists also complained that of the 765 houses owned by Newry Urban District Council only 22 had Protestant tenants, while Protestants constituted slightly more than one-fifth of the population. To Eddie McAteer's complaint that 'Derry has the melancholy distinction of being the worst housed community in the whole of the Six Counties,' Unionists replied that between 1947 and 1958, 2,400 houses were built by the local authority and the Housing Trust in the city, of which 1,000 had gone to Protestants and 1,400 to Catholics. Unionists argued that Catholics had a lower marriage rate than Protestants but a higher fertility rate; in other words, Catholic families were relatively fewer and larger. Accordingly, they argued, the comparing of houses allocated with overall population percentages produced ratios unduly favourable to the Catholic point of view.[142]

It was, however, also true that Nationalists, even if they wished to favour their own in local government, did not have the same opportunity as Protestants, since they controlled only eleven local authorities out of seventy-three.[143]

The basic religious-political division within Northern Ireland society extended to the personnel of the political parties as well: it was rare to find Catholic Unionists or Protestant Nationalists. In 1959, when Sir Clarence Graham, an ex-officio member of the Ulster Unionist Party's Standing Committee, suggested that Catholics should be able to join the Unionist Party and be selected for Parliament, another member of the committee, Sir George Clark, Grand Master of the Grand Orange Lodge of Ireland, rejected this, arguing: 'It is difficult to see how a Catholic, with the vast differences in our religious outlook, could be either acceptable within the Unionist Party as a member, or for that matter, bring himself unconditionally to support its ideals.' The Prime Minister, Lord Brookeborough, supported this view, declaring: 'There is no change in the fundamental character of the Unionist Party or in the loyalties it observes and preserves. If that is called intolerance I say it is not the fault of the Unionist Party. If it is called inflexible then it shows our principles are not elastic.'[144] An election leaflet in the St George's district of Belfast in 1961 informed voters that the three Unionist Party candidates 'Employ over 70 People & have NEVER employed A ROMAN CATHOLIC.' Brookeborough described this as an 'unfortunate occurrence', though 'perhaps understandable' given that the official Unionists' opponents in the constituency were representatives of an extremely militant Protestant body.[145] For Unionists, such sentiments merely reflected the sectarian reality of Northern Ireland politics, and they were quick to point out that in the same election Nationalist politicians in Down Urban District appealed to the 'Catholic Electors of Downpatrick'.[146]

Throughout the nineteen-fifties and into the early sixties, Northern Ireland remained a fundamentally divided and sectarian society. Differences between the two communities pervaded all aspects of society. There was a marked difference in the economic status of the two communities, with Protestants tending to provide the business and professional classes, the larger farmers and the skilled labour, and Catholics the small farmers and the unskilled labourers.[147] Barritt and Carter found that Protestants in general felt superior to Catholics within the province's class structure. This sense of superiority was to be found at all levels. Where Protestants and Catholics were brought together as neighbours, workmates, or in some common social activity, the relationships sometime showed a delicate desire to discern and respect difference and sometimes a wish to emphasise them without respecting them. There were few examples of a readiness to ignore differences. Friendly relations existed within a consciousness of difference. The prudent kept off controversial subjects; the less prudent might have engaged in friendly banter but of a kind that always remembered the religious difference. The desire to emphasise differences without respecting them was to be seen in the flying of flags or the chalking up of slogans.[148]

The cultural significance for Unionists of loyalty to the Crown was illustrated by the passing of the Flags and Emblems (Display) Act (Northern Ireland), 1954, which gave symbolic and legal substance to the Unionist claim that Northern Ireland was the loyal British, as well as Protestant, part of Ireland. The Minister of Home Affairs, George Hanna, said that the Act was introduced so that loyal subjects who desired to fly the Union Jack would be afforded all the protection the legislature could give them. The second clause of the Act provided for the removal by the RUC of any emblem whose display seemed likely to lead to disturbance. Referring to the claim that this in effect banned the Republic's flag, Hanna declared he had no desire to ban the flag of any state with which the United Kingdom was at peace but that the 'Republican part of the island' claimed jurisdiction in Northern Ireland, through its Constitution, and therefore he believed that a person displaying the Tricolour as an indication of support for that claim was in fact alleging the right of a foreign country to govern Northern

Ireland, which he saw as 'very close to an act of treason.'[149] He explained that the Union Jack was the flag of 'their country and of the Kingdom of which they were proud to be citizens.'

Hanna rejected as 'ridiculous' the contention that the Union Jack was a party emblem. The fact, he said, that the Nationalist Party boycotted the 'national flag' did not make it the emblem of another party, for the Unionist Party made no special claim or right to it. The 'broad ... fundamental and undeniable fact was that the national flag was above and outside parliamentary party politics, just as the Crown was above and outside politics.' A condition, he said, precedent to membership of the Northern Ireland Parliament was the swearing of allegiance to the Crown; the Parliament's every legislative act was prefaced with the words 'Be it enacted by the Queen's Most Excellent Majesty,' and it was called into being and prorogued by the Crown; therefore, he concluded, it was wholly paradoxical that any person should openly declare that he did not recognise Her Majesty as their queen or the Union Jack as their national flag. If any man regarded the Union Jack with hatred or as the symbol of thraldom, Hanna advised them to stay away from any part of the United Kingdom. Brookeborough believed the Union Jack was 'sacred', the flag he had fought for, and fought under, in the Great War; and the reason it was revered by unionists was because it was an emblem of the Crown and constitution and of those loyalties and traditions and of the desire to live in the British way of life.[150] Whatever the conditions, unionists would rather suffer harsh penalties than be 'members of a Republic separated from the British Commonwealth.'[151]

One Unionist backbencher, Thomas Lyons, argued that 'God Save the Queen' was a national prayer and that the people who sang it used it to express their loyalty. As to the term 'nationalist', he asked if it was realised what a nationalist was: he believed that unionists opposed the Nationalist Party because 'we are British Nationalists while they are not.'[152] Therefore, Hanna claimed, 'in the Six Counties the flying of the Union Jack on one's own property is an act of loyalty' to the Queen and to the flag, both of which expressed loyalty to 'our native land ... the Six Counties of Northern Ireland.'

The oath of allegiance Hanna considered an oath that the person taking it would bear true allegiance to Her Majesty the Queen.[153] Unionists denied that such men as Carson had broken their oaths of allegiance when they threatened rebellion against the British Government that sought to impose Home Rule on them during the Ulster Crisis of 1912–14. In every case, argued another backbench

Unionist, Archibald Wilson, they were oaths of allegiance to the King, and the action that men like Carson took was to prevent an alien state pushing them out of the United Kingdom—in other words, to 'remain faithful to the King to whom they had remained faithful.' The oath of allegiance in Wilson's opinion was one of the fundamentals of the British constitution. He argued that within the terms of the oath of allegiance to Queen Elizabeth II the people of Northern Ireland could vote, argue and debate the laws of their Parliament, both inside and outside that Parliament, even taking matters to the courts; but if, under that oath, force was used to break their allegiance, then unionists reserved the right to use force to resist this.[154]

Nationalists, however, protested at the compulsory declaration of allegiance to the monarch for public employment. A similar feeling existed about the flying of the Union Jack and gatherings and processions intended to be a declaration of loyalty to the Crown. Nationalists demanded the right to show flags and emblems and to hold meetings and demonstrations to illustrate their loyalty to another state.

Other matters that caused tension were the right to play the Republic's national anthem, 'Amhrán na bhFiann', and to remain seated when 'God Save the Queen' was played.[155] Cahir Healy, when referring to the ceremonial trappings of monarchy, told the British House of Commons that it was 'notable that the more primitive people are, the greater their desire for ceremonial. The very progressive and intellectual people aim rather at simplicity.'[156] During the celebrations for the coronation of Queen Elizabeth II the Nationalist representatives at Stormont and Westminster issued a proclamation repudiating her authority, stating:

> Whereas we, the undersigned, are the elected representatives of the greater portion of Ireland over which the British Crown and Government claim sovereignty and jurisdiction ... and whereas Queen Elizabeth of England has been crowned with the title of Queen of Northern Ireland ... now we, in the name of the people we represent ... hereby repudiate all claims now made or to be made in the future by or on behalf of the British Crown and Government to jurisdiction over any portion of Ireland or of her territorial seas.[157]

Northern Ireland remained a highly religious society. It was estimated that in the nineteen-sixties the proportion of church attendance was probably higher than in England at the turn of the century and for Protestants as much as six times higher than in England in the sixties. Probably more than 50 per cent of Catholics had an active connection with their church. The religiosity of both communities had an effect on community relations. Barritt and Carter found that many Protestants viewed the Catholic Church as a vast international empire, run on 'totalitarian' principles and instantly obeying the regulations of the Pope. The Catholic Church's view was that of a church involved in a long struggle against oppression and persecution, especially during the days of the penal laws; it was paternalistic, giving the parish priest the influence and reverence that naturally belonged to an educated man serving a poor community. Many Protestants believed that the Catholic Church taught that salvation was to be found only in communion with it and that in consequence they were regarded by Catholics as heretics doomed to eternal damnation. Protestants protested against what they saw as Catholic priests' interference in politics in support of Nationalist candidates and therefore, in the opinion of Unionists, engaged in treason against the Queen.[158]

Protestant-Catholic relations were such that on the death of Pope Pius XII in October 1958 the Northern Ireland Government advised against the attendance by the Governor at a requiem Mass, warning:

> The larger proportion of the population in Northern Ireland would not favour attendance by, or representation of, His Excellency at such a ceremony. The more vocal and extreme elements would voice disapproval. This could exacerbate public reactions to IRA activities. The religious community concerned, having regard to the political attitude they adopt and support in Northern Ireland, and having regard to the standard of conduct they maintain vis-à-vis Government House, will not expect, indeed would be surprised—not to say confused—at attendance or representation.[159]

Catholics complained of Protestant clerical intervention in politics, particularly with reference to the Orange Order. On Orange platforms, Government ministers and clergy mingled a religious and political appeal, emphasising that the maintenance of the Union with Britain was essential if Protestant civil and religious liberties in Ireland were to be safeguarded. An Orange parade could have very different meanings from those it possessed for Protestants.[160] For Catholics this was interpreted as a demonstration of control of territory, a demonstration of Protestant power, and proof that nothing had changed in almost three hundred years since the Battle of the Boyne in 1690.[161]

Marriage between Protestants and Catholics remained rare and was actively discouraged in some quarters. In May 1951, for example, Bishop Farren asked of Catholics if their young people went into dangerous surroundings, if they had to seek their amusement among non-Catholics in non-Catholic [dance] halls, where the standard of purity was not as high as it was among Catholics, could they expect their young people to come out of those halls as good as they went into them ... If you allow your children to be contaminated by those not of the Fold, then you can expect nothing but disaster ... It is too late whenever a dangerous friendship is formed which may lead your girl along the road to hell before she is prepared to give up the boy to whom she is attached or make your boy cry out that he prefers Barabas to Christ and will give up his Church and his soul rather than give up the girl with whom he has become infatuated ... We want to live in peace and harmony with non-Catholic neighbours. Our religion teaches charity. But the Salvation of your soul comes first ...[162]

Barritt and Carter described religious relations in Northern Ireland as a 'cold war', with each side profoundly conscious of the wrongness of the other but neither, on the whole, ready to carry condemnation to its limit. The nature of Northern Ireland society, both its churches and its schools, helped to reproduce communal divisions. In 1960, 41 per cent of the school population was Catholic and 59 per cent Protestant; at least 98 per cent of all Catholic primary school children attended Catholic schools.[163] Apart from the removal of the opportunity for friendship between schoolchildren there were other factors in the school system that added to division. Broadly, non-Catholic schools taught English history, with Irish history taught as an incidental to English history. Catholic schools were more likely to teach Irish history in its own right, and to treat it as the story of heroism in maintaining national feeling under foreign rule. Another difference was that in Catholic schools Irish was taught as a recognised subject. Most Protestants regarded Irish as a dead and useless language, while some Catholics thought of it as an important part of their birthright. Many Protestants complained that Catholic schoolchildren were being deliberately taught to look on all Protestants as wrong and wicked and were carefully trained to be anti-British nationalists. Catholics denied they taught hatred of Protestants and instead complained that Protestants were taught to hate the Catholic faith and to mistrust Catholics as people.[164]

It appeared that little had changed in rival communal perceptions in the four decades since partition. Any attempt to change or challenge the foundations of these divisions could destabilise the very basis on which the citizens of Northern Ireland's polarised community could live in relative peace with one another.

3

Civil Rights and Civil Strife

1963–1969

O'NEILLISM

In 1963 Lord Brookeborough resigned after twenty years as Prime Minister of Northern Ireland and was succeeded by Captain Terence O'Neill, who had been Minister of Finance for seven years. O'Neill had an Anglo-Irish landed background; among his ancestors were the ancient Ulster O'Neill family and the English Chichester family. Born in 1914 and educated at Eton, he had a traditional background for a Unionist leader and had also served in the British army during the Second World War.

O'Neill aimed for a better-planned economy based on the recommendations of the Matthew and Wilson economic reports, which had been commissioned by the Unionist Government. The economic circumstances of the nineteen-sixties were favourable for economic modernisation. Despite the decline of the staple industries, gross domestic product per head in Northern Ireland increased ahead of the United Kingdom as a whole. The main reasons for this were increased investment in manufacturing, a great deal of it coming from outside companies, and high levels of public sector investment, while the natural increase in the population maintained the problems of unemployment and emigration. By the time Brookeborough resigned, unemployment stood at 10 per cent.

The Wilson Plan of December 1964 proposed the acceptance of the irreversible decline of the staple industries and the creation of a modern economic infrastructure with an initial £450 million investment and extra grants from government sources, which would attract mostly foreign investment and new industries to the province. This plan became the basis of O'Neill's economic policy and was implemented by Brian Faulkner at the Ministry of Commerce.

O'Neill believed that the economic benefits of the Union could be used to integrate Catholics into the Northern Ireland state. He rejected the charge of 'apartheid' in Northern Ireland: where this existed, O'Neill claimed, it was almost entirely from a voluntary separation from the mainstream of public and social life.[1] The first aim in community relations, O'Neill argued, was to discard the unrealistic. He said that an *Irish Times* editorial that had expressed the hope that one day the North would embrace the republican heritage of Robert Emmet and Theobald Wolfe Tone was the kind of wishful thinking that for too long had held back the 'sane tide of reality in Irish affairs.' O'Neill argued that 'anyone who thinks the Protestant community in Northern Ireland is ever going to embrace the GAA, the Irish language, and the Fenian Brotherhood is being as realistic as someone who expects one day to see a banner of Queen Victoria carried in a Hibernian parade.'

Equally, O'Neill disagreed with those who advocated a kind of reciprocal emasculation, with 'no National Anthem or Loyal Toast to offend the other side; no outward signs or symbols of Nationalism to offend the other.' This approach was misconceived, he believed, because the state had a right to call on all its citizens to support the constitution. The whole basis of constitutional government would be debased, he argued, if the state were not to expect of its citizens the 'minimum duty of allegiance.' This would not involve the total surrender of one point of view to another, nor a sweeping under the carpet of major differences on points of principle: what he wanted to see was the 'occupation of a broad area of middle ground by reasonable men and its steady widening in the course of time.'

O'Neill doubted whether the people of Ireland, North and South, really brooded over the events of 1690 and 1798, instead believing that they were more concerned with the value of their take-home pay, with job security, and their children's education. He believed that in the great majority of issues that confronted a modern government the terms 'Catholic' and 'Protestant' were irrelevant. He wondered whether it would be possible for organisations to reach out across denominational barriers, for example in the field of voluntary effort, for the good of the community, and he looked forward to a day when Protestant people would decorate a youth club in Catholic Andersonstown and a young Catholic might read to a bedridden old woman on the Protestant Shankill Road.[2]

O'Neill decided it was time to help heal the divide in internal and external politics. He hoped to demonstrate that the historical divisions within Northern Ireland and between Northern Ireland and the Republic could not be allowed to stand in the way of the community spirit, without which O'Neill believed Northern Ireland would not be able to realise its full economic and social potential. He regarded Craigavon's remark that Northern Ireland possessed 'a Protestant

Parliament for a Protestant people' as having 'some relevance in its historic setting of the troubled twenties, but it is no more representative of the present spirit of Ulster Unionist politics than the declarations of Stanley Baldwin are of conservatism in the sixties.'[3] O'Neill argued that the Northern Ireland Government of the twenties and thirties faced appalling problems of physical violence and economic distress; but now Northern Ireland was making real progress, and all its people were sharing in ever-growing prosperity, realising the benefits of the British connection.[4]

O'Neill denied that because he spoke of a 'new Ulster', the Ulster of Carson and Craig was dead. 'We are building, certainly; but we build upon their foundations.' But, he argued, it was not enough just to be part of the United Kingdom: Ulster should be a progressive part of that kingdom, and he wanted to secure the prosperity of the United Kingdom for the people of Northern Ireland. 'It must be our aim', he argued, 'to demonstrate at all times, and beyond any possible doubt, that loyalty to Britain carries its reward in the form of a fuller, richer life.'[5]

For O'Neill, Unionism was an expression of his membership in the British nation. He believed that

> the fundamental purpose of Unionism ... is to preserve a parliamentary union with Great Britain unbroken, as far as we are concerned, since the start of the nineteenth century. Those who oppose us will attempt to convince you that Northern Ireland is some kind of last-minute expedient. It is well to remember that this area has been within the United Kingdom since the days of Napoleon ... Some people attach little importance to the question of nationality. They may regard nationalism as a passing phenomenon, and national pride as a bar to greater world unity. Others see the nation solely as a kind of paymaster, worthy of support only for what one gets out of it. For these people, 'Ask not what your country can do for you' is a meaningless phrase in a materialistic world. But the sort of Unionism in which I believe sees more in our ancient link with Britain than an historical accident or an economic convenience. He sees in it a chance to play a useful and rewarding part in events far beyond the local scene ... Are you not proud to be part of a nation which twenty years ago triumphed over the most evil tyranny the world has ever known? A nation, moreover, which then proceeded, with magnanimity and good judgement, to convert its imperial heritage into a commonwealth of independent states?[6]

O'Neill's primary loyalty was to Britain and the British state. In 1966, remembering the sacrifice of the 36th (Ulster) Division at the Battle of the Somme fifty years earlier, O'Neill emphasised how Unionism meant sacrifice for the Union between Great Britain and Northern Ireland.

We in Northern Ireland hear a great deal about the word 'loyalty'. But it is worth while to ask the question: what lies behind the display of the Union Jack and the other outward signs of our attachment to Queen and country? I am one of those who believe that patriotism is better demonstrated than proclaimed. For much of the time—and let us face up to this—Ulster's attachment to Britain is of great benefit to us. It guarantees our standard of living; it makes it possible for us to develop here all the services of a modern industrial state. It is easy to be loyal, when the rewards of loyalty are so material and so self-evident.

But patriotism, like marriage, demands a loyalty to the country which is 'for better for worse; for richer, for poorer; in sickness and in health.' If it provides benefits, it also expects sacrifices.[7]

O'Neill's first task as Prime Minister was to halt the electoral advance of the Northern Ireland Labour Party. In the Westminster election of October 1964 the NILP had polled 103,000 votes, though it won no seats. In the 1965 Stormont general election the Ulster Unionist Party's manifesto stated that the prime objective of the next five years was to create new employment, cater for the unexpected increase in population, and reduce unemployment as much as possible. The Unionist Government said it was striving to develop economic co-operation with the Government of the Republic. O'Neill explained: 'We seek no enemies. To those who will grasp it, the Red Hand of Ulster is extended in friendship.' He emphasised that the Government was prepared to fight on its economic record and that he would make no mention of the IRA issue in election speeches.[8] He promised 65,000 new jobs, 64,000 new homes, improved social services, more schools and hospitals, advances in agriculture, and a modern road system. To the electors he stated: 'I appeal to YOU to help me build over the next five years an even better Ulster for you and your children.' He believed the Ulster Unionist Party could attract Catholic voters, arguing, 'We must get away from this facile assumption that the Roman Catholic population is identical with ... the "Nationally minded people",' and he thought many voters would find in the Unionist Party's programme something far more relevant to their needs than the 'platitudes of an outdated Nationalism.'[9] O'Neill saw Unionism's opponents offering only doctrinaire ideas and threadbare policies: socialism was 'rooted in the class struggle of the Thirties'; nationalism was 'bogged down in the emotions of the Twenties'; only Unionism 'turns its face to the promise and hope of the Seventies.'[10]

O'Neill's concentration on the economic benefits of the Union successfully turned back the tide of socialism in Northern Ireland, and the NILP lost their two solidly Protestant seats in Woodvale and Victoria, while their majority in Pottinger was halved. The NILP's vote went down in every constituency, and their total vote, despite three extra candidates, was 66,323, some 10,000 less than in 1962.[11]

O'Neill shocked many of his supporters when, in January 1965, he suddenly met the Taoiseach, Seán Lemass, at Stormont, secretly and without prior Cabinet approval. O'Neill took this dramatic step because he claimed that the defence of Ulster's constitution had been the motivation of his entire political life. He had worked to secure Ulster's constitution against any threat from outside the United Kingdom. In the past this had taken two forms: the 'despicable and cowardly attacks' launched from across the border and a 'more insidious and potentially more dangerous' campaign of political propaganda, aimed at discrediting unionism and at showing the world that it was the loyal people of Ulster who were the cause of strife and disharmony in Ireland. This was behind his invitation to Lemass in 1965, in which he wanted to establish two things: firstly, that Northern Ireland's existence, its Parliament and Government, was a fact the Republic had to reckon with and that the 'grandiose and empty' territorial claims of the Irish Constitution to Northern Ireland were exposed for the vanity they were when a Southern prime minister drove through Stormont's gates; and secondly, by showing that it was not Unionists who represented any impediment to practical co-operation or a decent neighbourly relationship, that it was not they who were aggressors. O'Neill described his meeting with Lemass as an initiative to 'clothe our constitutional status with a new moral authority,' to make it clear that it was not Northern stubbornness but Southern interference that hampered the development of friendship and mutual respect.[12]

Following this thaw in North-South relations, Eddie McAteer, leader of the Nationalist Party, announced after a visit to the Taoiseach in Dublin that his party would become the official opposition at Stormont, for the first time in Northern Ireland's history. O'Neill continued to make overtures to the Northern nationalist community, as in June 1963, with public condolences to the Catholic primate, Cardinal Conway, on the death of Pope John XXIII, and in April 1964 by visiting a Catholic school. O'Neill broke with tradition when he decided that the message of sympathy on the Pope's death should be sent by the Prime Minister on behalf of the Northern Ireland Government. He felt this departure from previous practice was desirable in view of the change in public opinion and also as a gesture that change was recognised, even though at this juncture it was not possible to go as far as half-masting flags.[13] The message read: 'Please accept from the Government of Northern Ireland our sympathy on the great loss which your church sustained on the death of your spiritual leader. He had won acclaim throughout the world because of his qualities of kindness and humanity.'[14]

In making these gestures, O'Neill claimed that at all times he had kept before him the vital words of section 1 (2) of the Ireland Act, 1949, which declared that Northern Ireland would remain part of His Majesty's Dominions and of the United Kingdom as long as the Parliament of Northern Ireland desired it. This meant, he argued, that it was 'we here, and our successors in time to come who will determine the constitutional destiny of this Province.' The implications of those words lay at the root of his whole domestic policy. O'Neill explained to the Northern Ireland House of Commons:

I want the House to understand that I am a Unionist, a convinced Unionist, not for today, or for yesterday but for the far distant future. I want our descendants to live, as we have lived, under the Union Jack and enjoying all the benefits of the British connection. And because this is my wish, because I want to secure the Constitution not just for our time but for the foreseeable future, I want to show every citizen of Ulster, every section of Ulster the benefits of the British connection are all to share.

I want to see a day on which anti-partitionists will only be a tiny minority of eccentrics in this House. I know there are those who feel that a community which already represents over one-third of our population and has over 50 per cent of the children of school age can just be written off as a source of support for our Constitution and status. I believe such an attitude is defeatist. I prefer to say across the historic divide: 'This is your country too. Help us to make it all it could be.'[15]

CIVIL RIGHTS

Within the Catholic community, liberalising developments also appeared to be evolving. Openings made for Catholics in the nineteen-fifties, through the impact of the Education Act, 1944, and economic diversification, had by the mid-sixties created a much-strengthened Catholic middle class, who looked beyond the traditional role of serving their own community. The new Catholic graduates went mainly into teaching and the medical and legal professions, since public employment was dominated by Protestants. They also seemed to want to liberalise and modernise traditional nationalist politics, in order to participate not only in the economic and social life of Northern Ireland but in its political life also. For these groups the Republican movement and the IRA did not offer a promising policy.

Some Catholics, however, frustrated with the lack of evidence of reform, began to form themselves into political pressure groups. The first of these was the Campaign for Social Justice. This was formed out of the Homeless Citizens' League in Dungannon in May 1963, which was led by Conn and Patricia McCluskey, who also founded the CSJ. The HCL arose out of a challenge to Dungannon Urban District Council by a group of housewives when they submitted a petition to the council complaining that while they were in cramped or unsanitary houses, or living with relatives, Protestants, some from outside the area, were getting houses as soon as they applied.

Dungannon was evenly balanced between Protestants and Catholics, but control of the council was in Unionist hands. The East ward was predominantly Protestant, the West ward predominantly Catholic; but the Central ward, which had half the population of either of the other two, returned the same number of councillors and had a majority of Protestants. The result was that fourteen Unionists were returned against seven 'anti-Unionists'. Any expansion of housing could thereby alter the political composition of the Council. The HCL did not express the grievances of all Dungannon Catholics but of a particular section, that of young married couples and families living with relatives or in inadequate housing. What was different about it was that it took direct action, such as squatting in prefabs due to be demolished.

The founders of the Campaign for Social Justice were motivated by what they saw as the ineffectuality of Nationalist representatives in putting the minority's case. Although its membership was confined to thirteen professional people, and despite its avowal that it was non-sectarian, it was entirely Catholic. The CSJ was launched in Belfast on 17 January 1964 and differed from previous minority pressure groups in that it focused its efforts on British public opinion. It described the heart of the Ulster problem as

1. The fact that the Northern Ireland Parliament, which was subject to the authority of Westminster, had refused since it was set up by Britain, to give justice to the minority, and steadfastly ignored the appeals of the Parliamentary representatives of the minority.

2. That the Government of Ireland Act, which set up the Northern Ireland Administration had a Section 5 which was designed to give protection to the minority. It had failed to do so.

3. That every attempt to have the grievances of the minority discussed at Westminster was defeated by the existence of a 'convention' which prevented discussion of matters which were within the competence of the Parliament of Northern Ireland.[16]

While the CSJ saw itself as non-sectarian, many of its arguments against Catholic grievances in Northern Ireland echoed the arguments put forward by Nationalists over the previous forty years. In *Londonderry: One Man No Vote* the CSJ argued that the Northern Ireland state had been governed for over forty years by the Conservative and Unionist Party and that no Catholics were admitted to membership of this party. The CSJ accused the Ulster Unionist Party of consolidating its position by strengthening the economy of the eastern half of the state, predominantly Protestant, and encouraging few industries to set up in the western, predominantly Catholic, counties.

The CSJ accused the Unionist Government of making determined attempts in the recent past to 'further weaken and depopulate' the western counties.

1. There were two separate railway lines to Londonderry. In the interests of economy it became necessary to close one of them. The one axed traversed the western region. This has left Fermanagh, Tyrone and practically all of the county of Londonderry with no railway line whatever.

2. In order to further strengthen the relatively prosperous east, the government of Northern Ireland is to build a New City in County Armagh. Mr ... Copcutt ... its chief designer ... suggested the abandonment of the New City and that the development of Londonderry should be concentrated upon in order to give the province a reasonable balance.

3. The government in February 1965 accepted the Wilson Plan for economic development ... This report outlined four centres for rapid industrial development all within a 30 mile radius of Belfast, and none in the western counties.

4. In February 1965, the government also accepted the Lockwood

Report ... Here, Londonderry was rejected as the site for a new university, in spite of the fact that Magee University College [in Derry], a hundred year old institution, is at present providing for the first two years of university education in certain subjects.

The CSJ claimed that in the three Ulster constituencies 'where the Conservatives are in a minority' control was maintained by the manipulation of electoral boundaries. For example, in Londonderry the CSJ accurately pointed out that the electoral wards were gerrymandered as to size and composition, with the surplus Catholics in one large ward and two smaller wards composed of Protestants, so as to return two Protestant (or 'Conservative', as the CSJ called them) MPs to one Catholic, as follows:

Roman Catholic adults over 21	*Roman Catholic adults with local Government vote*
19,870	14,325 (inc. 257 company votes)

Conservative adults over 21	*Conservative adults with local Government vote*
10,573	9,235 (inc. 902 company votes)[17]

The issue of public housing had scarcely surfaced before the nineteen-fifties. The general condition of housing in Northern Ireland had been appalling. There had been few allegations of discrimination in the allocation of public housing, because there was little public housing to allocate. All this changed after 1945, when a large-scale public housing drive was launched. By 1961, 21 per cent of all housing in the province was public rented accommodation; by 1971 the proportion was 35 per cent. As public housing became more plentiful, so complaints about its allocation multiplied. The Housing Trust, set up in 1945, funded by the Northern Ireland Government and headed by an independent body of part-time members, selected tenants not just on the basis of need but on their ability to pay. The Housing Trust has generally been exonerated from any conscious desire to discriminate; this was not the case with regard to local authorities.

In Fermanagh, where Catholics formed a slight majority of the population, it was claimed that of 1,589 post-war council houses, 568 were let to Catholics and 1,021 to Protestants. The Cameron Commission concluded that there were many cases where councils had withheld planning permission, or caused needless delays, where they believed a housing project would be to their electoral disadvantage.

The commission concluded that in Unionist-controlled areas it was fairly frequent for housing policy to operate in such a way that houses allocated to Catholics tended, as in Dungannon Urban District, to go to rehouse slum dwellers, whereas Protestant allocations tended to go more frequently to new families. The total numbers allocated were therefore in rough correspondence to the proportion of Protestants and Catholics in the community; the principal criterion in such cases, however, was not need but the maintenance of the current political preponderance in the local government area.

The areas where allegations of discrimination in public housing persisted were, without exception, those west of the River Bann. Against the majority of councils there were no complaints. Cahir Healy even praised local authorities in Belfast, Antrim and Down, as well as the Housing Trust, for their fair play in serving needful ends. Belfast City Council, for example, was the largest local authority in the province. In those areas that did attract criticism the objection was not that Catholics were refused houses but that they were confined to those wards where they were already a majority, so as not to disturb the electoral balance. The Cameron Commission pointed out that in Londonderry, Catholics were rehoused almost exclusively in the South ward and in Omagh and Dungannon almost exclusively in the West wards. But it also remarked that in several of the areas the actual total of new housing had been substantial.

A survey by an American political scientist, Richard Rose, to test allegations of discrimination in housing found that 35 per cent of his Catholic respondents, as against 30 per cent of Protestant ones, lived in public housing. Taking account of income size, he found that in all but one income category the proportion of Catholics in subsidised housing was slightly higher than that of Protestants. Breaking down his figures by county and city, he found that the generally fair pattern remained. In four out of the eight counties and cities—Belfast, Derry (city), Armagh, and Tyrone—a majority of respondents in public housing were Catholics. The only evidence of bias against Catholics came when he tested for family size and found that among the very largest families (six children or more) there was a 12 per cent difference against Catholics in the proportion assigned public housing. This indicates that housing policies in individual areas, such as Fermanagh or Dungannon, could be very unfair, but that in many parts of Northern Ireland it was very fair.

Regional development, like housing, was relatively late on the scene, only appearing in the mid-sixties. The grievance was that Government decisions concentrated development in the east and neglected the west, even though the west needed more development. The suspicion was that the east was favoured because it was mainly Protestant, while in the west Catholics were a slight majority. Among the more controversial decisions were the Benson Report on railways in 1963, leading to the removal of the west's only railway line, cutting off Derry from Strabane, Omagh, and Dungannon; the Matthew Report in 1964, siting Northern Ireland's 'new town', Craigavon, in the east (Portadown); the Lockwood Report in 1965, rejecting Derry's claim for Northern Ireland's second university, despite the existence of a university college in the city; the Wilson Plan in 1965, which designated growth areas for Northern Ireland, concentrating them heavily in the east; and, in 1966, the closure of Derry's naval base.

Each of these decisions could be justified individually. The naval base closures were part of a general cut-back in British naval expenditure, from which Northern Ireland could not expect to remain immune. Railways in Northern Ireland were losing money, and, as in Britain and the Republic, the Government was obliged to close lines to limit losses; in fact the Benson Report had recommended the closure of both lines to Derry. The Matthew Report was not a regional plan for Northern Ireland as a whole but, as one of the civil servants involved explained, a means of circumventing a long-running dispute between Belfast City Council and the Ministry of Health and Local Government over the rehousing of Belfast's surplus population: the new city grew out of the need to solve this problem. The Lockwood Committee produced reasoned arguments for concluding that the Coleraine area best fulfilled the requirements of a site for a new university, among them the availability of an area large enough to allow for expansion, a criterion that the existing university college in Derry could not meet. Finally, Unionists could point to sound practical reasons why entrepreneurs preferred to settle in the east of the province: that was where skilled labour, docks and communications were most concentrated.[18]

The CSJ and its supporters had a far stronger case with regard to public employment. If all grades in public employment were lumped together, there appeared to be little if any underrepresentation of Catholics. In 1951, of 3,476 local authority workers of all kinds, 1,096, or 32 per cent, were 'nationalist' (by which was meant Catholic). This was close to the proportion of Catholics in the adult population. Rose, in his 1968 survey, found that 16 per cent of Protestants and 13 per cent of Catholics reported that they or someone in their family were, or had been, publicly employed. However, the moment one distinguished lower grades from higher ones, marked discrepancies appeared. In 1951 just over 40 per cent of manual labourers were 'nationalists', but of the 1,095 senior posts only 130, or 12 per cent, were held by 'nationalists'.

The Cameron Commission was satisfied that the Unionist-controlled councils it investigated had used their power to make appointments in a way that benefited Protestants. For example, in October 1968 only 30 per cent of Londonderry City Council's administrative, clerical and technical employees were Catholics, and in County Fermanagh no senior council posts and relatively few others were held by Catholics. Similar figures were found for the Northern Ireland civil service. The only Catholic to reach the rank of permanent secretary was A. N. Bonaparte-Wyse; after his retirement in 1939 no other reached the same rank until Patrick Shea in 1969. The CSJ reported that of 319 officials down to the rank of deputy principal officer, twenty-three, or 7 per cent, were Catholics. Catholics were also underrepresented on statutory bodies and among the highest ranks of the employees of such bodies. The CSJ listed twenty-two public bodies, with a total membership of 332, of whom forty-nine, or 15 per cent, were Catholics. In the publicly owned gas, electricity and water industries the imbalance against Catholics seems to have reached down through all levels. The census of 1971 showed that of 8,122 people employed in those industries only 1,952, or 15 per cent, recorded themselves as Catholics. An overall working figure shows that in 1971, of 1,383 senior government officials, including ministers, MPs, senior government officials and senior officers in local authorities, 11 per cent described themselves as Catholics, compared with 31 per cent of the population as a whole.

Against the CSJ claims of discrimination as the sole cause of these discrepancies there are other factors to be considered, such as Catholics being underrepresented because of their lower educational standards. This point was made by Barritt and Carter, who pointed out that three-quarters of the grammar school and university population was Protestant, so that it would be reasonable to expect at least that proportion of Protestants among the holders of higher posts. However, as Barritt and Carter also pointed out, the proportion of Protestants was considerably higher than that. It may also have been true that Catholics were unwilling to serve, or were discouraged by their co-religionists from serving. Patrick Shea records that Catholic civil servants were viewed with suspicion by other Catholics, because 'we had joined the enemy; we were lost souls.' A Southern journalist, Desmond Fennell, met a prominent Nationalist who told how a friend had remarked to him that 'it was a bad day for the Nationalists when a

Catholic was appointed a Supreme Court judge—it had sounded good to be able to say that the Supreme Court hadn't a single Catholic judge!'[19]

Yet, even when taking account of these factors, it seems evident that some discrimination did occur. Terence O'Neill recalled that when he was Minister of Finance in the nineteen-fifties he had to face a campaign against him in the Cabinet because it was believed that since he had taken up office Catholics were being encouraged to join the civil service. Patrick Shea was held for many years at the rank of principal officer, and his permanent secretary finally told him that 'because you are a Roman Catholic you may never get any further promotion. I'm sorry.' Shea eventually received promotion, but only several years later and after a change of department.[20]

The CSJ sought to use all the means at its disposal for disseminating information about discrimination against the Catholic community. When the British Prime Minister, Sir Alec Douglas-Home, visited Northern Ireland in March 1964 and stated that recourse could be had to the courts, the CSJ's legal advice led it to the conclusion that the 'discrimination practised by local authorities is not capable of review by the courts under the terms of the Government of Ireland Act 1920 or under any other statutory provisions.' The CSJ believed that section 5 of the Government of Ireland Act, 1920, which legislated against religious discrimination in enactments of the Northern Ireland Parliament, did not apply to religious discrimination in the exercise of executive powers granted to the Northern Ireland Government, did not appear to prevent discrimination in the exercise by others of powers or duties imposed by Acts of the Northern Ireland Parliament, and, in particular, did not give any redress against discriminatory acts by local authorities in the exercise of their duties.

As an alternative to the courts, the CSJ focused on British Government intervention in Northern Ireland's affairs as a means of forcing the Unionist Government into reforms. When Downing Street informed the CSJ that section 75 of the Government of Ireland Act 'preserves the supreme authority of the Parliament of the United Kingdom—not of Her Majesty's Government in the United Kingdom—over all persons, matters and things in Northern Ireland,' the CSJ concluded:

(1) The Parliament of the United Kingdom has the ultimate responsibility for discrimination in Northern Ireland, but the [British] Prime Minister is unwilling to ask Parliament to intervene.

(2) Despite the fact that the British Prime Minister told us that allegations of discrimination could be dealt with by law, he is now either unable or unwilling to let us know how this can be done.

We are left wondering if Sir Alec spoke in error, or in fact he has no real interest in the problem of the minority and the facts of religious discrimination in Northern Ireland.[21]

In their correspondence with Douglas-Home, the CSJ felt that they had not achieved much, except a formal admission that under the terms of the Government of Ireland Act, 1920, the Westminster Parliament retained supreme authority over Northern Ireland affairs. From this, according to Brian Gregory, secretary of the CSJ, 'our people are now thoroughly aware of this fact, and in that sense a new situation has been created. They believe that if something can be done, and if it's right and just and proper that it should be done, then it will be done by the present Government at Westminster.'[22]

Catholic political expectations were raised by the election of Harold Wilson's Labour Government in 1964. Patricia McCluskey of the CSJ informed an adviser of Wilson's:

We have been greatly pleased and encouraged by the achievement of your party at the General Election ... Not for generations has there been such hope in this community; and this hope has been created by Mr Wilson's action in recognising the disabilities under which the minority in Northern Ireland has to work.

The Prime Minister, in letters to our organisation, has been so sympathetic, and has given us such heart that it is impossible to assess the amount of good will already generated here towards the new Labour Government at Westminster.[23]

However, Wilson and the new Government remained unwilling to become embroiled in Northern Ireland's affairs. Wilson told McCluskey that the Labour Party believed that before steady progress could be made in solving Northern Ireland's problems there had to be changes in the parliamentary representation of Northern Ireland, both at Westminster and Stormont. Wilson, pointing out that the NILP was opposed to discrimination, argued that this was the most immediate way of furthering their cause and called on the CSJ to give active support to NILP candidates in the general election of 1964.[24] As Wilson explained to another correspondent, while acknowledging that the Labour Party and the British Government were opposed to all forms of discrimination on religious or other grounds and that it was intended to 'take all action in our power to eliminate it,' he had to take into account the fact that matters such as they were discussing fell under the provisions of the Government of Ireland Act, 1920, and within the remit of the Northern Ireland Government and Parliament. In view of the constitutional position 'it would not be proper for me to comment on the matters to which you draw attention, or to seek to intervene.'[25]

However reluctant Wilson was to intervene, he could not avoid the mounting pressure for him to do so. This took shape in the formation of the Campaign for Democracy in Ulster in June 1965. The CDU was established by rank-and-file members of the British Labour Party, mainly of Irish extraction. Its original aims were:

1. To secure a full and impartial inquiry into the administration of government in Northern Ireland, and into allegations of discrimination in the field of housing and employment.

2. To bring electoral law in Northern Ireland into line with that in the rest of the United Kingdom, and to examine electoral boundaries with a view to providing fair representation for all sections of the community.

3. To press for the incorporation of the Race Relations Act to be extended to include Northern Ireland and that it be amended to include religious discrimination and incitement.

Paddy Byrne, vice-president and driving force of the CDU, argued that the organisation was concerned

> only with obtaining full British democratic standards for the people of Northern Ireland, to which they are entitled as British subjects. We hold that the 'Border' is irrelevant to the issue ... As far as the CDU is concerned, the Tory-Unionists who rule Northern Ireland can build a wall around the six-counties if they wish, but we do insist that all citizens on the British side of the wall enjoy full British benefits.

Byrne, a Dubliner who been a member of the Republican Congress in the thirties, was motivated by his socialism, hoping that Belfast workers would be 'freed from the fear of what might befall them if Ulster were not kept "Protestant"' and 'would vote according to their class interest and return not one but perhaps five socialists to Westminster.' The *CDU Newsletter* argued that the interests of working-class people were identical, whether Catholic or Protestant, and that they should forget irrelevant religious differences and concentrate on obtaining social justice and civil and religious liberty for all.[26]

The CDU was sponsored by over a hundred Labour MPs and peers at

Westminster; but what kept up its momentum was the election of Gerry Fitt to the British Parliament. Fitt had been returned in 1958 as an Irish Labour member of Belfast City Council. In 1966 he won the West Belfast seat for Westminster from the Unionists, and at Westminster he made effective use of the material collected by the CSJ. He organised several trips to Northern Ireland for sympathetic Labour MPs, notably on the occasion of the Londonderry riots of 5 October 1968, when he himself received a head injury. A CDU conference held in London in January 1968 called on all CDU MPs to use whatever methods were available to question the legality of the convention that prevented the discussion of Northern Ireland affairs at Westminster.

Harold Wilson was constantly pressured by the CDU MPs on the Northern Ireland issue, and he was also aware of the sizable Irish immigrant vote in his own constituency. Nevertheless he took the attitude that Terence O'Neill had made more progress in the area of discrimination and human rights in three years than all his Stormont predecessors had in forty years and so preferred informal talks as a means of achieving change. When Wilson, at such a meeting in May 1966, pressed O'Neill on the concern that was felt on the Labour back benches at the lack of constitutional reform, the latter gravely underlined the threats to his position, how he had moved so fast by Northern Ireland standards that he felt there must be a period of consolidation or else a dangerous and possibly irresistible tide of reaction would set in.[27]

At about this time the concept of an organised civil rights movement arose from elements of the Republican movement. Following the end of its border campaign, the IRA had suffered from factionalism and defeatism. Sinn Féin, as the political arm of the movement, began to consider constitutional options and adopted left-wing policies to broaden its appeal. The new policy offended many militarist traditionalists, as well as many of the movement's devout Catholics, and frustrated those new and younger members who favoured military action. The idea of a civil rights campaign in Northern Ireland originated from a conference of Wolfe Tone Societies, which were offsprings of the Republican movement. The intellectual leaders of the societies were two Dublin academics, Anthony Coughlan and Roy Johnston. They believed that unionism was built on discrimination and the artificial division of Protestant and Catholic workers, who would no longer oppose each other if this machinery of discrimination, the Northern Ireland state, was destroyed.

How can Unionism possibly survive when Protestant and Catholic are no longer at each other's throats, when discrimination has been dealt a body-blow? ... This is the most progressive outcome to the present situation ... the destruction of the machinery of discrimination ... the unfreezing of bigotry ... the achievement of the utmost degree of civil liberties possible, freedom of political action, an end to the bitterness of social life and divisions among the people fostered by the Unionists ... They would permanently weaken the basis of Unionism, and towards these objectives the energies of the progressive people in the North should be bent in the coming months ... Force O'Neill to CONCEDE MORE THAN HE WANTS TO OR THAN HE CAN DARE GIVE without risking overthrow by the more reactionary elements among the Unionists. Demand more than may be demanded by the compromising elements that exist among the Catholic leadership. Seek to associate as wide a section of the community as possible with these demands, in particular the well-intentioned people in the Protestant population and the trade union movement.[28]

Although the initiative in setting up the Northern Ireland Civil Rights Association was very much that of Johnston, Coughlan, and the Dublin Wolfe Tone Society, the civil rights movement, when it emerged, was composed of those who, like the IRA, had revolutionary aims but were in a minority and those who, like the CSJ, were reformist, who were in the ascendancy. On 29 January 1967 a civil rights body was launched in Belfast. A thirteen-member steering committee was set up with, among its members, representatives from the CSJ, the Communist Party, the Belfast Wolfe Tone Society, Belfast Trades Council, the Republican Clubs, the Ulster Liberal Party, and the NILP; Robert Cole of the Young Unionists, chairman of Queen's University Conservative and Unionist Association, was subsequently co-opted onto the committee. Officially brought into existence on 9 April 1967, the Northern Ireland Civil Rights Association in its constitution laid out its objectives as:

1. To defend the basic freedoms of all citizens.
2. To protect the rights of the individual.
3. To highlight all possible abuses of power.
4. To demand guarantees for freedom of speech, assembly and association.
5. To inform the public of their lawful rights.

By the summer of 1968 the NICRA's leadership was ready to countenance public protests. In June 1968 Austin Currie, a young Nationalist MP, squatted in a Dungannon house that had been allocated to a young Protestant woman who was the secretary of a solicitor who was a Unionist parliamentary candidate; a Catholic family who had previously squatted in the house had been evicted, and a number of other Catholic families in the area had been denied houses. The NICRA fixed 24 July 1968 as the date for a protest march into the centre of Dungannon. Two thousand protesters assembled in Coalisland, accompanied by nationalist bands, to be faced by 1,500 loyalist counter-demonstrators, led by Rev. Ian Paisley. Although there had been two minor clashes with the RUC, the march passed off peacefully and had been well controlled by the organisers.

REACTIONS

Despite the fact that O'Neill offered no structural reform of the Northern Ireland state, hoping instead that long-term economic improvements would lead Catholics into accepting the existence of Northern Ireland, a number of fringe loyalist groups became increasingly concerned about 'O'Neillism' and its departure from the 'traditional unionism' of Carson and Craigavon. The Protestant fundamentalist Ian Paisley took his concern into the streets in a campaign to alert his co-religionists to the dangers he perceived from O'Neillism. Paisley, the son of a Baptist minister, was reputed to have begun preaching at the age of sixteen. In 1951 he founded the Free Presbyterian Church in the Ravenhill Road area of Belfast. It was in 1963 that his interest in political action developed. He organised a march to protest against the decision by the Lord Mayor of Belfast to half-mast the Union Jack on City Hall to mark the death of Pope John XXIII, leading more than a thousand members of the National Union of Protestants to protest at the decision and to adopt a resolution expressing the movement's concern 'at the lying eulogies now being paid to the Roman anti-Christ by non-Romanist Church leaders in defiance of their own historic creeds.'[29]

Paisley led opposition to O'Neill through the Ulster Constitution Defence Committee, of which he was chairman, and was soon able to form the Ulster Protestant Volunteers. This was open only to Protestants, but not members of the RUC, except for the exclusively Protestant B Specials. The UCDC constitution declared that it and the UPV, which it governed, were one united society of 'Protestant patriots pledged by all lawful methods to uphold and maintain the Constitution of Northern Ireland as an integral part of the United Kingdom as long as the United Kingdom maintains a Protestant monarchy and the terms of the [seventeenth-century] Revolution Settlement.' The UCDC had a committee of twelve, originally called together by Paisley. Its rules declared: 'No one who has ever been a Roman Catholic is eligible for membership. Only those who have been born Protestants are eligible for membership.' Each meeting of the UCDC and UPV was to be opened with a reading from the Authorised Version of the Bible. Each member had to be prepared to pledge their first loyalty to the society, even when its operations were at variance with any political party to which the member belonged. Any member associated with or giving support to any subversive or lawless activities would be expelled. The UCDC and UPV pledged to 'maintain the Constitution at all costs. When the authorities act contrary to the Constitution the body will take whatever steps it thinks fit to expose such unconstitutional acts.'[30]

Rose's survey, conducted in 1968, found that although in institutional terms the Free Presbyterian Church was no more than one among many small sects, a person who did not attend a Free Presbyterian church or subscribe to Paisley's newspaper, the *Protestant Telegraph*, could still agree with much that was said in it and could be regarded as a 'Paisleyite' in political if not church-membership terms. Defining Paisleyism at its broadest—endeavouring at all costs to keep Northern Ireland Protestant—more than half the Protestants in the province could be classified as Paisleyites. A survey by National Opinion Polls in 1967 found that 32 per cent of Protestants said they usually agreed with what Paisley said, while 58 per cent usually disagreed. There was only a difference of 1 per cent between the view of members of the Church of Ireland and members of the Presbyterian Church. A more detailed analysis of those with Paisleyite sympathies showed that there was a tendency for such people to cluster in the Belfast working class. But Paisleyites were not confined to these districts: there was some Paisleyite sympathy everywhere, among young and old, men and women, the middle class and the working class, and in towns and the countryside as well as Belfast.[31]

The improvement in community relations was measured in 1967 by Rose, who found that most Catholics and Protestants—65 per cent and 56 per cent, respectively—believed that community relations had improved since O'Neill became Prime Minister, although, crucially, this did not necessarily change their political outlook. While a majority of Catholics, even those in public employment, rejected the constitutional settlement, only 5 per cent of the total population thought religion was a barrier to getting a job. However, Rose's 'Loyalty Survey' denied O'Neill's theory that Catholic allegiance to the state could be bought with economic benefits, and it found that an increase in Catholic support and compliance, resulting from higher income or the receipt of welfare, was limited or non-existent. The theory of buying allegiance failed because it assumed that individual aspirations, personal economic benefits, were solely satisfied by the provision of those economic benefits: instead the survey found a concern by Catholics with *collective* well-being, that is, the well-being of the Catholic community. Catholics who were offered economic benefits by the Unionist regime readily accepted them but would not give allegiance in return, because they believed there remained other Catholics who were discriminated against or suffered unemployment because of the Unionist regime.[32]

The chances that there might be some change in support across sectarian lines appeared small. The Loyalty Survey found that the very things that drew so many Protestants to the Ulster Unionist Party were the things that repelled Catholics; the repulsion that existed was not of a kind that could be bridged by minor alterations or better public relations, for there were gulfs between the parties. Moreover, the actions these parties took to maintain their own support sustained the discord that deprived the Unionist regime of its full legitimacy. Because none of the parties were seen to be standing for civil rights, they failed to provide an institutional focus for the grievances of part of the population. This provided an opening for extra-parliamentary civil rights groups to become strong in 1968. In 1969 the civil rights groups lost support because they were associated with non-violent political action. Paramilitary groups, such as the UVF and IRA, began to draw support because they stood for the use of force to achieve political ends. Voting was not seen in Northern Ireland as an instrument for changing policies but as a duty, or a means of expressing substantive loyalties.

The survey emphasised that religion was a barrier preventing voters floating between the two major parties. The two parties were virtually exclusive on religious grounds: 95 per cent of Unionist voters were Protestant, and 99 per cent of Nationalist voters were Catholic. Very few people showed an inclination to cross religious lines in their voting.[33]

The results showed that few were apathetic about the use of violence. There was no apathy among Protestants when the Unionist regime was thought to be endangered: a majority of those surveyed, 52 per cent, endorsed the use of violence to keep Northern Ireland Protestant. The reasons given were few, simple, and unambiguous: defence of Protestantism and the British connection and opposition to Catholicism and the Republic. A big majority of Catholics, on the other hand, disapproved of the use of force to end partition. Force was disliked in principle and rejected as impractical. Catholics, often the losers in repeated violent combats in Northern Ireland, had practical reasons for avoiding conflict. A majority of Catholics, on the other hand, were more prepared to give conditional or unconditional approval to the holding of parades or meetings banned by the Government.

The survey therefore found that large numbers of Protestants and Catholics endorsed the breaking of basic political laws; they differed only in the ways in which they were prepared to break them.[34] This did not mean that the people of Northern Ireland supported lawlessness: on the contrary, 83 per cent of Protestants and 71 per cent of Catholics could name no law that they thought could be broken.[35] It was only on the question of the constitution and political laws, such as the Special Powers Act, that Protestants and Catholics countenanced law-breaking.

The survey found that nearly everyone in Northern Ireland had a sense of national identity, but there was no collective agreement about what the nation was.

	Protestant %	Catholic %	Total %
British	39	15	29
Irish	20	76	43
Ulster	32	5	21
Sometimes British, sometimes Irish	6	3	5
Anglo-Irish	2	1	1
Don't know	1	—	1

Very few people in Northern Ireland completely changed their national identity. Party identification also showed very limited differences between generations. Only 1 per cent appeared to have switched, between generations, from unionism to nationalism or vice versa.

The most noteworthy and consistent trend concerned belief in discrimination against Catholics. Younger people were readier to say that discrimination existed than were older people, providing a greater impetus for Catholics to reject the Unionist regime.[36] Thus, despite the apparent improvement in community relations and new manifestations in political groupings, it appears that, beneath the surface, communal perceptions and attitudes remained polarised.

Political tension began to rise as soon as the NICRA embarked on a series of public marches and demonstrations. Large-scale disturbances were prevented until 5 October 1968, when a civil rights march, banned by the Minister of Home Affairs, William Craig, was held in Derry. This led to serious rioting and confrontations with the RUC. The events of 5 October signalled the genesis of the latest phase of the Troubles. Television coverage had a profound impact, showing the RUC batoning demonstrators, including MPs. For the first time the Unionist leadership had to defend their system. Craig responded by claiming that the NICRA was infiltrated by the IRA and that majority opinion inside the NICRA was 'communist'; this was a genuinely held belief but not one accepted by British politicians or media, which focused instead on the NICRA's emotive slogans of 'British rights for British citizens' and 'One man one vote', which referred to the differences between Northern Ireland's and Britain's local government property qualifications.

The report of Lord Cameron into the disturbances identified them as arising from the following immediate circumstances:

(1) The Northern Ireland Civil Rights Association did not directly plan or control the march which was left to a local and purely *ad hoc* Committee.

(2) No properly thought out plans of action were available if the march was stopped by police.

(3) Stewarding was ineffective and no adequate communication system was available.

(4) Some of the marchers were determined to defy the Minister's order. They accepted the risk that some degree of violence would occur, believing that this would achieve publicity for the Civil Rights cause in Great Britain.

(5) A section of extremists actively wished to provoke violence, or at least a confrontation with the police without regard to the consequences.

(6) The police were determined that the Minister's order should be made effective on this occasion and by a display, and if necessary, use, of force to deter future demonstrators from defying ministerial bans.

(7) Hooligan elements wholly unassociated with the Civil Rights

demonstrators later took advantage of a minor clash ... to cause a serious riot ... wholly unassociated with the Civil Rights demonstration itself.

(8) The police handling of the situation ... was ill co-ordinated and ill conducted.

(9) The Minister's order had already caused irritation and resentment in Londonderry, and swelled the number of demonstrators, and was no doubt a subsidiary cause of the trouble which occurred.[37]

On 5 November 1968 O'Neill, Craig and Brian Faulkner were summoned to London to meet Harold Wilson for consultations. After the meeting Wilson reassured unionists that there would be no transfer of Northern Ireland to the Republic without the consent of the Northern Ireland Parliament. However, the following day in the British House of Commons, while supporting O'Neill, Wilson called for an impartial inquiry into the events of 5 October and for early changes in the local government franchise.

On 22 November 1968, in response to British pressure, the Unionist Government issued a five-point reform programme. This involved a new points system for the allocation of houses by local authorities; an ombudsman to be appointed to investigate complaints; a Development Commission to take over the local government powers of Londonderry City Council; the abolition of the Special Powers Act as soon as it was safe to do so; and, with regard to the local government franchise, the abolition of the company vote, which gave more than one vote to businesses.

This was too little and too late for many within the NICRA. The CSJ was of the opinion that the reforms fell short of reasonable requirements, for a number of reasons, the first of which was that the Government had not undertaken to 'establish British standards,' for there remained, they claimed, a quarter of a million people with no vote. Secondly, the reforms did not undertake, by excluding gerrymandering, to give 'just and fair' representation to those who opposed the Ulster Unionist Party. The points system proposed for housing allocation was open to alteration by local authorities and therefore 'could be modified to suit local Unionist needs.' Nor was there any commitment to extending the Race Relations Act to Northern Ireland, nor undertaking in 'unequivocal simple language' to repeal the Special Powers Act.[38]

On 17 November 1968 the Nationalist Party adopted a policy in favour of non-violent civil disobedience, after a two-hour specially convened conference in Dungannon. Eddie McAteer said the party had been driven to this decision by 'desperation'; they did not ask for any concessions from the Government, rather they 'demanded the minimum of what we are rightly entitled to' after 'half a century of contempt and scorn at Stormont.'[39]

The CSJ and anti-Unionists (as those within the civil rights movement called themselves) generally doubted the sincerity of O'Neill and his reform programme. *Spotlight Ulster* had complained that the 'myth' that O'Neill was a liberal 'appears to have taken root at Westminster.' This belief, based on 'pious statements' about better relations with the Nationalist opposition, was a 'grave mistake', it warned. Similarly, Patricia McCluskey wrote that it 'would be difficult to think of anything favourable to say about British Labour Government policy as far as it concerns the Northern Irish Roman Catholic minority.' She recalled that when the Labour Party was first elected the CSJ had said, 'At last, we are going to see the better side of the British—Mr. Harold Wilson has not only acknowledged the Catholic minority's plight, but has promised to act to put things right. Surely now we will see British justice, of which we have heard a lot of praise, in action, and at its best.' But, as month followed month and nothing happened, 'old doubts again arose.' The CSJ's Labour friends, said McCluskey, counselled patience until Labour was returned with a bigger Westminster majority. But, following an increased Labour majority in 1966 and no evidence of reform in the Queen's Speech at Stormont, 'our last hopes have been dashed,' for it offered no easement in discrimination. The proposed abolition of the university seats and the business votes, comprising only a few thousand people, were 'vaguely irrelevant measures ... so there is nothing of consequence ...'[40]

While the reforms failed to satisfy nationalists, they had the effect of enraging many unionists, who resented London interference, believing that Westminster did not understand the peculiarities of the Ulster situation. In particular, William Craig was publicly suggesting that it might be better for Northern Ireland to go it alone rather than be 'sold down the river' by London. Craig had become MP for Larne in 1960 and as Government chief whip from 1962 to 1963 held a key role in the choice of O'Neill as Prime Minister. He became Minister of Home Affairs in the O'Neill Government and Minister of Health and Local Government in July 1964. After a spell as Minister of Development he had returned to the post of Minister of Home Affairs in October 1966. Craig's speeches had become increasingly violent, and he seemed to be attempting to undermine O'Neill's position within the Unionist Party. On 28 November 1968 he made a speech at the Ulster Hall, repeated a week later, that caused controversy when he displayed a lack of enthusiasm for the Government's ombudsman plan and also criticised standards of democracy in countries where Catholics were in the majority.

Craig claimed that Ulster was facing a very difficult time, with 'all this nonsense centred around civil rights, and behind it all there is our old traditional enemy exploiting the situation.' He argued:

> We ... in this Unionist Party ... would resist every effort that was made to put us into a United Irish Republic, and we resolved that for many reasons, but for two principal reasons, there was an identity of heritages between us and our fellow citizens in Great Britain. There was and is great economic value to be attached to the link with Great Britain. And there was also another factor that some people are scared to talk about and this factor is the difference between our concept of democracy and that of a Roman Catholic country such as Ireland ... When you have a Roman Catholic majority you have a lesser standard of democracy. I have no doubt that whatever might happen between us and Great Britain, and God forbid that anything might ever happen, it would not follow that we would unite with the rest of Ireland ... There is the binding concept of democracy here in Ulster—government of the people, by the people, for the people. In the Republic, government of the people, by the people, for the people, is subject to the overriding decision on any matter concerning faith and morals.

Craig claimed that in Northern Ireland, Catholics had never been hindered or hampered in any way in their pursuit of their religion and never denied any basic human rights.[41] Catholics, he said, had different standards of democracy, because 'their religious faith dictates that it must be that way. We just couldn't accept those standards. Churches certainly have a place to play in our community ... but they have no authority or jurisdiction over Parliament or Government.'[42]

The civil disturbances at the end of 1968 again put the cross-border relationship under strain. When the Taoiseach, Jack Lynch, publicly declared that partition was the root cause of these disorders, O'Neill was forced to respond. At a meeting of the Commonwealth Parliamentary Association in November 1968 he explained the perceptions that shaped Unionist views of the relationship between Northern Ireland and the Republic and the pressures such statements from Southern leaders placed on him.

If the United Kingdom Government and the United Kingdom Parliament were to make a declaration tomorrow in favour of a United Ireland, it would achieve nothing really practical within Ireland. The choice must clearly be between a union by coercion [and] a union by consent—and let there be no doubt that we in Ulster do *not* consent to it; or an acceptance of the position as it actually exists. Do not be deceived by the slogans demanding that England should get out of Ireland. We *have* an Irish Government in the North. My colleagues and I are Irishmen too; but our crime in Southern Irish eyes is that of being Irishmen who are loyal to the Crown, and to a constitutional union with Britain which has embraced us for over 150 years. Please remember that what is now Northern Ireland was part of the United Kingdom when Nelson fought at Trafalgar and Wellington at Waterloo ... For we are British, and determined to remain British. We value our British citizenship, and are prepared to take the rough with the smooth in exercising it ... Your British citizenship has never been threatened, as ours has been. If at times we seem to you stiff and defensive, it is because constant attacks have been made upon all that we hold most dear. Not only verbal attacks ... but also physical brute force, exercised by armed bands of IRA, based in the Republic, whose forays into our territory [took place] as lately as 1956–62 ... The perpetrators of these acts always openly stated that their aim was to force Northern Ireland into an Irish Republic. Through all this long period of provocation, be it noted that the Ulster people did not once retaliate, angered and grieved though they were. What we ask in Northern Ireland is to be allowed to make up our own minds about our own destiny. That is enough. That is all we seek. We do not intervene in the domestic affairs of the South of Ireland. No terrorist bands from the North have sought to coerce the South. Leave us in peace, and there will be peace—peace in which the Governments in Ireland, North and South, may get on with the things which really matter.[43]

On 30 November 1968 attention was once again focused on communal tensions in Northern Ireland when in Armagh the RUC had been fully stretched keeping civil rights demonstrators and Paisley's supporters apart. With tensions rising, O'Neill felt it necessary to appeal directly to the people of Northern Ireland for calm. This appeal was broadcast on television on 9 December 1968. O'Neill warned his audience that 'Ulster is at the crossroads,' making clear his view that a Northern Ireland based on the interests of any one section of the community, rather than on the interests of all, could have no long-term future. He blamed a minority of agitators in Londonderry for the recent trouble but admitted that grievances, real or imaginary, had been piling up for years. He explained that the Government's duty had been to uphold law and order and to look at the underlying causes of dissension. As O'Neill saw it, if this had not been done the Government would have been faced with mounting pressure internally, from those seeking change, and externally, from British public and parliamentary opinion, which had been disturbed by the events in Londonderry. This was why the Government had decided to press on with a continuing programme of change to secure a 'united and harmonious community.' To disaffected Protestants, O'Neill warned that Harold Wilson had made it clear that if the Northern Ireland Government had not faced up to its problems, Westminster might act over Stormont's heads.

> There are, I know, today some so-called loyalists who talk of independence from Britain—who seem to want a kind of Protestant Sinn Féin. These people will not listen when they are told that Ulster's income is £200 million a year but that we can spend £300 million—only because Britain pays the balance … These people are not merely extremists. They are lunatics who would set a course along a road which could only lead at the end into an all-Ireland Republic. They are not loyalists but *disloyalists*: disloyal to Britain, disloyal to the Constitution, disloyal to the Crown, disloyal—if they are in public life—to the solemn oaths they have sworn to Her Majesty the Queen.

O'Neill appealed for a swift end to the growing disorder throughout Northern Ireland, warning that 'as matters stand today, we are on the brink of chaos, where neighbour could be set against neighbour.' To the civil rights demonstrators he argued that the changes introduced were genuine and far-reaching and that the Unionist Government was totally committed to them. If the civil rights campaigners were not entirely satisfied, he pleaded that Northern Ireland was a democracy and asked them to call their supporters off the streets so as to allow a favourable atmosphere for change to develop. To those who saw the changes as a threat to Northern Ireland's position within the United Kingdom, O'Neill said: 'Unionism armed with justice will be a stronger cause than Unionism armed merely with strength.' The changes, he argued, amounted to this: that in every aspect of Northern Ireland's life, justice had not only to be done but seen to be done by all sections of the community. Finally, O'Neill asked:

What kind of Ulster do you want? A happy and respected province, in good standing with the rest of the United Kingdom? Or a place continually torn apart by riots and demonstrations, and regarded by the rest of Britain as a political outcast? ... Make your voice heard in whatever way you think best, so that we may know the views *not* of the few but of the many. For this is truly a time of decision, and in your silence all that we have built up could be lost.[44]

The speech elicited a favourable response from Eddie McAteer of the Nationalist Party and the Catholic primate, Cardinal Conway, and a suspension of marches until 11 January 1969 was announced.

On 11 December 1968 O'Neill, buoyed by apparent public support, sacked Craig from the Cabinet. The disagreement between Craig and O'Neill centred on two fundamentally different interpretations of Northern Ireland's position within the United Kingdom. Craig claimed that Northern Ireland had a federal relationship with Britain, which meant that the Westminster Parliament and the Northern Ireland Parliament each had their own sphere of responsibility, into which the other Parliament could not interfere. Craig had declared: 'I would resist any effort by any Government in Great Britain ... to interfere with proper jurisdiction of the Government of Northern Ireland.' Craig argued that section 75 of the Government of Ireland Act, stating that the Westminster Parliament retained the supreme authority over all persons, matters and things in Ireland, was merely 'a reserve power to deal with an emergency situation,' and he found it 'difficult to envisage any situation in which it could be exercised without the consent of the Government of Northern Ireland.'[45]

Craig was not arguing for a unilateral declaration of independence, and he believed that O'Neill had misunderstood his argument regarding the issue. He pointed out that he had never used the term and never advocated the loosening of ties between Britain and Northern Ireland. But he had argued strongly that there should be changes in the United Kingdom's constitution as a whole to establish a federal system of government throughout the kingdom. Craig preferred to see federal parliaments in Scotland, Wales, and the English regions. He even predicted that if the United Kingdom did develop a federal system then the Republic, realising that its economy and future development were tied up with Britain's, might want to take part in that federation.[46] In fact Craig stood for a 'united Ireland under the Union Jack.'[47] For him, although the Northern Ireland constitution was founded on an Act of the United Kingdom Parliament, it was more than a mere Act of

Parliament: it represented an agreed settlement between London, Dublin and Belfast of the Home Rule controversy. Craig argued that any interference or change in the Northern Ireland constitution without the consent of the Northern Ireland Parliament would be an infringement of that settlement, and he pointed out that since the 1920 Act successive British Governments, regardless of which political party was in power, had confirmed that any change in Northern Ireland's constitutional position required the consent of the Northern Ireland Parliament. From this he concluded:

> The independence of the Parliament of Northern Ireland is in fact the cornerstone of our constitutional position within the United Kingdom. The powers and functions of the Parliament and Government of Northern Ireland must be regarded in the absence of any agreement as inviolable ... Section 75 of the 1920 Act does provide for the United Kingdom Parliament overriding powers, but both in theory and practice, in statute and convention, it is of very limited effect and certainly doesn't extend to varying Northern Ireland's constitution ... The rightness and strength of this position is a fundamental principle of democracy.[48]

In contrast, O'Neill asked those who supported Craig to understand that a failure to face up to the constitutional realities was in itself a threat to the status that Unionists valued so much. Referring to section 75 of the 1920 Act, O'Neill argued that the Westminster Parliament had acted with restraint towards Northern Ireland only because it would be clearly absurd to establish a representative assembly there with certain powers and then, for no good or sufficient reason, seek to override those powers. But, he warned, the fact that it was a convention that Westminster should not interfere in Northern Ireland's affairs did not mean that Westminster did not have the legal right to do so.

> I am afraid that it follows too, that if a convention is the prevailing and generally accepted principle of Parliament, based upon what seems sensible and realistic to it, equally that practice can be changed if the will of Parliament itself changes. If one thinks about this for a moment, it is self-evident. However strong the force of convention ... it cannot be stronger than the force of the law. And since Parliament can amend its own Acts, equally it is free to set aside its own conventions.[49]

CIVIL STRIFE

The day after Craig's removal from office a meeting of Unionist Party MPs at Stormont gave overwhelming support to O'Neill and his policies, although four abstained. Craig's position seemed to have been undermined by the success of O'Neill's 'crossroads' speech, and the Prime Minister appeared to have bought himself a breathing-space. By the end of the year an 'I back O'Neill' campaign, organised by the *Belfast Telegraph*, received over 150,000 letters of support. His position, however, was still vulnerable to the fears that gripped many of the unionist community, which could be galvanised by events. For example, on 31 January 1969 Anthony Peacock, the new Inspector-General of the RUC, aroused NICRA and nationalist anger, but echoed the suspicions of many Protestants, when he claimed that he had evidence for IRA support for the civil rights movement, stating: 'I do not think they are organising it, but it fits in with their long-term plans for uniting Ireland forcibly.'[50]

From within the Unionist Party, O'Neill came under attack from his predecessor, who challenged the fundamentals of O'Neill's reform programme. Lord Brookeborough, in a television interview, attacked O'Neill on the question of 'one man one vote' and spoke on the question of easing discrimination against Catholics. Asked if something could have been done to ease discrimination, Brookeborough replied: 'Yes, it could have been done, but it would have been politically difficult because of the antipathy of the Roman Catholics and the fact that they were backing the IRA. They were out to defeat Northern Ireland and shoot our people.' Asked who the disloyalists were, he replied, 'Most of them Catholics.' 'I am not', he insisted, 'criticising their religion,' but 'they won't do anything about the Union Jack, they won't take their hats off, they won't stand up when "God Save the Queen" is played, and very naturally with very severe restrictions as a result.'[51]

Brookeborough summed up the view that Northern Ireland had to remain a Protestant state, explaining that Catholics were not given positions of power because 'how can you give somebody who is your enemy a higher position in order to allow him to come and destroy you?' Catholics, 'plus or minus five per cent perhaps,' had remained 'anti-partitionists' above all else. He was not even happy to be called an Irishman, because of the 1916 Rebellion.[52]

Northern Ireland was plunged into further communal disturbances following the decision on 20 December 1968 by People's Democracy, a radical student group, to undertake a four-day protest march from Belfast to Derry, starting on 1 January 1969. PD was distinct from the civil rights movement, in that it was a student organisation, predominantly composed of young people, and with international links and influences. In contrast the NICRA was predominantly made up of branches in provincial towns that were rooted in traditional nationalism and republicanism. PD had affiliated with the NICRA, but only as a tactical ploy. It had no constitution or recorded membership. At any meeting any person attending was entitled to speak and vote, with decisions at any meeting open to review at a subsequent meeting. There was no subscription or membership fee, with funding coming from collections or well-wishers. PD had arisen out of a coalition of student groups at Queen's University, and the catalyst for its formation was the decision of William Craig to proscribe the Queen's University Republican Club, which had been formed in March 1967 after Craig had announced a ban on commemorations of the 1867 Fenian Rising and the proscription of Republican Clubs throughout Northern Ireland. A joint action committee became a nucleus for organising student action after the October 1968 march in Derry.

PD's march in January 1969 was denounced by both Nationalist and civil rights leaders, and a week later Ronald Bunting, Paisley's assistant, advised the marchers to avoid loyalist areas. There were confrontations with loyalists throughout the route as the march deliberately passed through Protestant areas. By the time the protest reached Burntollet Bridge, near Derry, the number of marchers had grown to several hundred. At Burntollet the marchers were confronted and attacked by about two hundred loyalists, including off-duty B Specials. The arrival of the marchers in Derry and that of the RUC in the Catholic Bogside saw further violence erupt. According to one of its leaders, Bernadette Devlin, People's Democracy had been aware that the march could provoke confrontations with loyalists, and the function of the march was to relaunch the civil rights organisation as a mass movement and to expose O'Neill so as to 'pull the carpet off the floor to show the dirt that was under it.' In doing this Devlin was aware that 'we wouldn't finish the march without being molested.'

Another PD leader, Michael Farrell, was well aware of the Protestant hostility the march would arouse in the south Derry area through which the marchers would pass, but he had not expected the full extent of the ensuing violence. He believed the march would force the Northern Ireland Government to either confront the loyalists or drop its pretensions about reform. The purpose of the march was to upset the status quo, with the result that the loyalists might back down, the Northern Ireland Government might fall, or the British Government might intervene in Northern Ireland's affairs, reopening the Irish question after fifty years. The march, according to Farrell, was based on the civil rights march from Selma to Montgomery in Alabama in 1966, 'which had exposed the racist thuggery of America's deep South and forced the US government into major reforms.' Farrell considered People's Democracy not just a part of a civil rights movement but 'a revolutionary assembly'. He had taken part in the civil rights agitation so as to radicalise the Catholic working class and radicalise the civil rights demands themselves. Now he wanted PD to 'complete the ideological development of the Catholic working class' and to 'develop concrete agitational work over housing and jobs to show the class interests of both Catholics and Protestants.' But, as another senior figure in the movement, Eamonn McCann, was to reflect, 'we failed absolutely to change the consciousness of people. The consciousness of the people who are fighting in the streets … is sectarian and bigoted.'[53]

The PD march, and the ensuing violence, had once more raised the political temperature within Northern Ireland, and there was more serious rioting in mid-January, in Newry and in Derry again. The consequences of the loyalist attack on what was to them an extremely provocative march was arguably the point where the Northern Ireland political situation was transformed from being primarily about civil rights to the more ancient disputes about religious and national identities. The report of Lord Cameron into the disturbances during 1968 and 1969 listed the general causes of the disturbances as

(1) A rising sense of injustice and grievance among large sections of the Catholic population … in particular, in Londonderry and Dungannon, in respect of (i) inadequacy of housing provision by certain local authorities, (ii) unfair methods of allocation of houses built and let by such authorities, (iii) misuse in certain cases of discretionary powers of allocation of houses in order to perpetuate Unionist control of the local authority.

(2) Complaints of discrimination in the making of local government appointments, at all levels but especially in the senior posts, to the prejudice of non-Unionists and especially Catholic members of the community, in some Unionist controlled authorities.

(3) Complaints in some cases of the deliberate manipulation of local government electoral boundaries.

(4) A growing and powerful sense of resentment and frustration

among the Catholic population at failure to achieve either acceptance on the part of the Government of any need to investigate these complaints or to provide and enforce a remedy for them.

(5) Resentment, particularly among Catholics, as to the existence of the Ulster Special Constabulary ... as a partisan and paramilitary force exclusively recruited from Protestants.

(6) Widespread resentment among Catholics ... at the continuance in force of regulations made under the Special Powers Act, and of the continued presence in the statute book of the Act itself.

(7) Fears and apprehensions among Protestants of a threat to Unionist domination and control of Government by increase of Catholic population and powers, inflamed by the activities of the Ulster Constitution Defence Committee and the Ulster Protestant Volunteers.[54]

In particular, Cameron concluded that the leadership, organisation and control of the Derry demonstration was ineffective and insufficient to prevent violent or disorderly conduct among certain elements. Cameron also highlighted the early infiltration of the NICRA, both centrally and locally, by 'subversive left-wing and revolutionary elements' that were prepared to use the civil rights movement for their own ends and were ready to exploit grievances in order to provoke and foment disorder and violence in the guise of supporting a non-violent movement. This infiltration was assisted by the declared insistence of the NICRA that it was non-sectarian and non-political and its consequent refusal to reject support from whatever quarter it came, provided that support was given and limited to the aims of the NICRA.

Cameron was referring to the presence of IRA members within the organisation, who regarded the NICRA as a stalking-horse for the achievement of other radical and revolutionary objects, namely the abolition of the border, the unification of Ireland outside the United Kingdom, and the setting up of a 32-county all-Ireland workers' socialist republic. Cameron also argued that People's Democracy provided a means by which politically extreme and militant elements could and did invite and incite civil disorder, with, as a consequence, the polarising and hardening of opposition to civil rights claims. Cameron claimed that the PD leadership represented and propagated political ideas that were politically more extreme than the objects for which the NICRA had campaigned and represented a threat to the stability and existence of the Northern Ireland constitution. He found that although the NICRA was especially dedicated to 'non-violence', the term was given a particular and limited meaning by certain of the leadership of People's Democracy. Cameron concluded that

in their vocabulary it is not violence to link arms and by sheer weight and pressure of numbers and bodies to press through and break an opposing cordon of police. If the police resist such pressure then it is the police who are guilty of violence—and if such 'violence' is offered then a 'defensive' violent reaction is permissible.

Cameron and his colleagues considered this view of the PD leaders Farrell, McCann and Kevin Boyle as 'metaphysical nonsense divorced from the world of reality' and considered the battering-ram pressure of a crowd with linked arms to breach a physical barrier in the shape of a police cordon as 'just as much in the way of force to achieve an object as the use of batons by police to achieve the dispersal of a hostile crowd.'

In contrast, the Derry Citizens' Action Committee, formed as a direct result of the disorder in Derry on 5 and 6 October 1968, had determined from the outset that its protests should be non-violent. Led by its chairman, John Hume MP, the DCAC organised protests such as sit-downs and a number of marches, which passed off peacefully. During the Derry riot of 3 January 1969 Hume and his colleagues used all their powers and influence to disperse the rioters, but were not successful.

The Cameron Commission concluded that while there was evidence that members of the IRA were active in the NICRA there was no evidence that they were in any sense dominant or in a position to control or direct its policy.[55] Cameron also concluded that the RUC's handling of the Londonderry demonstration of 5 October 1968 was in certain material respects 'ill co-ordinated and inept' and that there was a use of unnecessary force in the dispersal of the demonstrators, only a minority of whom had acted in a disorderly and violent manner. The wide publicity given by press, radio and television to particular episodes inflamed and exacerbated feelings of resentment against the police, which had already been aroused by their enforcement of the ministerial ban. Available police forces did not provide adequate protection to the People's Democracy marchers at Burntollet Bridge nor on 4 January 1969 in Londonderry. There were instances of police indiscipline and violence towards persons unassociated with rioting or disorder on 4 and 5 January in Londonderry, and this provoked serious hostility to the police, particularly among the Catholic population there, and an increasing disbelief in their impartiality towards non-unionists.

On the Protestant side, the Cameron Commission found that the deliberate and organised interventions by the followers of Paisley and Bunting, especially in Armagh, Burntollet, and Londonderry, substantially increased the risk of violent disorder on occasions when the NICRA demonstrations or marches were to take place and were a 'material contributory cause' of the outbreaks of violence that occurred after 5 October 1968, seriously hampering the RUC in their task of maintaining law and order.[56] The commission had no doubt that those who controlled and organised the Ulster Protestant Volunteers were those who organised and controlled the Armagh counter-demonstration. Further, at a meeting at the Guildhall in Londonderry, Bunting had appealed publicly for UPV recruits as well as intimating arrangements for a concentration of his supporters at Burntollet Bridge the following morning, for the avowed purpose of 'harrying and hindering' the People's Democracy march. The ambush of the marchers, the arrangements for providing missiles of all kinds there and the instruction to attackers to wear white armbands all pointed to a carefully planned and prearranged operation. The commission was left in no doubt that the interventions of Paisley and Bunting in Londonderry and Armagh, and the threatened marches of Bunting elsewhere, 'were not designed merely to register a peaceful process ... however much they profess the contrary ... Both these gentlemen and the organisations with which they are so closely and authoritatively concerned must, in our opinion, bear a heavy share of direct responsibility for the disorders in Armagh and at Burntollet Bridge and also for inflaming passions ...'[57]

Cameron stressed that it was right to see the measures taken by Unionists to ensure supremacy in certain local authorities in their historical context, because when these measures were taken the existence of Northern Ireland was felt to be threatened, and in many quarters only Protestants were regarded as 'loyal' to the British Crown and connection. Therefore, Cameron concluded, it was considered justified to use any measures that preserved Unionist, and therefore Protestant, power. Correspondingly, before 1939 local government was less important to the ordinary citizen than it was in 1968, particularly because local authority housing schemes were much less extensive, and public education, health and welfare services were relatively underdeveloped by comparison. In addition, many Catholics had withheld all but a *de facto* recognition of the state and of the local administration established thereunder. 'In such a historical context, it was only natural that the scheme of local government should in some measure reflect and be a reaction to religious and political conflicts in society.'

Cameron pointed out that certain local authorities controlled by Catholic majorities pursued precisely analogous policies: for example, Newry Urban District Council employed very few non-Catholics. It was also fair to say that even the least representative Unionist councils had rehoused large numbers of Catholics, though not always in the numbers their proportion of large families and slum dwellings had justified and not always in the most appropriate locations.

Cameron noted the continuing fears and apprehension that arose on the Protestant side. It was noticeable that these tensions increased as the civil rights movement gathered momentum and demonstrations increased in number and size. The reaction of the unionist side tended to become more hostile and emotionally charged, and the development and organisation of counter-demonstrations made serious disorder more likely as time went on. The likelihood of such clashes was heightened by inflammatory speeches from various quarters and in particular from Dr Paisley's organisation. These fears had a solid and substantial basis both in the past and even in the present, given the non-recognition of Northern Ireland by the Republic of Ireland and the ambiguous attitude of the Roman Catholic hierarchy in Northern Ireland; the hostility of a proportion of Catholics to the Northern Ireland constitution and to Great Britain; the continuing IRA activity and attacks; the steady decline of the Protestant population in the South; and the influence of Roman Catholic doctrines there on the Irish Government, displayed in matters of censorship, birth control and other health matters, as well as the Catholic Church's attitude to mixed, that is Catholic and Protestant, marriages.

All these factors were illustrative of what Protestants expected if Catholic political domination were to be achieved. Not least of these fears was a privately and publicly expressed concern that in the course of time the Catholic element in Northern Ireland could 'out-breed' the Protestant element and thereby produce a Catholic majority. The corollary of this fear or belief was not only that such an event would produce widespread discrimination against Protestants and a general lowering of living standards but that Northern Ireland's continued existence as part of the United Kingdom would be in jeopardy. Therefore, ran the argument, it was essential to ensure the maintenance of Unionist and Protestant governmental supremacy. A major factor in determining Unionist attitudes towards the NICRA was the wide existence of a 'sincerely and deeply' held fear that that organisation was an 'essentially Catholic if not Nationalist and Republican manifestation, unjustified by genuine grievance or complaint in fact.'[58]

THE FALL OF O'NEILL

Politically, events were now changing rapidly. On 24 January 1969 Brian Faulkner resigned from the Northern Ireland Cabinet in protest at the decision by O'Neill to hold an inquiry—the Cameron Commission—into the communal disturbances, which Faulkner considered an abdication of Government responsibility that would place the Unionist Government in the position of appearing to be forced against its will to grant reforms. In particular, Faulkner realised that 'one man one vote' in local government elections was now regarded by many Unionists as an important issue that must not be conceded, and he argued that the Government should either decide to resist the pressures being put on it or accept that there were other changes, including reform of the local government franchise, that were desirable and necessary, and put this view with honesty and determination to the people. Not taking these decisions, Faulkner believed, could only damage the trust between people and the Unionist Government and consequently reduce the capacity of the Government to give any real lead to the community.[59]

It was significant that Faulkner—who was ultimately to agree to concessions to the minority that would have been unthinkable in 1969—had come to the conclusion that the support that was given to the NICRA was not dependent on its specific civil rights aims or grievances but had become for nationalists and republicans a new way of getting at the Unionists and discrediting Stormont to the outside world. Faulkner argued that, irrespective of the ideals of those who started the civil rights movement, 'subversive elements were quick to realise the opportunities and to jump on the bandwagon.' Issues such as the local government franchise were believed by many Unionists to be merely a cover for destabilising the state.

> The fact that 'One man one vote' became the banner under which the CRA marches took place was, I believe, no coincidence. It sounded, to a world attuned to such protests, a positive humanitarian cry from an oppressed people. It also seemed to involve a very basic right—not many people would stop to ask, on seeing such a slogan, if it referred to the important elections for the parliaments at Westminster and Stormont where in fact one man one vote was as much part of the electoral system as elsewhere in the United Kingdom, or to local council elections where there was still a ratepayers franchise. Many well-meaning but ill-informed people,

even in Britain were under the impression that the 'evil Unionist government' had made it illegal for Catholics to vote in elections. From such initial misconceptions much of Westminster's subsequent mishandling of the situation arose.[60]

Eight days after Faulkner's resignation, as tensions mounted within the Unionist Party, twelve Unionist MPs issued a demand for O'Neill's removal in order to keep the party united. In response, an increasingly isolated O'Neill announced the dissolution of Parliament and called a general election. Called the 'crossroads election' by O'Neill, it was held on 24 February 1969. After decades of a rigid party system dominated by the Unionist-Nationalist split, the election saw a proliferation of candidates; it also saw the splitting of the Ulster Unionist Party. In some constituencies the UUP supported the Prime Minister and selected a pro-O'Neill candidate, while other constituencies, which opposed O'Neill, selected candidates with a similar outlook but who were deemed 'official' O'Neill candidates. Thus, some unofficial candidates supported O'Neill's reformist policies, while some official candidates opposed them.

O'Neill hoped there would be a substantial increase in the numbers of Catholics voting for the Unionist Party and claimed there would be no sectarian element in his, or his colleagues', campaign. 'Equal citizenship', he declared, 'for all the people of Northern Ireland within the United Kingdom; that is a fundamental principle, and I look for support to all who believe in it, regardless of religious affiliations.'[61] O'Neill's manifesto, which he styled a declaration of political principle as well as a statement of policy, contained three key passages:

1 The [Unionist] party will work to heal those divisions in our community which have so far prevented Northern Ireland from fulfilling its best hopes.

2 A united Ulster could make an even greater contribution to the life of the United Kingdom and the world.

3 Every policy and every action of a Unionist Government will be designed to ensure that all Ulster citizens continue to enjoy the benefits of the British connection, not just in high standards of service but in high standards of tolerance, fairness and justice.[62]

In a personal manifesto, Brian Faulkner also made a direct appeal for Catholics to support the Unionist Party. The Unionist manifesto had made no explicit mention of Catholics, but Faulkner declared: 'From my point of view Roman Catholics are very welcome indeed to come into the Unionist Party and the only qualification for membership is a determination to maintain the constitutional position.' He also pledged to use all his energies in support of vigorous industrial development for 'all our citizens' in Northern Ireland.[63]

In opposition to O'Neill, William Craig accused the Prime Minister of being the 'greatest supporter of Mr Paisley,' because a lack of leadership within the Ulster Unionist Party meant that those who looked to it for leadership were now turning to Paisley.[64]

Paisley's Protestant Unionists contested the election because of 'the policy of appeasement of ... O'Neill which threatens the Union, particularly his weak-kneed attitude to the IRA front organisation known as the "Civil Rights Movement".' The cardinal principle of the Protestant Unionists was that Ulster should remain an integral part of the Union, with full parity of benefits, services, and also rates and taxes. The defence of the Union was to be established by law and order, involving the strengthening of the RUC and the mobilisation of the B Specials, the 'real bulwark of Ulster against her enemies.' The Protestant Unionists also called for the restoration of the Stormont Parliament's sovereignty and the demonstration that justice would be done, in the courts and other Government administration, on the basis that 'every section of the community must be dealt with fairly.'

Protestant Unionists denied that they were repressive and reactive and instead claimed to stand for full civil and religious liberties for all Northern Ireland's people, 'particularly Roman Catholics, whose freedom from authoritarianism is of great concern to us.'[65] Paisley, in a television broadcast, claimed that O'Neill had broken his word on the question of Northern Ireland's constitution, having said he would never meet a Southern leader except when the South recognised Northern Ireland, but instead 'smuggled' Lemass into Stormont, a man who had taken part in the 1916 Rebellion, whose 'hands are stained with the blood of our kith and kin.' Paisley claimed O'Neill had a threefold plan to destroy Northern Ireland, involving breaking up the Ulster Unionist Party, setting candidate against candidate; then forming a coalition with the Nationalists; and finally establishing a united Ireland under pressure form Harold Wilson. Protestant Unionists, on the other hand, stood for the constitution and 'everything our fathers fought and died for.'[66]

Paisley's political and religious beliefs were diametrically opposed to those of Terence O'Neill. Paisley spurned gestures towards the Catholic community, arguing that good community relations could never be achieved by the selling of one's principles. He did not believe that either the Protestant or Catholic churches would change their doctrines, although he believed, as an 'uncompromising Protestant', that this did not necessarily mean that both sections of the community need be at loggerheads. Paisley claimed not to believe in hypocrisy and so made no apology for his Protestantism; and although he accepted that this meant that many Catholics in his own constituency would not be prepared to vote for him, if and when he stood for election, he did not believe that this meant he would not give them honest representation.[67] He did not deal with his constituents on a religious level; he never asked a man his religion or political philosophy: they could be a 'Jew ... an Orangeman, a Roman Catholic, a Protestant, an agnostic or an atheist.' He claimed: 'I am just as sectarian as the Queen, who takes a vow that she must be a Protestant. If you are saying I am sectarian then you have got to say that the British Constitution is founded on sectarianism.'[68] Paisley declared: 'I am not opposed to Roman Catholics ... I am against the system, not the people. The Roman Church is constantly attacking the Ulster Constitution. They do not fly the Union Jack and never stand for the singing of "God Save the Queen".'[69]

Paisley's evangelical Protestantism lay at the heart of his unionism. Paisley defined his loyalism thus:

> I am loyal to Jesus Christ, the only Head and King of the Church. I am loyal to the Bible, which I believe in every part is the infallible rule of faith and practice. I am loyal to the principles of the great Protestant Reformation, and refuse to barter my heritage for a mess of ecumenical pottage. I am loyal to the Queen and throne of Britain, being Protestant, in the terms of the Revolution Settlement.[70]

On the question of his Britishness, Paisley saw no contradiction between his definition of loyalty and his Britishness.

> Our flag is the Union Jack, and I think that declares exactly where we stand. I believe that Ulster's future is with Great Britain, but I distinguish between loyalty to the Throne and our attitude to any particular political Party. The voters of Ulster owed no allegiance whatsoever to the Government ... but they still claim to be loyal citizens because their allegiance was to the Crown and Constitution and not to any political Party.[71]

The civil rights platform was represented by a number of candidates in the election, which saw the demise of the Nationalist Party with the election of Catholic politicians such as John Hume, who were to dominate Catholic politics for years to come. In Derry, Hume believed it had been clear for some time that the Nationalist Party was disintegrating, with opposition emerging against it in all constituencies. He thought this was an indictment of its leadership and its failure to weld people into a fighting parliamentary force. Hume was seeking a mandate for a movement based on 'social-democratic principles', with open membership for people and their involvement in policy-making. He had become aware that for a long time there was a growing frustration in anti-Unionist circles, especially among the young, and a need for a fresh approach. The evidence of opinion polls suggested that only 6 per cent of the electorate now supported the Nationalist Party.[72]

With a turn-out of 72 per cent, the election saw thirty-nine Unionists returned, of whom twenty-four were 'official' Unionists and three 'unofficial' Unionists who supported O'Neill, while ten 'official' Unionists were opposed and two undecided. O'Neill's official Unionists took 31 per cent of the poll and unofficial Unionist supporters 13 per cent, against the 13 per cent of anti-O'Neill official Unionists. The Nationalist Party lost three seats to civil rights candidates but retained six seats; in Belfast, Republican Labour won two seats, as did the NILP. O'Neill was disappointed that more Catholics had not supported the pro-O'Neill candidates at the polls and believed that had they done so a rejuvenated and reformed Unionist Party would have been returned to Stormont and Catholics given new heart to see that moderation produced results, while Protestant extremists would have seen that to win seats, attention would have to be paid to moderate opinion.[73]

On 23 April 1969 a series of bombings of public buildings and utilities, such as Belfast's main water supply, further undermined O'Neill's position, as the attacks were believed to be the work of the IRA; in fact they were carried out by a revamped UVF, which was attempting to destabilise the O'Neill administration. On the same day as the bombings the Northern Ireland Government had finally announced that it would accept universal adult male suffrage in local government elections, thus conceding the civil rights demand of 'one man one vote'. Although the Unionist Party accepted this move, it did so by a narrow majority, and O'Neill was further weakened when Major James Chichester-Clark, the Minister of Agriculture, resigned from the Government, claiming that the timing of the introduction of the measure was wrong.

Increasingly it had become clear that O'Neill had failed to rally the Unionist Party around him; and on 28 April 1969 he announced his resignation. The following evening, in a television broadcast, he reflected how 'a few short weeks ago, you, the people of Ulster went to the polls. I called that election to afford you the chance to break out of the mould of sectarian politics once and for all. In many places, old fears, old prejudices and old loyalties were too strong.'[74] O'Neill's reforms had proved too much for many Protestants and too little for many Catholics. Expectations that the administration was either unable or unwilling to deliver had raised the political temperature to a level where subterranean divisions erupted in communal violence. O'Neill's long-term goal had been to integrate Catholics into the political ideology of Unionism. As he explained,

> it is frightfully hard to explain to Protestants that if you give Roman Catholics a good job and a good house, they will live like Protestants, because they will see neighbours with cars and television sets. They will refuse to have eighteen children; but if a Roman Catholic is jobless, and lives in the most ghastly hovel, he will rear eighteen children on national assistance. If you treat Roman Catholics with due consideration and kindness, they will live like Protestants in spite of the authoritarian nature of their Church.[75]

So far as O'Neill was concerned, Northern Ireland could have continued to enjoy the privileged position of being the only part of Ireland to enjoy a British standard of living. 'Instead,' O'Neill believed, 'she chose to put all this at risk in the interests of maintaining a Protestant ascendancy that had ceased to have any meaning anywhere else in the United Kingdom.'[76]

THE TROOPS ARRIVE

On 1 May 1969 James Chichester-Clark succeeded Terence O'Neill as Prime Minister of Northern Ireland, beating Brian Faulkner by seventeen votes to sixteen in an election by Unionist MPs at Stormont. In an effort to unite the party behind him, the new Prime Minister brought Faulkner back in to the Cabinet, as Minister of Development. Two other critics of O'Neill, John Taylor and John Brooke, received junior posts, in the Ministry of Home Affairs and Ministry of Commerce, respectively. Chichester-Clark accepted that O'Neill's reforms were to continue and also conceded that local government boundaries had to be redrawn by an independent commission. Following this, the NICRA announced that it would be easing up its campaign of agitation.

On 12 July 1969, however, serious rioting again broke out throughout

Northern Ireland. Sectarian rioting in July and early August was contained by the RUC, but on 12 August 1969 a parade by the Apprentice Boys of Derry led to riots as the marchers passed the Catholic Bogside area. Rioting then spread to other parts of Northern Ireland, and after days of rioting an exhausted RUC was no longer able to contain the disturbances. On 14 August 1969, to relieve the RUC, the British Government agreed to the Northern Ireland Government's request for the deployment of British troops on the streets of Northern Ireland.

In assessing the causes of the disturbances, Lord Scarman, appointed to inquire into the riots, concluded that while the Catholic minority was developing in its power, a feeling of insecurity was affecting Protestants, who became the more determined to hold their traditional summer parades, particularly those in Belfast and Londonderry. In these circumstances, Scarman concluded, sectarian conflict was to be expected, unless the police were strong enough to prevent it. However, they were not strong enough. The total strength of the RUC was approximately 3,200. In addition there was available the Ulster Special Constabulary, whose total strength was about 8,500. Of these some three hundred had been fully mobilised for duties with the RUC; the rest were part-time volunteers, who could not be effectively used in the event of sectarian conflict. No other police were available. Behind the police stood the British army, which, in the last resort, was available to assist the civil power. Its use, however, created the problem that, while law and order were the responsibility of the Northern Ireland Government, the operational control of the army always remained with the United Kingdom Government. If the Northern Ireland Government called out the Special Constabulary they ran the risk of deepening the conflict; if they called for the aid of the British army they had to submit to the operational control of Whitehall.

With the Protestant community determined to hold its traditional July parades, the danger was that the Catholic community, as a result of recent events, would not be inclined to let the marches go by without protest. In June 1969 there were troubles associated with Orange church parades and a ceremony of unfurling a new banner at the Orange Hall in Dungiven, a predominantly Catholic town. But the situation in the province as a whole did not become serious until July, when the approach of the traditional marches of the twelfth heightened tension everywhere. Disturbances, which arose by way of the minority's response to Protestant marches, occurred on 12 July in Londonderry, Dungiven, and Belfast, in the neighbourhood of Unity Flats and in the

Ardoyne. In Londonderry the disturbances had been particularly severe, and the Derry Citizens' Action Committee, which had been the focal point for minority actions there, was superseded by a more aggressive body, the Derry Citizens' Defence Association, which took over the defence of the Bogside.

There was serious rioting by Protestants on the Shankill Road, near Unity Flats, in the early days of August. On the twelfth the traditional Apprentice Boys' parade was due to take place in Londonderry. As the parade passed through Waterloo Place some youths threw stones at the marchers. From this incident three days of rioting resulted in Londonderry, spreading to Belfast. The same day there was a serious riot in Coalisland, and the following day rioting broke out in Dungannon, for the second time in three days. Disturbances spread to other centres on the same day. There was serious trouble in the Falls Road in Belfast and other riots in Newry and Armagh. The scale of the Londonderry riots was such that they were beyond the ability of the police to suppress or control them. At five o'clock on 14 August the civil authority asked for military assistance, and the British army entered Londonderry.

The spreading of the disturbances owed much to the deliberate decision by some minority groups to relieve police pressure on the rioters in Londonderry, including the NICRA, whose executive decided to organise demonstrations elsewhere in the province so as to prevent the reinforcement of the police in Londonderry.[77] In taking this decision the NICRA leadership did not advocate violence, but the course of action did offer the chance of violent clashes with the police.[78] Chichester-Clark made a television broadcast in which he stated, in relation to the Londonderry rioters: 'We want peace not vengeance. If the rioters withdraw peacefully to their homes and observe the law no attempt will be made to exploit the situation.' The NICRA attempted to mediate a truce, but this floundered when Bernadette Devlin could not give an assurance to the Prime Minister that the RUC would not be followed by rioters if they withdrew from the Bogside.[79]

Later that evening the Taoiseach, Jack Lynch, made his own television broadcast, in which he said it was evident that the Stormont Government was no longer in control of the situation. Indeed, he argued that the present situation was the inevitable outcome of the policies pursued for decades by successive Stormont Governments. It was clear, he stated, that the Irish Government 'can no longer stand by and see innocent people injured and perhaps worse.' Claiming that the RUC was no longer accepted as an impartial force and that the deployment of the British army would be unacceptable, the Irish

Government requested the British Government to apply to the United Nations for the urgent despatch of a peace-keeping force to the Six Counties. Lynch announced that with so many injured, his Government had directed the Irish army to establish field hospitals in County Donegal, adjacent to Derry, and at other points along the border. He concluded by saying that

> the reunification of the national territory can provide the only permanent solution for the problem, [and] it is our intention to request the British Government to enter into early negotiations with the Irish Government to review the present constitutional position of the 6 Counties of Northern Ireland.[80]

Lynch's speech was regarded as a provocation in many Protestant and unionist circles and as an encouragement by some Catholic activists. Patrick Kennedy MP, who was present on the Falls Road on 13 August, explained: 'You had a situation, a very tense situation, here in Belfast, and, because of the Derry situation, this tension was heightened on the Falls, in my opinion ... by the Taoiseach's speech of 13 August.'[81] Chichester-Clark attacked Lynch's speech as unnecessary and irresponsible and 'not statesmanship but the effusions of a hostile propaganda.' He disputed the Taoiseach's claim that the police had attacked the people of Londonderry and repeated that there would be no change in Northern Ireland's position as an integral part of the United Kingdom without its consent, 'and we do not consent, nor will we consent in the future.'

Chichester-Clark claimed that the events in Northern Ireland were not the agitation of a minority seeking by lawful means the assertion of political rights but the 'conspiracy of forces seeking to overthrow a Government democratically elected by a large majority.'[82] The cause of the disorder, in his opinion, was to be found in the activities of 'extreme Republican elements and others determined to overthrow our State.' Chichester-Clark ruled out a coalition with members of the opposition, arguing that there was one prerequisite if a coalition was to succeed: however divided on means, its members must agree on vital ends. But in Northern Ireland the position was that most of the opposition was opposed to the Government party on the most fundamental of all issues: the very existence of the state itself.[83]

Lord Scarman, in his report on the communal violence, rejected the underlying assumptions of both Catholic and Protestant interpretations of the disturbances. The mass of interviews and submissions from throughout Northern Ireland led Scarman to conclude that although mistakes were made and certain individual officers acted wrongly on occasions, the general case of a partisan police force co-operating with Protestant mobs was found to be devoid of substance. Since most of the rioting developed from action on the streets started by Catholic crowds, the RUC were more often than not facing Catholics, who, as a result, came to feel that the police were always going for them, baton-charging them—never the 'other'. It was clear from the evidence presented that, by July 1969, the Catholic minority no longer believed the RUC was impartial and that Catholic and civil rights activists were publicly asserting this loss of confidence. Faced with the distrust of a substantial proportion of the whole population, and short of numbers, the RUC had lost the capacity to control a major riot.

There had, however, been six occasions in the course of the disturbances when the police, by act or omission, were seriously at fault. This included the lack of firm direction in handling the Londonderry disturbances on 12 August, when the RUC incursion into the Bogside was seen by the inhabitants there as a repetition of events in January and April 1969, when the police had also entered the Bogside, leading many, including moderates, to think that the police should be resisted; and the failure of the police to prevent Protestant mobs burning down Catholic homes in Belfast on 14, 15 and 16 August. The Scarman Tribunal concluded, however, that the 'criticisms we have made should not ... be allowed to obscure the fact that the RUC struggled manfully to do their duty in a situation which they could not control. Their courage ... was beyond praise.'[84]

Although there was undoubtedly an IRA influence at work in the Derry Citizens' Defence Association, in the Ardoyne and Falls Road areas of Belfast, and in Newry, Scarman concluded that these elements did not start the riots or plan them. Indeed the evidence was that the IRA was taken by surprise and did less than many of their supporters thought they should have done. While the NICRA did not start any riots, it did help to spread the disturbances on 13 August. However, some within the NICRA leadership regarded the disturbances of 13 August as disastrous. Kevin Boyle, press officer of the NICRA, a law lecturer at Queen's University and a prominent member of People's Democracy, was convinced that the events of August 1969 'put back my ideals much further than they put back the Unionist Government's.' Frank Gogarty, chairman of the NICRA, admitted some responsibility for the Protestant backlash of 14 and 15 August when he said:

In this matter I am afraid that we all on the Executive underestimated the strength of militant Unionism at this time, and had we foreseen the holocaust which did occur in mid-August we most certainly would not have entered on such an enterprise as we did ... We underestimated the influence which possibly many right-wing Unionist politicians had when they slandered us as subversive. We did not really believe that this slander would have been believed as strongly by many Protestants as it seems it was.

Protestant participation in the disorders was largely that of reaction to disturbances started by Catholics, though there were exceptions. Their reaction was particularly fierce in Belfast in mid-August, when it took the form of violent eruptions into Catholic areas—the Falls, Divis Street, and Hooker Street. There was, however, no province-wide organisation sponsoring a policy of disturbance. The only centre where there was evidence of a Protestant organisation actively participating in the riots was Belfast, where the Shankill Defence Association participated in disturbances on the Crumlin Road and in the Falls. Nevertheless, as the shadow of the IRA appeared on the Catholic side, so that of the UVF did on the Protestant side. The evidence accumulated by Scarman suggested that the public utility explosions in April 1969 were the work of these extremists, directed against the Unionist Government of the day. Scarman found that Ian Paisley's role in the events of August was similar to that of political leaders on the Catholic side. He concluded that Paisley neither plotted nor organised the disorders and that there was no evidence that he was a party to any of the acts of violence investigated; nevertheless Scarman argued that those who lived in a free country had to accept the powerful expression of views opposed to their own and warned that Paisley's spoken words were 'often powerful and must have frequently appeared to some as provocative: his newspaper was such that its style and substance were likely to rouse the enthusiasm of his supporters and the fury of his opponents.'[85]

In conclusion, Scarman found that 'there was no plot to overthrow the Government or to mount an armed insurrection.' But while there was no conspiracy, in the sense in which this term is normally used, there was evidence that once the major riots had occurred in Londonderry, Belfast, Armagh, and Dungannon, which were not deliberately started, they were continued by elements that found expression in bodies 'more or less' loosely organised, such as People's Democracy and the various local defence associations associated with the NICRA and several action committees. However, the riots themselves were a different matter, and neither the IRA nor any Protestant organisation nor anybody else planned a campaign of riots. They were communal disturbances arising from a complex political, social and economic situation. More often than not they arose from slight beginnings: but the communal tensions were such that, once begun, they could not be controlled ... On one side people saw themselves, never the 'others', charged by a police force they regarded as partisan: on the other, police and people saw a violent challenge to the authority of the State. These attitudes were the creature of recent events. Their own interpretations of the events of 1968 and early 1969 had encouraged the belief among the minority that demonstrations did secure concessions, and that the police were their enemy and the main obstacle to a continuing programme of demonstrations, while the same events had convinced a large number of Protestants that a determined attempt, already gaining a measure of success, was being made to undermine the constitutional position of Northern Ireland within the United Kingdom. In so tense a situation it needed very little to set going a major disturbance.[86]

With the deployment of British troops dramatically altering the situation, Chichester-Clark flew to London to meet Harold Wilson. The outcome of this meeting was the Downing Street Declaration of 20 August 1969. Declaring that 'the Border is not an issue,' the United Kingdom Government reaffirmed that nothing that had happened in recent weeks meant a derogation from successive pledges by the British Government that Northern Ireland should not cease to be a part of the United Kingdom without the consent of the people and Parliament of Northern Ireland. The British Government reaffirmed its responsibility for Northern Ireland's affairs as 'entirely a matter of domestic jurisdiction' and affirmed that it would take full responsibility for asserting this principle in all international relationships. The Northern Ireland Government was informed that the troops had been provided on a temporary basis in accordance with the United Kingdom Government's ultimate responsibility and that they would be withdrawn when 'law and order has been restored.'

The Northern Ireland Government reaffirmed its intention of taking into the 'fullest account at all times' the views of the United Kingdom Government, especially in relation to matters affecting the status of citizens within that part of the United Kingdom, and their equal rights and protection under the law. Both Governments agreed that 'it is vital that the momentum of internal reform should be maintained' and that in all legislative and executive decisions of Government 'every citizen of Northern Ireland is entitled to the same equality of treatment and freedom from discrimination as obtains in the rest of the United Kingdom, irrespective of political views or religion.'[87]

Instead of being appeased, both Unionists and anti-Unionists attacked Chichester-Clark. Ian Paisley responded by stating that Harold Wilson had capitulated completely to the Catholic hierarchy, the IRA, the NICRA, and those who had always opposed Ulster's constitution, as seen by the agitation for the abolition of the Special Constabulary. Paisley claimed that 'if you want to destroy a country pull out the teeth of her defence forces and she will be an easy prey.' Warning that loyalists could next see their constitution suspended, Paisley was willing to contemplate physical opposition: 'If the forces of the British Crown are going to support the IRA to destroy this Province, then we are prepared to do as our fathers did and fight for our freedom.'[88]

The *Civil Rights News Service Bulletin* responded to the Downing Street Declaration by arguing that the reaffirmation of the constitutional relationship between Britain and Northern Ireland did not mean that Stormont's powers could not be progressively reduced and Stormont eliminated altogether; the border was not an issue, 'but Stormont is.' If Northern Ireland was 'entirely a matter of domestic jurisdiction,' then Westminster had to accede to demands to take over complete political control; the B Specials should be completely disarmed and disbanded; and the RUC had to be reformed, in particular their control removed from Stormont's Ministry of Home Affairs, to be decentralised or reorganised in such a way as to guarantee future impartiality.[89] The bulletin concluded:

> One thing has become clear since the London agreement. Unionists believe in the unity of the 'United Kingdom' only in so far as it suits them. The Unionist Party is an anomalous hybrid of social elements. The controlling element is the aristocracy and business bourgeois community. They are intent on the maintenance of power for the privilege power gives. They require the support of the Protestant working class to maintain this hold on power, and lend to it a superficial impression of democracy. This is done by maintaining the siege mentality, the IRA scare, and by making them feel that, as poor as they are, they are better off than the Catholics who want their jobs ... Now that unity within the United Kingdom is being reinterpreted, the hardline of the Unionist Party are demonstrating that their

interests are not British but the selfish maintenance of their own privilege. They are now attempting to create in working-class Protestant minds the idea that the Westminster Government is involved with the Dublin Government in a conspiracy to reunite Ireland. Unionists are not interested in the Union.[90]

What the evidence, from survey data and the perceptions of the participants themselves, suggests is that many of the old fears, myths and prejudices that Protestants and Catholics held of each other at the state's formation survived well into the second half of the twentieth century. While many of the leading actors might perceive themselves as adopting new perspectives, they were not only prisoners of the fears of their own communities but were also, as we shall see, fundamentally governed by traditional interpretations of their opponents' ideology.

4

The Collapse of the 1920 Settlement

1969–1976

THE RISE OF THE PROVISIONALS

The outbreak of communal violence in Northern Ireland had produced a crisis in the Republican Movement, many of whose members were dissatisfied with the IRA's response and its apparent failure to protect the Catholic population from Protestant mob violence. Slogans in Belfast declaring *IRA—I Ran Away* illustrated to many Republicans the inadequacy of their response.

It was an IRA extraordinary army convention, held in the middle of December 1969, that finally brought the dissatisfaction with the movement's leftist politics into the open and divided the IRA. Those dissatisfied with the movement's policy in the North—led by Seán Mac Stiofáin, Ruairí Ó Brádaigh, and Dáithí Ó Conaill—decided that if the leadership secured a majority at the convention, reducing the IRA to what they considered a 'cog in a Marxist political machine,' they would regroup and reorganise the Republican Movement. Mac Stiofáin, born in London, had been sentenced to eight years in prison for stealing arms from Felstead School in Essex. After his release in 1959 he became involved in intelligence work for the IRA. Dáithí Ó Conaill was to become a leading strategist for the Provisional Republican Movement from 1972 to 1986. Wounded in the 1956 border campaign, he had worked as a teacher in County Donegal, and was credited with the invention of the car bomb.

At the 1969 extraordinary army convention there were two critical proposals: firstly, that the IRA should enter a 'national liberation front' in close connection with organisations of the radical left; and secondly, that the Republican Movement should end its policy of parliamentary abstention from the Dublin, London and Belfast parliaments. It was the second proposal that presented, for traditionalists like Mac Stiofáin, the clear-cut issue of whether to choose between the acceptance of the institutions of partition and upholding the basic Republican principle of Ireland's right to national unity. Mac Stiofáin and his supporters opposed anything to do with 'communist organisations', on the basis of their 'ineffectiveness, their reactionary foot-dragging on the national question and their opposition to armed struggle. We opposed the extreme socialism of the revisionists because we believed that its aim was a Marxist dictatorship, which would be no more acceptable to us than British imperialism or Free State capitalism. We believed that every country must travel its own road to the kind of socialism that suits it best.'

After the convention had passed both of the contentious motions, Mac Stíofáin and his allies held their own convention, at which they pledged their allegiance to the 32-county republic proclaimed at Easter 1916 and established by Dáil Éireann in 1919. A Provisional Executive and a Provisional Army Council of seven were then elected (the term 'Provisional' referring to the claim that the extraordinary army convention had been improperly convened and that its decisions were therefore not irrevocable).[1] The Provisionals' Caretaker Executive of Sinn Féin reiterated that, since its foundation in 1905, Sinn Féin had consistently denied the British Parliament's right to rule in Ireland. Similarly, Provisional Sinn Féin refused to recognise the two 'partition parliaments' in Dublin and Belfast, forced on the Irish people. Provisional Sinn Féin's alternative was the 1919 all-Ireland republican Dáil, and it remained the task of Sinn Féin to lead the Irish people away from the 'British' six-county and 26-county parliaments and back towards the reassembly of the 32-county Dáil, which would then legislate for all Ireland.[2]

Ruairí Ó Brádaigh stated that Provisional Sinn Féin had reorganised on the basis of 'one allegiance only—adherence to the Republic of Easter Week and we declare [that] the sovereignty and unity of the Republic are inalienable and non-judicable.'[3] Deasún Breatnach, writing in An Phoblacht, explained that although the split had occurred for more than one reason, at its core was a question of ethics. Oaths of allegiance, or their equivalent declarations of loyalty to a monarch, state or constitution were regarded as sacred, for it was the 'calling of God to witness that what we say is true and that we will do as we promise.'

To put it bluntly: We cannot live the lie of false oaths and declarations; we cannot swallow the lie of participating in—and thereby perpetuating—parliamentary assemblies which have their being in Britain's alleged right to decide what kind of administration Ireland is to have and how far she will be permitted to conduct her own affairs. We cannot break our covenant of truth with either the dead or the living.[4]

An Phoblacht argued that to achieve its objectives the Republican Movement had to be based on the 'common working people of Ireland, North and South, Protestant, Catholic and Dissenter.' This would involve a massive education programme for the leadership and rank and file and would involve a 'spiritual motivation', involving the restoration of Irish.[5] But Mac Stiofáin emphasised that the most urgent task facing Republicans was to provide all possible assistance to 'our people' in the North, left defenceless against the violence of 'sectarian bigots'. The Irish people, he warned, would never be free until British rule was overthrown and the 'free Gaelic Republic of all Ireland' was established. And he reminded Republicans that the 'Irish Republic was proclaimed by the only way possible—by force of arms—and only by force of arms can the Republic we seek be established.'[6]

Early in January 1970 the Provisional Army Council met to decide military policy for the reorganised movement. With the summer marching season of 1970 as the most likely flash-point, the Provisional IRA, as the military wing of the breakaway movement was now called, determined that the most urgent priority would be area defence from loyalists and the British army. All energies would be devoted to providing material, financial and training assistance for Northern IRA units. As soon as it became feasible and practical the Provisional IRA would move from a purely defensive position to a phase of 'combined defence and retaliation.' After a sufficient period of preparation, when the movement was considered strong enough and the circumstances ripe, it would go into the third phase, launching an all-out offensive action against the 'British occupation system'.[7]

To the Provisionals the responsibility for the impending military conflict lay with Britain's illegal partition of Ireland. In Mac Stiofáin's view,

> the blame lay squarely on England, and with the Irish politicians and church leaders who propped up the status quo and the British connection. As for condemning force, England could not hold any part of Ireland except by military force. When that force was exercised against the population, the troops who exercised it became legitimate targets for Republican resistance fighters.
>
> As an individual, I was sorry for anyone's death, whether Irishman or Englishman. No doubt as individuals there were those on the British side who felt that too. But this did not prevent their

soldiers from volunteering to harass and kill the people of another country which they knew next to nothing about. There was no conscription in the British army ... Every man in it was a professional taking his military chances for money and promotion. If a soldier had any doubts, he could buy out or not re-enlist. But if he was in the North, it was nobody's fault but his own. An unjust system was crashing down around him. He had no idea why, but he was ready to shoot those who did know, smash up homes and arrest innocent men and women. In doing so, he called a guerrilla army into existence against him.[8]

Security force policy and activity played into the hands of the Provisionals, convincing many of the Northern Catholic population that the British army were not there to defend them. The failure to ban the 1970 Orange parades, and the massive arms search and curfew of the Lower Falls Road that followed, itself provoked by Provisional IRA sniping, were described by a senior civil servant as 'the turning point in our policy in Ulster.' In his judgment 'it was then that the army began to be viewed in a different light. Before they had been regarded by the bulk of the Catholic population as protectors. That operation turned things absolutely upside down.'[9]

The trouble began on 3 June 1970 when an Orange march, making its way from the city centre along the Crumlin Road, was diverted near the Ardoyne. Two nights of Protestant rioting ensued, accompanied by gunfire. Following more Orange marches on 27 June, fierce rioting occurred in north and east Belfast, which saw the first sustained military action by Provisional IRA snipers, in the grounds of St Matthew's Catholic Church on the Lower Falls Road, firing for five hours in the course of prolonged intercommunal rioting. During the day five Protestants and one Catholic were shot dead and twenty-six people wounded.

The following day about five hundred Catholic workers were expelled from the Harland and Wolff shipyards in east Belfast by Protestants. The same day James Chichester-Clark warned that a serious situation had arisen and that stern measures were to be taken. Following this the commander of the British army in Northern Ireland announced that anyone carrying a gun was liable to be shot.

This was soon followed by the Falls Road curfew, which lasted for thirty-four hours, except for a two-hour break to allow shopping, over an area of the Lower Falls covering about fifty streets. A British army search of the area uncovered 100 firearms, 100 home-made bombs, 250 pounds of explosives, 21,000 rounds of ammunition, and 8 two-way radios. During the curfew, gun battles between the British army and both wings of the IRA, the Provisionals and the 'Officials'—those who had remained loyal to the original IRA leadership—resulted in five civilian deaths, including two snipers, and the injuring of sixty people, including fifteen soldiers. Residents claimed that the troops caused unnecessary damage, stole property, and abused local people during the searches. It was at this point that relations between the British army and the Catholic working-class population of Belfast turned for the worse.[10] The result of this more aggressive policy against the Republican heartland alienated Catholic opinion, as Paddy Devlin, an NILP Stormont MP opposed to the Provisional IRA, recalled.

> The military, cock-a-hoop with their illegal takeover of the Falls, proceeded to put the boot in with a vengeance. Cars were stopped and the occupants ordered out to be humiliated or searched in a most degrading way. Homes were raided and ransacked at random. Pedestrians were halted and questioned as they walked innocently along the streets. The measures intensified as more and more troops poured in. Everybody in the Falls was subject to this unjustifiable repression, no one was immune. Even as an MP, I was subject to constant harassment and suspicion by the military. Overnight the population turned from neutral or even sympathetic support for the military to outright hatred of everything related to the security forces. As the self-styled generals and godfathers took over in the face of this regime, Gerry Fitt and I witnessed voters and workers ... turn against us to join the Provisionals. Even some of our most dedicated workers and supporters ... turned against us.[11]

With increased support, the Provisional IRA's campaign was stepped up from the bombing of 'economic targets' to attacks on British army personnel. On 6 February 1971 Gunner Robert Harris became the first member of the regular British army to be killed in the current phase of the Troubles when he was shot by a Provisional IRA gunman. On 28 February RUC members were issued with bullet-proof jackets after two unarmed RUC men were machine-gunned to death in another Provisional IRA attack. In March the Provisionals began a systematic campaign of attacking off-duty RUC officers and bombing police stations. Early in the same month three off-duty soldiers, two of them brothers, aged seventeen and eighteen, were shot in the back of the head after being lured from a Belfast pub by Provisionals. The widespread revulsion at the killings increased Protestant pressure on

Chichester-Clark to pursue a tougher security policy, including the rearming of the RUC, which had been disarmed as part of the reform programme.

At this time the 'Official IRA' were also active in paramilitary violence. (The Officials were also dubbed the 'Stickies', because of the introduction of self-adhesive Easter lilies for their annual Easter collection.) The Provisional IRA, however, soon outstripped the Officials, building their strength from local defence committees in Belfast and being widely perceived as defenders of the Catholic community from loyalist mob attacks. The tension between the Official and Provisional IRA was intense in 1970–71, and in March 1971 there was a fierce gun battle between the two groups in the Lower Falls area of Belfast, in which one man was shot dead and several wounded while the British army stood aside.[12]

In 1972 Cathal Goulding, the Chief of Staff, was to lead the Official IRA into declaring a cease-fire and was strongly critical of the Provisionals' bombing campaign, calling it inhuman in moral terms and provocative in political terms.[13] In contrast, governed by their perception of the Northern conflict, the Provisional IRA's leadership saw their campaign as morally justified until the British state disengaged from Ireland.

To accommodate Northern Protestants the Provisionals announced their Dáil Uladh policy, which would see the establishment of a nine-county Ulster parliament within a federal Ireland. Peadar Mac Gaotháin, secretary of Comhairle Uladh, explained that what the Republican Movement envisaged was not simply a united Ireland but a 'New Ireland—United and Free.' As all power derived from the people, to give power back to the people it was envisaged that there should be four provincial parliaments, under a central parliament. The latter would control foreign affairs, defence, finance, and the monetary system, while agricultural services and social welfare would be devolved to the provincial parliaments. Dáil Uladh, it was argued, was the solution to the partition problem. The big stumbling-block to any solution, according to the Republican Movement, had always been the unionist fear of being swamped in a Catholic-dominated republic. In this analysis, 'unionist intransigence lies in the fear of the loss of power … and without the power to administer their own destiny, the Northern Unionists would never be content within a United Ireland.' Therefore the answer seemed to be to allow the Protestant people to control one of the four parliaments in a nine-county Ulster, where they would still have a majority, and 'with the bogey of the border removed the old issues would become irrelevant, and we would see for the first time in our tragic history, a normalisation of politics along "left", "right", "centre", rather than religious divides.'

The fear for Catholics of any future Protestant misrule would be diminished by the size of the minority in the new Ulster, by the constitution, and by the central Irish parliament. With the old fears removed, 'Catholic and Protestant culture could flourish side by side and the nation would draw strength from ... diversity, rather than allow hatred to breed from it.' In the new republic, 'Catholic, Protestant and Dissenter could retain their identity and still find common identity as Irishmen.'[14]

In announcing Dáil Uladh on 11 August 1971, the Provisional Army Council appealed to the

Protestants of Ulster to involve themselves with their fellow-countrymen in establishing a Provincial Parliament. For too long British politicians and sectarian perverts have divided our people in order to secure their own vested interests irrespective of the cost to Catholic, Protestant and Dissenter. The agony and suffering of our people recognises no religious divide. In this time of strife, we appeal to all Irish people to unite for the defeat of British imperialists who have been in the past and even now exploiting irrelevant past dissensions to maintain their presence and influence in Ireland.[15]

Asked how Protestants would react if the British withdrew from Northern Ireland, Ruairí Ó Brádaigh replied that 'if Britain disengages that door would be closed,' the time having arrived for work on the Republican Movement's social and economic programme and going to the Protestant people and telling them that they did not want the twenty-six county state to dominate the six-county state. He regarded the likelihood of a 'backlash' by Protestants as 'overrated', based on the understanding that Britain stood at their back. But with Britain washing its hands of the situation, Ó Brádaigh thought that, given that the majority of Protestants were 'hard-headed, sensible and very realistic,' they would come to realise that the best thing to do would be to participate in the building of a new Ireland. If they decided to fight, which he regarded as hypothetical, then a 'peace-keeping force' would have to deal with the situation. Ó Brádaigh appealed to Protestants on the grounds that the Provisionals believed in making a 'fresh start', getting down to the question of 'national reconstruction', to which Protestants had a contribution to make. He also felt that Protestants, like Catholics, had suffered cultural alienation and that they would like to 'see all of us enjoying our cultural heritage. We believe in the separation of Church and State and the building of a pluralist society.'[16]

In September 1971 the Provisionals put forward their proposals for peace. These involved the immediate cessation of the British forces' 'campaign of violence against the Irish people'; the abolition of Stormont; a guarantee of non-interference with a free election to establish Dáil Uladh, and a new governmental structure for the entire country; the release of all 'political prisoners', tried or untried, in Ireland and Britain; and a guarantee of compensation for all those who had 'suffered as a result of direct or indirect British violence.'[17]

POLITICAL REALIGNMENTS

Elsewhere within the Catholic community the demise of the Nationalist Party in the 'crossroads' election created an opportunity for a realignment in constitutional Catholic politics. In Derry, John Hume, the civil rights activist, called for a new social-democratic and anti-Unionist movement that would transcend the sectarian divide. This would involve:

1. The formation of a new political movement based on social-democratic principles, with open membership and elected executives to allow complete involvement of the people in the process of decision making.

2. A movement that must provide what has been severely lacking at Stormont—a strong energetic opposition to conservatism—proposing radical social and economic policies.

3. A movement that must be completely non-sectarian and committed to rooting out the fundamental evil in our society—sectarian division.

4. A movement that would be committed to the idea that the future of Northern Ireland should be decided by the people and that there should be no change in its constitutional position without the consent of the people.[18]

In January 1970 Hume called for the amendment of section 5 of the Government of Ireland Act, 1920, to guarantee civil rights in all the fields that had been in question over the past year. He believed that while the constitutional question was allowed to remain the central party political question, the hopes of moving away from fixed political positions into 'normalised politics' of a left-right variety were dim. There was no chance, he said, of the Unionist Party casting aside sectarianism as a political weapon, for 'their whole past is built upon it. Their whole future depends on it.' He challenged the Unionist view that those who wished to remove the border were disloyal citizens, claiming that 'anyone who believed that the people's best interests were served by an alternative Constitution was absolutely loyal.'[19]

This emphasised a view common to the new generation of Catholic civil rights leaders, which they shared with their Nationalist Party predecessors, that unionism was based on a permanent sectarian ascendancy. The young Nationalist Party MP Austin Currie claimed that Unionists realised that a united Ireland would be a threat to their privileges and powers. These, however, would be wiped away by the reforms being imposed from London. Currie believed that those who identified with unionism were 'now asking what they had in common with the lords, majors, captains and commanders who represented them … They were beginning to realise that it was the same families who had ruled since [the Ulster rebellion of] 1641.'[20]

Similarly, Gerry Fitt echoed many of the beliefs of previous advocates of republican socialism in his assessment of unionism. Fitt defined himself as a strong socialist with a belief in a united Ireland. He believed that the Protestant working class had been 'deluded' into the belief that they were superior to the Catholic working class, while the Catholic working class had been made to believe that they were inferior. In 1970 Fitt felt there were signs that the Protestant and Catholic working class were now coming together so that Northern Ireland could have a 'real "polarisation" of the right and left divisions.' He predicted that if the anti-Unionists got increasing Protestant support it would 'spell the death-knell for the Unionists in Northern Ireland' and that 'this will eventually lead to a united Ireland Republic where the working class interests will be paramount … A process of education and enlightenment will bring home to the Unionists that we are all Irish; that this is our own country and our future is tied up in a 32-county Ireland.'[21]

Likewise, Hume saw Unionists as primarily Irish and argued that in the North of Ireland there was a large group 'who had no identity such as the Prime Minister, Chichester-Clark, who was afraid to say whether he was Irish or British.' That confusion, Hume argued, ran through the whole unionist community.[22] He compared the Unionist ruling class and its supporters to the white ruling elites in Rhodesia and South Africa. He pointed out what he considered the basic contradictions within unionism, scrutinising the link between Britain and the Unionists and asking:

Is the maintenance of the link with Britain the real first principle and motivating factor of Unionism? ... Loyalty to the Crown is always loudly proclaimed by the Unionist Party and its supporters ... Yet, when His Majesty's Parliament at Westminster showed signs of willingness to grant Home Rule ... the Unionist Party ... was ... pledged to take up arms against the Crown ... 'Not an inch.' Originality or liberalism of any sort can only lead to a crack in the wall. This, added to the essential puritanism which has long been evident, has meant the drying up of the cultural roots of the Northern Unionists. And many parts of the North, which had long periods of cultural activity are culturally dead today, and are dull uninteresting places ... There is, today, little evidence of any real traditional culture amongst them. These hysterical outpourings on gable walls, or the red, white and blue kerbstones, painted with detail and defiance are pathetic evidence of all to which they have to cling. It is really little wonder that there should be such confusion amongst them about their identity, or that they should be such recent signs of striving for a sense of one ... Loyalty to what? It is clear that the 'real principles' of Unionism have little to do with loyalty to the Crown or to the Union Jack. They have more to do with the maintenance of a system of power and privilege. It is the defence of this that is ... one of the consistent themes of Unionism. 'What we have we hold,' 'No surrender' and 'Not an inch' are the most prominent of Unionist slogans which give the key to what Unionism is all about—what they have they hold.[23]

Common to all these interpretations was the belief that Unionists sought power in order to maintain a Protestant ascendancy over Catholics. This interpretation also denied that Unionist opposition to a united Ireland was based on a sense of British nationalism, for Ulster Protestants were ultimately perceived as part of the Irish nation. The anti-Unionists therefore saw the ultimate removal of sectarianism, of the Unionist control of power in Northern Ireland, as leading to a united Ireland, since the core of unionism was believed to be the reproduction of Protestant political, economic and social dominance.

But while the anti-Unionists shared many of the views of the cultural and political interpretations of unionism that the Provisionals held, where they fundamentally dissented was in their attitude to violence. Like Cardinal Conway, the Catholic primate of All Ireland, they did not accept that 'a million Protestants' could, or should, be bombed into a united Ireland. The principle that the consent of Ulster Protestants should be sought for any change in the constitutional status of Northern Ireland was a fundamental shift in Catholic politics, and for the first time it was argued that it was not the territory of Ireland that was divided but the Irish people. John Hume, for example, concluded that the tragic happenings at the beginning of the century had left Ireland with two confessional states, which, because of their very nature, had contributed to a narrowness and insularity that had prevented the development of the generosity of spirit and breadth of vision necessary for the problem of division in Ireland to be solved in a manner acceptable to all.

> The result has been that to many Irish Unity has come to mean the conquest of one state by the other rather than a partnership of both where both traditions combine in agreement to create a new society in Ireland, a pluralist society where all traditions are cherished and flourish equally … The border in Ireland is the psychological barrier between the two sections of the community in the North built on prejudice, sectarianism and fear. To remove it requires the eradication of sectarianism and prejudice. This can only come through the development of understanding and friendship. This is the real task which faces anyone who genuinely wants to solve the Irish problem. The weakness of this approach is that it is undramatic. It does not offer an instant and glorious solution. It offers only a hard unpopular road of accepting that it will take patience and a long term plan which should be worked out painstakingly. Its virtue is that it is the only road … It cannot come about by coercion or violence, because a problem of sectarian division and prejudice is only deepened and strengthened by violence. It would not resemble in any way the unity that seems to be envisaged by some of those in Dublin who talk of their 'own people' and whose loudly proclaimed 'pure republicanism' seems to me to be nothing more than the pursuit of 'Catholic victory'.

Hume concluded that an essential first step along this road was equality and justice in the North. Equal citizenship was an essential prerequisite to the reconciliation that was necessary to break down the sectarian barriers. When these barriers went, the 'real border will have gone and the solution to what has become known as the "Irish Question" will be easy to achieve.' Hume went on to argue that right-wing Unionists were right when they said that reform and civil rights could lead to an end of Northern Ireland as they knew it; but where they were wrong was to assume that it would lead them into an Ireland where the Northern Protestant would be trampled on and their rights of conscience infringed. 'No-one', claimed Hume,

> is entitled to assume that when we talk of unity we are talking of assimilation into the present state south of the border. Such unity as envisaged would be a unity under an entirely new Constitution, one which all sections would have a say in drafting and one which would provide a framework for a pluralist society in Ireland in which the rights of conscience and religious liberty would be upheld. It would be a society that would be much richer than what we have known in that it would have the full and free participation of all our traditions, unfettered by the negative dissensions that have wasted so much energy in the past, energy which would then be devoted to the positive construction of the whole country.

Hume thought that more and more Northern Protestants were asking what was their 'real identity and are prepared to openly discuss the pros and cons of a united country.' They were, he claimed, 'disenchanted and disillusioned' with the instability of the Northern state and realised that the Unionist Party could only survive as a party of prejudice, injustice, and sectarianism. In short, he concluded,

> to create a truly united country we need a truly united people, not a united piece of earth. In that task we need not to overcome the Northern Protestant but to seek his co-operation, help and assistance. When he realises fully that the unity proposed is a unity sought with his agreement and his participation then surely a vision opens up of an Ireland that can be an example to other countries in the world with serious and bitter problems of community division. Is there any other way in which we can create a society in Ireland where Catholic, Protestant and Dissenter can work together as equals for the betterment of us all? Those are the sentiments of a Northern Protestant [Theobald Wolfe Tone] who founded the republican tradition in Ireland.[24]

These views crystallised in the formation of a new political party, the Social Democratic and Labour Party, in 1970. The SDLP's constitution set out the formal aims of the party:

1. To organise and maintain in Northern Ireland a socialist party;
2. To promote the policies decided by the party conference;
3. To co-operate with the Irish Congress of Trades Unions in joint political or other action;

4. To promote the cause of Irish unity based on the consent of a majority of people in Northern Ireland;

5. To co-operate with other labour parties through the Council of Labour and co-operate with other social democratic parties at an international level;

6. To contest elections in Northern Ireland with a view to forming a government which will implement the following principles:

(a) the abolition of all forms of religious, political or class discrimination; the promotion of culture and the arts with special responsibility to cherish and develop all aspects of our native culture.

(b) the public ownership and democratic control of such essential industries and services as the common good requires.

(c) the utilisation of its powers by the state, when and where necessary, to provide employment, by the establishment of publicly owned industries.[25]

The upheavals of 1968–1970 also saw the formation of the Alliance Party of Northern Ireland, which had its origins in the New Ulster Movement, formed in January 1969 as a pressure group to promote moderate and non-sectarian policies, calling for the creation of a Community Relations Commission and the centralised control of public housing. Many of its members—it claimed a membership of seven thousand in 1969—were to become active in the Alliance Party. The party itself was launched in April 1970, and although its leadership was at first drawn from people previously unknown in politics, it gained support from a section of Unionists who had backed Terence O'Neill. Although its main base to start with appeared to be middle-class, it absorbed many people who had formerly backed the NILP. It got an early boost in 1972 when three sitting MPs joined it—two Unionists and one Nationalist.

According to John Hunter, chairman of the Policy Committee, the Alliance Party was anti-sectarian. It considered itself the only party in Northern Ireland to recognise sectarianism as *the* major problem; it recognised that the 'natural' Northern Ireland political division was not that of left-right politics but a division between sectarians and non-sectarians, rejecting the left's view that non-sectarians could only come from one particular class. The Alliance Party was to be 'progressive' and 'unique' in its outlook; it should also, Hunter believed, be undogmatic, and was to be a 'Northern Ireland Party', in that it claimed no connection with any political grouping outside Northern Ireland. This meant a continuing British connection, recognising the economic advantages accruing from this but also accepting that 'we have a distinct cultural heritage which is neither solely Saxon nor solely Celtic, but unique to ourselves. We are Northern Irishmen ...'[26]

Oliver Napier, joint chairman of the Alliance Party's Political Committee, summed this up by arguing in early 1971 that

> all of us in Northern Ireland are an integral part of a single great cultural heritage ... a true mixture of Gael and Gall ... of Celt and Norman ... of Native Irish and Scot ... We are culturally an Irish people. We are proud of being Irish ... But our cultural nationality has no connection with legal citizenship. We are British citizens. There is no inconsistency between being culturally Irish and legally British. Is the Scot no less a Scot because he is British? ... There is no such thing as a 'British cultural nationality.' British is a legal definition for neighbouring peoples who have come together in one national unit. Within the United Kingdom there are four peoples, English, Irish, Scots and Welsh ... We proclaim that we in Northern Ireland are all one people, united by race ... culture ... history ... by one common destiny.[27]

UNIONIST POLITICS

Northern Ireland's Prime Minister, James Chichester-Clark, had inherited an unenviable situation from his predecessor. He was faced with continuing demands for reform, from the Northern Catholic community and the British Government, while facing increasing grass-roots opposition to the reform programme from within the Ulster Unionist Party. He was not assisted by continuing calls from the Government of the Republic for the British Government to settle the Irish question once and for all, which merely fuelled the Unionist sense of siege and added to the internal Unionist pressures on Chichester-Clark. In late August 1969 Jack Lynch again reiterated his belief that the 'unnatural and unjustified partition of Ireland' was at the heart of the Ulster problem. 'No long-term, much less a permanent, solution can be contemplated without having full regard to its existence,' Lynch stated. The Taoiseach and his Government recognised that the border could not be changed by force and that it was their policy to 'seek the reunification of the country by peaceful means,' declaring that the Irish Government was prepared to discuss a federal solution with the British Government to end partition. Chichester-Clark responded by calling Lynch's statement 'ill-judged and unhelpful' and stating that Northern

Ireland was 'no concern of Mr Lynch or his Government.'[28]

In September 1969, when Lynch emphasised the two aspects of his Northern policy—firstly a renunciation of force in any circumstances as a way of resolving the partition question, and secondly an acknowledgment that any Irish union not rooted in consent would be a negative and even destructive union—Chichester-Clark welcomed these clarifications. However, he regretted that these points had not been made in earlier pronouncements, at a more sensitive moment, when the Irish Government's deployment of troops on the border had given rise to Unionist fears that the Republic was going to intervene militarily in Northern Ireland, 'and so into a situation already overladen with fear a new fear was injected.' Chichester-Clark believed that Lynch's hopes for a closer North-South relationship could not be realised if the people of the South did not accept that

> however much they [the Irish Government] disapprove of the present Government of Northern Ireland, it is there because the people of Northern Ireland put it there ... Nor can any proper view be formed of the attitude of the North unless one accepts that the loyalty of the vast majority here to Britain and to the Crown is an intense and deeply rooted thing ... Every nation like every individual has a right to its aspirations. All we ask is that our aspirations in Northern Ireland should not be overlooked.[29]

Turning to the Northern Catholic population, Chichester-Clark gave an assurance that Catholics were welcome in the Unionist Party, not just as voters but as party members. He rejected the use of the term 'minority' to describe Catholics as a 'silly expression', since 'all of us are in a minority on some issue or other'; it was misleading to assume that Catholics constituted one collective body, with identical views on religious, political, social or other issues.[30] He called on the Unionist Party to kick out those 'two-timers' who wanted to 'run Ulster with the gun and the strong-arm tactics of the bully.' He argued: 'You can be a Unionist or you can be a Protestant Unionist. You cannot, with any honesty, pretend to be both at the same time.'[31]

This was to prove too revolutionary a concept for many Unionist Party members. While Chichester-Clark sought to introduce reforms that he hoped would reduce Catholic alienation from the state, his Government in turn was faced with the prospect of alienating its own supporters with every reform introduced. The Hunt Report led to far-reaching reforms in Northern Ireland's local security forces in 1969, recommending an unarmed RUC and the replacement of the Special

Constabulary, with a new part-time force under the British army commander, as well as a police reserve. The B Specials held a unique position within Unionist mythology as the personification of the Northern Ireland state's ability to protect itself from internal and external attack.

At talks in London with Harold Wilson, Chichester-Clark agreed to the suggestion that the British army commander in Northern Ireland should be director of security operations. Following this meeting, Wilson gave a television interview in which he indicated that the Special Constabulary would be phased out. This was denied by Chichester-Clark, who felt undermined by the comments. He declared that 'the Specials are not being disbanded' and that 'I would have resigned at once if there had been any proposal to leave us naked to attack.' Instead, and unconvincingly, he argued that only the name and organisation of the Specials would change and that this had been the fate of many regiments of the British army. All members of the Special Constabulary would be receiving a letter explaining the changes, and there would continue to be an opportunity for 'loyal men to serve Ulster.'[32]

But the Northern Ireland Government was forced to admit that it was bowing to London pressures when Chichester-Clark revealed it had hoped to 'modernise' the Specials but that these hopes had been frustrated by the decision of the Hunt Committee to set up the Ulster Defence Regiment in its place. The situation, explained Chichester-Clark, was that when the new regiment was proposed it was made clear that 'if we did not go for the new local defence force we would have had them disbanded over our heads by the Westminster Government.'[33] Many Unionists perceived the disbanding of the B Specials as undermining Northern Ireland's status within the United Kingdom. After fifty years of controlling its own affairs, the Unionist Government's reform programme, introduced under pressure from London, was seen as revolutionary.

In October 1969 a Ministry of Community Relations was established to advise other departments on community relations and to administer the financing of projects for improving amenities in urban areas suffering from social deprivation. The following month a Commissioner for Complaints, independent of the Northern Ireland Government and reporting to the Northern Ireland Parliament, was appointed to deal with individual grievances against local councils and public bodies. An Electoral Law Act introduced universal adult suffrage for local government elections and lowered the voting age for all elections to eighteen. The Macrory Report on local government reform, completed in May 1970 and accepted in December 1970 by the Stormont administration, recommended the abolition of the old system of local government and its replacement with twenty-six district councils. It also established area boards to control health, education and library services, these new services to be the responsibility of the Northern Ireland Parliament. This was followed in April 1971 by a Local Government Boundaries Act, providing for the appointment of a Boundaries Commissioner to recommend boundaries and names for the new districts and the electoral districts and wards into which they would be divided.

In May 1971 an independent system of public prosecutions was established, and the Northern Ireland Government announced the appointment of a Director of Public Prosecutions, responsible to the Northern Ireland Attorney-General, who in turn was answerable to the Northern Ireland Parliament, replacing the RUC's responsibility for prosecutions. And, on 27 October 1971, G. B. Newe, a Catholic, was appointed Minister of State in the Prime Minister's Department at Stormont, becoming the first Catholic to hold a ministerial position since the statelet's formation.

In 1970 evidence of opposition to the reform programme was apparent when the Prime Minister was ousted from his own Unionist Party constituency association in Castledawson. When he sought re-election at the annual meeting, Chichester-Clark, who had been vice-chairman of the association, was beaten by a 53-year-old bus driver. The new secretary explained that 'our idea in opposing him was to let the Government see just how strongly the ordinary members of the Party feel at the present time.'[34] The Prime Minister also suffered a setback when two Stormont by-elections in April 1970 returned Ian Paisley for Terence O'Neill's old constituency and William Beattie for South Antrim as Protestant Unionists.[35]

In response, Chichester-Clark warned the Unionist Party that it faced 'a choice between a Government pursuing reasonable policies of fairness and justice for everyone, and not going back on the changes that have been made or direct rule from London.'[36] He appealed to members of the community to help him. He complained that the vast majority of people had remained silent and called on them to 'become activists ... They must stir themselves to show that they have opinions too.'[37]

But, in an atmosphere of an increasing bombing and shooting war, this support was not forthcoming. Indeed the Prime Minister's position became increasingly insecure, and in August 1970 confusion raged over whether or not Chichester-Clark had received a vote of confidence from his own constituency.[38] A month later the executive committee of his constituency association passed a resolution deploring the formation of a central housing authority without a mandate from the Northern Ireland Parliament or people.[39] The dispute culminated in the decision of the constituency association in October 1970 to join the West Ulster Unionist Council, a pressure group within the Unionist Party that opposed the reform programme,[40] although this decision was later reversed.[41]

The Prime Minister's fiercest critic within the Unionist Party was William Craig, who continued to attack Chichester-Clark as he had O'Neill, telling him to 'pack up your bags and get back to your farm.' He was highly critical of the Government's policies, in particular those concerning the disarming of the RUC and the disbanding of the Special Constabulary. Craig looked forward to the formation of a new, traditional Unionist government; in the meantime he appealed to his supporters to 'see that the conspiracy against this land of ours does not succeed.'[42]

More evidence of Unionist disaffection came in September 1970 when more than two hundred delegates from Unionist Party constituency associations west of the River Bann gave their unanimous approval to a pamphlet drawn up by the West Ulster Unionist Council. It called for the rearming of the RUC and the formation of a strong reserve force to support the regular police, as well as pronouncing its opposition to the new central housing authority and the reorganisation of local government. The last two objections were made on the grounds that these changes would 'undermine the democratic rights of the local people of the province.'[43] This was followed by a vote of no confidence by the Unionist Party executive in the Government's law and order policies.[44] Grass-roots fears were not eased when Chichester-Clark told Stormont that the Government was considering further reforms, such as the introduction of PR for Stormont and local elections.[45]

Following riots in the Shankill area of Belfast a demand was made by over 150 leading Unionists in January 1971 for the resignation of Chichester-Clark. They signed a requisition for an emergency meeting of the Ulster Unionist Council to debate the motion

> that this council, recognising with increased anxious concern the abysmal and costly failure of the Government to maintain law and security in this community, calls upon it to resign so that a new

administration may urgently attempt to save the country from impending disaster.[46]

1971 did not see Chichester-Clark's position ease. The Provisional IRA moved to the offensive, and the murder of the three young soldiers in March 1971 was the signal for a new loyalist campaign demanding Chichester-Clark's resignation. On 18 March 1971 the beleaguered Chichester-Clark flew to London for talks with the new Conservative Prime Minister, Edward Heath. He pressed for a new security initiative, but Heath offered only an extra 1,300 troops.

Two days later Chichester-Clark resigned. In his resignation statement he emphasised that one of the reasons for the failure to restore law and order to Northern Ireland's streets was the unrealistic expectations many Unionists had of the Northern Ireland Government's ability to suppress the Provisional IRA campaign.

> I have decided to resign because I can see no other way of bringing home to all concerned the realities of the present constitutional, political and security situation … It is apparent that public and parliamentary opinion in Northern Ireland looks to the Northern Ireland government for measures which can bring the current IRA campaign swiftly to an end. I have expressed to British Ministers the full force of this opinion and have pressed upon them my view that some further initiative is required. While they have agreed to take any feasible steps open to them to intensify the effort against the IRA, it remains the professional military view—and one which I indeed have often expressed myself—that it would be misleading the Northern Ireland community to suggest that we are faced with anything but a long haul, and that such initiatives as can be taken are unlikely to effect a radical improvement in the short term …[47]

INTERNMENT

Three days after Chichester-Clark's resignation, Brian Faulkner defeated William Craig by 26 votes to 4 in a vote by Unionist MPs at Stormont to become Northern Ireland's sixth Prime Minister. On his appointment Faulkner described his most important aim as the restoration of

> confidence throughout the entire community. Without that all else would be futile. Obviously the kernel of our immediate problem is the law and order situation. Let me say right away that I am convinced

that what we need on this front are not new principles, but practical results on the ground in the elimination not only of terrorism, but of riots and disorder. The basic principle must clearly be that the rule of law shall operate in all parts of Northern Ireland, so that the security which goes with the rule of law can be enjoyed by all our citizens ...[48]

Faulkner's first meeting after his election was with General Tuzo, commander of the British army in Northern Ireland. Tuzo was concerned that the army's practice of 'minimum force' was not a policy that could be lightly changed under the law of the United Kingdom. On the other hand, Faulkner pressed the view that this should not simply mean the containment of the increasing terrorist activity, and he pressed on Tuzo his belief that it had been a mistake for the British army to be seen as a 'mere "peace-keeping" force', with no obligation to 'seek out and destroy the terrorist.' By the end of the discussion Tuzo and Faulkner had agreed that more effective progress could be made in hindering the movement of terrorists, cutting their supply lines, and getting more information on their activities and personnel.[49]

Faulkner had come to the conclusion that a more effective enforcement of existing security policies was required, and to this end a small high-powered branch of the Northern Ireland Cabinet Office was established for the co-ordination of security policy and the servicing of the Joint Security Committee. A senior civil servant was appointed security adviser, as a link with British army headquarters at Lisburn and special adviser to the Northern Ireland Cabinet.[50]

On 1 April 1971 Faulkner flew to London for a meeting with the British Prime Minister. Heath took a tough line on the issue of security. He assured Faulkner that Northern Ireland's position within the United Kingdom was 'inviolate' for as long as that was the democratically expressed will of the people there, and he emphasised that the British Government would not act as a 'Big Brother', pushing the Stormont administration around in public: he wanted a two-way relationship, so that Stormont would have adequate authority and resources to carry out its responsibilities, while paying attention to the London perspective. He was particularly emphatic that the IRA had to be beaten, and he pressed for more security measures, such as the blocking of minor cross-border roads, which the Provisional IRA were using to mount attacks from the Republic. The question of internment was raised, and General Tuzo informed the Prime Ministers that plans were ready for its implementation if necessary.[51]

Back in Northern Ireland, on the political front Faulkner suggested the setting up of three functional committees at Stormont, covering the social services, the environment, and industry. Without executive powers the committees would review and consider Government policy and provide a means of 'expressing legitimate parliamentary interest in the overall quality of government proposals and performance.' The committees would be composed of not more than nine members each, broadly representative of party strengths in the Northern Ireland House of Commons. The addition of three new committees to the existing Public Accounts Committee would mean that the opposition, and in particular the SDLP, would provide at least two chairmen. This, Faulkner argued, would allow the House of Commons to perform its functions of scrutiny and control more effectively, permit genuine and constructive participation in the work of Parliament by all its members, and encourage the development of much greater specialisation and expertise. As a final enticement Faulkner hinted that other constitutional changes, such as the introduction of PR, could be introduced in the future. He concluded his offer by asking to start with three committees, 'see how they go, learn from our experience, but above all let us trust one another.'[52]

Faulkner had identified four main blemishes on Stormont's record and performance as a Parliament. These were insensitivity on the Government front bench to the contribution backbenchers could and wished to make to the life of Parliament; the inability of successive oppositions to feel that they were achieving anything positive by their parliamentary membership; the tendency to concentrate too much discussion on 'things of no real, ultimate importance'; and the fact that many of the most experienced and talented elements of the community had not an adequate parliamentary voice. But, he cautioned, as long as Northern Ireland's politics was divided along religious lines, so long would a religious minority be a political minority. For democracy to mean anything, Faulkner argued, the will of the majority must still decide fundamental issues.[53]

On three points the Northern Ireland Government was 'unable to admit of any compromise whatever.' These were:

(a) the maintenance of Northern Ireland as an integral part of the United Kingdom in accordance with the statutory guarantee of the Northern Ireland Act 1949;

(b) the preservation in Northern Ireland of the processes of democratic Government, as represented by a democratically elected Parliament with an executive responsible to it; and

(c) absolutely firm and unequivocal resistance to all and any organisations seeking to advance political or constitutional causes in Northern Ireland by violence or coercion.[54]

The SDLP's response was generally favourable, though cautious. Austin Currie praised Faulkner for speaking of 'genuine and constructive participation'; Gerry Fitt 'read his remarks with great care and we hope we shall be able to co-operate with him.' By the end of the opening debates on the proposals the SDLP appeared to have accepted them wholeheartedly.[55] However, the prospects of a new departure in political discourse were dashed by the deteriorating security situation. Despite the spreading violence, the security forces had caused relatively few civilian deaths; but on 25 May 1971 Faulkner announced at Stormont that 'any soldier seeing any person with a weapon or seeing any person acting suspiciously may fire either to warn or may fire with effect, depending on the circumstances and without waiting for orders from anyone.'[56] The statement was considered significant because it appeared to supply an open political justification for any future contentious shooting involving the British army. This was not lost on the SDLP, and Paddy Devlin warned that 'if authority is now being put into the hands of soldiers ... we will withdraw from parliament.'

On 8 July 1971, after four successive nights of rioting in Derry between Catholics and the British army in which stones, petrol bombs and gunfire had been directed at troops, Séamus Cusack was shot by a soldier and later died from loss of blood. The army claimed that Cusack had been aiming a rifle when shot, a claim denied by rioters and bystanders. More rioting followed, and Desmond Beattie was also shot dead by British troops. On this occasion the army claimed that Beattie had been about to throw a nail bomb when shot; again local people claimed the dead man had been unarmed.

On 11 July 1971 John Hume and several other SDLP MPs announced their decision to withdraw from Stormont if an inquiry was not held into the Derry killings.[57] The SDLP was responding to pressures emanating from its grass roots. It was feared that the emotional anger aroused by the killings could be channelled into support for the Provisionals. Máire Drumm, a Provisional leader, told a meeting in the Bogside on 11 July that 'the only way you can avenge these deaths is by being organised ... until you can chase that accursed army away. I would personally prefer to see all the British army going back dead ... You should not just shout "Up the IRA". You should join the IRA.'[58]

Within the SDLP, Fitt and Devlin accepted reluctantly the decision to boycott Stormont, Devlin believing that 'just at a time when there might be signs that we might be getting somewhere, the old nationalist knee-jerk reaction of abstention was brought into play,' which Fitt and Devlin feared would clear the way for the Provisionals to dictate the agenda.[59] On 12 July 1971 the SDLP justified its decision to withdraw from Stormont by pointing out that it had continually urged restraint on its supporters and tried at all times to give 'responsible leadership'. But, it continued,

> there comes a point where to continue to do so is to appear to condone the present system. That point, in our view, has now been reached ... The British government must face up to the clear consequences of their intervention of August 1969 and reveal their determination to produce a political solution which will be meaningful and acceptable to those present. Without such evidence we cannot continue to give our consent to a continuation of the present situation ... If our demand is not met ... we will withdraw immediately from parliament and will take the necessary steps to set up an alternative assembly of elected representatives to deal with the problems of the people we represent, and to become the authoritative voice to negotiate a political solution on their behalf ...[60]

Catholic alienation from the state now reached a new low point with the introduction of the internment of terrorist suspects without trial under the Special Powers Act. Faulkner, who made the decision to implement internment, felt that the decision was one that was virtually forced on him. The Provisional IRA campaign had reached an unprecedented level of ferocity in the summer of 1971. By July 55 people had died violently; in the first seven months of 1971 there were over 300 explosions and 320 shooting incidents, and over 600 people received hospital treatment for injuries. All this was happening in a small province of one-and-a-half million people; proportionate figures for the whole of the United Kingdom would have meant over 2,000 dead and, in seven months, 11,000 bombings, 11,600 shootings, and 22,000 people injured. Faulkner recalled: 'In 1971 people were not hardened to violence, or resigned to accepting it as a background to daily life; they were demanding that the Government do something to stop it, and stop it quickly.' There appeared to be only one unused weapon in the Government's arsenal: internment. During Chichester-Clark's premiership Faulkner had argued against internment, concerned that it should only be used as a weapon of last resort and fearful that Catholic 'no-go' areas—in which barricades had been erected to keep out the security forces—had undermined the RUC's intelligence, on which any successful internment operation would depend. A series of city bombings in July 1971 tipped the scales, and Faulkner concluded that internment had to be introduced. The British army and RUC suggested a wide swoop involving the arrest of over five hundred people; this was aimed principally at the Provisional and Official IRA, since the security forces were adamant that at that time there was no evidence of organised terrorism by Protestants that could justify their detention. After consultation with the British Government, the decision was taken to implement internment.[61]

On 9 August 1971, in a series of dawn raids, the British army attempted to arrest 452 men, although only 342, mainly from the Official IRA, were captured. Of those arrested, 105 were released within two days; the rest were detained. The immediate result was an upsurge in violence. In the Ardoyne area of Belfast two hundred Protestants were forced out, setting fire to their homes as they left, rather than let them be occupied by Catholics. Eventually 2,000 Protestants were left homeless, while 2,500 Catholics left Belfast for refugee camps set up in the Republic. By 12 August, 22 people had been killed and 7,000 people, mostly Catholics, were left homeless as their houses were burned. In the year before internment, 34 people had been killed; 140 were to die in 1971. On 1 September 1971 a series of explosions over two days saw 39 people injured by Provisional IRA bombs in towns throughout Northern Ireland. On 30 September another Provisional IRA bomb exploded in a bar on the Shankill Road, killing two men and injuring thirty others. The incident, condemned by the Official IRA, led to sectarian clashes the next day.[62]

Nationalists were angered by allegations that those arrested during the internment operation had been ill-treated, and the Unionist Government was forced to set up a committee of inquiry under Sir Edmund Compton to investigate the charges. The Compton Report concluded that people had not suffered physical brutality but that there had been 'ill-treatment'. It found that although there had not been any torture there had been 'in-depth' interrogation, involving hooding, forcing detainees to stand with their arms against walls for long periods, and the use of 'white noise' and deprivation of food and sleep to cause confusion. While the committee had investigated charges made by forty detainees, only one gave evidence to it.[63]

For the Provisional IRA the value of internment was most striking in its effect on its personnel strength; it claimed that only fifty-six of its members had been interned. During the following few weeks properly integrating new members into the movement and putting them to work caused serious difficulties in several areas; the Provisionals' strength was further increased by Official IRA units coming over.[64] Following the introduction of internment, the Provisionals changed operational tactics and moved from selected bombings to a widespread bombing campaign against previously selected economic targets, with the aim of forcing the security forces to extend their 'saturation policy' to non-nationalist areas, offering more targets. The Provisionals also intensified attacks against the RUC and the Ulster Defence Regiment, who were treated as 'legitimate combat targets, whether on duty or not, armed or not, in uniform or not.'[65]

In response to internment, the SDLP called on Catholics to withdraw from all aspects of public life. Meeting in Dungannon, the SDLP, Nationalist and Republican Labour MPs announced that they regarded internment as 'further proof of the total failure of the system of government in Northern Ireland' and condemned the British Government's actions in 'clearly taking a course of repression.' The MPs called on

all those who hold public positions in Northern Ireland, whether elected or appointed, to express their opposition by immediately withdrawing from those positions and to announce their withdrawal publicly and without delay ... We call on the general public to participate in this protest by immediately withholding all rent and rates. We expect one hundred per cent support from all opponents of internment ...

At a meeting in Coalisland on 22 August 1971, 130 councillors from twenty councils unanimously agreed to withdraw immediately from their elected positions. In Derry thirty prominent Catholics, including the vice-chairman of Londonderry Development Commission, withdrew from their offices in protest against internment. The UDR saw approximately two hundred Catholics withdraw from the force. About a quarter of all Catholic council households, encouraged by the SDLP, participated in a rent and rates strike. To counter the strike the Payment for Debt (Emergency Provisions) Act (Northern Ireland) was passed, granting retrospective powers to Government departments, private landlords and building societies to recoup debts from wages and state benefits.[66]

Opposition MPs met in an 'alternative assembly', called the Assembly of the Northern Irish People, in Dungiven on 26 October 1971. The assembly's failure to make a significant impact was emphasised by the fact that it held only two plenary sessions. It was, however, a moderately successful propaganda exercise, designed, as John Hume explained, 'to demonstrate clearly that a large section of this community has withdrawn its consent from the system of government. No system of government can survive if a significant section of the population is determined that it will not be governed ...'[67]

A survey conducted in 1973 and 1974 among Northern Ireland men aptly demonstrated the polarity of views on internment between Catholics and Protestants. Of the Protestant respondents, 19 per cent agreed that internment was a strong cause of the Troubles, compared with 67 per cent of Catholics. Similarly, only 3 per cent of Protestants were recorded as having had a member of their family or a close friend interned, compared with 34 per cent of Catholics. Activity by the security forces was also more widespread in Catholic areas: only 3 per cent of Protestant respondents had had their homes searched, compared with 24 per cent of Catholics. A survey in 1972, focusing on working-class Catholic political activists, found internment the dominant issue to the exclusion of all others. 80 per cent approved of parliamentary abstention, and 90 per cent favoured the rent and rates strike.[68]

According to Hume, the SDLP were not prepared to sit at Stormont, or to assist in the drawing up of reform plans with the British Government, until the removal of the 'real roots of sectarian discord ... the system of government created by the Government of Ireland Act 1920.' The British army, Hume continued, was now defending Unionist power and privilege, as contained in that system of government.

> British policy in Ireland today is dictated, as it has been since 1912, by the threat of the Right-wing Unionists. There can be no real solution till the British Government face up squarely to this threat ... When the power of the threat is broken, the solution to the Irish question will be remarkably easy.[69]

Austin Currie explained how an important element in shaping the SDLP's response to internment was the attitude of the party itself, and particularly that of the MPs, towards Faulkner; the 'confidence gap' between them and Faulkner was considered 'unbreachable'. Faulkner's close identification with the Orange Order, his 'tricky Dicky' image, his 'shoot to kill on suspicion' speech, and 'occasions ... when he had tried to pull the wool over our eyes,' all contributed to a perception, for the SDLP, that the 'opposite of what he said was taken to be nearer the truth.' The SDLP claimed that the alienation of the non-unionist community embraced not only those who had never identified with the

Stormont system but also those of the professional and business class who had been prepared to play a full part in Northern Ireland's life, particularly under O'Neill. But, said Currie, the alienation was so total that even if the SDLP had wished to talk it would have been impossible; 'but', he later admitted, 'we had no desire to talk … We were committed to ending the Stormont system of government.' By refusing to talk to Faulkner and the British Government, by initiating a civil disobedience campaign and symbolising their rejection of the system through the alternative assembly, the SDLP believed it could 'end internment, end Faulkner and end the System.'[70]

From the Unionist perspective, Faulkner believed that the SDLP had a choice: either to have real and effective participation in Northern Ireland's affairs, with a chance to do genuine constructive work together, or to have the 'instant' politics of exploiting every issue as it arose, without consideration of the long-term effects.[71] Assessing the SDLP's attitude, he argued:

In our country today we sometimes hear from apologists who say, or who imply, that the physical violence we see around us is justified by other things—what they call the 'institutional violence' of the system under which we live … I do not deny that a minority has felt itself to have some grievances. But of what dimension have these grievances been? Has there been persecution so gross that the minority have been driven from the land—or has it on the contrary more than held its place numerically in the total population? As a matter of fact the minority here has increased by almost a quarter during 50 years of so-called misrule and oppression. Compare this with the situation in the Republic where the Protestant minority has, in the same period, dwindled to less than half its former strength. Has its separate religious and cultural identity been ruthlessly suppressed—or has it, on the other hand, been assisted by massive public finance to maintain and expand an extensive system of schools in which that identity has been fostered? … Is every political opponent ruthlessly persecuted or are Opposition Members, who have set up a sham Parliament and encouraged citizens to disregard their obligations to the State, nevertheless free to disseminate their ideas through all the media of communication?

Of course there are people in this and every other community with grievances against the 'system'. There are, alas, many thousands amongst the majority here who are unemployed, or poorly housed … who may well feel … that more should be done for them. But no one has yet suggested that there would be moral justification for them to make a protest in the form of killing or maiming, totally at random, some unfortunate number of their fellow-citizens.[72]

While recognising that, because of the historical political allegiances of Northern Ireland, the 'political minority' had no prospect of coming to power, Faulkner echoed the Unionist belief that 'no one should imagine that this special position gives any minority the right to veto the operation of Government': the majority remained the majority, and the rights of unionists were not to be disregarded. 'We have no wish to dominate or to be unfair,' said Faulkner, 'but if intolerable demands are made of us we shall certainly stand firm and say, "Thus far and no further."' While the Northern Ireland Government was willing to see community progress occur, it was not willing to 'throw overboard everything we stand for.' Faulkner warned against believing that moves on the political front would have the slightest effect on the IRA or their sympathisers, for while it was to be hoped that in the future, when the current wave of terrorism had been 'put down', political progress would help ensure that terrorism did not again take root, in the short term no political initiative would mollify the IRA: the only way to deal with them was to militarily defeat them.[73]

Faulkner appealed to those members of the Catholic community who, for him, seemed to show concern only for their co-religionists to consider whether 'this is not the ultimate in sectarianism.' He described the SDLP's position, influenced by their attitude to internment, as a 'great negative—they won't do this, they won't do that. You in the SDLP have chosen to ride on the back of the tiger,' he accused; 'to use escalating violence as an excuse to escalate your demands.' There were no suggestions in the summer of 1969, he pointed out, for the changes the SDLP now demanded.

In the 'new pattern of government and administration which is now evolving,' claimed Faulkner, the 'keynote will be absolute fairness.' He listed fairness in elections and the drawing of boundaries; control of the new local authorities; fair representation on area boards, committees, and public authorities; fair housing; and machinery for investigating complaints and public employment.[74] He accused those Catholic politicians who 'whipped up anti-Government feeling' of, regardless of their intentions, creating a climate in which gunmen and bombers could count on more passive shelter and support than would otherwise have been the case. These politicians, who he believed were nurturing a 'persecution complex' among vast numbers of the population, 'now look like the sorcerer's apprentice who, having invoked powers beyond his control found that they eventually swept him before them in their path.' The result was that the Northern Ireland community was suffering the horrors of a guerrilla war.[75]

Turning to the Unionist community, Faulkner urged Protestants not to look on every Catholic demand for a 'bigger say in things' as a veiled attempt to undermine the state from within. He remained convinced that a very great number of Catholics would 'like this community, and the politics of this community, to be concerned with bread and butter issues—with the raising of living standards, the creation of better job opportunities for themselves and their children, better houses, better services and so on'—people who wished to participate in the full life of the Northern Ireland community. He warned that 'we as Unionists would be making a great mistake if we did not welcome and foster such a spirit.'[76]

Faulkner accepted that although it was not their responsibility alone that there had been a rigid political polarisation in the community, being in government for an uninterrupted fifty years had created problems for Unionists, and 'we should ask ourselves honestly how much effort we, as a party, have made in the past, not just to persuade our Catholic fellow-citizens that Unionism is the best course for Ulster, but that they really have a part to play in Unionism themselves, not just as voters but as party members, candidates and public representatives.' In Northern Ireland's present state Faulkner admitted that it was not easy to make such changes in practice, but he believed that Unionists had to be clearly seen to be making their party open and welcoming to any good citizen of Northern Ireland.[77] He stressed that 'Catholic' was not synonymous with 'Nationalist' or 'Republican' and that it was of great importance for Northern Ireland's future stability that members of that faith could play a part in government.

> As leader of the Unionist Party, I shall want to satisfy myself that our Catholic citizens are not merely able, but encouraged to join our Party, to participate in its work, and to run for public office on its platform. Indeed I look forward to the day when my Unionist colleagues on [the] Front Bench will be Protestant and Catholic, and no one will ever think it worthy of comment. Neither Unionism nor Ulster will survive in the long run if we take any other course.[78]

This did not mean, however, that Faulkner was prepared to accept Jack Lynch's demand for Northern Ireland ministerial positions to be allocated on a sixty-forty power-sharing basis between Unionists and non-Unionists, with Faulkner calling this 'ridiculous' and vowing that 'no republican will sit in a Cabinet headed by me. To my mind it would be a contradiction in terms to have a coalition in Government of politicians who disagreed on such a fundamental issue as the existence of the constitution of the very State itself.'[79]

Faulkner felt it was necessary to explain the Unionist position directly to the Southern political elite, and he accepted an invitation from Edward Heath to attend a two-day tripartite summit with Lynch at the British Prime Minister's official residence, Chequers, in September 1971. Faulkner attended so as to put two fundamental issues before Lynch. The first was that there was an urgent need for Lynch's Government to clamp down on subversive activity from within the Republic, which, he told Lynch, was ultimately as big a threat to himself as to Northern Ireland. Secondly, he told Lynch how misguided he was in giving even moral support and succour to those, such as the SDLP, who were refusing to play a constructive part in the Northern Ireland community. He felt that the Republic's Government, fed on an 'unremitting diet of biased reports' about Northern Ireland, had stumbled into policy mistakes out of basic ignorance.

Faulkner claimed that the meeting gave him the opportunity to tell the Southern Government that the Unionists were unwavering in their resolve to remain British.[80] He felt that Southern attitudes to Northern Ireland were

the very source of the poison itself—for it is in the South that the whole romantic, violent, blood-stained 'physical force' tradition of Irish Republicanism has its home. Too many of their political leaders have been nurtured in that tradition to break fully free of it; too many have honoured the graves of yesterday's assassins to be wholly resistant to today's. They have shown no ability to understand or sympathise with a million of what they themselves claim to be their fellow Irishmen ... Yet there was another course possible—the course Craig and Cosgrave mapped out in 1925 but which 'ran into the sands' of de Valera republicanism. It is the course of recognising things as they are, without shedding any hope or aspiration that they might one day be otherwise. It is the course of patience, which acknowledged that only mutual good can come out of mutual respect and co-operation.[81]

But the space Faulkner needed in which to even attempt to build a unionism capable of reaching across the sectarian divide stood little chance of being achieved, given the deteriorating security and political situation in Northern Ireland. Unionists felt under pressure from both the Republic and Britain. In November 1971 Harold Wilson, now leader of the opposition, had produced a 'fifteen-point plan' leading to a united Ireland. Faulkner believed that the effects of Wilson's plan were dangerously explosive, by raising the hopes of the Provisional IRA and at the same time increasing the fears of the unionist population and the readiness of the more militant among them to create organisations that could be used to frustrate any future government actions interpreted as giving effect to this plan. From the moment he made this speech Wilson was regarded with suspicion and a lack of confidence by the whole spectrum of Ulster unionism.[82]

THE RISE OF LOYALIST PARAMILITARISM

The sense of siege felt by the Ulster Protestant community from the Provisional IRA campaign, the irredentism of the Republic's Government and the pressure for continuing reforms from the SDLP and the British Government had an impact far beyond the Unionist elite. The fears of working-class Protestants were crystallised in September 1971 with the formation of the Ulster Defence Association, established by the merging of a wide range of Protestant vigilante and paramilitary groups. The UDA's motto was Cicero's *Cedant arma togae*—'Let war yield to peace'—chosen because 'every UDA member considers that LAW properly functioning in a stable community is at all times preferable to a situation whereby LAW is subservient to the machinations of church or … party'; but the law was now 'in disrepute in Northern Ireland because it does not exist in every rook and cranny of our land.'[83] The UDA's long-term aim was the 'DEFENCE of ULSTER against ALL who would destroy her'; its short-term aims were the 'restoration of law and order to every street in N. Ireland,' to 'prevent further disintegration of our society,' and to 'begin rebuilding our Community both materially and spiritually.'

The UDA's aims were to establish an organisation that would be able to take over 'in the event of a complete breakdown of law and order' and to operate as a pressure group to ensure that its policies were 'kept to the forefront of political activity.' Its rules stated that there would be no political activity internal to the organisation: no MPs were to be admitted; there were to be no religious mentors or any direct religious influence, for the organisation was to 'remain secular'. However, it was decided that because of the present situation in Northern Ireland, in which a STATE OF WAR exists, no Roman Catholic can become a member. We state categorically that there are many Roman Catholics who pose no threat to the community, nor would they willingly take part in any activity detrimental to the well-being of the Community. However, since these people have friends/relations in areas under PROVO control, they are subject to pressure and thus pose a security risk ... We do not advocate discrimination against anyone except those who actively seek to destroy our state by MURDER, TERRORISM, INTIMIDATION, and FALSE PROPAGANDA.[84]

The UDA and the older UVF chose the term 'loyalist' as opposed to 'unionist'—terms generally used interchangeably up to this point—with a loyalist now defined as someone who was determined to do his utmost to ensure the continued existence of the state, to safeguard his heritage and his way of life.[85]

The growth of loyalist paramilitarism was related to the increasing levels of violence and the perception that the security forces could not contain violent republicanism. In 1969 the Troubles had claimed thirteen lives—one RUC man and twelve civilians. In 1970 there were twenty-five violent deaths—two RUC men, the rest civilians, many killed in intercommunal violence. But in 1971 there were 174 deaths. Of these, 11 were RUC men, 115 were civilians, and 43 were soldiers.

In 1971 the Provisionals had broadened their campaign by attacking the economic fabric of Northern Ireland. Shops and factories, mainly Protestant, were bombed. There were thirty-seven serious explosions in April, forty-seven in May, and fifty in June. In addition to this, British army bomb disposal units disarmed between 200 and 600 pounds of explosives in every month of 1971. As the level of violence increased, new targets were added when the Provisional IRA began to bomb Protestant pubs. In May, drinkers in the Mountview Tavern on the Shankill Road were seriously injured by a bomb. On 29 September a bomb at the Four Step Inn killed two and injured twenty.[86] There was widespread anger in Protestant working-class areas at the level of violence and the apparent inability of the security forces to deal with it. The UDA News declared:

1. Our Community, the one consisting of Roman Catholics and Protestants, is no longer in EXISTENCE. When the SDLP and their supporters, the Roman Catholics withdrew their support from participation in our ... community they severed the bond between us

… The bond was the love we shared for our native land … for each other's views and traditions …

2. We can no longer afford to be sentimental. We can no longer sustain friendship for nationalists when such friendship is an obstacle to us in the protection and preservation of our community …

3. … As in any war friendships must be set aside. IT'S THEM and US.[87]

For many loyalists the abolition of the B Specials had created a gap in Northern Ireland's defences that the newly formed UDR had failed to fill. The UDA was overwhelmingly working-class and was organised on military lines; at its peak, in 1972, it had a membership of between forty and fifty thousand. The great majority had full-time jobs and played little part in the day-to-day running of the organisation. The hard core were often unemployed and spent much of their time either working for the UDA or frequenting local pubs and clubs. The UDA provided a medium through which the frustrations of young working-class loyalists could be channelled by manning local barricades and taking part in marches and demonstrations.[88]

As the Republican assault on the state intensified, the pressure within Protestant working-class areas to retaliate began to grow. One woman vented her anger in *UDA News*, exclaiming:

I have reached the stage where I no longer have any compassion for ANY NATIONALIST, man, woman or child. After years of destruction, murder, intimidation, I have been driven against my better feelings and the way my mum and dad brought me up to take the decision … IT IS THEM OR US. What I want to know is this, where the HELL are the MEN in our community; have they any PRIDE? Have they any GUTS? Why are they not organised in, not defence, but COMMANDO GROUPS? Why have they not started to hit back in the only way that these nationalist bastards understand. That is ruthless, indiscriminate killing. 'What's that?' some lily-livered Protestant without a backbone is saying 'you can't come down to their level' … To whom does he think he is talking too? I was burned out of Ardoyne where I was born and reared for nineteen years. My brother was run out of New Barnsley. My father's firm was blown up. Now mine. If I had a flame thrower I would roast the slimy excreta which pass for human beings … FROM NOW ON ITS ME AND THEM. WHAT ABOUT YOU?[89]

For many working-class Protestants the conflict was between people who supported the British connection, who were in the majority, their religion being Protestant, and their opponents who wanted a united

Ireland, who were 'adherents of the Roman Catholic Church which unlike its Protestant counterpart fosters and murders the Nationalistic dream.'[90] Many loyalists found it difficult to accept that many in Britain regarded their efforts to repel the enemies of Northern Ireland's place within the United Kingdom as 'un-British'. *Official UDA News* argued in response to a British Cabinet minister calling it 'un-British behaviour' for people in the Shankill to confront British troops by replying, 'We do not profess to be British, we are British,' claiming that it was 'un-British' to allow the deaths and maimings of British citizens, 'un-British' to suspend a democratically elected government, as Stormont was in 1972, and 'un-British' to use British troops to smash a protest by British citizens.[91] The loyalist paramilitaries also reflected a widely held view among the Protestant population, which found it difficult to accept the allegiance of Catholics to what most Protestants regarded as a 'foreign country'. One loyalist asked his 'Catholic Fellow Citizens':

> Can we meet each other halfway? Can we not accept that we have more in common with each other than I have with the English or you with the Southern Irish. Can we not for the sake of our kids accept that we are both citizens of N. Ireland and work from that basis ... Can we not both be proud of being Ulstermen and just leave it at that? ... You must forget any humiliation, real or imaginary, you have suffered; you must forget any discrimination, actual or imaginary ... I must forget that in the past 4 years I have been branded as a bigoted master ... that I have been terribly humiliated by the abolition of the USC, suspension of Stormont, etc.; I must forget that I have been made to eat dirt ... Are the Scots any less Scottish for being part of Gt. Britain and associated with England? Are the Welsh ... less Celtic ... Both of these nations have accepted they are British citizens of the British Isles. We are also British ... Like the Welsh and the Scots, let us put our past behind us and work with our fellow Britains [sic], to secure a better future for ourselves, here in N. Ireland.[92]

Loyalist anger and frustration with the apparent refusal of Catholics to pledge allegiance to the Northern Ireland state, coupled with the increasing Provisional IRA bombing campaign, provided the impetus for loyalist paramilitaries to move towards a systematic campaign of sectarian assassination. Although Peter Ward, a young Catholic barman, had been murdered by the UVF in 1966, it was not until 1972 that loyalist paramilitary murders exhibited a systematic pattern, as opposed to the Protestant mob violence of 1969–1970. An illustration of this was provided by the bombing of McGurk's Bar on 14 December 1971 by the UVF, which had lain largely dormant since 1966, initially identified as an 'own-goal' IRA bomb that had detonated prematurely. The attack killed fifteen people, including three women and two children. The report in the Woodvale Defence Association newssheet illustrated a tendency to equate the entire Catholic community with violent Republicanism:

We would wish it to be known, while sympathy is extended to the families of those killed, it should be noted that these people have never once condemned the IRA. In fact, they claim the IRA would have given a warning. Let us remind those people the IRA gave no warning at the Springfield Road Police Station, where a 30 lb bomb was placed just one foot from children standing in the hallway ... Is it possible that the Roman Catholics believe that the IRA only give warnings when they, the Roman Catholics, are in danger? This is possible, for the hatred they possess for the Protestant Community leaves them blind to everything else, and they will at all times support any organisation or army whose sole purpose is to destroy anything or anyone who is Protestant.

Loyalist attacks on Catholics varied considerably in the amount of planning involved; generally, though, it was very little. No design was formulated among the UVF or UDA leaderships to begin a campaign of killings against Catholics: rather, as one leader of a vigilante group explained, 'We never planned to go on the kill. There was no time when we sat down and said "That's it. Stiff a Taig [murder a Catholic]" ... No, it was ground up. One or two volunteers just started doing it.' Separate teams of 'Ulster Freedom Fighters'—a cover name for the actions of UDA members—did what they liked and claimed responsibility using a code name.

Probably the first loyalist attack on an individual Catholic chosen at random, as distinct from those killed in gun battles, was in April 1970, when an Ardoyne man was shot and wounded on his way home from a pub. The first such fatality was Bernard Rice, a sixty-year-old member of the Catholic Ex-Servicemen's Association, who was shot dead on the Crumlin Road on 8 February 1972. In the next eighteen months over two hundred other murders, mainly against uninvolved Catholics, were to follow. These attacks, justified as revenge for IRA attacks on the state and on individual Protestants and to deter further attacks, were defended by one loyalist, who claimed, 'If we hadn't done something, they'd have been all over us. We had to stop them. Tribal survival. We had to hit back.'[93]

THE IMPOSITION OF DIRECT RULE

The event that eventually came to symbolise the bankruptcy of Stormont, and of British policy in Northern Ireland, was that of 30 January 1972, known as Bloody Sunday. Thirteen men, all apparently unarmed, were shot dead, and seventeen wounded, by members of the Parachute Regiment in Derry. Another man died later.

The shooting began at the end of a banned civil rights march attended by nearly ten thousand people, when part of the crowd tried to climb over a street barrier and were forced back by the British army using rubber bullets and spray from a water cannon. More than a hundred youths threw stones and iron bars at the troops, and a running battle continued for more than ten minutes. It was never established who fired the first shots. Major-General Robert Ford, Commander of Land Forces in Northern Ireland, later denied that the army had fired first and said, 'There is absolutely no doubt that the Parachute Regiment opened up only after they were fired on.' There were counter-claims that a loyalist sniper opened fire as Bernadette Devlin was about to speak to the crowd, while nearly twenty years later a television documentary suggested that members of the Official IRA, acting independently, may have fired on the army. In August 1973 the official inquest recorded an open verdict on those killed.

The events of Bloody Sunday created a wave of anger throughout the Catholic community. In a debate in the British House of Commons, Bernadette Devlin, speaking of the Home Secretary, Reginald Maudling, said: 'The minister got up and lied to the house. Nobody shot at the paratroops, but someone will shortly …' She then ran across the floor of the house and physically assaulted Maudling. In Dublin, during an anti-British demonstration, the British embassy was burned down after being attacked by a mob of more than twenty thousand.

The months after Bloody Sunday were to be no less violent. In late February 1972 a 50 lb Official IRA car bomb exploded at the 16th Parachute Regiment's barracks at Aldershot, England, killing five kitchen staff, a gardener, and a Catholic chaplain. On 4 March 1972 the Abercorn restaurant in Belfast was bombed by the Provisional IRA, resulting in the death of two people and the injury of 130, including two sisters who were shopping for a wedding dress, both of whom lost both legs. On 20 March 1972 six people were killed and more than a hundred injured by a 100 lb Provisional IRA car bomb in Lower Donegall Street, Belfast. The Provisionals had given no warning, but a hoax call had deliberately led shoppers to where the bomb was planted.

The deteriorating situation led the British Prime Minister, Edward Heath, to announce on 24 March 1972 the suspension of the Stormont Parliament for one year, after the Northern Ireland Government refused to accept giving up control of security powers to Westminster. Heath told the House of Commons that the British Government held the view that the transfer of the security powers to Westminster was an indispensable condition for progress in finding a political solution in Northern Ireland.

In his letter of resignation as Prime Minister, Faulkner claimed that the transfer of security powers 'is not justifiable and cannot be supported or accepted by us. It would wholly undermine the powers, authority and standing of this government.'[94] But, as Patricia McCluskey, one of the original members of the Campaign for Social Justice, explained, the perception of the Catholic minority had evolved, between 1969 and 1972, through a dynamic alienation process that had produced the conditions in which Westminster had little option but to impose direct rule.

> The non-Unionist minority, mostly Catholics, began to feel at long last [in 1969], not alone had they new protection but even a chance to prosper under the reluctant New Order ... However as the new system was merely as yet an expression of the will of the Parliament at Westminster, which had set up the state of Northern Ireland, and as the hard-line Unionists in that state were loud in their denunciations of all reforms proposed, the minority, especially in the Catholic ghettos, still remained suspicious and sullen, suffering from the shock and anger aroused by the Unionist mobs who had burned thousands of them out of house and home ... With the advent of a new British Conservative Government there appeared to be changed attitudes. The Unionists 'harder-line' directives went into the Catholic areas to re-establish 'law and order'. Force was met by force ... The army by its inept handling of the situation and its support of the Unionists had now firmly consolidated the position of those in the Catholic areas who refused to 'trust anything in uniform.' This was exactly how the Unionist wanted it to be. The army was now, according to them, and with appropriate support from Westminster, acting in a proper way and doing what every loyalist and Unionist required ... beating the minority back into submission.[95]

The Northern Ireland (Temporary Provisions) Act, 1972, suspended the Northern Ireland Government and vested all powers of the Governor and Government in a newly created Secretary of State for

Northern Ireland. The Act provided that the Northern Ireland Parliament was to stand prorogued and that Orders in Council, having the same validity and effect as Acts of the Northern Ireland Parliament, would have the power to legislate for 'any purpose for which the Parliament of Northern Ireland has power to make laws.' Such Orders in Council had first to be approved by both houses of the Westminster Parliament but, being a form of delegated legislation, could not be amended in either house; provision was also made whereby an Order could become law immediately. As a consequence, minimal parliamentary time was given to the scrutiny of Northern Ireland laws, with policy formulation vested in a non-elected Commission, established by the Act and appointed by the Secretary of State to give 'advice ... on such matters connected with the discharge of his functions.'[96]

The abolition of Stormont created alarm throughout the unionist community. No longer did the Unionist Party or its supporters, after fifty years of power, control the destiny of Northern Ireland. Unionists were fearful of what would happen next. Just before the suspension of Stormont, William Craig, now the leader of Ulster Vanguard, a fringe organisation within the Unionist Party, threatened to form a provisional government, telling a rally of sixty thousand people in Belfast that if and when the politicians failed the unionist community, it might be 'our job to liquidate the enemy.'[97] Motivated by the fear that Northern Ireland was about to be forced out of the United Kingdom, Craig claimed that Ulster would rather 'go it alone' than be absorbed into an Irish republic. He proposed that Faulkner should call a general election and show the British Government what the Protestant majority's feelings were. If Westminster did not like this, then Protestants would oppose any interference, and 'we would hold Ulster in trust as a dominion for the Crown until such time as there are realistic policies.'[98] The first priority for the Vanguard movement would be the restoration of a Northern Ireland Parliament, ideally within the United Kingdom, but if that was not possible then Northern Ireland should have a new constitution outside the United Kingdom. 'We will not be one bit less British for that,' Craig insisted, for the allegiance of the Ulster people was to the Queen, not to the British Parliament, and, 'like our fathers and grandfathers, we will hold this country in trust for the Queen.'[99]

Vanguard represented a call for a return to the 'traditional unionism' of a culturally one-dimensional Protestant British Ulster. The executive committee of Ballymena and District Vanguard Club, while it called for

'A New Society Evolved Based On "Equal Rights for ALL—Special Privileges for NONE",' also declared that 'ALL Loyalists Must Have ONE Faith,' believing that 'All Loyalists believe in God since it is impossible to be a true loyalist and not believe in God. We must have faith to believe that we are now preparing to fight a battle on behalf of Jesus Christ, who will return very soon as "King of all Nations on the face of the whole earth".'[100] A Vanguard Declaration of Intent and Covenant to Act, modelled on the Ulster Covenant of 1912 and distributed at meetings in February 1972, declared:

> We, as loyal subjects of Her Majesty the Queen, Loyalists of Ulster, do hereby declare our intent to maintain Ulster's allegiance to the Crown, our British heritage, traditions and way of life and more specifically to prevent the inclusion of Ulster in the Irish Republic.
>
> In furtherance of this intent it is our preference to maintain our present constitutional position as an integral part of the United Kingdom, having a Parliament of Northern Ireland ... not to be abrogated except by their own consent.
>
> We now solemnly covenant that if this agreement is departed from without the consent of the Parliament of Northern Ireland having a mandate from the people for that purpose we shall assert our right to take whatever action we consider best to safeguard our loyal cause ... such action to include, if there is no alternative, the establishment of an independent British Ulster ... We are firmly persuaded that by no law can the right to govern those whom we represent be bartered away without their consent ... The present United Kingdom Government ... may drive us forth from a Constitution which we have ever loyally upheld, they may not deliver us bound into the hands of our enemies ...[101]

Brian Faulkner, on the other hand, rejected such notions, calling the 'vision of an independent Ulster, self-supporting and self-sufficient ... a myth.'[102] Faulkner believed that the manufacture of a synthetic Ulster loyalty was impossible. The Unionist Party had always existed to safeguard the Union and maintain British citizenship and allegiance to the Crown, and it was not dependent on any feeling of close affinity with any particular race or people. Loyalty, said Faulkner, was the basic factor in Irish politics. 'In Ulster we have conflicting loyalties which have produced a fundamental breach between two political communities. There are those who regard themselves first and foremost as "British", and those who would never accept any other description other than "Irish".' He regarded as impossible any suggestions that these two loyalties could be submerged into one immediate loyalty to Ulster.[103] Faulkner and his supporters actively supported the Union and did not 'merely accept it in a tepid and equivocal manner.' It asserted British citizenship as its 'birthright' and claimed that the Northern Ireland people appreciated a 'common and true bond of identity and friendship with the rest of the United Kingdom.' This meant that the relationship between Northern Ireland and the rest of the United Kingdom 'involves rights and obligations on both sides. Ulstermen have the same right to pressurise and persuade as Scotsmen, Welshmen and Englishmen.'[104]

While the Ulster Protestant community suffered the trauma of losing its parliament, the Provisional IRA, encouraged by the imposition of direct rule, proclaimed 1972 the 'year of victory'. At the beginning of March 1972 the Provisionals announced their terms for negotiations with the British Government:

1. Withdrawal of British troops in the North from the streets to barracks as a prelude to eventual evacuation, coupled with an acknowledgement by the British government of the right of the Irish people to determine their future without interference by that government.
2. Abolition of Stormont.
3. A total amnesty for political prisoners.[105]

Now, with the second of their demands achieved, the Provisionals announced on 22 June 1972 that they would suspend their military activities, provided British forces publicly reciprocated. As a result of this action they hoped there would be meaningful talks between the 'major parties' in the conflict, in their view themselves and the British Government. William Whitelaw, the first Secretary of State for Northern Ireland, agreed to Provisional demands for Republican prisoners to have 'special-category status', allowing them more visits and the use of civilian clothes. At the time Whitelaw believed that the concessions were 'fairly innocuous'; but for the Provisionals this was seen as conceding that their prisoners were prisoners of war. On 7 July 1972 Whitelaw and other British ministers met Provisional IRA members in London. The IRA delegation included Seán Mac Stiofáin, Séamus Twomey, Dáithí Ó Conaill, Gerry Adams (released from detention for the meeting), Ivor Bell, and Martin McGuinness. The Republican delegation demanded that the British Government publicly recognise the right of the people of Ireland, acting as a unit, to decide the future of Ireland and to declare its intention of withdrawing all

British forces from Irish soil, such a withdrawal to be completed on or before the first day of January 1975. Pending such a withdrawal, British forces were to be withdrawn immediately from all 'sensitive' areas. The Republican delegation also reiterated its demand for the release of all political prisoners.

The two delegations clashed over the actions of British troops in Northern Ireland when Whitelaw claimed that troops would never open fire on unarmed civilians, which was forcefully disputed by Martin McGuinness, who recalled Bloody Sunday and the cases of Séamus Cusack and Desmond Beattie in Derry. A fundamental difference between the British and the Provisionals occurred on the question of all-Ireland elections and Irish self-determination. For the British the unit of self-determination was Northern Ireland, while for the Provisionals the whole of Ireland was the unit. Whitelaw brought up the objection that the British Government had several times given constitutional guarantees to the majority in Northern Ireland. This was rejected by the Provisionals, who protested that this guarantee came from the Ireland Act, 1949, passed by the British House of Commons, and 'no act of that parliament could not be set aside by another.' In the Republican view these guarantees 'were not insurmountable problems. All that was required to remove them was a simple majority in the House of Commons.' Therefore, in the Provisionals' view, the solution to the Irish question rested not on persuading the unionist community to accept a united Ireland but on persuading the British to legislate for a united Ireland in the British House of Commons.

Realising that Whitelaw would face opposition from within his own party for such an agreement, the Provisionals were prepared to accept a secret memorandum along these lines, witnessed and entrusted to a person of international standing, such as the Secretary-General of the United Nations. If this was forthcoming they were willing to extend the deadline for completion of a withdrawal by one year, to 1976, giving the British three-and-a-half years to arrange an orderly withdrawal of their forces. They gave the British Cabinet a week to respond to their demands. On the question of the truce, the Provisionals proposed that twenty-four hours' notice should be given by either side before breaking it.[106]

Whitelaw revealed his meeting with the Provisionals to the House of Commons a week later, calling the IRA's ultimatums 'absurd', which no British Government could ever concede. He later wrote that 'the meeting was a non-event. The IRA leaders simply made impossible demands which I told them the British government would never concede. They were in fact still in a mood of defiance and determination to carry on until their absurd ultimatums were met.'

The incompatibility of the two views meant that the two-week truce ended on 13 July 1972, with the death of three soldiers and a civilian; on the following day four civilians and a soldier were also to die. Five days later the hundredth soldier to die in the current phase of the Troubles was shot by a sniper in Belfast, while on 21 July the Provisional IRA set off twenty-six bombs in Belfast, including one in a bus station, killing 11 people and injuring 130, an incident that became known as 'Bloody Friday'; some of the bodies were so badly dismembered that they had to be swept up and collected in plastic bags. Further Provisional IRA bomb attacks in the County Londonderry village of Claudy and at a customs post in Newry in late July and early August left a further seventeen people dead, including three Provisional IRA members.[107]

With the talks between the Provisional IRA and the British Government illustrating the incompatibility of each side's aims, the British Government was made aware that any solution in Northern Ireland was going to involve a long haul. Northern Ireland, unlike the British withdrawal from empire that involved counter-insurgency operations, was not some far-off colony but an integral part of the United Kingdom, a mature liberal democracy. An alternative approach was therefore needed, and the one adopted was the use of the criminal justice system and the concept of the rule of law. This process began in earnest with the Diplock Report, published in December 1972, which was concerned with the problem of dealing with terrorist violence other than by internment. The report marked the advent of a policy in which the use of prosecution through the courts was gradually to replace executive detention in an attempt to bury the distinction between political violence and 'normal' crime. The report provided the basis for the Northern Ireland (Emergency Provisions) Act, 1973, which, although later amended, continued as the basis of anti-terrorist legislation.

At the time when Lord Diplock reported, the problems with the existing system were those of securing arrest, gathering evidence and securing convictions against suspected terrorists in the face of intimidation against witnesses and juries, and the possibility of perverse acquittals by juries. Diplock considered that the problems of perverse acquittals and the intimidation of juries were sufficient to justify the suspension of trial by jury in favour of trial by a single judge in cases involving 'scheduled', or terrorist, offences. The second major recommendation related to the admissibility of confessions obtained from suspects, because of the lack of evidence provided by witnesses, whether as a result of intimidation or of communal support for paramilitaries.[108]

Merlyn Rees, the Labour Secretary of State for Northern Ireland from 1974 to 1976, set up the Gardiner Committee to examine the operation of the Emergency Powers Act, which, when it reported in January 1975, argued that the continued existence of special powers should be limited in duration and scope, with a long-term solution to Northern Ireland's problems requiring social reforms, especially in the fields of housing, community relations, and possibly a Bill of Rights. The Gardiner Committee criticised special-category status, introduced by Whitelaw, claiming that it virtually meant the loss of disciplinary control by the prison authorities. As a result Rees announced the phasing out of special-category status from 1 March 1976; and in 1980 Humphrey Atkins, the incoming Conservative Secretary of State, stopped all new admissions to this category. At the end of 1976 the total of special-category prisoners was more than 1,500; by the middle of 1978 it had dropped to about 800. Prisoners who would normally have been placed in compounds were now put in cells, and eight new blocks, each with a hundred cells, were built at the Maze prison, formerly known as Long Kesh (commonly called the H Blocks, because of their design).[109]

In July 1976 Rees announced the conclusions of the Ministerial Committee on Law and Order, established the previous month. The strength of the RUC was to be increased, and the RUC Reserve was to replace the British army and RUC in operations that required less specialised training, while the Ulster Defence Regiment was to have an increased full-time complement and to take more responsibility for routine security tasks. By the end of 1976 British army strength had been reduced by six thousand from its 1972 level and RUC strength increased by a thousand, while the RUC Reserve was more than doubled, from 1,900 to 4,670. A new Chief Constable, Sir Kenneth Newman of the London Metropolitan Police, was appointed to oversee the new policy of 'police primacy'.[110] The use of locally recruited security forces—the RUC and UDR—in the forefront of the war against paramilitaries was commonly known as 'Ulsterisation', with a concentration on 'normal' policing activities rather than military operations alone.[111] A central element of this new strategy was the policy of returning the primary responsibility for law and order, including security, to the RUC, with the British army now operating in a support role.

POWER-SHARING AND THE SUNNINGDALE AGREEMENT

Politically, with the ending of the 1972 Provisional IRA cease-fire, the British Government moved to find common ground between Northern Ireland's constitutional parties. On 25 September 1972 William Whitelaw called a three-day conference to be held at Darlington in England. The conference achieved little, with only the Unionist Party, Alliance and NILP attending; the SDLP boycotted the conference in protest at the continuance of internment. Despite the boycott, the British Government was aware that the SDLP sought a far greater role for the Catholic community in the government of Northern Ireland. While John Hume had wished to see the abolition of Stormont, he was also worried about the implications of direct rule, which he saw as a return to the system of government established by the Act of Union in 1801. What the SDLP required was a new Northern constitution that would allow all sections in the North to share power.[112] Hume was arguing that there were deeper reasons for unrest in Northern Ireland than the question of civil rights, such as the need for all the community to have a share in decision-making.[113] The main cause of the unrest, according to Hume, was the fact that a large section of the community had never been given an opportunity to participate in the moulding of the society of which they were part.[114]

Taking this feeling into account, in October 1972 the British Government published The Future of Northern Ireland, which set out its thinking on the Northern Ireland question and from which successive Governments have deviated little. It stated that Northern Ireland would remain part of the United Kingdom as long as the majority of people wished it to be so, while a partial transfer of sovereignty, whether geographical (through a redrawing of the border with the Republic) or jurisdictional (such as joint sovereignty between the British and Irish Governments), was excluded. It called for an examination of the nature of any future affirmation of Northern Ireland's constitutional status and of the possibility of cross-border co-operation with the Republic at executive or consultative levels—the so-called Irish dimension.

The Government was lukewarm on the question of the 'total integration' of Northern Ireland into the British political system, such as making direct rule permanent, on the grounds that the majority of political parties there were opposed to it. It argued that this would represent a reversal of the traditions of half a century, impose a new legislative burden on the Westminster Parliament, and be unacceptable to the Irish Government, making co-operation with it more difficult.

The choices laid down relating to the creation of a local body to replace Stormont were a Council (a purely executive authority), a Convention (a limited law-making body), or a Parliament or Assembly (a powerful legislature) and Executive.

The discussion paper described the British Government's concerns in Northern Ireland as threefold. Firstly, Northern Ireland should be internally at peace, because a divided and strife-ridden province was bound to disturb and weaken the whole United Kingdom. Secondly, Northern Ireland should prosper, so that it could contribute to and not detract from the prosperity of the United Kingdom. And thirdly, Northern Ireland should not offer a base for any external threat to the security of the United Kingdom.

So long as Northern Ireland remained part of the United Kingdom, the British Government declared that the Westminster Parliament had to remain the sovereign authority over all persons, matters and things in Northern Ireland, and the ultimate acceptance of that authority had to be a necessary condition of the financial, economic and military assistance from which Northern Ireland benefited as part of the United Kingdom. A recognition of the right of self-determination of the people of Northern Ireland did not exclude the legitimate interest of other parties, however. The discussion paper argued that to say that it would be wrong to terminate the relationship between Northern Ireland and the rest of the United Kingdom against the wishes of a majority in Northern Ireland was not to say that it was for Northern Ireland alone to determine how it should be governed as part of the United Kingdom, since 'its association with Great Britain involves rights and obligations on both sides; it is to say that insistence on membership of the United Kingdom carries with it the obligations of membership including acceptance of the sovereignty of Parliament as representing the people as a whole.'

In the discussion document the British Government made it clear that whatever arrangements were made for the future administration of Northern Ireland they had to take account of the province's relationship with the Republic and that there was an obligation on the Republic to reciprocate. Such an agreement should seek the acceptance of Northern Ireland's present status within the United Kingdom as well as the possibility, compatible with the principle of consent, of a subsequent change in that status, should make possible effective consultation and co-operation in Ireland for the benefit of North and South, and should provide a firm basis for concerted governmental and community action against terrorist organisations. The British

Government declared that it favoured, and was prepared to facilitate, the formation of a Council of Ireland to operate at intergovernmental and interparliamentary level, provided that any Northern Ireland executive might '(a) consult on any matter with any authority of the Republic of Ireland' and (b) 'enter into any arrangements with any authority of the Republic' in respect of any matters transferred by Westminster to the executive.[115]

To reassure Unionists, a border poll, as promised at the suspension of Stormont by Edward Heath, was held on 8 March 1973 but was boycotted by the nationalist community. To the questions 'Do you want Northern Ireland to remain part of the United Kingdom?' and 'Do you want Northern Ireland to be joined with the Republic of Ireland outside the United Kingdom?' 591,820 voters—approximately 58 per cent of the electorate—voted for the union with Great Britain, while 6,463 voted for union with the Republic; 425,800 people—approximately 42 per cent of the electorate—boycotted the poll.

On 20 March 1973 the British Government issued a White Paper entitled *Northern Ireland Constitutional Proposals*. It called for a Northern Ireland Assembly of about eighty members, elected by PR. It was the Government's view that the Assembly's Executive could no longer be solely based on any single party if that party drew its support, and its elected representation, from any one section of a divided community. In effect this meant that Unionists would have to share power with Nationalists at government level. The Secretary of State was to act as a mediator between the parties to discover whether an Executive could be set up that would command 'widespread support' in the community. The White Paper also outlined the policy towards the 'Irish dimension'. After elections to the Assembly the British Government would convene a conference with the Government of the Republic and representatives from Northern Ireland to discuss the acceptance of the present status of Northern Ireland, effective North-South co-operation, and provision for concerted action against terrorism.[116]

The Unionist Party leader, Brian Faulkner, supported the White Paper on the grounds that it offered the only realistic chance of ending the violence, by giving Catholics a stake in Northern Ireland's government. Faulkner called the White Paper a 'constructive document ... Basically it passes the criterion laid down in our *Unionist Blueprint*.'[117] This document had listed three conditions that had to be fulfilled before meaningful North-South co-operation could be achieved. These were the acceptance by the Republic of the right of

Northern Ireland's people to self-determination, translated from a verbal commitment into political and constitutional action; a thorough-going review of extradition arrangements in Ireland, with a preference for Britain and Ireland to be made a common law enforcement area; and the establishment of an Inter-Governmental Council, whose members would be drawn equally from the Northern and Southern Governments, to discuss co-operation in economic and social maters. On the last point the Unionist Party was adamant in its rejection of any attempt by the Republic to interfere in Northern Ireland's internal affairs and its refusal to allow any Council of Ireland to 'become a stage on the road to Irish unity.'[118]

Faulkner recognised that the White Paper fell short in some areas: the names of many of the new institutions indicated a reduced status, the office of Governor was to be abolished, and there was to be no return of security powers. But Faulkner focused on the positive points, such as the winning of the battle for a legislative assembly with greater financial freedom than before and an executive government, which, although not simply committee government supported by other parties, was not necessarily out of touch with the Unionist Party's proposals for a role for 'all reasonable men', which did not necessarily mean one-party government. As for security, Faulkner argued that no assembly could maintain peace, order, and good government; however, in view of the deterioration of security since direct rule it would be wise to let Westminster clear up the mess it had allowed to develop before the Assembly would take on the responsibility for law and order. Faulkner also claimed that the Council of Ireland envisaged in the White Paper was almost identical to that proposed by the Unionist Party, arguing that Ulster's position in the Union was even more secure, in that the consent of the people would be required for any change.[119]

The British Government then introduced the Northern Ireland Assembly Act, 1973, providing for the holding of elections to a single-chamber Northern Ireland Assembly (rather than Parliament) of seventy-eight members, to be elected by PR. Further legislation, enshrined in section 1 of the Northern Ireland Constitution Act, 1973, and known as the 'constitutional guarantee', defined Northern Ireland as the unit of self-determination for deciding whether Northern Ireland was to remain within the United Kingdom.

It is hereby declared that Northern Ireland remains part of Her Majesty's dominions and of the United Kingdom, and it is hereby affirmed that in no event will Northern Ireland or any part of it cease to be part of Her Majesty's dominions and of the United Kingdom without the consent of the majority of the people of Northern Ireland voting in a poll held for the purposes of this section.

The Act renamed existing Government departments and established an Executive consisting mainly of the political heads of these new departments and presided over by a 'Chief Executive Member' (rather than Prime Minister). Section 2 of the Act made the formation of a 'broadly based' Executive the prerequisite for the devolution of legislative power to the Assembly. To ensure a 'strong link between the Assembly and the Executive, to involve majority and minority interests alike in constructive work and to provide for the active participation of all its members,' the Assembly was obliged to establish consultative committees to advise and assist the head of each department in the formulation of that department's policy. The head of each department was also to be the chairman of the relevant consultative committee, which, so far as was practicable, was to reflect in its membership the balance of the Assembly's parties. Section 32 of the Act provided that the office of Governor of Northern Ireland ceased to exist. Matters excepted from the Assembly's jurisdiction were the same as those in the 1920 Act, although controversial matters such as the appointment of magistrates and judges other than those of the Supreme Court, the franchise relating to local and Assembly elections, prosecutions and security policy were also excluded.[120]

Faulkner differed from most commentators in interpreting the new power-sharing scheme as not providing an absolute right for the SDLP to be in government and believing that it was conceivable that an uncooperative SDLP could pave the way for a coalition of the Unionist and Alliance Parties involving elected representatives of the Catholic community. Most important of all for Faulkner was the second clause of the Constitution Act, which stated that the people of Northern Ireland would remain citizens of the United Kingdom unless they decided otherwise in a poll. The border poll was central to Faulkner's attitude to the SDLP, since it was a doctrine of traditional republicanism that Ireland as a whole was a political unit and that only a vote of the whole country was valid in determining the future of any part of it. Faulkner believed that now the poll was in the Constitution Act, any party seeking participation in government would have to accept the validity of a vote of the Northern Ireland people alone, and if the SDLP did so they would be abandoning doctrinaire nationalism for the more practical task of preserving the interests of their supporters and making Northern Ireland a better place for all to live in.[121]

Faulkner also believed that a rejection of the proposals would discredit unionism abroad and in Britain, seriously injuring the position of unionists as citizens of the United Kingdom. In the end the scheme appealed to Faulkner because it guaranteed Northern Ireland's position within the United Kingdom and would, for the first time, secure the support of all three major British parties for the Union. He further considered that it was closer to the Unionist Party's proposals than any of the others; and he was aware, from trips to Britain, of the possibility of being presented with a much less acceptable scheme. His main reservation was the fact that the scheme not did not transfer police powers to the new Executive.

Having come to a decision that they would work with the scheme, Faulkner and his colleagues published a pamphlet entitled *The White Paper: A Constructive Approach*. The section on power-sharing declared:

> We have one important reservation. There can be no place in any new Executive for those who are not prepared to accept the right of the people of Northern Ireland to decide their future by a free vote, to accept that decision and to work for the benefit of the community inside the framework thereby decided …

Faulkner and his supporters adopted the formula that 'we are not prepared to participate in government with those whose primary objective is to break the Union with Great Britain.' This, he believed, would not exclude the SDLP from participating in the Executive, for the Constitution Act laid down an oath for members of the Executive to take:

> I swear by Almighty God that I will uphold the laws of Northern Ireland and conscientiously fulfil, as a member of the Northern Ireland Executive, my duties under the Constitution Act 1973 in the interests of Northern Ireland and its people.

Faulkner believed that this was an oath that no Republican dedicated to the destruction of Northern Ireland could take. 'If any other party is prepared to take this oath in good faith it will provide a starting point for discussion about power-sharing,' he argued; but 'no party can be in government and support rent and rates strikes.' Taking the second clause of the Constitution Act and the border poll together, Faulkner claimed that any politician taking this oath would be supporting that provision.[122]

On 27 March 1973 Faulkner won an important vote in the Ulster Unionist Council, the governing body of the Unionist Party, which turned down a motion to reject the White Paper by 381 votes to 231. On 30 March some of the disaffected minority among the Ulster Unionist Party, led by William Craig, resigned to form the Vanguard Unionist Progressive Party. In June 1973 Faulkner emphasised the difference among Unionists, stating that only those who accepted the party pledge to support the White Paper could be officially endorsed in the forthcoming Assembly elections, with Faulknerites termed 'Official Unionists'. However, the vice-president of the UUC, Rev. Martin Smyth, illustrated the differences within the party when he reassured the 'unpledged' candidates that they would not be disowned by the party.

When, therefore, on 28 June 1973 the elections for the Northern Ireland Assembly were held, the Ulster Unionist Party went to the polls split from top to bottom on the question of accepting the White Paper. The elections saw a 72 per cent turn-out of voters. Twenty-four 'Official Unionists' or Faulknerites were elected, receiving 29 per cent of valid first-preference votes, nineteen SDLP members, with 22 per cent of the first-preference votes, eight Alliance Party members, with 9 per cent, and one NILP member, with 3 per cent. The anti-Faulkner Unionists had a total of twenty-six members, consisting of eight members of Ian Paisley's Democratic Unionist Party with 11 per cent of the first-preference vote; seven Vanguard members with 11 per cent; three West Belfast loyalists with 2 per cent; and eight 'unpledged' Unionists with 9 per cent. Faulkner's Unionists were now in a minority. The death of one Official Unionist and the election of another as Speaker left Faulkner with 21 Assembly members whom he could rely on, against 27 anti-Faulkner Unionists.[123]

On 8 October 1973 the unpledged Unionists within the Ulster Unionist Party, led by Harry West, called for Faulkner's resignation as party leader over the issue of power-sharing. On 23 October the party's Standing Committee gave its support to Faulkner's Assembly members taking part in a power-sharing executive, but only by 132 votes to 105; and on 20 November the UUC turned down a proposal to reject power-sharing by only 379 votes to 369. Harry West, from within the Ulster Unionist Party, and Paisley and Craig outside, were opposed to power-sharing with the predominantly Catholic SDLP, because of its aim of a united Ireland, which it shared with its predecessor, the Nationalist Party. These Unionists believed that the SDLP would seek to destroy Northern Ireland's position within the United Kingdom from within the power-sharing Executive. Paisley stated that his opposition to power-sharing with the SDLP was because 'they claim they want a united Irish Republic … Certainly … not … a united Ireland under the Crown, so the … party are Republicans' and therefore opposed to Northern Ireland's membership of the United Kingdom.[124] Craig contrasted the idea of a coalition government in Britain with the Northern Ireland situation: in Northern Ireland politicians were not simply quibbling about bread-and-butter issues and the everyday problems of running the country but were quarrelling about the fundamental issues and principles that lay behind the state. This division, he argued, struck at the very existence of Ulster as a British community, and the SDLP was still committed to its 'fundamental and primary' objective of creating an all-Ireland republic.[125]

Despite this opposition, the power-sharing Executive managed to take its first faltering steps towards taking power in the province, and on 22 November 1973 the make-up of the Executive was announced. Faulkner was made Chief Executive and Gerry Fitt, leader of the SDLP, Deputy Chief Executive. There were six other Unionist members, five SDLP members, and two Alliance Party members.

Attention now turned to what sort of relationship was to develop between Northern Ireland and the Republic. In talks at Sunningdale in England in December 1973, Faulkner and delegations from the SDLP, the Alliance Party, the British Government and a new Fine Gael-Labour coalition Government in the Republic agreed the formula for the contentious Council of Ireland. A joint British and Irish Government communiqué announced that the Council of Ireland was to have a Council of Ministers consisting of seven members of the Northern Ireland Executive and seven members of the Irish Government and to have 'executive and harmonising functions and a consultative role' but with decisions being made only by a unanimous vote. There would be a Consultative Assembly, with thirty members from the Executive and the same number from the Dáil, having advisory and review functions. There would also be a permanent secretariat to service the institutions of the Council and to 'supervise the carrying out of the executive and harmonising functions and the consultative role of the Council.'

Regarding co-operation on security matters, article 10 of the communiqué promised an Anglo-Irish special commission to discuss amending laws on extradition, the creation of a common law enforcement area, in which an all-Ireland court would have jurisdiction, and the extension of the powers of domestic courts to try extra-territorial offences. Article 15 provided for the Republic and the Executive setting up two Police Authorities, to which appointments would be made after consultation with the Council of Ministers; the Police Authorities would then seek to improve 'community identification with and support for the police services.' Article 5 of the agreed communiqué addressed the question of the Republic's territorial claim to Northern Ireland in the form of parallel declarations by the Irish and British Governments, stating:

The Irish Government fully and solemnly declared that there could be no change in the status of Northern Ireland until a majority of the people of Northern Ireland desired a change in that status.

The British Government solemnly declared that it was, and would remain, their policy to support the wishes of the majority of the people of Northern Ireland. The present status of Northern Ireland is that it is part of the United Kingdom. If in future the majority of the people of Northern Ireland should indicate a wish to become part of a united Ireland, the British Government would support that wish.[126]

THE UWC STRIKE AND THE FALL OF THE EXECUTIVE

With hindsight it seems that the flaw in the Sunningdale Agreement was that those involved had completely different views on what it entailed. Faulkner was convinced that the Ulster Unionist delegation had come off best during the negotiations. Formal co-operation against terrorism had been agreed for the first time, and although the lawyers had not yet produced any agreed means of closing the 'political offence' escape, the Unionists were confident that a high-powered joint legal commission would do so within a few weeks. On the recognition of the constitutional status of Northern Ireland, Faulkner claimed that the achievement had been even more decisive. Unionists, he claimed, had, for the first time since de Valera laid claim to Northern Ireland, achieved a recognition by the Republic of Northern Ireland's right to self-determination within its existing boundaries. They had also received an informal commitment that the constitutional claim would be removed at the earliest opportunity.

The price we had paid for this progress ... lay in the structure of the Council of Ireland. The Council of Ministers had a valuable practical role in formalising co-operating on security and social and economic matters. In a very real sense getting the Dublin Government to treat Northern Ireland representatives as equals on an inter-governmental body underlined their acceptance of partition ... The other appendages of the Council—the Consultative Assembly, the Permanent Secretariat, the executive functions of the Council of Ministers—fell in my mind into the 'necessary nonsense' category. They were necessary to get the co-operation of the SDLP and the Dublin Government. But nothing agreed at Sunningdale infringed on the powers of the Northern Ireland Assembly by which everything would have to be approved and delegated. Given the overwhelmingly Unionist composition of that body and the unanimity rule in the Council of Ministers we were satisfied that the constitutional integrity of Northern Ireland was secure.[127]

The SDLP, however, had a different view of what the Council of Ireland would mean. Paddy Devlin explained that the general approach of the SDLP to the talks

was to get all-Ireland institutions established which, with adequate safeguards, would produce the dynamic that could lead ultimately to an agreed single State for Ireland. That meant, of course, that SDLP representatives would concentrate their entire efforts on building up a set of tangible executive powers for the Council which in the fullness of time would create and sustain an evolutionary process. All other issues were governed by that approach and were aimed generally at reducing loyalist resistance to the concepts of a Council of Ireland and a power-sharing Executive.[128]

The SDLP had in fact made it clear in 1972 that it regarded it as an 'unchallengeable fact' that Northern Ireland was 'inherently unstable'. Any re-examination of the 1920 settlement had to take place, not in a purely Six-County context but in an Irish context. Secondly, the means by which the original settlement was arrived at—the threat of violence by a minority unwilling to accept the wishes of British and Irish representatives at the beginning of the century—was considered essentially undemocratic and placed a question mark over the legitimacy of the Northern Ireland state. Thirdly, the means by which the state's area was arrived at were deliberately based on a sectarian head count, providing a permanent sectarian domination, which was a recipe for permanent instability. Fourthly, those who objected to Catholic ascendancy in the Republic were in reality objecting to the results of partition, which institutionalised the differences between the two main traditions, creating a Protestant ascendancy in the North and a Catholic one in the South, thereby preventing the positive interaction of one tradition upon the other, 'which a unified state would have provided.' Finally, the SDLP argued that in the second half of the twentieth century, at a time when Europe was looking to the future with a vision of ending old quarrels, 'we in this island cannot remain in the seventeenth century ... It is not beyond the wit and ingenuity of the Irish people—all its sections—to devise amongst themselves a means whereby they can live together in peace and harmony.' This required no imposed settlements but agreements freely arrived at without any outside interference.

According to the SDLP, it followed from this that Britain would not again attempt to impose a settlement in Ireland. The key to its role now lay in its making an immediate declaration that Britain believed that it would be in the best interests of all sections of the community in both countries 'if Ireland were to be united on terms which would be acceptable to all the people of Ireland.' Such a declaration would contain no hint of coercion but would make it abundantly clear that 'this is Britain's view and it is one she will positively encourage.' This, the SDLP stressed, was not a demand for immediate Irish unity, because of the inherent problems in its implementation, which would take time and would require the setting up of 'democratic machinery' to resolve. In the meantime an interim system of government for Northern Ireland would be set up that would be 'fair to all sections.' Assuming that Protestant loyalty would remain partly to Britain and partly to themselves as a people, and assuming that Catholics would in general continue to give their loyalty to Ireland, then 'immediate unity' would mean defeat for Protestants and victory for Catholics, while the maintaining of the British constitutional link would mean defeat for Catholics and victory for Protestants. Therefore, the SDLP believed, either path would mean the 'continued existence of political violence by dissident minorities.' Any *interim* system of government would therefore have to give fair expression to those present basic loyalties, including an acceptable system of security and policing that would ensure an effective end to political violence.

The SDLP had proposed that the British and Irish Governments agree on a treaty accepting joint responsibility for an interim system of government, to be known as the 'Joint Sovereignty of Northern Ireland', reserving to themselves all powers relating to foreign affairs, defence, security, policing, and financial subvention. Two Commissioners would act jointly as the 'Representatives of the Sovereign Powers' to sign all legislation passed by a Northern Ireland Assembly, consisting of eighty-four members and elected for four years by PR, to legislate in all matters, including taxation, except those reserved to the sovereign powers. A Chief Executive would be elected by a fifteen-member Executive, elected by PR by the Assembly's members. A Constitutional Court of three judges would hear appeals on constitutional law and pronounce on the constitutionality of legislation referred to them from the Court of Appeal and the Commissioners; the flags of both sovereign states would have equal status; Northern Ireland's inhabitants would have the right to claim either Irish or British citizenship; and there would be no representation in either the Westminster or Dublin Parliament.

> It must be made clear that the translation of the declaration by the British Government on the question of Irish unity into a reality is the most difficult and delicate of all our proposals to implement. The very mention of Irish Unity creates the impression of Catholic victory with which it has come to be associated. It is necessary therefore to make clear from the outset that the unity we seek is an entirely new concept and that the New Ireland that should evolve will be one which will still Protestant fears and will have the agreement and consent of all sections of opinion in Ireland. To achieve this the machinery which will bring it into being must be such as to give full confidence to the Protestant Community … that the kind of Ireland which will emerge will be one, in which their rights are fully and adequately protected and in which they would be subjected to no sectional or sectarian domination and in which they would play a full role.

Accordingly, the SDLP proposed a National Senate of Ireland, which would have equal representation from the Dáil and the Northern Ireland Assembly. The basic function of the Senate would be to plan the 'integration of the whole island by preparing the harmonisation of the structures, laws and services of both parts of Ireland and to agree on an acceptable constitution for a New Ireland and its relationships with Britain.' Although the SDLP visualised no preconceived concept of a New Ireland being placed before the Senate, it concluded that 'we would envisage the emergence of a Parliament for the whole of Ireland.'[129] Clearly, the Sunningdale Agreement sat comfortably with the SDLP's long-term aim of creating a new Ireland by evolution.

While Sunningdale was the basis for raising SDLP hopes of ultimate Irish unity, for many unionists it spelt the end of the union with Britain. Ian Paisley had rejected talks with Whitelaw in November 1973 because anti-power-sharing Unionists were not invited to the

Sunningdale talks. The White Paper had stated that the elected representatives of Northern Ireland's political parties would be invited to the tripartite conference; but the Executive parties and the Irish Government feared that the loyalists would disrupt the proceedings and disclose confidential details. Paisley and Craig were eventually invited, but only to give their views and not to act as participants; this proved unacceptable to them, as they considered it undemocratic.

On 5 December 1973 Faulkner suffered a setback when five of the Ulster Unionist Party's seven Westminster MPs announced their decision to ally themselves with Harry West. The following day six hundred delegates from Unionist Party constituency associations, Craig's Vanguard group, Paisley's Democratic Unionist Party and the Orange Order met to form an umbrella political organisation, the United Ulster Unionist Council. The UUUC criticised the recognition given to Northern Ireland by the Republic's Government in the Sunningdale Agreement as wholly inadequate. Paisley noted that the Irish Government's declaration on the status of Northern Ireland, in article 5 of the agreed communiqué, gave no definition of what the Republic thought Northern Ireland's status was and was separate from the British Government's declaration, which stated that Northern Ireland was part of the United Kingdom. The Irish Government, Paisley pointed out, did not define Northern Ireland's status as a part of the United Kingdom for the simple reason that it would be against the Irish Constitution, which defined Northern Ireland as part of the Republic. Therefore, Paisley said, the Faulknerite claim that the Irish Government recognised Northern Ireland as part of the United Kingdom was false,[130] for 'you cannot recognise Northern Ireland as part of the United Kingdom and then claim Articles 2 and 3 which say that it is part of the all-Ireland Republic. You cannot have both things.'[131]

Paisley went on to sum up how many Unionists regarded the Southern state, from whose side of the border Provisional IRA attacks were often launched and from which Provisional IRA members could not be extradited if they pleaded that their offences in Northern Ireland were 'political'.

> Nothing enrages the Loyalist people more than the fact that across the Border is a safe sanctuary. Yet it is the Ministers of that country who are going to have a say in the running of our police. They would not even defend the police. That country gives sanctuary to the people who shoot the police here and yet they are going to have a say in the running of the police.[132]

But it was opposition to the Council of Ireland that was to seal Faulkner's fate. On 4 January 1974 the UUC rejected the Council of Ireland by 427 votes to 374, and Faulkner was forced to resign as Ulster Unionist Party leader three days later; on 22 January 1974 he was succeeded by Harry West. The British general election of February 1974 saw Faulkner's position further undermined when UUUC candidates won eleven of the twelve parliamentary seats, with 51 per cent of the votes. Faulknerite Unionists polled only 13 per cent of the votes.

Within the new Unionist Party leadership Harry West, James Cunningham, president of the UUC, and Sir George Clark, chairman of the Standing Committee of the UUC, dedicated themselves to 'maintaining our British heritage and citizenship' and stood by the broad principles of the 1972 *Unionist Blueprint*. A significant development in their proposals was that, as Craig had previously argued, they now advocated that the Union's future would be best secured if Northern Ireland were to achieve a federal rather than a devolved status within the United Kingdom, so that any new institution of self-government could not be swept away, as the Stormont Parliament had been. It was now evident, they said, that Northern Ireland's independence within the British constitution needed to be protected by law: 'convention' was not enough after Unionists had been told, from the time of Attlee's tenure as British Prime Minister, that the British Government's view was that no change could occur in Northern Ireland's constitution without its free agreement. West and his colleagues argued that it was Faulkner and his supporters who had deviated from traditional Ulster Unionist Party policy and had gravely misrepresented the attitudes and principles of unionism in their dealings with the British Government.[133]

The view that it was Faulkner who had departed from 'traditional unionism', and the confusion this caused for many Unionists, was summed up in the Orange Order's *Orange Standard*, which argued that even the term 'unionist' had recently changed its connotation for many. Previously it was one that stood for the union of Britain and Northern Ireland on religious, social and political grounds and the refusal to accept that the Republic had any right to involve itself in Ulster's affairs. Now, for some, a 'unionist', while determining to maintain the British connection, could recognise Southern involvement in Ulster's business, at least to the extent of sharing views and acting together with the Republic on matters of common interest in a council with executive powers. The *Orange Standard* described the differences between 'traditional unionism' and '1973 Constitution Act unionism' in one word: 'irreconcilables!' The attitude of the Grand Lodge of Ireland was distaste for the Executive in its 'alliance of unionism and republicanism, and our abhorrence of a Council of Ireland as envisaged by Sunningdale.'[134]

A former Stormont MP, Professor Kennedy Lindsey, summed up the fear the Council of Ireland held for anti-Faulkner unionists when he argued that it was to be the main instrument for bringing about Irish unification through the gradual transferring of powers to it. The 1973 White Paper, he claimed, had laid down that a prime objective of the council would be the possibility of a subsequent change in Northern Ireland's status; therefore, the mere existence of the council 'with such an objective' was an admission that Ulster's place within the United Kingdom was not conceded permanent recognition by either Westminster or Dublin. This, he said, would be a permanent monument to the Provisional IRA campaign and an incitement to new campaigns. The representatives of a Northern Ireland Assembly, it was argued, would have little more standing than those of a county council and, with inadequate or hostile Westminster backing, would be in no position to negotiate on equal terms with an independent 'alien power' determined to discredit and absorb it. Furthermore, the Council of Ireland would be an admission that the Republic had an interest in Ulster beyond that which could be claimed by a 'normal foreign state' and would give the Republic an ill-defined right to pose as protector of the 'Ulster rebel minority'. Would Westminster, asked Lindsey, have the will or the inclination to stand against the Republic as a 'recognised interested party'?[135]

Elsewhere in the Ulster Protestant community, loyalist paramilitaries reacted to Sunningdale by forming an Ulster Army Council, an umbrella paramilitary group offering support to loyalist politicians who opposed the Council of Ireland. The UVF's publication Combat believed that 'one does not have to be a genius to realise that within ten years, or less,' the elements of the Council of Ireland would be used 'as the structure for a 32 County Parliament for a United Irish Republic.' In the meantime it would 'act as a provisional Parliament pending the total reunification of the island.'[136]

On 23 March 1974 the Ulster Workers' Council, a new loyalist group, threatened civil disobedience unless new Assembly elections were held. The UWC constitution described it as a non-violent organisation, not aligned to any paramilitary group or political party, firmly believing in loyalist unity and willing to work with any other group to 'obtain a secure future for Ulster.' It sought to embrace the aspirations of all sections of loyalist workers and was pledged to 'fight Irish Republicanism and all forms of Communism.' Among the objects of the UWC were:

(a) To promote and maintain the allegiance of Northern Ireland (Ulster) to the British Throne and Succession and to preserve the union between Ulster and Gt. Britain, the same being based on the consent of the parties thereto.

(b) To maintain Ulster's relationship with the British Commonwealth of Nations.

(c) To seek the restoration in Ulster of democratic institutions designed to preserve the British heritage.

(d) To oppose and resist all attempts to assimilate, or merge Ulster with the Irish Republic.[137]

On 15 May 1974 the UWC called for a general strike, which began with power cuts and the closure of factories, such as the Harland and Wolff shipyards. The strike was run by a co-ordinating committee of between thirteen and fifteen members, chaired by Glen Barr of the UDA and Vanguard and including the party leaders Paisley, West, and Craig. The head of the UDA, Andy Tyrie, and the head of the UVF, Ken Gibson, were also among the leaders. A system of passes was issued by the UWC so as to maintain essential services by allowing those employed in them to reach their work and to cross the barricades set up by paramilitaries.

Then, on 17 May 1974, twenty-two people were killed and over a hundred injured when three car bombs exploded in Dublin; five more were killed and twenty injured by a car bomb in Monaghan. Both the UVF and the UDA denied responsibility for the atrocities, and it was to be twenty years before responsibility was admitted by the UVF. As Northern Ireland was brought to a standstill and loyalist paramilitaries erected barricades and intimidated workers from entering their place of work, Harold Wilson, returned as British Prime Minister in the general election and underestimating the groundswell of Protestant support for the stoppage, made a television and radio broadcast describing the strike as a 'deliberate and calculated attempt to use every undemocratic and unparliamentary means.' He went on to state that many in Northern Ireland were 'sponging on Westminster and British democracy.'

That remark in itself was enough to drive Protestant doubters into the arms of the strikers, and Northern Ireland became ungovernable. On 28 May 1974, with the new Labour Secretary of State, Merlyn Rees, unwilling to deploy British troops against workers, Brian Faulkner resigned as Chief Executive, on the grounds that the degree of consent required to support the Executive did not exist at that time. He recommended to Rees that negotiations between the UWC and the Northern Ireland Office should take place; Rees declined to accept this proposal. The administration of Northern Ireland then reverted to the Secretary of State, and on 30 May 1974 the Assembly was prorogued; it was officially dissolved in March 1975.[138]

THE CONSTITUTIONAL CONVENTION

After the failure of Sunningdale, the British Government announced in July 1974, in another White Paper, that legislation would be introduced to provide elections for a Constitutional Convention, which would throw the responsibility for finding a constitution for Northern Ireland on Northern Ireland's elected representatives. The Government, however, set certain conditions that had to be met. Firstly, there had 'to be some form of power-sharing and partnership because no political system will survive, or be supported, unless there is a widespread acceptance of it within the community'; therefore 'there must be participation by the whole community ...' Secondly, as Northern Ireland shared a land frontier with the Republic, any political arrangements 'must recognise and provide for this special relationship. There is an Irish dimension.'

The Northern Ireland Act, 1974, reintroduced direct rule and provided for this Constitutional Convention. The elections to the Convention, held on 1 May 1975, had a 66 per cent turn-out, with the UUUC winning 55 per cent of first-preference votes and 47 seats. The SDLP won 17 seats with 24 per cent of the first-preference votes, the Alliance Party eight seats with 10 per cent, Faulkner's Unionist Party of Northern Ireland five seats with 8 per cent, and the NILP one seat with 1 per cent.

During the Convention the UUUC recommended that Northern Ireland remain an integral part of the United Kingdom, represented in the United Kingdom Parliament but administered by an assembly and an executive empowered to legislate and govern. Any new Northern Ireland parliament would have the same powers as those in the Government of Ireland Act, 1920, including those relating to law and order. Although the UUUC rejected the use of PR in elections, it claimed that 'consideration' could be given to ways in which representation could be given to 'significant' but 'scattered' minorities.

Government power-sharing was rejected, and instead a parliamentary system of backbench committees would be established, to 'make parliament and opposition more effective,' covering each department of government. The committees would consist of eight or ten members drawn equally from government and opposition supporters. In addition, the committees would be empowered to scrutinise all the activities of their departments, and each committee would be involved in the process of legislation relating to its department.

The UUUC proposed that a Bill of Constitutional Rights be enacted, whereby the existence and the powers of a Northern Ireland parliament would be entrenched and Westminster legislation could not be passed affecting either without the prior consent of the parliament and people of Northern Ireland. On the issue of external relations, (*a*) it would be the responsibility of the British Government, in consultation with the Northern Ireland Government, to ensure that Northern Ireland's interests were adequately represented in international affairs; (*b*) any proposed institutionalised association or other constitutional relationship with the Republic was rejected; (*c*) the security problem, which was considered to stem from the policy pursued by successive Governments of the Republic, could best be remedied by an extradition treaty; and (*d*) economic problems common to Northern Ireland and the Republic might be tackled by both Governments, separately but working together, on schemes of mutual benefit, although not in the form of a joint institution such as the Council of Ireland.[139]

The UUUC policy position emphatically rejected what it regarded as a system of executive government or power-sharing at government level, which was in essence 'an imposed or compulsory' coalition of political parties or elected representatives. It believed that a multi-party government could come into existence

(i) By agreement between Parties before an election and [if it] obtains approval from the electorate.

(ii) Where the largest Party in Parliament has not an overall majority and needs to obtain it by agreement with another Party. At best this can only be a short term government.

(iii) Where an emergency or crisis situation exists and parties by agreement come together in the national interest for the duration of the crisis.[140]

The SDLP, in contrast, argued that a new approach was needed, not one that had ulterior ultimate objectives but one that, while respecting and recognising the aspirations and culture of each tradition, allowed for the freely agreed evolution of both institutions and attitudes, which, in the end, would produce a 'normal political society' based on egalitarian principles. In the SDLP's view, only the 'path of partnership' between the two traditions and between both parts of Ireland would lead to this. The SDLP accepted that there was a 'British dimension', which was the declared wish of a majority of Northern Ireland people to remain part of the United Kingdom. But, argued the SDLP, membership of the United Kingdom had its duties as well as its rights and implied accepting the will of the British Parliament and the rights of all other United Kingdom citizens, including those of the minority in Northern Ireland.

During inter-party talks with the UUUC leadership on 27 August 1975, the SDLP set out five principles on which its policy was based.

1. Maximum devolved power to Northern Ireland Assembly and Government. All sections of the community represented at Government level.

2. Institution freely agreed between North and South.
Responsibilities:
a. Development of agreed matters of common concern in socio-economic field.

b. Standing agreement on security between North and South to be activated when the State of Emergency is declared in either part. Small North/South Security Council to implement and oversee the agreement and to operate only during state of emergency.

3. Policing powers to be devolved to the new administration.

4. Support for the new institutions to be fully given by all sections in Northern Ireland expressed through a referendum.

5. Request to South to give full support to institutions by means of a referendum of the people.[141]

The SDLP thought that the UUUC document, while championing the Westminster model of government, missed three significant aspects of the British tradition and parliamentary system that did not suit the Northern Ireland situation:

(a) the Swing of the Pendulum, which means that the Opposition of to-day can expect to be Government of to-morrow.

(b) a tradition of empiricism which ensures that the system is constantly adapted to meet the changing needs of society.

(c) a tradition of compromise which means that the political parties attempt constantly to find political accommodations.[142]

During inter-party talks between William Craig's Vanguard and the SDLP, Craig indicated a preference for a constitution based on the 1973 Act, or a 'Voluntary Coalition', with safeguards to prevent arrangements being unilaterally terminated. Craig believed that there was a real possibility that the electorate would support a coalition government if it worked well.[143] He had come to the conclusion that there could not be devolution of government at any level unless it enjoyed the consent of a 'very great majority' of the community: a simple majority was not enough. He felt that direct rule was not going to inject a feeling of confidence and stability into the province, and he feared that there could be an increase in IRA activity, motivated by a belief that the British Government was going to yield to them. If that state of affairs were to continue, then he feared that loyalist paramilitary capacity would increase, which would be a recipe for 'explosion rather than stability.'

Crucially, Craig now accepted that the SDLP 'has satisfied me … and, I think, the great majority of the people that it is prepared to accept the decision that Ulster remains inside the United Kingdom for as long as the majority of our people want that.' Craig considered this a 'big step forward' for the SDLP, as it recognised the will of 'our people' to maintain the Union. With regard to the SDLP's aspiration for a united Ireland, Craig recognised its right to work towards this aspiration but thought that until such time as there was a democratic decision to change the current position of Northern Ireland within the United Kingdom, full honour and support had to be given to all the institutions of the state. It was therefore unreasonable to talk of power-sharing in the sense of a condominium or joint authority, as the SDLP had previously argued for. Craig wanted SDLP members to make it clear that when they were talking about institutionalising the relationship with the Republic they were not trying to create any sort of constitutional device in the form of an all-Ireland set-up. If this was left unclarified in the minds of the majority community, he warned that fear and suspicion could inhibit any worthwhile developments.[144]

But Craig's idea of a 'voluntary coalition', which was rejected by the UUUC, left him isolated. A resolution by Ian Paisley against 'republicans taking part in any future cabinet in Northern Ireland' was passed by 37 votes to 1, only Craig voting against. He and his three supporters in the Convention were then expelled from the UUUC. The UUUC report was endorsed by the Convention by 42 votes to 31. This proved unacceptable to the British Government, which dissolved the Convention. There would not be another serious effort by the British

Government to politically address the Northern Ireland problem for another decade.

5

The Long War

1976–1996

Since March 1972 Northern Ireland has been governed by a Secretary of State, who is a member of the British Cabinet, assisted by several ministers. The Northern Ireland Office was also created at that time, taking over the law and order functions of the Northern Ireland Ministry of Home Affairs and the responsibility for giving general advice to the Secretary of State on the political situation. Direct rule was seen as a temporary measure until a restructured devolved government could be returned to Northern Ireland. However, the inability of the warring parties to find an acceptable political settlement led to the gradual entrenchment of direct rule as the least unacceptable form of government for Northern Ireland.

In 1976 the Department of the Civil Service was separated from the Department of Finance, renamed in 1982 the Department of Finance and Personnel. The Department of the Civil Service was dissolved and its main function transferred to the Department of Finance and Personnel. In addition, various functions of the Department of Finance were transferred to other departments. Six new departments were also created: Economic Development, Environment, Education, Health, Social Services, and Agriculture. The four categories of expenditure within the responsibility of the Secretary of State were law and order and protective and other services provided by the NIO; social security benefits; certain national agricultural support schemes transferred to the Department of Agriculture; and other expenditure by Northern Ireland departments.[1]

Local government in Northern Ireland remained the poor relation of central government and was significantly different from the system operating in Britain. The Macrory Report in 1970 had established twenty-six district councils (some since renamed city or borough councils) and the creation of appointed area boards to decentralise the administration of education services. The recommendations were subsequently passed into law by the Local Government (Northern Ireland) Act, 1972.

Macrory's proposals were, however, superseded by the abolition of Stormont in 1972. The responsibility for regional services now rested with the British Government under direct rule, working administratively through the NIO. From this point on the functions of district councils were confined principally to certain regulatory services, for example the licensing of cinemas and dance halls, building regulations, environmental health, and the provision of a limited range of services such as street cleaning, refuse collection, cemeteries and crematoria, and amenities. The two main functions of health services and of education and public libraries were operated through area boards, on which there was local council representation. The result was a one-tier system of local government, with regional services provided by boards accountable to British ministers, largely through nominees rather than elected representatives.[2]

The democratic deficit in local government was also reflected at the parliamentary level. On a small number of matters Northern Ireland was legislated for at Westminster in the same way as the rest of the United Kingdom—by a full Act of Parliament; the great majority of its laws, however, took the form of Orders in Council, a type of delegated legislation. What was dealt with by way of Order in Council for Northern Ireland would be dealt with by way of an Act of Parliament for the rest of the United Kingdom. They could not be amended by Parliament but had to be accepted or rejected in their entirety. Furthermore, parliamentary debate on the principle contained in the Orders in Council was severely limited, lasting approximately two to three hours.[3]

In effect, central government dictates the policy process and the allocation of resources and services in Northern Ireland. Certain features of public spending stand out. For example, the growth of dependence on benefits, linked to increasing unemployment, meant that between 1973/74 and 1987/88 social security spending grew in real terms by 102 per cent. Equally, continuing political unrest guaranteed that expenditure on law and order would also rise disproportionately. A further distinctive feature has been the endurance of a form of corporatism, a product of the nineteen-seventies Labour Governments. Throughout the seventies a number of new institutions were established to assist in the industrial development process. The Local Enterprise Development Unit was established in 1971 to provide a channel for assistance to small firms, normally in the manufacturing sector, and in rural areas to redress the eastern bias of overseas investment, although the LEDU's remit was later extended to cover the service sector and small-firm development in the greater Belfast area. The Northern Ireland Finance Corporation was established in 1972 to provide loans, guarantees and equity capital to industrial undertakings threatened with contraction or closure but with good prospects of long-term viability. The replacement of the NIFC with the Northern Ireland Development Agency in 1976 represented a broadening of the scope of the agency, following on Scottish and Welsh precedents. The NIDA was established with a strong investment banking function, with a remit to set up state industries, to improve and strengthen Northern Ireland's firms, to encourage joint ventures, to acquire licences and patents and introduce these to firms in Northern Ireland, and to facilitate the reorganisation, modernisation or, if necessary, orderly running down of an undertaking or industry. In 1982 the NIDA was in turn replaced by the Industrial Development Board, whose main strategy was the revitalisation of home industries, the sharpening of industrial skills, particularly in marketing, research and development, and technology transfer; and the better identification of foreign investment activities.[4]

Despite these efforts, unemployment remained a perennial problem. In 1974 unemployment reached a post-war low point of 5 per cent, but this was short-lived. The numbers unemployed doubled between 1970 and 1979 and doubled again between 1979 and 1982. Thereafter the rate stabilised and showed signs of decline in the nineteen-nineties. Northern Ireland nevertheless retained its place at the top of the United Kingdom unemployment league, with 14 per cent, compared with an average of 10 per cent, although this was lower than that of the Republic. Long-term unemployment was now assuming major significance, with the proportion of those unemployed for more than one year increasing from 30 per cent in 1979 to over 53 per cent by 1994. The corresponding figures for the United Kingdom as a whole were 25 per cent and 38 per cent. 18 per cent were unemployed for five years or more, compared with 4 per cent in the United Kingdom as a whole.[5]

From the nineteen-sixties onwards two related factors have been significant in the productive base of Northern Ireland's economy. The first was the long-term contraction in areas of traditional employment such as agriculture, engineering and shipbuilding, and linen manufacture. The numbers employed in manufacturing, for example, have halved since 1950. Secondly, structural reliance on declining industries is accepted as the reason for Northern Ireland's loss of manufacturing employment and poor economic position vis-à-vis the

United Kingdom. By 1991 the shipbuilding and engineering industry and the textiles and clothing industry accounted for only 30 per cent of manufacturing industry, compared with 62 per cent in 1971 and 77 per cent in 1952.

Control of the main manufacturing sectors has also passed out of local hands. By the nineteen-sixties the linen industry had almost disappeared, to be replaced by short-lived transnational investments in synthetic fibre production, dominated by firms such as ICI, Courtauld, and Enkalon; the recessions of the seventies, the oil crisis and cheap labour in non-industrial countries ended this investment. Shipbuilding firms, such as Short's and Harland and Wolff, lost jobs on a large scale and had to change ownership, often with large state assistance. It was also estimated that the Troubles, in the period 1971–1983, prevented the creation of about forty thousand extra manufacturing jobs.[6]

From the early seventies Northern Ireland has increasingly become a state-dependence economy. Public service employment and public expenditure rose dramatically. There was large-scale growth in employment in the public sector and in security employment for Protestant males. Employment in service industries rose from 53 per cent in 1973 to 69 per cent in 1991.[7]

Economics have also had knock-on effects in the basic political divisions in society. Social and economic factors appear to have contributed to Catholic alienation during the period of the present Troubles, particularly in fuelling the perception among Catholics that they are unfairly discriminated against. In 1971 it was found that there were three main ways in which Catholics were disadvantaged. Firstly, they were somewhat more likely than Protestants to be low in the socio-economic scale. Secondly, within each class there was a tendency for Catholics to cluster in the lower reaches, Protestants in the higher ones. Thirdly, Catholics were more likely to be found in industries with lower status and more unemployment, such as construction, while Protestants tended to be found in industries such as engineering, which ranked higher in pay and prestige.[8] The greatest gap between Protestants and Catholics was in unemployment rates. The 1971 census showed that Catholic males were 2.6 times more likely to be unemployed than Protestant males. The 1981 census revealed that little had altered and that Catholic males were still 2.4 times more likely to be unemployed.[9]

Controversy has raged over the reasons for such differences, particularly in unemployment levels. Discrimination is one factor suggested; others have been the existence of an informal or word-of-mouth network of recruitment, which benefits Protestants more, since they were more likely to be employed than Catholics. Other reasons suggested have been demographic factors, such as the fact that Catholics were more likely to live in peripheral areas of Northern Ireland, where employment was harder to obtain; that Catholics were more likely to be unskilled; and that Catholics were more likely to have large families, a characteristic that, for a variety of reasons, is associated with unemployment. The Standing Advisory Commission on Human Rights added other factors to the debate, such as the black economy, the reluctance of Catholics to join the locally recruited security forces, and the 'chill factor'—the impact of intercommunal hostility and fear, where members of one community are often reluctant to take up work in a work-place dominated by the other community or to travel to work through territory dominated by the other community.[10]

To combat discrimination in employment, in 1976 the British Government established the Fair Employment Agency, which at first concentrated on individual complaints of discrimination by employers. But relatively few complaints were made, and it was difficult to establish that there had been any deliberate discrimination. During the nineteen-eighties the agency shifted the focus of its work to more general investigations of patterns of employment in the principal sectors or firms, notably the civil service, other public sector employers, the universities, banking, and some large engineering firms. In almost every case it was found that more Protestants were employed than would have been expected and that some of the practices of employers were failing to give full equality of opportunity to Catholics.

The results of this external monitoring, particularly with regard to the civil service, persuaded the Government that more could be done by all employers to provide equality of opportunity if they were obliged to monitor the composition of their own work force. Under an amending Fair Employment Act, 1989, a formal obligation to this effect, supervised by a strengthened Fair Employment Commission, was imposed on all employers with more than twenty-five employees. The practical result is that, though there are no formal quotas for the numbers of Protestants or Catholics in any work-place, there is a considerable pressure on employers to take action to secure a reasonable balance. One of the achievements of the FEC has been to make it no longer acceptable in business circles to regard open or covert discrimination as either acceptable or unavoidable.[11]

There have been some changes in Catholic-Protestant employment patterns. In 1995 the annual report of the FEC noted that while Catholics were underrepresented in the work force, the gap had closed:

63 per cent of the work force was Protestant and 37 per cent Catholic, compared with 65 per cent and 35 per cent in 1990, while Catholics made up 40 per cent of those available for work.[12] From 1990 to 1996 the Catholic proportion of the work force had risen by more than 2 per cent. Catholics, however, were still twice as likely to be unemployed.[13]

The most spectacular change has been in the number of Catholics employed in the public sector. The pre-partition pattern suggests substantial Catholic underrepresentation as administrators and managers and in many of the core occupations of an expanding industrial society. By 1971 the basic pattern might be considered to have remained unchanged. After the introduction of direct rule, numbers in the public sector increased substantially, and responsibility for the principal social services was transferred from local authorities to the newly created Housing Executive, health and personal services boards, education and library boards, and the Northern Ireland civil service. While only twelve thousand people were employed by the civil service at the end of the nineteen-sixties, this had more than doubled by the middle eighties. By 1991, 50,657 Catholics worked in the public services, representing 36 per cent of all such employees, or 40 per cent if security occupations were omitted. Public employment represented 28 per cent of all economically active Catholics in employment. By the early nineties, therefore, just over 1 in 4 employed Catholics were employed in the public sector, representing over a third of employees. Catholic representation in senior public sector posts was 24 per cent in 1991—lower than Catholic public sector representation as a whole but a substantial advance in twenty-five years.[14]

There is a direct and obvious link between employment patterns and general levels of household prosperity. If there is greater unemployment in the Catholic community it is to be expected that Catholic households would have lower incomes than Protestant households. But equally significant differences in relative wealth and poverty are to be found within rather than between the two communities. The basic figures for gross household income show that while in 1987/88 the average household income, at £225 (sterling) per week, was far below the United Kingdom average of £270 per week, it was roughly the same as that for Scotland (£234), Wales (£228), the Republic (£220), and the north of England (£220). The equivalent figures for 1992 showed that the Northern Ireland average of £281 lagged somewhat behind those in the same regions (Scotland £314, Wales £295, north of England £285), but not appreciably.

The overall figures for Northern Ireland, however, conceal a substantial difference between those households that were recorded as Protestant, as Catholic, and as neither. The figures for 1988 indicated an average income for Protestant households of £228, compared with an average of £185 for Catholic households and £247 for those not allocated to either. The figures for 1990 showed no such disparity between Protestant and Catholic households (£253 each), while the unallocated households remained substantially better off (£324). The figures for 1992, however, showed a continuing though smaller differential, with an average income for Protestant households of some £290, compared with £264 for Catholic households and £308 for unallocated households. The resulting income per person is further affected by the fact that the average Protestant household of 2.7 people in 1988 and 2.5 in 1992 was slightly smaller than the average Catholic household of 3.3 people in 1988 and 3.2 in 1992.

But prosperity in Northern Ireland, as elsewhere in the United Kingdom, is unevenly divided within both communities, and the differences within each community are far greater than those between them. In 1987/88 the Northern Ireland figures of 13 per cent for the highest income group (over £400 per week) and 32 per cent for the lowest income group (less than £100 per week) were not appreciably different from those for Scotland, Wales, and the north of England.

Figures for Protestant and Catholic households in Northern Ireland show a similar widespread distribution, though there were, by a few percentage points, more Protestant households in the most prosperous group and a few less in the least prosperous group. In 1986/87, 30 per cent of Protestant households were in the lowest group (less than £4,000 per year) and 16 per cent in the highest (more than £15,000 per year), compared with 39 per cent and 9 per cent, respectively, of Catholic households; in 1988–1991 the equivalent figures for Protestant households were 27 per cent and 23 per cent, compared with 30 per cent and 17 per cent for Catholic households.[15]

The place of women in Northern Ireland's economic structure dramatically altered during the period of direct rule, assisted by the expansion of the service industries. From 1952 to the nineteen-nineties the female proportion of employees increased from 36 per cent to over 48 per cent in an expanded work force. Two crucial qualifications are needed, however. Firstly, women were concentrated in a very limited number of sectors and in low-paid, frequently part-time jobs in the service sector; secondly, although women's participation in the labour force increased, it remained below that of men. One of the more dramatic changes has been the increase in the number of married women in employment. In 1961 just under 30 per cent of married women had a paid job, compared with 59 per cent by the nineteen-eighties.[16]

Since 1971 there has been a significant change in the demographic pattern towards a more rapid growth in the proportion of Catholics in the population. Between 1926 and 1961 the balance in each of the six counties had remained remarkably stable, despite a substantially higher birth rate in the Catholic community. In that period many more Catholics emigrated to Britain and further afield to find jobs. Since 1971 the proportion of Catholics has increased from at least 33 per cent in 1971 to at least 40 per cent in 1991. This increase was probably due to a continuing higher birth rate among Catholic families compared with Protestant families and, in part, to a relative decline in emigration among Catholics.[17]

In political solidarity the two communities are more clearly defined and stable in their allegiances than those in comparable divided societies in Europe. About 85 per cent of those who vote regularly give their first preferences to parties that are clearly identified as Catholic or nationalist or as Protestant or unionist and only about 15 per cent to parties that promote themselves as intercommunal. In the 1992 Westminster election the main Unionist parties secured 50 per cent of the vote, the main nationalist parties 34 per cent, and other parties 15 per cent; in the district council elections of 1993 the equivalent figures were 49 per cent for the main Unionist parties, 34 per cent for the main nationalist parties, and 9 per cent for the centre parties.

The first significant trend is the gradual increase in the nationalist block. During the seventies the unionist block regularly accounted for about 60 per cent of the total vote, compared with between 25 and 30 per cent for the nationalist block and about 12 per cent for other parties. Though the centre block remained relatively stable, by the nineties there had been a significant shift of some 5 to 10 per cent from the unionist to the nationalist block. The main reasons for this were the increase in the proportion of Catholics in the population and the re-emergence of Provisional Sinn Féin as the organised voice of republicanism. A second significant feature has been the shifting of support among committed unionists between the Unionist Party and the DUP. In times of political crisis the DUP has been able to increase its support from its base of about 15 per cent to some 20 per cent and in European Union elections—in which Northern Ireland is a single constituency and Ian Paisley has been able to capitalise on his personal popularity—to about 30 per cent.[18]

The second half of the nineteen-eighties saw a fundamental change in Government policy on community relations, characterised by a number of features. Firstly, a clear and explicit community relations policy was established, which emphasised three objectives: (*a*) to increase opportunities for contact between Protestants and Catholics; (*b*) to encourage tolerance of cultural pluralism; and (*c*) to seek to achieve equality of opportunity for all citizens in Northern Ireland. Secondly, a community relations infrastructure was re-established with the creation of the Central Community Relations Unit in 1987 within the Central Secretariat of the Northern Ireland civil service and the creation of the Northern Ireland Community Relations Council in 1990. Thirdly, new legislation to combat discrimination in employment and a set of education reforms came into effect in 1990.

A number of factors influenced these policies. At a political level there was the political rise of Sinn Féin, the failure of the Northern Ireland Assembly's attempt at 'rolling devolution', and the seemingly endless cycle of violence. Secondly, there was external pressure on the British Government, such the MacBride Principles campaign in the United States against employment discrimination in Northern Ireland and the involvement of the Irish Government through the Anglo-Irish Agreement. Thirdly, there was pressure on the issue of fair employment from the Standing Advisory Commission on Human Rights, which reviewed the Fair Employment Act, 1976, and was critical of its effectiveness. A fourth factor was the increased concern about the need for specific community relations activity. An SACHR paper recommended the creation of a new Community Relations Agency.[19] The Government agreed to reconstitute a more general NICRC with the task of encouraging and financing intercommunity projects of all kinds, such as training workshops on community relations, anti-intimidation programmes, and the development of integrated schools, local history societies, and local cultural festivals. The promotion of 'two traditions' in all forms of cultural and artistic activity has been one of the main objectives of the NICRC.[20]

Reconciliation groups emerged in Northern Ireland for the first time in 1964 but mushroomed in the post-1969 period after the outbreak of communal violence. The focus of their activities varied and included the tackling of political issues, developing ecumenical understanding, and bringing children and families from the different traditions together. As community-based programmes evolved, mainly within the voluntary sector, and as the people concerned gained experience, their influence began to be felt in such areas as education, youth work, and community development. Eventually long-term programmes developed as experience of joint work accumulated. The importance of some of this work was later accepted by central government in the policy changes made with respect to 'education for mutual understanding', the Youth Service and community relations, and the establishment of the NICRC. More recent examples of this critical reconciliation tradition were the positive response of the Government to some proposals from the Committee on the Administration of Justice on police accountability, the lay visitor programme, and documents on the need for race relations legislation in Northern Ireland.

The range of reconciliation groups can be classified into four types: international communities of reconciliation, containing groups formed with the specific intention of acting as centres for reconciliation, such as the Corrymeela Community; local groups formed in the midst of hostility; groups formed out of the experience of violent bereavement; and children's community relations holidays.[21] A raft of policy commitments by central government, with associated legislative changes, have promoted discussion about community relations within Government and public bodies and have seen the establishment of internal audits by the Central Community Relations Unit within many Government bodies. Initiatives that have evolved in the wake of these policy impulses include the appointment of community relations officers in the twenty-six local government districts; the promotion of intercommunity contact schemes for schools; the creation of youth service agencies and a youth intercommunity contact scheme; and the anti-sectarian, anti-discrimination programmes of the trade union movement.[22]

Although teachers and academics had been active from the early seventies, the Government was more hesitant and cautious about suggestions that schools should be involved with community relations issues. Its first public commitment of any sort was the production in 1982 of a circular called The Improvement of Community Relations: The Contribution of Schools, which stated that 'every teacher, every school manager, Board member and trustee, and every educational administrator within the system has a responsibility for helping children learn to understand and respect each other.' This signalled the beginning of formal Government support. It led to the Education Reform (Northern Ireland) Order, 1989, which specified that two cross-curricular themes related to the issue of community relations be included in the curriculum. These were called 'education for mutual understanding' (EMU) and 'cultural heritage'.[23] The two subjects share many of their basic objectives. EMU has four objectives:

Objective 1:   Fostering respect for self and others
Objective 2:   Understanding conflict
Objective 3:   Appreciating interdependence
Objective 4:   Understanding cultural traditions.

'Cultural heritage' has three objectives:

Objective 1:   Interaction, interdependence, continuity and change
Objective 2:   Shared, diverse and distinctive features of different traditions
Objective 3:   International and transnational influences.[24]

Perhaps the most dramatic development in education over the twenty years has been the creation of integrated schools, which are attended in roughly equal numbers by Protestants and Catholics. By 1993 there were twenty-one integrated schools—seventeen primary and four post-primary—attended by approximately 3,500 pupils or about 1 per cent of the school population. The aim of the integrated schools is that they would be open to children from both Protestant and Catholic backgrounds, to those from other religious backgrounds and from backgrounds where there are no religious beliefs. In practice the schools are Christian in character, and the founders, parents, teachers and managers have developed workable procedures for the teaching of religion. The Education Reform (Northern Ireland) Order, 1989, included a number of provisions for encouraging the development of integrated schools, created a mechanism for financing them, and placed a statutory responsibility on the Government to support and promote integrated education.[25]

The games curriculum of many, if not most, schools is predominantly either 'Catholic' or 'Protestant'. Gaelic sports prevail in most Catholic schools, while games with a British pedigree, such as rugby union, hockey, and cricket, dominate in Protestant schools. There are, however, a group of sports, including soccer, basketball, and netball, that cut across the denominational split. Nevertheless, simply playing a game that is also played in the other community counts little towards assimilation if it is only done against 'them' and in the company of those from one's 'own side'. When schools participate in a common game, such as soccer, they often do so in ways that ensure that most Protestant and Catholic children never play together in the same team but only against one another. A subtle form of sporting apartheid is carried on outside the school gates by a huge network of voluntary sports organisations and governing bodies through which separate community affiliation is confirmed according to which games are played or watched, which teams are supported, and which clubs and societies are joined and patronised in later life. In this respect sport has developed as one of Northern Ireland's most important symbols of community identity. It has been estimated that, outside school, up to a quarter of a million people are actively involved in sport in Northern Ireland.[26]

The people of Northern Ireland have remained considerably more religious than those of Britain. The churches in Northern Ireland are more conservative or orthodox in their theology than their British counterparts. In the 1992–93 Social Attitudes Survey, 80 per cent of the sample saw themselves as belonging to a Christian denomination, compared with 56 per cent of the British sample. People in Northern Ireland were not only far more likely to belong to a religious organisation but were also more likely to attend church. 58 per cent of the Northern Ireland respondents were frequent church attenders, compared with 15 per cent of the British respondents. Within Northern Ireland 84 per cent of Catholics frequently attended church, compared with 52 per cent of Presbyterians and 45 per cent of Church of Ireland members.

The difference between the number of people in Northern Ireland with conventional Christian beliefs and the number in Britain with similar beliefs was very large. In religious belief the Anglican, Presbyterian and Methodist churches in Northern Ireland contained large conservative elements. A fifth of both Methodists and adherents of the Church of Ireland and more than a quarter of Presbyterians claimed a 'born-again' experience—a turning-point in one's life when one commits oneself to Christ. The theological divide between Northern Ireland and Britain was demonstrated in the fact that in no church in Northern Ireland were there more liberals than evangelicals, while in all three of the largest churches in Britain liberals outnumbered evangelicals. Similarly, more than a quarter of the members of each Protestant church in Northern Ireland were biblical literalists—that is, believing that the Bible is the literal word of God, true in every detail. Taking all churches together, there were twice as many literalists as modernists; in Britain, biblical literalism was very rare.[27]

The Troubles seem to have had an impact on definitions of national identity, confirming the cultural alienation of Catholics from the Britishness of the Northern Ireland statelet and an acceleration of Protestant cultural alienation from their Irishness. John Dobson, a Stormont MP for West Down, summed up this process in 1972 when he explained:

I have been British all my life and I wish to remain British. I consider myself to be Irish-British, just as there are Scottish-British and Welsh-British, but I am first and foremost British, and British I want to remain ... and every shot that is fired by the IRA, every bomb that is planted by the IRA ... reinforces my desire to remain British and that this country should remain an integral part of the United Kingdom.[28]

Increasingly, many Protestants, because of Republican violence, became uncomfortable with calling themselves primarily Irish, as Scots and Welsh people might. While Republicans saw their campaign as directed against the British state in Ireland, loyalists saw it as a campaign against Ulster Protestants, who saw themselves as British and Northern Ireland as their state. Protestants increasingly defined themselves as either British, British-Irish, or Ulster-British: the common denominator for all was Britishness, and the psychological identification of Northern Ireland with Britain remained.

The *UWC Journal* explained in 1975 that when a Northern Ireland citizen was quizzed about his nationality he was promptly reminded by anti-partitionists that 'he is really Irish, because he lives or was born in Ireland.' Much capital, it pointed out, had been made of this because some public figures had confessed confusion about whether they were Irish or British, while many loyalists, otherwise proud of their British allegiance, also reluctantly admitted to being Irish. In Northern Ireland, the *UWC Journal* argued, 'geography has made us Irish, but in nationality we are British as this is the political mode of government in Ulster.' It felt that a reaction against Irishness among Ulster Protestants did not necessarily mean a move towards an Ulster identity at the expense of their Britishness, and it asserted that

> as British Irish, and like other areas of the UK such as the West Country or Yorkshire, we do have a unique regional identity of our own, and have had for centuries ... But the time has now arrived many feel, when the name 'Ireland' in any context is a liability because of IRA activities, or by association with a southern government which has a reputation for being among the most backward and reactionary nations in Europe.
>
> The name 'Ulster' we believe is more appropriate and representative. It conveys more aptly the cultures and traditions of the North Irish people.
>
> But to return to that question—just as there are British Scotsmen we are British Irishmen ... or more correctly—British Ulstermen![29]

In 1968 it was found that there were three national labels of importance in Northern Ireland: British, Irish, and Ulster; ten years later these had collapsed into British and Irish. Protestants had become more inclined to see themselves as British and less identified with Ulster, while Catholics overwhelmingly identified with being Irish. The cumulative effect of Republican violence appears to have had the opposite effect of what the Provisional IRA intended: Ulster Protestants have become more British, at the expense of their Irishness. While Irishness and Ulsterness have oscillated in the choice of national identity among Protestants, their British identity has remained the strongest and indeed has been strengthened by the impact of the Troubles.

For Protestants, an Ulster identity implies an identification with Northern Ireland as a political region and an acceptance of its legitimacy. It seems that the term 'Northern Irish' began to gain acceptance for both Catholics and Protestants during the nineteen-seventies. In comparing six surveys on national identity, spanning the period of the Troubles, a clear pattern emerges. In 1968 less than two-fifths of the people described themselves as British, a fifth saw themselves as Irish, and a third saw themselves as having an Ulster identity. After a decade of the Troubles only 8 per cent of Protestants chose to describe themselves as Irish, while two-thirds identified themselves as British and 20 per cent chose the Ulster identity. Subsequent surveys showed a decreasing proportion of Protestants describing themselves as Irish and an increasing proportion seeing themselves as British. The attractiveness of the Ulster identity to Protestants declined strongly between 1968 and 1989, and the availability of the 'Northern Irish' label seemed to provide a viable alternative for those who felt a strong identification with their locality.

The 1991 and 1993 NISA surveys found the Ulster identity growing in popularity in comparison with the 1989 findings; however, the patterns found in 1994 were remarkably similar to those found in 1989, with 11 per cent of Protestants identifying themselves as Ulster and 15 per cent as Northern Irish.

Choice of national identity for Protestants, 1968–1994 (%)

	British	Irish	Ulster	Northern Irish	Other
1968	39	20	32	—	9
1978	67	82	0	—	5
1989	68	3	10	16	3
1991	66	2	15	14	3
1993	70	2	16	11	3
1994	71	3	11	15	—

Few Catholic respondents chose the Ulster identity in any of the surveys between 1968 and 1994. At the same time the proportion of Catholics choosing to describe themselves as Irish has fallen, from 76 per cent in 1968 to 62 per cent in 1994, while a sizable minority of Catholic respondents have chosen to describe themselves as Northern Irish in the NISA surveys in which this option has been available.

Choice of national identity for Catholics, 1968–1994 (%)

	British	Irish	Ulster	Northern Irish	Other
1968	15	76	5	—	4
1978	15	69	6	—	10
1989	10	60	2	25	4
1991	10	62	2	25	1
1993	12	61	1	25	2
1994	10	62	—	28	—

For Catholics the term 'Northern Irish' does not legitimise political boundaries or compromise their aspirations, as the term can refer to the geographically northern part of Ireland. Similarly, the 'Northern Irish' identity does not compromise the British identity of Protestants, as the term can be seen as derived from 'Northern Ireland', an officially designated region of the United Kingdom.[30]

These national divisions are reflected in the opposing opinions of unionists and nationalists regarding the cultural identity of the Northern Ireland state, such as flags and symbols and Orange marches. For unionists the British national anthem and the Union Jack represent the state institutions that exercise sovereignty over Northern Ireland and thereby provide a sense of security in the face of the risk of the unification of Ireland. For a unionist, if the Union Jack is not flown or 'God Save the Queen' is not played it is a sign that the link with Britain is being weakened. For unionists, the symbols of the Irish state are seen as irredentist and threatening, and they would prefer that they be controlled. The Tricolour is associated in some Protestant minds with religion as much as with the Irish state.

On the other hand, when nationalists see the British flag or hear the British national anthem they do not see them as representing the people or territory of the United Kingdom but as symbols of the state. Unlike unionists, nationalists have not got the same benign view of that state: for them it is an imposed order within Ireland in a most hostile form and is seen as an imperialist system. Not all nationalists share the level of hostility that Republicans display towards the British state: some are willing to respect the symbols, though they tend to feel that they are overused and unnecessary on many occasions. Nationalists have a sense of Irishness, whether or not they want the early reunification of Ireland. Some do not feel that reunification is possible in the present circumstances, but that does not lessen the wish to identify with the Irish people. An important expression of this identification is through the Tricolour and the Republic's national anthem, 'Amhrán na bhFiann'.[31]

A LOW-INTENSITY WAR

Between 1969 and June 1989 some 2,761 people were killed as a result of political violence in Northern Ireland. Of these, 862 (31 per cent) were members of the security forces, 364 (13 per cent) were paramilitaries, and 1,510 (55 per cent) were civilians.

The pattern of casualties indicates the main targets of both loyalist and republican paramilitaries. Loyalist paramilitary organisations killed 623 people. Catholic civilians were by far the primary victims (73 per cent), followed by Protestant civilians (18 per cent), other loyalist paramilitaries (5 per cent), republican paramilitaries (3 per cent), and security forces (2 per cent). The pattern is strikingly different for the 1,593 killed by republican paramilitaries. The security forces accounted for 53 per cent, followed by Protestant civilians (24 per cent), Catholic civilians (11 per cent), and other republican paramilitaries (9 per cent); loyalist paramilitaries accounted for only 1 per cent of the total. It is noticeable that 173 Catholic civilians were killed by republican paramilitaries, more than were killed by the security forces.[32] According to figures quoted by John Hume in 1990, 10 per cent of those killed during the Troubles of the previous ten years had been killed by the British army, 2 per cent by the RUC, and only 0.3 per cent by the UDR. By the same calculations, the Provisional IRA and other republicans were responsible for the murder of about 70 per cent of the 2,859 victims of violence.[33]

The British Government's response to the continuing political violence has been to combat it by criminalising those perpetrating it. The objectives of its security policy in Northern Ireland in November 1990 were:

(a) to maintain the rule of law

(b) to ensure that all the people of Northern Ireland are free to express their political opinions without inhibition, fear of discrimination or reprisal (*c*) to defend the democratically expressed wishes of the people of Northern Ireland against those who try to promote political objectives, including a change in the status of Northern Ireland, by violence or the threat of violence

(*d*) to create in Northern Ireland the condition for a just, peaceful and prosperous society in which local people can exercise greater control over their own affairs.

So that these aims could be achieved, the British Government considered the first priority to be the eradication of terrorism, from whatever section of the community it came. To this end, the strategy was to

(*a*) ensure that the police, supported by the armed forces, have the resources they need to undertake their difficult and dangerous work on behalf of the whole community

(*b*) provide a legal framework within which the security forces can act to defeat terrorism

(*c*) cooperate closely on security with the government of the Republic of Ireland

(*d*) seek and isolate the terrorists from the communities within which they operate.[34]

Not only did this policy result in a further remilitarisation of the RUC but the continuing Provisional IRA campaign inevitably led to significant increases in the size of the RUC and the UDR, with the latter, originally intended to be primarily a part-time force, becoming 46 per cent full-time by 1988. The effect of this was to replace regular British army personnel with Ulster Protestants.

The RUC quickly became involved in renewed controversy. By the early eighties the use of plastic bullets by the security forces, sometimes with fatal consequences, had become a controversial issue, and 1982 saw the first allegations of a 'shoot-to-kill' policy against the RUC. This led to the so-called Stalker Affair, in which John Stalker, the Deputy Chief Constable of Manchester, was suspended—because of allegations that were subsequently shown to be unfounded—from an inquiry into a number of lethal-force incidents involving the RUC. The investigation was taken over by Colin Sampson, the Chief Constable of West Yorkshire, and ultimately resulted in disciplinary proceedings against more than twenty RUC officers. Further controversy regarding the security forces arose in 1989 over damaging allegations of the leaking of security force documents to loyalist paramilitaries. An inquiry carried out by John Stevens, the Deputy Chief Constable of Cambridgeshire, found that while there had been some collusion with loyalist paramilitaries it was 'restricted to a small number of members of the security forces and is neither widespread nor institutionalised,' and he focused his main criticisms on the UDR rather than the RUC.[35]

Increasingly, intelligence was deemed essential to foiling Provisional IRA attacks, through the use of informers and of electronic and undercover surveillance. The controversy over the RUC's alleged shoot-to-kill policy necessitated their replacement by special units to ambush Provisional IRA active service units. Regular British army patrols rarely intercepted or killed members of IRA units, although the level of violence from that source had consistently declined. From 1976 to 1978 the Special Air Service in Northern Ireland killed ten people; seven of them were Provisional IRA members, but three had been innocent bystanders. In December 1978, SAS ambushes stopped for five years, until December 1983. However, the number of Provisional IRA deaths remained relatively small compared with deaths caused by that organisation: for example, during 1979–80 only one Provisional IRA member was killed by the entire British army in Northern Ireland,[36] while between 1983 and 1987 twenty Provisional IRA members were killed by the SAS or by the 14th Intelligence Company, the army's special surveillance unit. There was a feeling in security circles that the Provisional IRA had to be faced with occasional ambushes, because many members would not be deterred by prison sentences.[37] The most famous example of this was the SAS ambush of an ASU at Loughgall, County Armagh, in 1987. Eight IRA members were killed by the SAS as they bombed Loughgall police station.[38]

The brunt of IRA activity was increasingly borne by the locally recruited security forces. From the time of its establishment the UDR was seen by most Catholics as an undisciplined sectarian force. Although it did attract up to 18 per cent Catholic recruits in its early days, by the end of the eighties this had fallen to 3 per cent. While this was partly due to the high security threat to Catholic members, it also indicated that the UDR had a serious credibility problem in the eyes of the Catholic community. In July 1992 the UDR was merged with the Royal Irish Rangers, a regular British army regiment, to form the Royal Irish Regiment. The new regiment was to have full-time and part-time soldiers and to consist of one general service battalion of nine hundred members with worldwide responsibilities and up to seven home service battalions, with a total strength of six thousand for duty in Northern Ireland.[39]

The UDR had been a particular target for assassination by the Provisional IRA. Of the 159 members killed between its formation and the end of 1986, 129 were killed while off duty.[40] Such attacks were perceived by the Protestant community as a direct assault on that community by their Catholic neighbours. Up to 1990 more than forty thousand men and women had served in the UDR, many motivated by 'love of country' or of 'Queen and country' as much as by the financial rewards.[41] Out of 924 security force deaths in the Troubles between 1969 and 1992, more than half were members of the RUC, the RUC Reserve, or the UDR or RIR.[42] In 1992, 87 per cent of those employed in the RUC, RIR, prison service and publicly financed security positions were Protestants, 7 per cent were from the Catholic community, and the remainder were classified as non-determined.[43] Given that the locally recruited security forces were overwhelmingly Protestant, the great majority of those killed, many off duty in or outside their homes, were from that community. Many Protestants regarded the IRA campaign against the locally recruited security forces, and particularly part-time members of the UDR in border areas, as 'ethnic cleansing'. It was believed that the Provisional IRA chose the eldest sons, the wage-earners in border families, the sons who run the farms and businesses in a predetermined campaign to drive Protestants inland from the border and claim their land and living.[44]

The Provisional IRA made no distinction in killing UDR soldiers and members of the regular army. Dáithí Ó Conaill argued that 'members of the UDR and the RUC are members of the British Crown Forces engaged in a war of repression ... Anyone who wears the uniform of the British Crown engaged in a war of repression in Ireland is a legitimate target irrespective of what his religious beliefs are.'[45] The main objectives of the Provisional IRA's war strategy, as described by the 'Green Book', issued to each new member, were:

1. A war of attrition against enemy personnel which is aimed at causing as many casualties and deaths as possible so as to create a demand from their people at home for their withdrawal.

2. A bombing campaign aimed at making the enemy's financial interests in our country unprofitable while at the same time curbing long-term investment in our country.

3. To make the Six Counties as at present and for the past several years ungovernable except by military colonial rule.

4. To sustain the war and gain support for its ends by National and International propaganda and publicity campaigns.

5. By defending the war of liberation by punishing criminals, collaborators and informers.

A commitment to the Republican Movement was based on the 'firm belief that its struggle both military and political is morally justified' and that the Provisional IRA were the direct representatives of the 1918 Dáil Éireann, the product of the last all-Ireland parliamentary election. The Army Council of the Provisional IRA was therefore the 'legal and lawful government of the Irish Republic with the moral right to pass laws for, and to claim jurisdiction over, the whole geographical fragment of Ireland, its maritime territory, air space, mineral resources, means of production, distribution and exchange and all of its people regardless of creed or loyalty.' This belief, 'this ethical fact,' was supposed to give moral strength to all IRA volunteers. As the Provisional IRA's leadership was the lawful government of the Irish Republic, and with all other parliaments and assemblies claiming the right to speak for and pass laws on behalf of the Irish people being 'illegal assemblies, puppet governments of a foreign power, and willing tools of an occupying force,' IRA members were urged to believe 'without doubt' that all orders were the legal orders and actions of the Government of the Irish Republic. The Green Book explained:

> The Irish Republican Army as the legal representatives of the Irish people are morally justified in carrying out a campaign of resistance against foreign occupation forces and domestic collaborators. All Volunteers are and must feel morally justified in carrying out the dictates of the legal government … All Volunteers must look upon the British Army as an occupying force … the RUC, the Gardaí, the UDR and the Free State Army as illegal armies … and forces whose main tasks are treasonable and morally wrong, politically unacceptable and ethically inexcusable.

The long-term objective of the movement was the 'establishment of a Democratic Socialist Republic,' while 'the Brits out campaign is … our "National" short-term objective,' crucial to achieving the long-term objective.[46]

In 1974 the Provisionals appeared to believe that the UWC strike had radically altered British policy towards staying in Northern Ireland. An Phoblacht argued that the old unionist relationship with Britain was gone, 'smashed by the Loyalist rebellion.' It predicted that an independent Ulster would not be economically viable and appealed to loyalists on the basis that 'together we [the IRA and UWC] who smashed Sunningdale ... can build a better Ireland for all, if only we can learn to trust each other.'[47]

'Now that it seems more likely than ever that the Republican war aim will be achieved,' a contributor to *An Phoblacht* wrote, Republicans should look to what would be the impact of an independent Ulster arising from the UWC strike. From a Republican point of view, Ulster separatism was an 'advance on the previous situation. The formal political link with England would have been broken throughout Ireland,' and the political response to Ulster separatism should be the creation in Ulster of a 'pro-Ulster Irish nationalism'. Ulster separatism could only be fought effectively by an 'Ulster political patriotism working in the Irish nationalist interest,' the foundation of which was to be provided by the Dáil Uladh proposal.[48]

On 10 December 1974 talks took place between Protestant churchmen and six members of the Provisional IRA Army Council in Feakle, County Clare. A temporary unilateral truce, arising out of the Feakle talks, was called by the IRA on 20 December 1974, to last from 22 December to 2 January. British Government officials then held talks with Provisional Sinn Féin from 22 December to 17 January. On 2 January the Provisional IRA extended its cease-fire until 17 January. On that day, however, the cease-fire came to an end with the exploding of four bombs in London, with nineteen people being injured in another blast in Manchester. Then, on 9 February, the Provisional IRA announced an indefinite cease-fire to begin the following day. 'Incident centres', to be staffed by Sinn Féin members, were set up to monitor the cease-fire, in tandem with British Government officials.

The Provisionals appeared to have been spurred on by a belief that the British were prepared to disengage from Northern Ireland. According to Ruairí Ó Brádaigh, the IRA had received a message from the British over the Christmas period that the British Government 'wished to devise structures of disengagement from Ireland.' A bilateral truce lasted until 22 September 1975, with talks taking place between both sides throughout. Provisional IRA representatives offered to deliver a permanent cease-fire in return for a public declaration that Britain would withdraw from Ireland by a date to be negotiated. On 14 July 1975 Merlyn Rees, the Secretary of State, outlined in the House of Commons the British Government's response to the IRA's proposals. No interim custody orders had been signed since the start of the cease-fire, the size and frequency of British army patrols had been reduced, and the searching of homes had been scaled down. The intention was that if a permanent cessation of violence was achieved, security would be reduced to a 'peacetime level'; furthermore, if violence ended then detainees would be progressively released. Rees also revealed that talks had taken place with the UDA and UVF, and that the same opportunities existed for the Provisional IRA and the Official IRA.

During the talks with the Provisionals the British Government was represented by senior officials—Frank Cooper of the NIO and James Alan of the Foreign and Commonwealth Office—but no politicians. The Republican Movement was represented by Ó Brádaigh and Billy McKee, one-time commander of the IRA in Belfast. According to one source—the most senior British official involved—the talks were never about 'disengagement' but could have resulted in a complete withdrawal of the British army from internal security, in return for a genuine reduction in Provisional IRA violence and a move by them into politics. There was apparently great hostility from the Dublin Government to the discussions; the prospect of a British withdrawal 'was not real politics,' despite withdrawal being on the agenda.[49]

According to Ó Brádaigh, the truce failed for three reasons: '(a) the loyalist death squads immediately embarked on the greatest assassination campaign of innocent Catholics ... (b) the Dublin government indicated to the British that a withdrawal must not be contemplated ... [and] a key republican leader, Dáithí Ó Conaill, was singled out and hunted down by them ... and (c) ... the British did not deliver on their promise of the previous Christmas.'[50]

The return of the Provisional IRA to its campaign of violence saw some particularly brutal outrages. On 5 January 1976, as they returned home in a minibus, ten Protestant workers were murdered at Kingsmill, County Armagh, by the 'Republican Action Force', a cover name for the local Provisional IRA unit. As a result, Merlyn Rees announced the official deployment of the SAS in the south Armagh area. The Provisionals also focused on prestige targets, such as Christopher Ewart-Biggs, the British ambassador to Ireland, who was murdered when a land-mine exploded under his car in Dublin on 21 July 1976, and Jeffrey Agate, the English manager of the Du Pont factory in County Londonderry, who was shot dead on 2 February 1977. In the main, however, attacks on the security forces and commercial targets were the main focus of IRA activity, whether through sniping, bombings, or attacks on off-duty members of the RUC and UDR.

The most spectacular attack during this period was the assassination on 27 August 1979 of the Queen's cousin, the 79-year-old Lord Louis Mountbatten, together with his fourteen-year-old grandson, the Dowager Lady Brabourne and a seventeen-year-old boatman in a bomb attack in County Sligo. The same day Provisional IRA bomb attacks in Warrenpoint, County Down, killed eighteen British soldiers. Other attacks, however, continued to result in significant civilian deaths; in one such attack twelve people, all Protestants, were killed and twenty-three injured by an incendiary bomb at the La Mon House Hotel in County Down.

During this period the Irish Republican Socialist Party emerged, following a split in Official Sinn Féin. By March 1975 it claimed to have seven hundred members, including Séamus Costello, its leader, and the former MP Bernadette McAliskey (née Devlin). Ultimately the more militant supporters of the new party formed the Irish National Liberation Army. The most spectacular INLA success was the murder of Airey Neave, the Conservative Party spokesman on Northern Ireland, with a bomb placed under his car in the House of Commons car park on 30 March 1979. One of its most infamous acts was the killing of three church elders and wounding of seven others at a Pentecostal church at Darkley, County Armagh, under the cover of the 'Catholic Reaction Force', on 20 November 1983.

However, the main thrust of anti-state violence continued to come from the Provisional IRA. The Republican Movement did suffer some notable setbacks from the more aggressive security policies employed by the Secretary of State, Roy Mason, during the late seventies, particularly as a result of confessions extracted from terrorist suspects, often in controversial circumstances. The impact of Mason's security policies on the effectiveness of the Republican Movement was admitted in a Provisional IRA 'Staff Report', which stated that three-day and seven-day detention orders were 'breaking' the movement but blamed the IRA itself for not indoctrinating members with the 'psychological strength to resist interrogation.' The report also considered the Provisional IRA to be burdened with an inefficient infrastructure of commands, brigades, battalions, and companies; this old system was considered too familiar to the British and the RUC Special Branch. The report emphasised a return to secrecy and strict discipline, to be obtained by the creation of a new rank of education officer, to be available to give anti-interrogation lectures. The report argued that the Provisional IRA had to gear itself towards a 'Long Term Armed Struggle', based on putting unknown members and new recruits into a new cell structure. Ideally a cell would consist of four people, although rural areas would be treated separately. Existing battalion and company staffs were to be dissolved, with existing brigades to decide who passed into the reorganised cell structure. Cells would specialise as intelligence, sniping, execution, bombing and robbery cells and would operate as far as possible outside their own areas, to confuse British intelligence and expand the IRA's operational areas. In addition it was proposed that Sinn Féin should come under IRA organisers at all levels. Sinn Féin would also be radicalised in that it would agitate around social and economic issues that 'attack the welfare of the people'; it would also infiltrate other organisations to win support and sympathy for the Republican Movement.[51]

As both the Provisional IRA and British security forces began a war of attrition, the lack of an immediate threat to Northern Ireland's position within the United Kingdom saw a corresponding decline in loyalist violence. The calming of unionist fears was most graphically illustrated by the failure of another attempt at a political strike in 1977. On 25 April 1977 the United Unionist Action Council, led by Ian Paisley and supported by the UDA and UWC, announced that it would call a strike in May 1977 to protest against British Government security policy and demand the return of a majority-rule government. The UUAC issued an ultimatum to the Secretary of State, giving him seven days to meet their demands. Despite demonstrations and road-blocks in support of the stoppage, however, it made little impact. The main reason for the failure was the general lack of support from the unionist community and the Government's reaction, which was better planned and more decisive than in 1974. Roy Mason was excused from Cabinet duties and stayed in Northern Ireland throughout the strike, and the NIO also successfully played a delaying game with the electricity workers, whose support was crucial to the success of the stoppage. What the 1974 and 1977 strikes illustrated was that unionist unity existed only in extreme cases, when the very existence of Northern Ireland was believed to be threatened.

With a decline in, although by no means an end to, violence, loyalist paramilitaries turned their attention to political activity. In 1975 and 1976 there had been 114 and 113 loyalist murders; in 1977 and 1978 the numbers were 25 and 8, respectively.[52] Glen Barr, who had left the UDA in 1975, returned in 1977 to help form the New Ulster Political Research Group and produce a coherent political direction for the UDA. Over the next few years the UDA's leadership attempted to reassure Catholics that it had moved away from sectarian murder. Andy Tyrie, the UDA's 'Supreme Commander', explained in 1983: 'Normally the UDA would have reacted to the La Mon [Hotel] bombing. However, we decided not to because we felt that getting involved in indiscriminate violence would drive the ordinary decent Catholic behind the IRA ... If we come into serious conflict with the Roman Catholic areas ... for purely sectarian reasons, it will separate us again for another fifteen or twenty years.' The UDA, however, retained a right to make 'selective attacks on known Republicans, the people who lead their campaign, give the arms, and supply them with information.'[53]

The political programme advocated by the UDA was negotiated independence for Northern Ireland. Barr argued:

> We need to create a system of government, an identity, and a nationality to which both sections of the community can aspire. We must look for the common denominator. The only common denominator which the Ulster people have, whether they be Catholic or Protestant, is that they are Ulstermen. And that is the basis from which we should build the new life for the Ulster people, a new identity for them. Awaken them to their own identity. They are different. That they're not second-class Englishmen but first-class Ulstermen. And that's where my loyalty is.

The proposed constitution for an independent Ulster was based on that of the United States, with an elected president, who would choose an executive, preferably of academic and professional people rather than politicians. The executive would answer to committees drawn from an elected legislature. There would be a detailed Bill of Rights and a judiciary responsible for safeguarding civil liberties. In November 1978 this policy appeared as a document, *Beyond the Religious Divide*, and immediately attracted favourable responses from across the political divide, including that of Paddy Devlin of the SDLP.[54]

Tyrie supported independence because he foresaw the withdrawal of Britain from Ulster in his lifetime. Therefore, the 'Ulster people will have to make their choice. To be thrust into a united Ireland would be an anathema to any Protestant and it would be forcibly rejected by everyone who holds their Ulster identity close to their hearts.' Despite being in favour of independence, the UDA-inspired political party, the Ulster Loyalist Democratic Party, according to its manifesto emphasised that its aim was to 'achieve Ulster national sovereignty by the establishment of a democratic Ulster parliament' and the 'introduction of an agreed written constitution for Ulster, within the United Kingdom.' As its chairman, John McMichael—former secretary of the NUPRG and a UDA 'brigadier'—admitted, this was because 'we found that although people feel anti-Westminster and anti-English, they still have a great affection for the monarchy. So it would be independence within the EEC and the Commonwealth, which we think would be acceptable to many Roman Catholics.'[55]

Electorally, however, loyalist politicians with paramilitary connections received minimal support. Part of the problem for the UDA was that the idea of negotiated independence was anathema not only to Catholics but to the overwhelming majority of Protestants as well.

THE HUNGER-STRIKES

The adoption of the cell structure and the strategy of a lower intensity of conflict—the 'long war'—saved the Provisional IRA from military defeat. At the same time the Republican Movement's political fortunes were revived by the emotional trauma caused in the Catholic-nationalist community by the events of the 1981 hunger-strikes.

On the fifth anniversary of the ending of special-category status for terrorist offences committed after March 1976, the Provisional IRA leader in the H Blocks, Bobby Sands—serving a fourteen-year sentence for firearms offences—began a hunger-strike aimed at regaining political status. Before Sands embarked on his hunger-strike some three hundred Republican prisoners had, since the spring of 1978, stepped up their campaign for political status by wearing only a blanket. They refused to wash, leave their cells, or use toilet facilities, and the walls of many of their cells were covered with excreta by the prisoners. On 27 October 1980 seven Republican prisoners at the Maze prison—six Provisional IRA and one INLA—began a fast, demanding that they be allowed to wear their own clothes and be excused from prison work. The protest ended in confusion when, on 18 December 1980, the prisoners abandoned their fast because of a message from the new Conservative Secretary of State for Northern Ireland, Humphrey Atkins, and a document from the British Government clarifying earlier proposals and in effect, the prisoners believed, conceding their demands.

On 25 January 1981, however, Sands claimed that moves for a gradual co-operation between the prisoners and the prison administration had broken down. On 1 March he began fasting once more. The prisoners listed five demands: the right to wear their own clothes, no prison work, freedom of association, extra recreational facilities and more letters and visits, and the return of remission lost on protest.

On 5 March a unique opportunity arose for the hunger-strikers. Frank

Maguire, the independent nationalist MP for Fermanagh-South Tyrone, died, and Sands was nominated for the ensuing by-election. The SDLP withdrew their candidate, leaving voters to choose between Sands and the Unionist candidate. Sands, now forty days into his hunger-strike, was elected, beating Harry West by 30,492 votes to 29,046.

The British Prime Minister, Margaret Thatcher, was unmoved and declared: 'We are not prepared to consider special category status for certain groups of people serving sentences for crime. Crime is crime is crime; it is not political.' Humphrey Atkins added: 'If Mr Sands persisted in his wish to commit suicide, that was his choice. The government would not force medical treatment on him.' On 28 April the Pope's private secretary visited Sands in the Maze but failed to persuade him to end his hunger-strike.

Sands saw himself as a political prisoner, at war with an occupying power. On the first day of his hunger-strike he had written: 'I am a political prisoner because I am a casualty of a perennial war that is being fought between the oppressed Irish people and an alien, oppressive, unwarranted regime that refuses to withdraw from our land.' Sands believed and stood by the 'God-given right of the Irish nation to sovereign independence and the right of any Irishman or woman to assert this right in armed revolution.' Foremost in his mind was the conclusion that 'there can never be peace in Ireland until the foreign, oppressive British presence is removed, leaving all the Irish people as a unit to control their own affairs and determine their own destinies as a sovereign people, free in mind and body, separate and distinct physically, culturally and economically.' 'I am dying,' he wrote, 'not just to attempt to end the barbarity of H-Block or to gain the rightful recognition of a political prisoner but primarily because what is lost in here is lost for the republic and those wretched oppressed whom I am deeply proud to know as the "risen people".'[56]

On 5 May 1981, on the sixty-sixth day of his fast, Sands was the first of ten hunger-strikers to die; the last died on 20 August. In the House of Commons, Margaret Thatcher remarked: 'Mr Sands was a convicted criminal. He chose to take his own life. It was a choice that his organisation did not allow to many of its victims.' In contrast, on 7 May 1981 almost a hundred thousand people attended Sands's funeral in Belfast. The Catholic Bishop of Derry claimed: 'I would not describe Bobby Sands's death as suicide. I could not accept that. I don't think he intended to bring about his own death.' The Catholic primate, Cardinal Tomás Ó Fiaich, condemned the British Government's 'rigid stance' and warned that it would face the 'wrath of the whole nationalist population.'

On 12 May 1981 the Provisional IRA prisoner Francis Hughes, serving a life sentence for murder, died on the fifty-ninth day of his protest. The others who died were Raymond McCreesh (Provisional IRA) on 21 May after sixty-one days; Patsy O'Hara (leader of the INLA prisoners) on 21 May after sixty-one days; Joe McDonnell (Provisional IRA) on 8 July after sixty-one days; Martin Hurson (Provisional IRA) on 13 July after forty-six days; Kevin Lynch (INLA) on 1 August after seventy-one days; Kieran Doherty (Provisional IRA, elected TD in Cavan-Monaghan) on 2 August after seventy-three days; Thomas McElwee (Provisional IRA) on 8 August after sixty-five days; and Michael Devine (INLA) on 20 August after sixty-six days. Sixty-one other people died in violent incidents during the hunger-strikes. Fifteen RUC men, eight soldiers and seven members of the UDR died in bombings and shootings; five of the soldiers died in a land-mine explosion near Camlough, County Armagh. Thirty-four civilians were also killed, seven of them, including two girls aged eleven and fourteen, as a result of injuries from plastic bullets fired by the security forces. Another of the fatalities was a woman shot dead by the Provisional IRA while collecting census forms in Londonderry.

On the political front, Sands's electoral agent, Owen Carron, won the Fermanagh-South Tyrone by-election caused by the hunger-striker's death, defeating the Ulster Unionist Party candidate, Ken Maginnis, by 31,278 votes to 29,048 votes. In the district council elections of May 1981, candidates from several parties campaigning on the H Block issue polled 51,000 votes and won thirty-six seats. In the Republic nine H Block candidates polled nearly forty thousand first-preference votes, and two of the hunger-strikers were returned as TDs. The Northern Ireland Attitude Survey found that 57 per cent of Catholics agreed that 'the British government should stop treating people convicted of crimes which they claim were politically motivated as ordinary prisoners.'[57]

The hunger-strikes finally ended on 3 October 1981. While the Provisionals had been forced to accept that the Thatcher Government would not concede 'political status', they nevertheless won substantial concessions on several issues for the prisoners, such as being allowed to wear their own clothes at all times, but only after the fasting had ceased. After the hunger-strikes, violence increased, with the number of people killed jumping from 76 in the previous year to 101, shootings from 642 to 1,142, and bombings from 400 to 529.[58]

Of far greater significance in the long term was the radicalising effect of the protest on the Catholic population. Father Des Wilson, talking about the effect of the hunger-strikes in the Catholic ghettos of west Belfast, observed:

> There were people on marches against the government's treatment of the hunger strikers who had never been on a march before … As each death occurred, a number of things became possible which had not been possible before. It was now possible to speak respectfully of the IRA. To have done so before would have been to invite condemnation by Church and state … The trouble with a hunger strike is that so many honourable people in the past have used it and have been praised for it. You cannot now turn around and say a hunger strike is immoral and violent if you have said the opposite in the past … In Ireland a hunger strike is something which governments ignore at their peril …[59]

The electoral success enjoyed by Sinn Féin encouraged the Republican Movement to adopt a twofold strategy, symbolised by a senior Republican, Danny Morrison, at the Sinn Féin ardfheis in October 1981 when he asked, 'Who here really believes we can win the war through the ballot box? But will anyone here object if, with a ballot paper in one hand and the Armalite [automatic rifle] in the other, we take power in Ireland?' In elections to a new Northern Ireland Assembly in October 1982 Sinn Féin obtained 64,191 votes or 10 per cent of the valid poll, while the SDLP polled 118,891 votes or 19 per cent.[60] In the 1983 British general election Gerry Adams—soon to become president of Sinn Féin following the departure of traditionalists such as Ruairí Ó Brádaigh, who adhered to the traditional Republican stance of not participating in British elections—was elected MP for West Belfast with a majority of 5,445 over the SDLP candidate. Altogether the SDLP's share of the vote fell to 18 per cent, while Sinn Féin's increased to 13 per cent.[61]

According to Danny Morrison, elections were only one part of the overall struggle, as would be spectacularly evidenced in 1984 when a Provisional IRA bomb attack at the Conservative Party conference in Brighton came close to wiping out the British Cabinet. The main focus remained the armed struggle, because 'that's the only way to get the Brits out of Ireland.' The purpose of contesting elections was to 'completely undermine British propaganda, which states that Republicans have no support. They show that Republicans have popular support.' Sinn Féin criticised the SDLP's political strategy as 'collaboration'. Sinn Féin's objective was to break the grip the SDLP had in the nationalist community. The feeling within the Republican

Movement was that the only basis for direct talks with the British was for the British Government to make a declaration of its intention to withdraw from Ireland. A declaration by Britain that it was in favour of the long-term unification of Ireland was not sufficient, because, as Dáithí Ó Conaill explained, the British 'are absolutely notorious for double-dealing, for making a statement and then taking nine or ten different interpretations out of it. We want a clear-cut, unambiguous statement to the effect that they are leaving the country.' A settlement arising out of any Anglo-Irish process between the British and Irish Governments would not suffice, because this involved a closer association with Britain, and 'fundamental to Republicanism has been the concept of a separatist identity, the breaking of the connection completely. You must sever the connection absolutely.'[62]

THE ANGLO-IRISH PROCESS

After the fall of the power-sharing Executive in 1974, Paddy Devlin of the SDLP recalled that the fears of Northern Catholics were heightened to the extent that they not only felt under siege from loyalists but felt that their right to exist in the North had received diminishing backing from the British Government and less than lukewarm support from the Irish Government. He described Catholics as having been alienated by the fall of the Executive, while the British army had stood aside in 'obvious partisanship'.[63] The lesson of May 1974 for the SDLP, according to a senior member, Brian Feeney, was that Northern Ireland could not work as a political unit: it could work for unionists, for whom it was carved out, but when the British insisted that it must accommodate nationalists it could not operate, since the unit was being asked to perform the antithesis of the function for which it was designed. In some respects Feeney considered the power-sharing experiment necessary to show that Northern Ireland could not provide a framework for justice and peace.

The SDLP now believed that the British and Irish Governments faced an 'Anglo-Irish problem'. The SDLP sought

> justice and peace in that order. This requires absolute equality of status for the people we represent. Nothing less is acceptable, and to suggest anything less [for a] growing, powerful, self-confident, dynamic community is infuriatingly patronising. That status is unobtainable in N. Ireland because N. Ireland is nothing more than the last of the stratagems Unionists have devised since the 1880s to avoid living on equal terms with the rest of the people on the island. Unionists must

oppose equality of status for Nationalists or Northern Ireland ceases to have a reason for existing.

The British, said Feeney, had allowed the Unionists to twist their constitutional guarantee into a veto against any change at all. But Unionist consent was not necessary to bring in measures that gave justice to nationalists and did not affect unionists' rights, ethos or way of life. For example, Unionist consent was not forthcoming for the disbanding of the B Specials or the fall of Stormont. 'Unionists have no right to withhold consent to the principle of change while structures in N. Ireland deny their fellow citizens justice,' although Unionist consent was necessary where their way of life was affected, namely when political changes were involved. The British Government had to make it clear that a breach of British sovereignty was a *sine qua non* of any lasting settlement. Unionist consent to negotiations taking place was not necessary.[64]

John Hume argued that since 1971 a number of attempts had been made to get agreement internally on the North, but all had failed, because every attempt at an internal solution would 'founder on the rock of the [1973 constitutional] guarantee.' This, Hume concluded, left two choices: to 'keep on trying something you know is going to fail or you move on to a wider stage—the Anglo-Irish approach.' He advocated this approach because 'in the end we're not simply dealing with the question of the relations between Catholics and Protestants in the North; it's a question of relations within Ireland between North and South and relations between Britain and Ireland.'[65] Hume stressed that while any solution had to be acceptable to Protestants, that right 'is not an absolute right. It's a right that's qualified by the right of the minority to an acceptable solution and by the rights of the British and Irish governments who will be called upon to enforce or pay for any settlement.' All these parties would be involved in negotiations. Ideally, for Hume, the Anglo-Irish process would see the Governments start the process of negotiations, inviting the Northern parties. The ultimate result would be to see

the Unionists come in and ask for their independence. And then the real negotiations begin, because the first thing you ask when they ask for independence is, 'How do they get the consent of the minority for that?' Because you can't have an independent state if one third of the population is against it. How do you get the recognition of the South? How do you get the recognition of Britain, particularly for the financial arrangements that would be involved? So, immediately you're locked in to real negotiations for the first time. Then, in my view, we respond at that point by saying, 'We're not agreeable to independence but we are agreeable to autonomy.'

Hume defined the trade-off between independence and autonomy as an independent Irish state with a federal unit composed of what currently constituted Northern Ireland, coupled with an external Anglo-Irish Council.

At the end of the day I see the Unionist or Protestant position as saying two things. One, we're British, and two, we're Protestant. I'm not sure which they place the most emphasis on, and I'm not sure they're too sure themselves. The crisis of identity in that community is at the heart of the problem.

Protestantism, in my opinion, can be protected by the powers which the autonomous [federal Irish] state will have. The Protestant state would give Protestants absolute control over the thing they fear most—which is being subsumed into a Catholic state which is hostile to them. The Britishness would be protected by the Anglo-Irish Council, an institutional link with Britain which would provide for British citizenship. The Irishness of the minority would be protected by the federal link ... The only victim of the 1920 settlement was the minority in Northern Ireland ... not only in terms of economics, but also in terms which are essential to the cohesion of any state.

Most democratic states survive because they have an identity to which the whole population subscribes. Identity is the focus of order and authority. But the identity of the minority in Northern Ireland is not recognised. The minority have no source of authority.

That's why ambivalence on violence is not ambivalence on violence *per se* but an ambivalence on how to deal with it. And the ambivalence on how to deal with it comes from the absence of a central authority to which they can give their allegiance. Therefore an essential element to any solution has to be a recognition of the identity of the minority.[66]

The emphasis on an Anglo-Irish process signalled what Paddy Devlin and Gerry Fitt felt was a movement within the SDLP, associated with John Hume, towards a 'greening' of the party and a dilution of its socialism. The publication of a British Government consultative document on the government of Northern Ireland in November 1980, ruling out discussion of Irish unity, confederation, independence, or a change in the status of Northern Ireland, had brought about a split in the SDLP. Fitt resigned as leader, having wished to continue discussions with Unionists, even without an Irish dimension, commenting: 'Nationalism has been a political concept in Ireland over many, many years but I suggest that it has never brought peace to the people of the six counties. I for one have never been a nationalist to the total exclusion of my socialist ideas.'[67] Fitt was replaced as leader by Hume.

The rise in support for Sinn Féin following the hunger-strikes provided an important catalyst to the Anglo-Irish process. In an effort to consolidate the SDLP's position, constitutional nationalism throughout Ireland sought to reinvent its ideology through the New Ireland Forum in 1983 and 1984. The parties to the Forum, consisting of the main Southern parties and the SDLP, reaffirmed their shared aim of a united Ireland, pursued only by democratic political means and on the basis of agreement. They agreed that for nationalists a central aim had been the survival and development of an Irish identity, although

> for historical reasons, Irish nationalism may have tended to define itself in terms of separation from Britain and opposition to British domination of Ireland. The positive vision of Irish nationalism, however, has been to create a society that transcends religious differences and that can accommodate all traditions in a sovereign independent Ireland united by agreement. The aim of nationalists … in promoting Irish unity is to develop and promote an Irishness that demonstrates convincingly to unionists that the concerns of the unionist and Protestant heritage can be accommodated in a credible way and that institutions can be created which would protect such concerns and provide fully for their legitimate self-expression.

Perhaps the greatest significance of the Forum was its recognition that nationalists had 'hitherto in their public expression tended to underestimate the full dimension of the unionist identity and ethos.'[68] Although unionists generally ignored its deliberations, the evidence to the Forum of two brothers from the unionist tradition, Michael and Christopher McGimpsey, provided direct evidence of the Ulster Protestant commitment to the union with Great Britain, demonstrated on the question of unionism and its Britishness.

> [Michael McGimpsey] I think the real issue for the Unionist population of Northern Ireland is one of simple identity. We identify with the United Kingdom and regard ourselves as British. We have shared psychological bonds with the people of the United Kingdom, bonds of blood and history, common adversity, shared experience, shared emotional bonds. We are not so much saying we are against a

united Ireland as that we are pro-Union with the rest of the United Kingdom. We wish to remain British and intend to remain British ...

[Christopher McGimpsey] I am very proud of being Irish ... I do not define my Irishness as being ruled by a 32-county legislator in Dublin ... You can be Irish and British at the same time ... I define my Irishness as being an Irishman of Irish blood living in Ireland. I define my Britishness as being an Irishman of Irish blood living in that part of Ireland that did not secede from the rest of the United Kingdom ... I do not see the reconciling of the Irish and British traditions being dependent on unity. We must retain our Britishness because we are British. The only way we can retain our Britishness is with the border ... What a united Ireland is going to do is give you your Irishness but it is going to strip us of our Britishness.[69]

The Forum thus identified three elements of what it perceived unionists wanted to preserve: 'Britishness', Protestantism, and 'the economic advantages of the British link.' Exploring these, the Forum concluded:

Unionists generally regard themselves as being British, the inheritors of a specific communal loyalty to the British Crown. The traditional nationalist hostility to British rule is thus seen by unionists as incompatible with the survival of their own identity. Unionists generally regard themselves as being Irish even if this does not include a willingness to live under all-Ireland political institutions. However, many of them identify with Ireland and with various features of Irish life and their culture and way of life embrace much that is common to people throughout Ireland.[70]

This amounted to the first time that the representatives of Irish nationalism, North and South, apart from the Republican Movement, had officially recognised the right of unionists to their British identity. Previously, while admitting that the Northern Ireland people could consent to terminating Northern Ireland's position within the United Kingdom, nationalists had still defined unionists as an Irish minority.

However, the Forum did not allow the recognition of unionists' Britishness to undermine its goal of an 'agreed Ireland'. It defined 'agreement' as meaning that the 'political arrangements for a new and sovereign Ireland would have to be freely negotiated and agreed to by the people of the North and the people of the South.' The particular structure of political unity that the Forum wished to see established was a 'unitary state, achieved by agreement and consent, embracing the whole island of Ireland and providing irrevocable guarantees for the protection and preservation of both the unionist and nationalist identities.' A second model considered was that of a two-province non-denominational federal or confederal state based on the two existing entities of North and South. The third option was 'joint authority', described as the 'equal sharing of responsibility and authority for all aspects of the government of Northern Ireland by the governments of Great Britain and Ireland,' including external relations and diplomatic representation.[71]

The Forum concluded that the solution to the Northern Ireland conflict required new structures that would accommodate two sets of legitimate rights: 'the right of nationalists to effective political, symbolic and administrative expression of their identity' and 'the right of unionists to effective political, symbolic and administrative expression of their identity, their ethos and their way of life.'[72] The 'major realities' as identified by the Forum were:

(1) Existing structures and practices in Northern Ireland have failed to provide either peace, stability or reconciliation. The failure to recognise and accommodate the identity of Northern nationalists has resulted in deep and growing alienation on their part from the system of political authority.

(2) The conflict of nationalist and unionist identities has been concentrated upon the narrow ground of Northern Ireland. This has prevented constructive interaction between the two traditions and fostered fears, suspicions and misunderstandings.

(3) One effect of the division of Ireland is that civil law and administration in the South are seen ... by unionists, as being unduly influenced by the majority ethos on issues which Protestants consider to be a matter for private conscience ... On the other hand, Protestant values are seen to be reflected in the laws and practices in the North.

(4) The present formal position of the British Government, namely the guarantee ... has in its practical application had the effect of inhibiting the dialogue necessary for political progress ... of removing the incentive which would otherwise exist on all sides to seek a political solution.[73]

The last point was deemed to constitute in effect a unionist veto on 'any political change affecting the exercise of nationalist rights and on the form of government for Northern Ireland.' Finally, although the Forum recognised the Britishness of unionists, it was still argued that partition did not lie with the unionist resistance to a united Ireland but that the 'origin of the problem' remained the 'imposed division of Ireland which created an artificial political majority in the North.'[74]

THE ANGLO-IRISH AGREEMENT

While the British Government had less cause in the early eighties to worry about the possibility of dealing with terrorism on two fronts, it was confronted with the problem not only of continuing Republican violence but of increasing electoral support for Sinn Féin. Initial British reactions to the report of the New Ireland Forum were cool, summed up in Margaret Thatcher's 'out ... out ... out' response to its options for an 'agreed Ireland'. But the spectre of Sinn Féin overtaking the SDLP as the dominant nationalist party led the British to initiate discussions with the Irish Government in order to shore up the SDLP by reducing Catholic alienation within Northern Ireland. The outcome of this was the institutionalising of the Anglo-Irish process through the Anglo-Irish Agreement, signed by Margaret Thatcher and the Taoiseach, Garret FitzGerald, on 15 November 1985.

The origins of the agreement lay in an Anglo-Irish governmental process begun by Thatcher and the then Taoiseach, Charles Haughey, in 1980. A communiqué issued at the end of an Anglo-Irish summit meeting in May 1980 referred to the wish of both leaders 'to develop new and closer political co-operation between their two governments' and, with this purpose in mind, to hold regular meetings. The first meeting, in December 1980, promised to give special consideration to the 'totality of relationships within these islands.' It commissioned joint studies covering issues such as possible institutional structures, citizenship rights, security, economic co-operation, and measures to encourage mutual understanding.[75]

Relations between the two Governments cooled during the Falklands War in 1982, and the British Government once again turned to the search for an internal Northern Ireland settlement. A White Paper published in April 1982, *Northern Ireland: A Framework for Devolution*, proposed a 78-member single-chamber Assembly, elected by PR, possessing 'scrutinising, deliberative and consultative functions' but no legislative or administrative functions, although these could be devolved to the Assembly later in a form of 'rolling devolution'. These proposals were enshrined in the Northern Ireland Act, 1982, which sought to improve the processes and scrutiny of direct rule by establishing committees entrusted with monitoring the NIO departments. The main requirement for intercommunity consensus involved the Assembly not submitting any proposals unless they had the support of at least 70 per cent of its members, or a combination of the support of a majority of members and the Secretary of State's opinion that the proposals would command widespread community support.[76]

The SDLP, however, boycotted the Assembly, concentrating on the Anglo-Irish process. Following the fall of Haughey's Fianna Fáil Government and its replacement by a Fine Gael-Labour coalition, the British Government began secret discussions with the Irish Government to produce an agreement that would demonstrate that constitutional nationalism in Northern Ireland could deliver progress. Unionists became suspicious when they heard rumours of what the intergovernmental conversations entailed. In August 1985 the two main Unionist leaders, James Molyneaux, who had replaced Harry West as leader of the Ulster Unionist Party, and Ian Paisley, wrote to Margaret Thatcher expressing their concern about the secrecy surrounding the Anglo-Irish talks, and the future of constitutional politics in Northern Ireland, should an Anglo-Irish agreement accord the Republic any role in the direction or control of Northern Ireland's internal affairs. They stated that provided the United Kingdom's sovereignty over Northern Ireland remained undiminished, and provided the Republic's territorial claim to the North was withdrawn, they were willing to contribute to a process of British-Irish discussion and co-operation

(a) as members of a newly formed government of Northern Ireland meeting with opposite numbers in the government of the Irish Republic to consider matters of mutual interest and concern within the purview of respective departmental responsibilities, and

(b) as members of a devolved government comprising part of a United Kingdom delegation to talks with the government of the Irish Republic about matters of mutual interest and concern to both the states exclusive of those matters referred to in (a) above, and those touching upon United Kingdom sovereignty over Northern Ireland.

Molyneaux and Paisley submitted their view that a 'continuing SDLP veto' over internal political development, and a continued denial of local democracy in Northern Ireland in the wake of any Anglo-Irish agreement, could only further erode the confidence of the unionist majority in the constitutional process, with 'calamitous' consequences. Short of seats in a devolved government, the two Unionist leaders were prepared to consider 'any reasonable proposals' for the protection of minority interests in a new Northern Ireland Parliament.[77]

Thatcher replied by stating that she was convinced that the present dialogue with the Irish Government represented the best hope of improving co-operation in a number of areas, including security, and of promoting an enduring peace and stability in Northern Ireland. If the dialogue was to have a chance of producing useful results, she argued, it had to remain confidential until it reached a conclusion. She gave an 'unqualified assurance' that British sovereignty over Northern Ireland would be undiminished. By this she meant that 'first Northern Ireland will remain part of the United Kingdom for as long as a majority in the Province so wish; and secondly that whatever may emerge from our discussions with the Irish authorities, responsibility for the government of Northern Ireland will remain with UK ministers accountable to Parliament.' She hoped that the two Unionist leaders would accept that 'it must be the Government of the United Kingdom and Parliament that determine the policy to be adopted in respect of relations with other countries, including the Republic of Ireland.'[78]

Molyneaux and Paisley had specifically sought an assurance that undiminished British sovereignty over Northern Ireland would preclude any British-Irish machinery dealing only with Northern Ireland, rather than with British-Irish relations as a whole, and noted its omission in Thatcher's reply as an indication that such machinery was being planned by the British Government. This they saw as an infringement of British sovereignty over Northern Ireland. Molyneaux and Paisley did not accept that the Republic had in any way diluted its claim to the territory of Northern Ireland, and an indication by the Republic's Government that it was forced to accept the reality of the existence of Northern Ireland as a political fact was a far cry from *de jure* recognition. The two Unionist leaders accepted the right of the United Kingdom Government and Parliament to determine the policy to be adopted in respect of relations with other countries;

> we would contend, however, that if it is your intention to treat Northern Ireland as a distinct part of the Kingdom in terms of relations with the Irish Republic, then justice dictates that the people of Northern Ireland ... should be afforded the opportunity to accept or reject what your government has negotiated for the Province before the deal is finally struck. After all ... you insist that devolved government can only be restored to Northern Ireland if it 'is acceptable to both sides of the Community there.' We invite you to

state whether it is your government's policy to proceed with a British/Irish deal on Northern Ireland unacceptable to the majority in the Province, while the minority is to be permitted to continue to exercise a veto on devolution.[79]

The worst fears of the Unionist leaders were realised when, on 15 November 1985, the British and Irish Governments signed the Anglo-Irish Agreement. The agreement established an Inter-Governmental Conference dealing with political matters, security and related matters, legal questions, and the promotion of cross-border co-operation. Under article 2 (*b*) the British Government committed itself, 'in the interests of promoting peace and stability,' to making determined efforts to resolve any differences that arose within the conference with the Irish Government. Article 5 (*a*) stated that the Conference would look at measures to 'recognise and accommodate the rights and identities of the two traditions in Northern Ireland, to protect human rights and prevent discrimination.' Matters to be considered in these areas included measures to foster the cultural heritage of both traditions, changes in electoral arrangements, the use of flags and symbols, and the avoidance of social and economic discrimination. Article 5 (*c*) stated that 'if it should prove impossible to achieve and sustain devolution on a basis which secures widespread acceptance in Northern Ireland, the conference shall be a framework within which the Irish Government may, where the interests of the minority community are significantly or especially affected, put forward views on proposals for major legislation and on major policy issues, which are on the purview of the Northern Ireland departments.' On the status of Northern Ireland, article 1 of the agreement stated that the two Governments

(*a*) affirm that any change in the status of Northern Ireland would only come about with the consent of a majority of the people of Northern Ireland;

(*b*) recognise that the present wish of a majority of the people of Northern Ireland is for no change in the status of Northern Ireland;

(*c*) declare that, if in the future a majority of the people of Northern Ireland clearly wish for and formally consent to the establishment of a united Ireland, they will introduce and support in the respective Parliaments legislation to give effect to that wish.[80]

Unionist opposition to the agreement was total. On 23 November 1985 between 100,000 and 200,000 unionists attended a demonstration against the agreement at Belfast City Hall. All fifteen Unionist MPs resigned their seats in protest, under the slogan 'Ulster says no,' after which the marginal Newry and Armagh seat was lost to the SDLP deputy leader, Séamus Mallon. Despite this apparent setback the vote demonstrated Protestant opposition, with 418,230 voting against the agreement, and the collapse of support for the Alliance Party, which received only 32,095 votes, as Protestants voted for anti-agreement parties.[81]

On 3 March 1986 a Unionist 'Day of Action' shut down much of Northern Ireland's commerce and industry, followed by rioting in Protestant areas of Belfast and loyalist snipers shooting at the RUC. Later that month the banning of an Apprentice Boys parade in Portadown led to rioting between the RUC and loyalists, continuing over the following weeks and leading to the death of a young Protestant. Tensions between the RUC and loyalists ultimately led to over five hundred police homes being attacked and 150 families being forced to move out of vulnerable Protestant areas. The RUC Chief Constable, Sir John Hermon, later revealed that he was determined that there would be no repeat of the UWC strike of 1974 and that the RUC would be in the forefront in controlling public order; he declared that 'I was quite prepared, if necessary to see them [the RUC] sacrifice themselves.'[82]

Unionist opposition to the agreement, however, despite a reduction in violence, remained fundamental. Article 1 (a) was considered by the Unionist parties to go no further than earlier statements by Governments of the Republic and was virtually identical to the Irish declaration at Sunningdale. Article 1 (b) was described as merely a statement of existing fact and added nothing to the significance of article 1 (a). Unionists claimed that article 1 (a) and (b) was merely a statement of the factual position of Northern Ireland existing within the United Kingdom and of the current professed intentions of the two Governments. They argued that the article 'does not accord recognition to Northern Ireland and those who claim that it does … are either ignorant of the history of the question or are misrepresenting the position.' Furthermore, Unionists considered that article 1 was the weakest statement yet of the position of the British Government. Unionists recalled that in paragraph 5 of the Sunningdale Agreement in 1973 the British Government had declared that 'it was, and would remain, its policy to support the wishes of the majority of the people of Northern Ireland. The present status of Northern Ireland is that it is part of the United Kingdom.' Unionists noted that it was 'no longer the policy of Her Majesty's Government to support the wishes of the people of Northern Ireland, and that Her Majesty's Government are no longer concerned to identify the present status of Northern Ireland.' This latter point was considered significant in view of the differences between the British and Irish versions of the text of the agreement. In the former, the preamble began:

> Agreement between the Government of the United Kingdom of Great Britain and Northern Ireland and the Government of the Republic of Ireland

whereas the preamble to the Irish version read:

> Agreement between the Government of Ireland and the Government of the United Kingdom.

These differences, Unionists argued, taken with the failure to identify the status of Northern Ireland, left room for those who believed that Northern Ireland was, in Irish law, part of the Irish state to assert that the agreement accepted, or did not dissent from, that proposition. Unionists claimed that there had been a change in Northern Ireland's status, because the Northern Ireland people were affected by the agreement, which changed the processes and structures of government operating within Northern Ireland. They argued that the Governments of the United Kingdom and the Republic should have sought the consent of the people of Northern Ireland to that change.[83] In opposing the agreement, they concluded that

> the Agreement is the reward of the intransigence of the SDLP, coupled with the violence of militant republicanism ...
>
> The manner in which the Agreement was negotiated clearly indicates that it is designed to operate to the detriment of the people of Northern Ireland ...
>
> The Agreement does not give any added recognition to the status of Northern Ireland: rather than accept the right of the people of Northern Ireland to determine their future, the Agreement attempts to subvert that right ...
>
> The Intergovernmental Conference is a joint authority in embryo, which if allowed to develop will become the effective government of Northern Ireland ...
>
> The Agreement and Conference by acting over the heads of the elected representatives of the people of Northern Ireland undermines the status of those representatives ...
>
> The Agreement diminishes British sovereignty in Northern Ireland by admitting a foreign government into the structure and

processes of government of Northern Ireland: Northern Ireland is no longer a part of the United Kingdom on the same basis as Great Britain and the people of Northern Ireland are denied equality of treatment, status and esteem with their fellow citizens ...

The Agreement lacks the consent of the people of Northern Ireland ...

The changes in security and other policies adumbrated in the Agreement will only lead to greater insecurity and instability and ... this Agreement will not lead to peace and reconciliation ...

There is no prospect of devolution while the Agreement remains ... The requirements for devolution are unjust in that greater acceptance is required to diminish the Agreement than was needed to establish it ...

In total the Agreement is discriminatory, it does not provide for equality of treatment either within Northern Ireland or within the United Kingdom ... It is irreformable ... there are no changes which can make this framework acceptable ... [84]

Ian Paisley summed up the fears of many unionists when he said that he believed that 'whether Mrs Thatcher knew it or not, she was signing a document, the eventual outcome of which was a united Ireland.'

I think the British government said, 'Yes, we will go for a united Ireland.' The Secretary of State has said ... he doesn't believe the IRA can be defeated. Well, if they can't be defeated, then he must be preparing surrender terms for the British government. So the view of the people would be, 'Yes, the British government is trying to sell us out.' Absolutely.[85]

SDLP-SINN FÉIN TALKS

What became known as the 'peace process' began in talks between the SDLP and Provisional Sinn Féin in 1988. John Hume incurred considerable criticism for embarking on this course of action, particularly as it had followed relatively soon after one of the Provisional IRA's most infamous bombings, that of a Remembrance Day service in Enniskillen on 8 November 1987. Eleven people, all Protestants, were killed in the attack. During the talks the SDLP tried to persuade Sinn Féin that the British Government had taken up a neutral position on Northern Ireland's continuance within the Union. The SDLP argued that article 1 of the Anglo-Irish Agreement was evidence of this, and that in that Article, in the SDLP's view, the British government has made clear that if the people of the unionist and nationalist traditions in Ireland reach agreement on the unity and independence of Ireland, then the British government will legislate for it, facilitate it, and leave the people of Ireland, North and South, to govern themselves. In short, they are stating that Irish unity and independence are entirely a matter for those Irish people who want it, persuading those Irish people who don't. It is clear from Article 1 ... that the British government have no other interest at stake in the exercise of self-determination except that violence or the threat of violence shall not succeed. In this context the 'armed struggle' can only be a negative factor.[86]

Hume claimed that implicit in article 1 (c) was a declaration that the British had no interest of their own in staying in Ireland. In short, he claimed, the British Government was 'neutral in that it was no longer pro-Union. There is nothing, therefore, to stop the British government from becoming pro-Irish unity in their policies.' The SDLP's task was to persuade the British to move in that direction and to 'use all their considerable influence and resources to persuade the Unionist people that their best interests are served by a new Ireland, in which Unionist interests are accommodated to their own satisfaction and in which there is a new relationship with Britain.'[87] Article 1 of the Anglo-Irish Agreement, embodying the 'Unionist veto', was now regarded by the SDLP as a 'natural veto', because Unionist agreement was essential if Irish unity was to be achieved.[88] Hume asked Gerry Adams, the president of Sinn Féin:

1. Do you accept the right of the Irish people to self-determination?

2. Do you accept that the Irish people are at present deeply divided on the question of how to exercise self-determination?

3. Do you accept that in practice agreement on that right means agreement of both the unionist and nationalist traditions in Ireland?

4. If you accept 1, 2, and 3 would you then agree that the best way forward would be to attempt to create a conference table, convened by an Irish government, at which all parties in the North with an electoral mandate would attend? The purpose of such a conference would be to try to reach agreement on the exercise of self-determination in Ireland and on how the people of our diverse traditions can live together in peace, harmony and agreement. It would be understood in advance that if such a conference were to

reach agreement, it would be endorsed by the British government.

5. In the event of the representatives of the unionist people refusing to participate in such a conference, would you join with the Irish government and other nationalist participants in preparing a peaceful and comprehensive approach to achieving agreement on self-determination in Ireland? Would he in fact and in practice take up the challenge laid down by Wolfe Tone?

In reply, Adams said he accepted the right of the Irish people 'as a whole' to self-determination and recognised that unionists had 'democratic rights' but that those rights 'must not extend to a veto over the national rights of the Irish people as a whole.' The suggested conference would have to be held unconditionally, and the precondition of an IRA cessation of operations should not be attached to the proposal. Sinn Féin, however, did not believe that the proposed conference would be the best way forward, since it would be in the absence of a prior declaration of intention to withdraw from Ireland by the British. Instead Sinn Féin suggested:

1. That Sinn Féin and the SDLP agree with, and endorse, the internationally established principle of the right of the Irish people to national self-determination.

2. That Sinn Féin and the SDLP agree that Britain has no legitimate right to be in Ireland.

3. That Sinn Féin and the SDLP agree that the IRA is politically motivated in its actions and that IRA volunteers are not criminals.

4. That Sinn Féin and the SDLP agree that the British government and its forces in Ireland are not in a peacekeeping role.

5. That Sinn Féin and the SDLP would agree that failure to rule out nationalist participation in a devolved or internal six-county arrangement actually encourages the British to pursue such policies and in reality would protract the conflict.

6. That Sinn Féin and the SDLP agree on a common solution to the political situation existing in the six counties.

7. That Sinn Féin and the SDLP join forces to impress on the Dublin government the need to launch an international and diplomatic offensive to secure national self-determination.

Adams rejected the idea that the British Government was neutral and argued that *de facto* sovereignty over the two states in Ireland was exercised by the British and Dublin Governments. For Sinn Féin the exercise of Irish self-determination would involve the British

Government relinquishing its claim to sovereignty over the six-county state. Political, constitutional and psychological reasons, therefore, Adams argued, dictated that the British Government should be involved in any process that would realise the exercise of Irish national self-determination. Irish reunification as a stated British policy objective would constitute, as a first step, the minimum requirement of such an indication. In the absence of such a declaration, Unionists, assured by the veto conferred on them by the British Government, would feel no compulsion to move towards a consensus on the means to constructive British disengagement from Ireland.

For Sinn Féin the key questions were how to get the British Government to recognise Irish national rights, how to get it to change its present policy to one of ending partition and the Union within the context of Irish reunification, and, having done so, how to secure the co-operation of a majority in the North to the means of implementing those rights. Adams argued that Hume's claim that the British Government was in effect neutral

> ignores all the historic evidence of British domination in Ireland and is wholly contradicted by the events of the past twenty years, all of which point to the continuing commitment of the British government to impose its will by force on the Irish people through the dominance of the six-county state. In the face of British government injustice and oppression the SDLP, to substantiate claims that the British are neutral, can only point to Article 1 of the Hillsborough Treaty despite the fact that the loyalist veto is explicitly contained within this Article ... Sinn Féin ... in exploring the SDLP policy of 'unity by consent', was dismayed to discover that contained within this policy was a recognition of and acceptance of the loyalist veto. The SDLP now appear to accept as absolute the power of veto of a national minority to obstruct and thwart the democratic right of the Irish people as a whole to exercise national self-determination. This position is of course untenable for a party which claims to act in the interests of Irish nationalists.[89]

THE INTER-PARTY TALKS AND BRITISH-SINN FÉIN CONTACTS

Following the failure of these talks, political attention switched from intra-nationalist negotiations towards Nationalist-Unionist talks, in the form of the Brooke-Mayhew inter-party talks of 1991–92. These involved the British and Irish Governments and the four main

Northern Ireland constitutional parties—the Ulster Unionist Party, DUP, SDLP, and Alliance Party—who together, for the first time, explained their perceptions of themselves and each other. The talks owed their origins to the many 'talks about talks' conducted between local parties and the Secretary of State, Tom King, and his successor, Peter Brooke, which sought a new, broadly based agreement to supersede the Anglo-Irish Agreement. The talks involved three sets of relationships, or 'strands': those within Northern Ireland (strand 1), those between Northern Ireland and the Republic (strand 2), and those between the United Kingdom and the Republic (strand 3). All three strands would begin within weeks of each other, and nothing would be agreed until everything was agreed.

During strand 1 negotiations in 1992, conducted under the aegis of the new Secretary of State, Sir Patrick Mayhew, all the parties, with the exception of the SDLP, envisaged some form of assembly for dealing with Northern Ireland's internal affairs, to be composed of elected Northern Ireland representatives alone. In May 1992 the SDLP suggested that Northern Ireland should be run by six commissioners, with an assembly based on the European Parliament. Three of the commissioners would be elected in Northern Ireland by PR, while the British and Irish Governments and the European Community would each appoint one commissioner. There would also be a North-South council of ministers, which would deal with a wide range of issues, including economic and security matters. For the SDLP 'parity of esteem' for nationalists meant absolute equality in all aspects of political, cultural, social and economic life, including institutional North-South arrangements. They argued that the Republic's role in the internal affairs of Northern Ireland, through the Anglo-Irish Agreement, was there 'of right'. The SDLP rejected the other Northern parties' plan for a devolved assembly, arguing that they were based on the assumption that as part of the United Kingdom, Northern Ireland was 'an exclusively British political entity'.

> The SDLP contests ... that assumption ... that the significance of the Unionist community's Britishness is of greater significance to that community, than is the significance of its Irishness to the nationalist community ... Such an approach fails to render parity of esteem to both identities ... and the result would mean victory for one community over the other ... In contrast, the SDLP takes the view that since both identities are of equal significance to their respective communities, both must be given parity of esteem in new institutions.

It is on the basis of this requirement that the SDLP has approached its proposals for new institutions.[90]

This came as a considerable shock for Unionists and the Alliance Party. The Unionist Party argued that such a body as suggested by the SDLP 'is not consistent with the continued membership of NI within the UK.'[91]

Deadlock manifested itself in strand 2, dealing with North-South relations, while strand 3, dealing with the United Kingdom and the Republic, hardly got off the ground. In strand 2 the primary aim of the Unionist parties was the removal of the Republic's territorial claim and the creation of North-South bodies based on mutual respect and co-operation between a Northern Ireland Assembly and the Dáil but not a single executive North-South body acting on an all-Ireland basis. The position of the Ulster Unionist Party was that nationalists represented an Irish identity and an Irish dimension but that there was another Irish identity that nationalists appeared incapable of understanding, since it had not been defined exclusively by them. The Unionist Party felt that even while nationalists might now acknowledge unionists' Britishness they still believed that unionists were ultimately absorbable within the Irish nation, as represented by a united Ireland.

For Nationalists the real problem is their inability to accept the legitimacy of the Irish Unionist identity ... The Union with Great Britain is a Union in the hearts and minds of the Unionist people, and is something which we cannot change, even if we wanted to. This feeling of Britishness is so deeply ingrained as to be almost genetically encoded. It is not a device or artifice which has been imposed on an unsuspecting people; neither is it something Unionists wish to impose on those who have different political aspirations. But for Unionists their basic political heritage is their Britishness.

   Failure to recognise this is a fundamental and enduring mistake of Irish Nationalism ... Britishness is at the heart of Unionist philosophy ... the feeling of belonging; the feeling of sharing with our fellow-citizens in Great Britain in great national events; of being part of something larger than simply the six counties in the north-eastern corner of our island. It is a shared psychological bond; a shared emotional bond ... common bonds of history and of shared adversities, shared triumphs and shared sacrifices ... The British presence in Ireland is not merely the 12,000 regular troops stationed in Northern Ireland in support of the Civil Power. Neither is it simply the Secretary of State and the Administration at Stormont ... The real long-term British presence in Ireland is the one million plus Irish Unionists who live in the north-east of the island and who continue to demonstrate, through the ballot box, their wish to remain within the United Kingdom.

Because of this deep and fundamental principle of belonging, unity by consent, either now or in the foreseeable future, is not forthcoming.

Unionists have the right to say YES to a 32 county state ... but they also have the right to say NO ... The so-called guarantee to Unionists by the Westminster Parliament is simply an acceptance of reality. A vote in Westminster to expel Northern Ireland from the Kingdom could not stop those who support the union from feeling as they do, nor would it convince Unionists of the desirability of Irish unity.

For those who support the union and desire its continuance there is no contradiction in being Irish and British—just as there is no contradiction in being Scottish and British, Welsh and British or English and British ... Many of us are proud to be Irish, and will always hold ourselves so to be. But we are equally proud to be British and will always feel similarly committed to that sense of identity.

The Ulster Unionist Party considered that a historic breakthrough in North-South relations could best be achieved through the establishment of an Inter-Irish Relations Committee to facilitate business between the Belfast and Dublin administrations, in which the two could co-operate, as equals, in achieving social and economic benefits for the Irish people as a whole. It would further form an integral part of a larger body, a 'Council of the British Isles', rather than merely part of a Council of Ireland.[92] Unionists rejected an executive role for the Irish Government in Northern Ireland's affairs and pronounced themselves disappointed with the lack of generosity on the part of the South's negotiating team, particularly when the latter suggested that they could, rather than would, change the Republic's constitutional claim to the North.

Despite the failure to reach a settlement, the participants did identify a number of principles that should underlie any new political institutions in Northern Ireland. It was agreed that they should be

 a. based on democratic principles and reflect the wishes of the electorate;
 b. widely acceptable, in particular in the sense of providing an appropriate and equitable role for both sides of the community, such

that both the main parts of the Northern Ireland community should be able to identify with them and feel that their representatives have a meaningful function to perform;

c. stable and durable in the sense of not being dependent on a particular election result or political deal. The system should, so far as possible, be self sustaining;

d. capable of development, in response to changing political realities, with the agreement of all concerned;

e. workable, in the sense of being as straightforward to operate as possible;

f. such as to avoid any entrenchment of the main community division and to encourage the development of a society in which both main traditions would be respected;

g. such as to provide all constitutional political parties with the opportunity to achieve a role at each level of responsibility, and to have a position proportional to their electoral strength in broad terms;

h. able to function effectively, efficiently and decisively within clearly defined areas of responsibility;

i. innovative, in the sense of learning from and not merely modelled on any previous arrangements;

j. established within a defined relationship with UK institutions;

k. competent to manage any relationship developed in strand two of the talks;

l. capable of developing a direct relationship with EC [European Community] institutions;

m. capable of developing relationships with any devolved institutions in Great Britain present or future;

n. capable of securing public endorsement;

o. consistent with the maximum possible delegation of authority;

p. such as to ensure the greatest possible degree of parliamentary scrutiny of and public accountability for the exercise of powers of government within Northern Ireland.[93]

Unknown to most observers, at the same time that the inter-party talks had been taking place the British Government had had a secret channel of communication with the Republican Movement for three years. Mayhew later claimed that the channel had arisen out of an oral message from the Provisional IRA leadership, declaring that 'the conflict is over but we need your advice on how to bring it to a close.' Martin McGuinness of Sinn Féin emphatically denied that any such message was sent, claiming instead that the British Government had begun the contacts. Following the first alleged contact from Sinn Féin, the British Government responded by stating that 'any dialogue would follow from an unannounced halt to violent activity. We confirm that if violence had genuinely been brought to an end, whether or not that fact had been announced, then dialogue could take place.' The Provisional IRA did not provide the unequivocal response the British Government sought, instead asking: 'In plain language please tell ... as a matter of urgency when you will open dialogue in the end of a total end to hostilities.' The British response stated: 'If, as you have offered, you were able to give us an unequivocal assurance that violence has indeed been brought to a permanent end, and that accordingly Sinn Féin is now committed to political progress by peaceful and democratic means alone, we will ... publicly ... enter exploratory dialogue with you.'[94]

Sinn Féin claimed that a British MI5 officer, acting as a go-between, had accepted that a united Ireland would be the final result of any negotiations; the British Government, in turn, claimed that there had been no authorisation for such a statement.[95] On 19 March 1993 the British Government sent a message to the Provisionals explicitly stating its rejection of the position originally advocated by the SDLP and now adopted by Sinn Féin, that it should seek to 'persuade' unionists that their best interests lay in a united Ireland.

The British Government has no desire to inhibit or impede legitimate constitutional expression of any political opinion ... and wants to see included in this process all main parties which have sufficiently shown they genuinely do not espouse violence. It has no blueprint. It wants an agreed accommodation, not an imposed settlement, arrived at through an inclusive process in which the parties are free agents ... [But] the ... Government does not have, and will not adopt, any prior objective of 'ending partition.' The British Government cannot enter a talks process, or expect others to do so, with the purpose of achieving a predetermined outcome, whether the 'ending of partition' or anything else. It has accepted that the eventual outcome of such a process could be a united Ireland, but only on the basis of the consent of the people of Northern Ireland. Should this be the eventual outcome of a peaceful democratic process, the British Government would bring forward legislation to implement the will of the people ... But unless the people of Northern Ireland come to express such a view, the British

Government will continue to uphold the union, seeking to ensure the good governance of Northern Ireland, in the interests of all its people, within the totality of relationships in these islands.[96]

THE HUME-ADAMS TALKS

The disclosure that such contacts had taken place angered Unionists, even though it was clear that the British Government's private stance on Northern Ireland's position within the United Kingdom was the same as its public stance: that there should be a permanent end to violence. Unionists were again incensed when, following the collapse of the inter-party talks process, the reasons for the SDLP's reluctance to accept an internal settlement became apparent when it was revealed that John Hume and Gerry Adams were once again involved in discussions. Sinn Féin had also opened a channel to the Dublin Government, through an intermediary. Republicans argued that if there was to be peace in Ireland then Dublin would have to assume its 'national responsibility' and persuade the British Government that partition had been a failure and seek a change in British policy. Sinn Féin sought to pursue a peace initiative that would also be compatible with their goal of ending partition. Republicans had been encouraged by a speech by Peter Brooke in 1990 in which he stated that it was 'difficult to envisage a military defeat of the IRA.'

In 1992 Sinn Féin published *Towards a Lasting Peace in Ireland*, their analysis of how the deadlock in the North might be broken. It placed the onus on the two Governments, but particularly on the British Government, to work to secure change. It called on the British Government to 'join the persuaders,' to use its influence to convince unionists that their future did not lie within the Union. It also called on the Dublin Government to persuade the British that partition had failed, to persuade unionists of the benefits of reunification, and to persuade the international community that it should support a 'peace process' in Ireland.[97]

Following a meeting on 23 April 1993, Hume and Adams issued a joint statement declaring that an internal Northern Ireland political settlement with no Irish dimension was 'not a solution.' They accepted that 'the Irish people as a whole have a right to national self-determination' and that this view was 'shared by a majority of the people of this island, though not by all its people.' The exercise of self-determination was a 'matter for agreement between the people of

Ireland. It is the search for that agreement and the means of achieving it on which we will be concentrating. We are mindful that not all the people of Ireland share that view or agree on how to give meaningful expression to it. Indeed we cannot disguise the different views held by our own parties.'[98]

According to Adams, the basic principles underpinning the Hume-Adams agreement were:

1. The Irish people as a whole have the right to national self-determination.

2. An internal settlement is not a solution.

3. The exercise of self-determination is a matter for agreement between the people of Ireland.

4. The consent and allegiance of unionists are essential ingredients if a lasting peace is to be established.

5. The unionists cannot have a veto over British policy.

6. The British government must join the persuaders.

7. The London and Dublin governments have the major responsibility to secure political progress.[99]

The secret Hume-Adams negotiations angered and alarmed Unionists, who denounced the talks as evidence of a 'pan-nationalist front'. Amid increasing violence, particularly loyalist, on 23 October 1993 a Provisional IRA bomb exploded in a fish shop on the Shankill Road, Belfast, killing ten people and injuring fifty-seven; nine of the dead were Protestant shoppers, the tenth the IRA bomber. The Provisionals claimed that their intended target was members of the UFF. Gerry Adams was subsequently condemned for helping carry the coffin of the deceased bomber. In the days following the bombing, loyalist paramilitary attacks on Catholics resulted in four deaths, culminating on 30 October with UFF gunmen entering the Rising Sun bar in Greysteel, County Londonderry, to randomly fire at customers celebrating Halloween. Seven Catholics and one Protestant, a former UDR member, were killed. By the end of October 1993 a total of twenty-seven people were killed, the highest number for a single month since October 1976.

The violence shifted the emphasis away from the Hume-Adams agreement and back to the efforts of the British and Irish Governments to produce conditions that might tempt the paramilitaries into cease-fires. The outcome of inter-governmental discussions was the Downing Street Declaration of December 1993. In the declaration, the British Government, in an effort to remove the main Republican justification for violence, namely British imperialism in Ireland, declared that it had 'no selfish strategic or economic interest in Northern Ireland' and that its primary interest was to see 'peace, stability and reconciliation established by agreement among all the people who inhabit the island.' The role of the British Government was to 'encourage, facilitate and enable' the achievement of such agreement over time, through a process of dialogue and co-operation, based on the 'full respect for the rights and identities of both traditions in Ireland.' In this the British Government accepted that such agreement might take the form of a united Ireland, but crucially stated that

the British Government agree that it is for the people of the island of Ireland alone, by agreement between the two parts respectively, to exercise the right of self-determination on the basis of consent, freely and concurrently given, North and South, to bring about a united Ireland, if that is their wish.

The British Government thus rejected the Republican demand that the unit of self-determination should be the island of Ireland; concurrent referendums, North and South, still permitted Northern Ireland to self-determine its constitutional future and to consent, or not consent, to a change in its status, regardless of how the rest of Ireland voted.

For the Irish Government the Taoiseach, Albert Reynolds, agreed that it would be wrong to attempt to impose a united Ireland in the 'absence of the freely given consent of a majority of the people of Northern Ireland,' and he accepted, on behalf of the Government, that the 'democratic right of self-determination by the people of Ireland as a whole must be achieved and exercised with and subject to the agreement and consent of a majority of the people of Northern Ireland and must, consistent with justice and equity, respect the democratic dignity and the civil rights and religious liberties of both communities.'

Referring to the unionist position in Northern Ireland, Reynolds committed his Government to an examination of any elements in the democratic life and organisation of the Irish state that could be represented to the Irish Government, in political talks, as a real and substantial threat to the unionist way of life and ethos or that could be represented as not being fully consistent with a modern democratic and pluralist society. He then confirmed that, in the event of an overall political settlement, the Irish Government would—not could—put forward and support proposals for changing the Constitution that would fully represent the principle of consent in Northern Ireland.

Both Governments confirmed that democratically mandated parties that 'establish a commitment to exclusively peaceful methods and which have shown that they abide by the democratic process, are free to participate fully in democratic politics and to join in dialogue in due course between the governments and the political parties on the way ahead.' Reynolds suggested that democratic parties could consult together in a Forum for Peace and Reconciliation.[100]

CEASE-FIRES

The Downing Street Declaration did not meet the Republican Movement's demands on the question of consent, or on the role of the British Government as a persuader for a united Ireland. Sinn Féin, while accepting that Britain no longer had any selfish economic or strategic interest in staying in Ireland, was dissatisfied with the fact that the British Government did not state that it had no remaining political interest in Ireland, believing that it remained politically committed to the Union and seeing the weakening of the link with Northern Ireland as potentially the first stage in the disintegration of the United Kingdom.[101] Nevertheless, the declaration did increase the pressure on the Provisional IRA to declare an end to hostilities and to explore the possibilities for peace through dialogue. This occurred on 31 August 1994, when the IRA issued a statement announcing a cease-fire.

> Recognising the potential of the current situation and in order to enhance the democratic peace process and underline our definitive commitment to its success the leadership of Óglaigh na hÉireann [the IRA] have decided that as of midnight, Wednesday, 31 August, there will be a complete cessation of military operations ... Our struggle has seen many gains and advances made by nationalists and for the democratic position. We believe that an opportunity to create a just and lasting settlement has been created ... We note that the Downing Street Declaration is not a solution ... A solution will only be found as a result of inclusive negotiations. Others, not least the British government, have a duty to face up to their responsibilities ... [102]

The Republican Movement did not accept that its cessation meant that its fundamental principles were to be abandoned: rather, a new front in the struggle was being opened. The ten 'strategic objectives' set out by the Republican Movement for its supporters, referred to as TUAS (interpreted by many commentators as 'totally unarmed strategy' but later revised by others to 'tactical use of armed struggle'), were:

1. Affect the international and domestic perception of the republican position i.e. one which is reasonable;

2. To develop a Northern nationalist consensus on the basis of constitutional change;

3. To develop an Irish national consensus on the same basis;

4. To develop Irish-America as a significant player in support of the above;

5. To develop a broader and deeper Irish nationalist consensus at grassroots level;

6. To develop and mobilise an anti-imperialist Irish peace movement;

7. To expose the British and Unionists as the intransigent parties;

8. To heighten the contradiction between British unionism and Ulster loyalism;

9. To assist the development of whatever potential exists in Britain to create a mood/climate/party/movement for peace;

10. To maintain the political cohesion and organisational integrity of … SF so as to remain an effective political force.[103]

The IRA's cessation, however, was not enough to enable Sinn Féin to gain immediate and unconditional entry to all-party talks with the British Government and the Unionist parties. The British Government had remained sceptical of the IRA's sincerity, since its cease-fire statement did not refer to a permanent cessation. Consequently, the British Prime Minister, John Major, explained: 'We need to be sure the cessation of violence isn't temporary; that it isn't for one week or one month, but a permanent cessation of violence.' Sir Patrick Mayhew emphasised that there was a serious need to establish the permanence of the cease-fire, stating:

This is not just a piece of pedantry or nitpicking about a particular word. What lies behind it is the absolute essential importance that such talks and negotiations as may take place in future shall not take place under the implied threat that violence, which after all has gone on for so long, could be taken up again and renewed and resumed if people didn't behave during those discussions in a way which was congenial to the IRA.

In part this was a concern to reassure the unionist population, which remained suspicious of secret deals. Ian Paisley noted that the Provisional IRA had not used the term 'permanent' and added that the only way 'that you could prove that there would be a permanent cessation is by the surrender of their killing machine, their Semtex [explosive] stores, their guns, their mortars and their equipment.'[104]

In Washington, on 7 March 1995, Mayhew outlined a three-point plan for the 'decommissioning' or destruction of terrorist weapons that would allow Sinn Féin to join all-party talks. These were a 'willingness to disarm progressively'; agreement on the method of decommissioning weapons; and a start to the process of decommissioning as a 'tangible confidence building measure.'[105] The British and Unionist argument was that if the IRA cessation was permanent, then Republicans no longer needed their weapons of war. In contrast, the Irish Government, along with the SDLP, continued to take an optimistic view of the permanence of the cease-fire; and when, in October 1995, Gerry Adams said that statements by his party had shown that it was committed to 'the democratic and peaceful process', adding that 'it is self-evident that threats of any description from any quarter have no part in any such process,' the new Taoiseach, John Bruton, told the Dáil that this statement, and others, showed a 'significant and important new commitment on the part of Sinn Féin.' The Tánaiste, Dick Spring, argued: 'The crucial point is that the guns are silent.'[106]

The question of the attitude loyalist paramilitaries would adopt in regard to the cease-fire still remained. The period from 1990 to the cease-fires of 1994 saw an upsurge in loyalist violence. In the eight years from 1978 to 1985 loyalists were responsible for an average of 8.5 deaths a year. After the signing of the Anglo-Irish Agreement the average went up to 18.6 per year for 1986–1990. Loyalists killed 40 people in 1991, 39 in 1992, and 44 in the first eleven months of 1993. Much of this increase in activity came from the UDA, under its cover name of the UFF. This violence was brought about by a number of factors. Between 1988 and 1992 there was a thorough clearing out at the top of the UDA and a new generation came to power. The North Belfast brigadier was convicted of gun-running; the South Belfast and Mid-Ulster brigadiers were convicted of extortion; the political spokesman was killed by the IRA; the Supreme Commander lost a vote of no confidence; and the West and East Belfast brigadiers were arrested in connection with the Stevens inquiry into collusion between the UDA and the security forces. Jimmy Craig and Ned McCreery, senior figures in west and east Belfast, respectively, were killed by the UDA. Some members of the Derry leadership were stood down for inactivity; one was assassinated by the IRA. There was also a smaller but nonetheless marked increase in activity from the UVF, which had seen no recent changes in leadership.

The increase in loyalist violence was influenced by two environmental changes. Firstly, although the security forces arrested many UDA operators, mainly those involved in logistics rather than the gunmen themselves, these people were readily replaced by a considerable increase in the number of recruits to the UDA and the UVF. Secondly, within Protestant working-class communities there appeared to be an increase in the popular support for terrorism, allowing a greater increase in terrorist activities.[107]

> Some of the old leadership was corrupt, sitting back, not rocking the boat. In this way the Government was able to introduce the Anglo-Irish Agreement without any ... real retribution because they had informers ... A phrase I often hear ... mentioned ... is 'returning to the basic principles of the organisation' ... The UDA was always the last line of defence between us and an enforced United Ireland ... We can't trust the British Government and we can't trust anyone else ... Without us being here, it would be so much easier for our country, and our way of life to be taken from us.[108]

On 10 December 1993 the Combined Loyalist Military Command, consisting of the leaderships of the UDA, UVF and Red Hand Commando, set out its basic principles, making it clear that it would not tolerate any change in the constitutional status of Northern Ireland within the United Kingdom and that while cross-border co-operation could be explored, it should not take any institutional shape in the form of joint authority over Northern Ireland by the British or Irish Governments. The CLMC listed its basic principles as:

> 1. There must be no diminution of Northern Ireland's position as an integral part of the United Kingdom whose paramount responsibility is the morale and physical well-being of all its citizens.
> 2. There must be no dilution of the democratic procedure through which the rights of self-determination of the people of Northern Ireland are guaranteed.
> 3. We defend the right of anyone or group to seek constitutional change by democratic, legitimate and peaceful means.
> 4. We recognise and respect the rights and aspirations of all who abide by the law regardless of religious, cultural, national or political inclinations.
> 5. We are dedicated to a written constitution and bill of rights for Northern Ireland wherein would be enshrined stringent safeguards for individuals, associations and minorities.

6. Structures should be devised whereby elected representatives, North and South, could work together to explore and exploit co-operation between both parts of Ireland which would not interfere with either's internal jurisdiction.[109]

For a number of years many commentators had detected a tangible sense of increasing alienation among Protestants when describing their position within the United Kingdom. A nadir in relations between Northern Ireland and Britain, and the consequences for Protestant alienation, could be identified in 1985 with the signing of the Anglo-Irish Agreement. Subsequent political developments, from a unionist perspective, had copperfastened that agreement. The period since the signing of the agreement witnessed an annual increase in loyalist paramilitary violence. The agreement was identified by Protestants as a watershed in relations between the unionist community and the British Government, and for many it marked the beginning of the end of the union with Britain. But this did not mean that Protestants, particularly the loyalist paramilitaries, were going to take this quietly, and indeed many Protestants believed that instead of reducing terrorist violence the agreement had the reverse effect, making it worse.

The lack of democratic accountability within Northern Ireland was much resented by Protestants, with the Orders in Council system producing little debate on Northern Ireland legislation and a sense of powerlessness. Of the various legislative measures, fair employment legislation was most disliked and distrusted, and there was a feeling that reverse discrimination was now occurring, to the disadvantage of Protestants. There was also a clear view that Government investment was heavily biased in the direction of Catholic areas, because of a perception that this was where the real need lay. It was widely believed that every move by the Government was intended to placate Catholics, and this was seen by Protestants as a concession resulting from Republican violence. On the issue of security, the RUC were still generally seen as 'ours' rather than 'theirs', and some Protestants found it difficult to come to terms with the idea of a non-aligned police force. In general, many Protestants felt that security policies were too soft and that the RUC were being held back for political reasons; there was also a degree of bitterness that Republican violence was seen to be successful.

Protestants also felt that the media were biased, unsupportive, and often wrong in their facts, and for this reason it was thought that international sympathies were with the Catholics. The high profile of nationalist or Catholic culture was connected with the Protestant belief that one of the two cultures in Northern Ireland was better presented publicly, with the result that Protestant culture was thought of as less exciting and complex.

The consequence of Protestant alienation was that the issue of growing Protestant violence, and a growing private acceptance of this violence, might lead to the consideration of some sort of 'civil war'. This change in the reaction to violence came, it was argued, from feelings of fear, isolation, and betrayal. There was also little enthusiasm for political dialogue, as the failure of talks between politicians had led to feelings of anger and frustration, with John Hume and the SDLP blamed for their breakdown. Violence and the economic situation were being blamed for the emigration of the best of the young Protestants to Britain.

What was described in public as 'Protestant alienation' in essence reflected a perception that the social and constitutional bulwarks and defences for Protestants were being steadily and persistently eroded. Politically, Protestants were nervous about peace and the changes this might bring, which might include a reduction in the essential Britishness of Protestants, and were determined that such an accommodation would not be bought by violence. The issue of openness and secrecy was a major concern for Protestants, in that they needed to be reassured that they were involved in the thinking, planning and negotiation of their own future, because the negative side-effect of a policy that believed that a degree of secrecy was necessary if any progress was to be made was Protestant suspicion and anger. The socio-economic dimension arose from concerns about, and perceptions of, discrimination, bias and unfair treatment between the two communities, the central issues appearing to be employment and investment and how these should be allocated and distributed, with a view that Protestant communities were disadvantaged in respect of Government investment, grants, and projects.[110]

Aware of some of these anxieties, and to politically reassure Protestants, the British Government appended to the British copy of the Downing Street Declaration the following clarification:

The joint Declaration does not:
in the absence of majority consent
* commit the British government to join the ranks of the persuaders for a united Ireland
* set any time scale for a united Ireland to come about nor indicate that this is even probable

* commit the people of Northern Ireland to joining a united Ireland against their democratic wishes
* establish arrangements for the exercise of joint authority between the British and Irish governments over Northern Ireland
* assert the value of achieving a united Ireland nor assert the legitimacy of a united Ireland
* derogate in any way from UK sovereignty over Northern Ireland, nor diminish the constitutional guarantee
* contain any reference or implicit commitment to the withdrawal of British troops from Northern Ireland
* give Sinn Féin any immediate place at the Talks table
* sideline the valuable round of meetings with the Northern Ireland parties ...[111]

With assurances that there had been no secret deals with the Provisionals, on 13 October 1996 the CLMC followed the IRA and declared a cease-fire. The permanence of this cease-fire

will be completely dependent upon the continued cessation of all nationalist/republican violence. The sole responsibility for a return to war lies with them ... In the genuine hope that this peace will be permanent, we take the opportunity to pay homage to all our Fighters, Commandos and Volunteers who have paid the supreme sacrifice. They did not die in vain. THE UNION IS SAFE.[112]

Resentment within Republican circles grew, however, as the British Government continued in its refusal to pressure the Unionists into all-party talks while there was no determinant of the permanence of the IRA cease-fire. To reassure the unionist community generally, John Major also promised that any political agreement would have to be subject to approval in a referendum. Nationalists, on the other hand, became convinced that the electoral arithmetic within the House of Commons, which saw the Conservative Government's small majority relying on the Ulster Unionist Party's support in crucial parliamentary votes, caused the British Government to place survival in power above the peace process. The fall of Albert Reynolds's coalition Government in December 1994 demonstrated that Republicans could not hope to dictate the course of the peace process. The new Taoiseach, John Bruton of Fine Gael, was widely believed to be far more sympathetic to Unionist sensibilities then his predecessor.

In an effort to prevent the collapse of the peace process, in February 1995 the British and Irish Governments published their joint discussion documents, *Frameworks for the Future*. Part I, a British Government proposal, suggested a one-chamber Northern Ireland assembly of ninety members elected by PR. All-party committees were to oversee the work of Northern Ireland departments, while the Assembly would be chaired by a directly elected panel of three people.

Part II referred to North-South institutions, which were to 'promote agreement among the people of the island of Ireland; to carry out on a democratically accountable basis delegated executive, harmonising and consultative functions over a range of designated matters to be agreed; and to serve to acknowledge and reconcile the rights, identities and aspirations of the two major traditions.' Such institutions would be created to 'cater for the present and future political, social and economic inter-connections on the island of Ireland,' enabling representatives, North and South, to enter 'agreed dynamic co-operative and constructive relationships.' Membership would consist of department heads from the Northern Ireland assembly and the Republic; areas where harmonisation would take place would include agriculture and fisheries, industrial development, consumer affairs, transport, energy, trade, health, social welfare, education, and economic policy. The objective of the new North-South body would be to 'provide a forum for acknowledging the respective identities and requirements of the two major traditions; express and enlarge the mutual acceptance of the validity of those traditions; and promote understanding and agreement among the people and institutions in both parts of the island.' The remit of the body would be 'dynamic', making possible the progressive extension, by agreement, of its functions to new areas, with its role developing to keep pace with the 'growth of harmonisation' and 'greater integration' between the two economies. John Major emphasised that 'nothing in these Frameworks will be imposed' and affirmed that 'I cherish Northern Ireland as part of the United Kingdom and it will remain so for as long as this reflects the democratic wish of a greater number of its people.'

The British Government described its main political objective in Northern Ireland as the bringing about of a

comprehensive political settlement which would return greater power, authority and responsibility to all the Northern Ireland people, on an agreed basis, and take full account of Northern Ireland's wider relationships with the rest of the United Kingdom and the rest of the island of Ireland ... such an overall agreement being secured by reference to the principles in the Joint Declaration ... It is essential that any outcome is acceptable to the people. The Government have already undertaken to submit any outcome from the Talks process to a referendum in Northern Ireland ...[113]

The Unionist parties were forthright in their rejection of the contents of the Frameworks documents, which reminded them of Sunningdale and the Council of Ireland, fearful that they encompassed a process whereby an all-Ireland government could evolve by stealth without a formal transfer of sovereignty from the United Kingdom to the Republic. The Ulster Unionist Party saw them as a sop to the Provisional IRA and warned its supporters that 'great efforts will be made to persuade you that the benefits of a continuing ceasefire are a fair price to pay for the sacrifice of your British identity. A ceasefire with terrorists retaining their weapons and bombs is not peace ... These papers cannot be considered as a basis for discussion, only rejected in their entirety.'[114]

Concern among the unionist community crystallised during the 'marching season' at the 'Siege of Drumcree' in July 1995, where a confrontation occurred when Orangemen were prevented from marching along what they considered a traditional route, which passed along the nationalist Garvaghy Road in Portadown. Eventually the marches were let through, providing what many unionists regarded as the first political victory since the Anglo-Irish Agreement. A repeat of the Drumcree siege a year later was to plunge community relations in Northern Ireland to what many observers saw as their lowest point ever.

The principal casualty of the Frameworks documents was the Ulster Unionist Party leader, James Molyneaux, who, with his position undermined after his suggestion that his parliamentary party had an 'understanding' with the Conservative Government, resigned on 28 August 1995. In a surprise result, David Trimble, the MP for Upper Bann and a prominent participant in the first Drumcree confrontation, was elected leader of the Unionist Party on 8 September 1995. Trimble believed that there was no evidence that the IRA was committed to exclusively peaceful methods, commenting: 'The private army is being maintained; the weapons are still there, the punishment beatings continue, murders are occurring. The political representatives of this body are using language which is wholly inconsistent with a commitment to peaceful methods, because implicit in their language is the threat of a resumption of violence.' The goal of Trimble and of the Unionist Party was the establishment of some form of assembly that could be the forum for debate between Unionists and Sinn Féin, which would have established a democratic mandate in a period when there was no violence; but Republicans had not fulfilled all the requirements of the Downing Street Declaration and therefore, in the Unionist view, had not qualified for participation in all-party talks.[115]

On the eve of the visit of the American president, Bill Clinton, to Northern Ireland the British and Irish Governments attempted to kick-start the peace process once more with a summit meeting in London to announce a 'twin-track' strategy. The Governments noted their aim of achieving all-party talks by the end of February 1996, and invitations were sent to all parties to participate in preparatory talks. At the same time an international body, chaired by the former US Senator George Mitchell, was set up to look into the decommissioning issue.[116]

The Mitchell Report was delivered on 24 January 1996 and concluded that paramilitary organisations would not decommission any arms before all-party talks. It suggested that parties should consider an approach whereby some decommissioning would take place during the process of all-party negotiations, rather than before, as was the British view, or after, which was Sinn Féin's view. Those involved in all-party negotiations should affirm their commitment to a number of fundamental principles of democracy and non-violence. The parties should be committed to democratic and exclusively peaceful means of resolving political issues; should undertake the total disarmament of all paramilitary organisations, such disarmament to be verifiable to the satisfaction of an independent commission; should renounce for themselves, and oppose any efforts by others to use, force or threats of force to influence the course of all-party negotiations; should agree to abide by the terms of any agreement reached in all-party negotiations and to resort to democratic and exclusively peaceful methods in trying to alter any aspect of that outcome they might disagree with; and should take effective steps to prevent punishment killings and beatings. Among a number of possible confidence-building measures, the report noted that an elective process could make such a contribution 'if it were broadly acceptable with an appropriate mandate and within the three-strand structure.'

At Westminster, John Major, while accepting the report, revealed that the British Government was ready to introduce legislation to allow an elective process. He argued that there were two ways to advance all-party talks: 'The first is for paramilitaries to make a start to decommissioning before all-party negotiations. They can—if they will. If not, the second is to secure a democratic mandate for all-party negotiations through elections specially for that purpose.' John Hume attacked the election proposals, saying: 'It would be utterly irresponsible for any party to play politics with the lives of those people. It would be particularly irresponsible for a government to try to buy votes to keep themselves in power.' Major replied that from the outset he had tried to 'prevent the killing, the bloodshed, the hatred ... that has dominated too much of the lives of British citizens in Northern Ireland ... I am prepared to take risks for that but I am not prepared to buy votes for it.'[117]

A defining moment had been reached in the peace process. On 4 February 1996 the IRA cease-fire ended with the detonation of a massive bomb in an underground car park near Canary Wharf in London. Two men were killed, more than a hundred were injured, and more than £85 million worth of damage was caused. The Provisional IRA blamed the British Government for the ending of its cease-fire, claiming that the IRA had risen to the challenge created by its cessation and that time and again selfish party and sectional interests had been placed before the rights of the people of Ireland. The British Government rejected such an analysis, with Sir Patrick Mayhew commenting that 'those who have said the government hasn't moved fast enough are really saying "You haven't responded to our threats fast enough so here's another one to smarten you up."' For Unionists the bombing merely confirmed what they had believed all along: that the IRA cease-fire was merely a tactic, with Ian Paisley summing up this feeling when he said he was 'sorry that so many people were gulled into believing the lies of the IRA and Sinn Féin that there will be no return to violence.'[118]

For the Republican Movement, the IRA cease-fire had itself been regarded as a major concession. What the ending of the cease-fire illustrated was that while Sinn Féin had moved some way towards recognising that the Northern Ireland conflict was not merely between Britain and the Irish people, significant ideological barriers remained between its own and other parties' interpretations of the conflict. Considerable differences existed in particular between all constitutional nationalist parties and Sinn Féin regarding the question of consent. In February 1996 this became clear when Sinn Féin was unable to subscribe to the report of the Forum for Peace and Reconciliation, which stated that the consent of a majority in Northern Ireland was required for any new agreement, describing this as providing a 'unionist veto'.[119]

The Forum, a meeting of all the main nationalist parties, including Sinn Féin, as well the pro-Union Alliance Party, was an attempt to integrate the Republican Movement into peaceful political dialogue. At the Forum the SDLP and Sinn Féin adopted fundamentally differing interpretations of the nature of the Northern Ireland problem. The SDLP argued that the 'conflict of the two identities in Northern Ireland is the essence of the problem, and the failure to provide structures of accommodation for both its continuance.' The unionist community, as the SDLP understood it, 'perceives itself as British with an underlying Protestantism which finds a strength in allegiance to the British Crown, relative to the latter's essential Protestantism,' which saw the aspirations of nationalists 'as a threat to its identity, and as being incapable of tolerance and respect for the unionist ethos, its heritage, tradition and civil liberties.' As a consequence, to protect their identity unionists 'felt a need to exercise total control and power exclusively.'[120]

Sinn Féin, however, continued to argue that 'British interference lies at the root of the political conflict on this island.' While accepting that all shared a degree of culpability for the unresolved conflict, it was Sinn Féin's contention that 'the primary responsibility in all of this rests with Britain. It is because of British policy that our conflict exists and only a change in British policy can create the atmosphere necessary to resolve it.'[121] While the SDLP saw the conflict as between two identities in Ireland, Britishness and Irishness, or as a divided people, Sinn Féin continued to see the conflict in traditional nationalist terms, as a division of territory, with the primary responsibility, and the ability to resolve it, lying with the British Government. Gerry Adams believed that

> unionism and loyalism require a Protestant ascendancy—that is their *raison d'être*. Their political philosophy expresses loyalty to the union with Britain precisely and solely because that union has, to date, guaranteed them their privileges and their ascendancy ... What republicanism has to offer loyalists is equality ... The loyalists have a desperate identity crisis. They agonise over whether they are Ulster-Scots, Picts, English or British ... Yet they are not British. Loyalism is not found in Britain itself, except as an Irish export. There are no cultural links between the loyalists and the British, no matter how much the loyalists scream about their 'British way of life' ... The loyalists are Irish ...[122]

Since Sinn Féin did not accept the Unionist claim that Ulster unionism was a variant of British nationalism or patriotism, Republicans argued that partition propped up unionism by perpetuating discrimination against Northern nationalists. The divisions in Ireland were the work of previous British Governments. Sinn Féin believed that the achievement of equality for nationalists in the North would erode the very reason for the existence of the statelet, for unionists had traditionally supported the Union because it gave them a 'superior status in relation to nationalists. Once they are treated on equal terms with nationalists ... this must inevitably reduce their advantage in practice and undermine the rational basis of the unionist doctrine.'[123] Given that Republicans saw unionists as a national minority within the Irish nation, Sinn Féin could not subscribe to the concept of unity by consent: as Adams explained,

we subscribe to the classic, democratic position of Irish nationalism. Britain's partitioning of Ireland turned the Irish unionist minority into an artificial majority in the Six-County area. Unionists are not— and do not claim to be—a nation with a right to national self-determination. Unionists are a national minority, a religious/political minority, with minority rights, not majority rights ... While nationalists deny that unionists have any right of veto over British or Irish policy directed at seeking to dissolve the union, most nationalists and republicans recognise as a matter of pragmatism that it is desirable in practice that the consent, or assent, of as many unionists as possible should be obtained to the practical steps required to bring about ... a united Ireland ... I have consistently argued that the consent and allegiance of unionists is needed to secure a peace settlement. But the argument that the consent of a national minority, which has been elevated into a majority in an undemocratic and artificially created state, is necessary before any constitutional change can occur is a nonsense ... It ignores the reality that in British and international law the British government, if it wishes can legislate itself out of Ireland ... We believe that the consent of the present-day unionists could, in fact, be won over time ... to reunification, provided that the two governments, and primarily the British government, made that the basis of their policy. That is why nationalists want Britain to 'join the ranks of the persuaders' ...[124]

While it was apparent that many unionists and nationalists still held fundamentally misconceived ideas of each other, the Troubles had at least forced many throughout Ireland to reappraise some of their perceptions; but for Republicans, the recognition of unionists' Britishness, and their right to define themselves as such, remains the quantum ideological leap to be made by the Republican Movement.

Notes

Chapter 1 (p. 1–55)

1. Buckland (1973a), xiv.
2. Bowman (1982), 11–12.
3. Eamon Phoenix, 'Northern Nationalists, Ulster Unionists and the development of partition, 1900–1921' in Collins (1994), 109–10.
4. Ibid., 75–6.
5. Hickey (1984), 62–3.
6. Hennessey (1993), 27–33.
7. *House of Commons Debates*, vol. 42, col. 1615, 10 Oct. 1912.
8. *News Letter*, 15 Mar. 1918.
9. Alvin Jackson, 'Irish Unionism, 1905–21' in Collins (1994), 41–2.
10. *Report of the Proceedings of the Irish Convention, 1918*, 5–6.
11. Kendle (1989), 188.
12. *House of Commons Debates*, vol. 127, col. 990–1, 29 Mar. 1920.
13. *Weekly Northern Whig*, 20 Nov. 1920.
14. *House of Commons Debates*, vol. 129, col. 1289–90, 18 May 1920.
15. Harris (1993), 52–3.
16. Phoenix (1994b), 36–7.
17. Ibid., 41.
18. Ibid., 43.
19. Ibid., 48–51.
20. Ibid., 54–5.
21. *Irish News*, 7 Dec. 1918.
22. Phoenix (1994b), 76.
23. Ibid., 83.
24. *House of Commons Debates*, vol. 134, col. 925–7, 8 Nov. 1920.
25. Ibid., col. 1441–2, 11 Nov. 1920.
26. Ibid., vol. 129, col. 165–6, 10 May 1920.
27. Bardon (1992), 494.
28. Follis (1995), 93–4.
29. Bardon (1992), 494.
30. Coogan (1970), 44.
31. *Weekly Northern Whig*, 27 Nov. 1920.
32. Ibid., 17 July 1920.
33. Kennedy (1988), 121.
34. Ibid., 50–2.
35. *Weekly Northern Whig*, 30 Oct. 1920.
36. *House of Commons Debates*, vol. 132, col. 1111, 26 Dec. 1920.
37. O'Halloran (1987), 52.
38. Bardon (1992), 468–9.
39. Phoenix (1994b), 87–8.

40. *Weekly Northern Whig*, 31 July 1920.
41. Follis (1995), 12–13.
42. Phoenix (1994b), 91–2.
43. *House of Common Debates*, vol. 132, col. 731–2, 22 July 1920.
44. *Weekly Northern Whig*, 14 May 1921.
45. Ibid., 30 Apr. 1921.
46. Phoenix (1994), 107–9.
47. Ibid., 119–123.
48. *Weekly Northern Whig*, 7 May 1921.
49. *Irish News*, 7 May 1921.
50. Ibid., 11 May 1921.
51. Bowman (1982), 47.
52. Ervine (1949), 411.
53. Phoenix (1994b), 129.
54. Ervine (1949), 419.
55. Follis (1995), 29.
56. *Weekly Northern Whig*, 16 July 1921.
57. Ibid., 23 July 1921.
58. Ibid., 20 Aug. 1921.
59. Phoenix (1994b), 148–50.
60. Ibid., 152–3.
61. Mansergh (1991), 184.
62. *Northern Ireland House of Commons Debates*, vol. 2, col. 1149, 7 Dec. 1922.
63. Phoenix (1994b), 154–6.
64. *Irish News*, 4 Jan. 1922.
65. Ibid., 5 Jan. 1922.
66. Ibid., 9 Jan. 1922.
67. Phoenix (1994b), 139.
68. Ibid., 141.
69. Follis (1995), 88.
70. Campbell (1994), 271–3.
71. Phoenix (1994b), 170.
72. *Weekly Northern Whig*, 28 Jan. 1922.
73. Phoenix (1994b), 173–5.
74. Ibid., 182.
75. Follis (1995), 153.
76. *Weekly Northern Whig*, 11 Feb. 1922.
77. Ibid.
78. Ibid., 8 Apr. 1922.
79. Phoenix (1994b), 204–10.
80. O'Halloran (1987), 141–2.
81. Ibid., 99.
82. Harris (1993), 112–14.

83. *Weekly Northern Whig*, 1 Apr. 1922.
84. Ibid., 6 May 1922.
85. *Northern Ireland House of Commons Debates*, vol. 2, col. 223–9, 28 Mar. 1922.
86. Buckland (1979), 213–15.
87. Follis (1995), 98–100.
88. Campbell (1994), 278.
89. Follis (1995), 86.
90. Ibid., 108–9.
91. O'Halloran (1987), 134.
92. Ibid., 137.
93. Harkness (1983), 36–7.
94. *Northern Ireland House of Commons Debates*, vol. 2, col. 596–8, 23 May 1922.
95. Ibid., col. 1152, 7 Dec. 1922.
96. Follis (1995), 154.
97. Ibid., 156–7.
98. Phoenix (1994b), 263–4.
99. *Irish News*, 15 Feb. 1923.
100. Ibid., 21 Feb. 1923.
101. *Weekly Westminster*, 28 June 1924.
102. Harkness (1983), 38–9.
103. *Northern Ireland House of Commons Debates*, vol. 2, col. 1207, 7 Oct. 1924.
104. Harkness (1983), 39–40.
105. PRONI, D2991/B/1/10A, Healy to editor of *Irish Independent*, 30 Nov. 1925.
106. *Irish News*, 4 Dec. 1925.
107. Ibid., 8 Dec. 1925.
108. Ibid.
109. Ibid., 4 Dec. 1925.
110. Harris (1993), 21.
111. Ibid., 29.
112. Ibid., 200.
113. Ibid.
114. Buckland (1979), 247–56.
115. PRONI, CAB 9B/101/1, Proportional Representation: Abolishing the System of Proportional Representation in Local Government Elections.
116. PRONI, CAB 9B/101/1.
117. Hadfield (1989), 52–4.
118. PRONI, CAB 9B/101/1.
119. Buckland (1979), 231–2.
120. Ibid., 223–6.
121. Ibid., 236–9.

122. *Irish News*, 15 Feb. 1923.
123. PRONI, D2291/E.
124. PRONI, CAB 9B/13/1, Ministry of Home Affairs Memorandum, 8 Mar. 1923.
125. Ibid., Ministry of Home Affairs Memorandum, 24 Mar. 1923.
126. Ibid., 8 Mar. 1923.
127. Ibid., Redistribution of Electoral Areas in County Fermanagh.
128. Ibid., Memorandum on Redistribution in Tyrone.
129. J. Whyte, 'How much discrimination was there under the unionist regime, 1921–1968?' in Gallagher and O'Connell (1983), 6.
130. Buckland (1979), 240–1.
131. PRONI, D2991, 'The Nationalist Party in Northern Ireland, 1921–55' by Eamon Phoenix.
132. PRONI, D2991/A–B, McManus to Healy, 1924.
133. *Éire*, 29 Mar. 1924.
134. PRONI, D2991, 'The Nationalist Party in Northern Ireland, 1921–55' by Eamon Phoenix.
135. *Fermanagh Herald*, 18 Feb. 1928.
136. Northern Ireland House of Commons Debates, vol. 8, col. 2280–2, 25 Oct. 1927.
137. Ibid., vol. 9, col. 2809, 30 Oct. 1928.

Chapter 2 (p. 56–120)
  1. Harkness (1983), 50.
  2. Buckland (1981), 74–5.
  3. Harkness (1983), 49–50.
  4. Michael Connolly and Andrew Erridge, 'Central government in Northern Ireland' in Connolly and Loughlin (1990), 22.
  5. Buckland (1981), 74.
  6. Harkness (1983), 52–4.
  7. Bew, Gibbon, and Patterson (1995), 64.
  8. Harkness (1983), 55.
  9. Michael Connolly and Andrew Erridge, 'Central government in Northern Ireland' in Connolly and Loughlin (1990), 23.
 10. Walker (1985), 61.
 11. Harkness (1983), 69.
 12. Walker (1985), 61–2.
 13. Ibid., 59.
 14. Harkness (1983), 70.
 15. Ibid., 63.
 16. Farrell (1976), 130.
 17. PRONI, D2991.
 18. *Irish News*, 18 Nov. 1933.
 19. PRONI, CAB 9B/200/1, Bates to Craigavon, 2 July 1932.

20. Walker (1985), 75–6.
21. *Northern Ireland House of Commons Debates*, vol. 16, col. 1090, 24 Apr. 1934.
22. Ibid., vol. 2, col. 422, 23 May 1922.
23. Ibid., col. 425–6.
24. Farrell (1976), 90.
25. *Northern Ireland House of Commons Debates*, vol. 16, col. 1114–20, 24 Apr. 1934.
26. Ibid., vol. 8, col. 2283–4 25 Oct. 1927.
27. Ibid., vol. 16, col. 1077–82 24 Apr. 1934.
28. Ibid., vol. 8, col. 2308–9 26 Oct. 1927.
29. Ibid., vol. 16, col. 1101–5, 24 Apr. 1934.
30. Walker (1985), 76–7.
31. PRONI, D2991/A–B, Healy to Inskip, 16 Aug. 1935.
32. *Irish News*, 24 July 1935.
33. Ibid., 14 Aug. 1935.
34. Ibid., 24 Aug. 1935.
35. Ibid., 30 Aug. 1935.
36. PRONI, D2991, Calendar.
37. PRONI, D2991/A–B, Healy to de Valera, 23 Oct. 1935.
38. Ibid., Gilmore to Healy, 25 Oct. 1935.
39. Ibid., Healy to Gilmore, 27 Oct. 1935.
40. PRONI, D2991/D/9, Oct. 1935.
41. *Irish News*, 5 Nov. 1935.
42. PRONI, D2991, Calendar.
43. PRONI, D2991/A–B, 16 Sep. 1936.
44. Ibid., Donnelly to Healy, 25 Sep. 1936.
45. Ibid., Healy to Donnelly, 27 Oct. 1936.
46. Ibid., Donnelly to Healy, 30 Oct. 1936.
47. Ibid., Nugent to Healy, 12 Oct. 1937.
48. Lee (1989), 34.
49. Dunn and Hennessey (1996), 193–4.
50. *Fermanagh Herald*, 7 Oct. 1933.
51. Dunn and Hennessey (1996), 193.
52. *News Letter*, 18 May 1937.
53. Hadfield (1989), 243.
54. *Irish News*, 3 May 1937.
55. Ibid.
56. Ibid., 3 Feb. 1938.
57. Ibid., 5 June 1937.
58. Ibid., 6 May 1937.
59. Ibid., 7 May 1937.
60. *House of Lords Debates*, vol. 59, col. 563, 7 Oct. 1924.
61. *Irish News*, 30 Mar. 1938.

62. Ibid., 13 Jan. 1938.
63. Ibid., 14 Jan. 1938.
64. Ibid., 21 Feb. 1938.
65. Ibid., 14 Jan. 1938.
66. Ibid., 15 Jan. 1938.
67. Ibid., 18 Feb. 1938.
68. Ibid., 28 Nov. 1938.
69. *Irish Press*, 29 June 1937.
70. Ibid., 25 Feb. 1938.
71. PRONI, D2991/B/145, Maguire to Healy, 20 Jan. 1938.
72. *Irish Press*, 15 Jan. 1938.
73. Ibid., 26 Jan. 1938.
74. PRONI, D2991/B/145, Healy to Fay, 28 Oct. 1938.
75. PRONI, D2991/A–B, Healy to editor of *Irish Press*, 14 Jan. 1938.
76. Buckland (1979), 112–15.
77. Harkness (1983), 58–9.
78. *Irish News*, 28 Apr. 1938.
79. PRONI, D2991/D/9.
80. PRONI, D2991/A–B, Healy to Murney, 11 Sep. 1938.
81. Ibid., Murney to Healy, 16 Sep. 1938.
82. Ibid., 19 Sep. 1938.
83. Ibid., Healy to Murney, 21 Sep. 1938.
84. Ibid., 30 Sep. 1938.
85. *Irish Press*, 12 Dec. 1939.
86. PRONI, D2991/A–B, Stewart to Healy, June 1940.
87. *Irish Press*, 26 June 1940.
88. Ibid., 28 June 1940.
89. Barton (1995), 123.
90. Farrell (1976), 151–4.
91. PRONI, D2991/A–B, Feb. 1940.
92. *Northern Ireland House of Commons Debates*, vol. 22, col. 1907, 4 Sep. 1939.
93. Fisk (1985), 207.
94. *Northern Ireland House of Commons Debates*, vol. 2, col. 2491, 29 Oct. 1940.
95. Fisk (1985), 211.
96. Barton (1988), 160.
97. Ibid., 162.
98. Fisk (1985), 217.
99. Barton (1995), 79–81.
100. Ibid., 84–7.
101. Ibid., 44.
102. Ibid., 46.
103. Ibid., 87–9.

104. Ibid., 123.
105. Ibid., 17–19.
106. Ibid., 52–3.
107. *Northern Ireland House of Commons Debates*, vol. 30, col. 1965–71, 8 Oct. 1946.
108. Bew, Gibbon, and Patterson (1995), 82–4.
109. Ibid., 97–104.
110. Harkness (1983), 108–11.
111. Wichert (1991), 47–8.
112. McCabe (1991), 117–21.
113. Farrell (1976), 184.
114. McCabe (1991), 130–5.
115. *Northern Ireland House of Commons Debates*, vol. 32, col. 3364–8, 30 Nov. 1948.
116. Ibid., col. 3704–5, 1 Dec. 1948.
117. Farrell (1976), 177–9.
118. Ibid., 181–3.
119. PRONI, D2291, Calendar.
120. Farrell (1976), 204–5.
121. PRONI, D2991/A–B, Healy to Costello, July 1954.
122. Ibid., Healy to Costello, Nov. 1954.
123. PRONI, /D2991/B/24, McGill to Healy, 2 Sep. 1955.
124. PRONI, CAB 9B/125/4.
125. PRONI, D2991/A–B, Healy to Lodge-Curran, Mar. 1955.
126. *Belfast Telegraph*, 4 May 1955.
127. Farrell (1976), 209.
128. *Belfast Telegraph*, 16 May 1955.
129. Farrell (1976), 209–10.
130. Bell (1979), 283.
131. Smith (1995), 67–8.
132. Farrell (1976), 215.
133. Bell (1979), 291.
134. Farrell (1976), 216–21.
135. Bew, Gibbon, and Patterson (1995), 115–18.
136. Ibid., 124–5.
137. Ibid., 128–31.
138. PRONI, CAB 9B/205/1, Memorandum, Oct. 1932.
139. Buckland (1979), 243–5.
140. Barritt and Carter (1962), 93.
141. PRONI, CAB 9B/205/1, appendix B, Appointments to Official Positions.
142. Ibid., appendix A, Allocation of Houses.
143. Whyte (1983), 6.
144. Wichert (1991), 67–8.

145. PRONI, CAB 9B/205/1, Brookeborough to Bishop of Manchester, 21 June 1961.
146. *Down Recorder*, 12 May 1961.
147. Barritt and Carter (1962), 54–5.
148. Ibid., 57–8.
149. *Northern Ireland House of Commons Debates*, vol. 38, col. 586–91, 10 Feb. 1954.
150. Ibid., col. 647–50, 11 Feb. 1954.
151. Ibid., col. 2766, 19 Oct. 1954.
152. Ibid., col. 711, 11 Feb. 1954.
153. Ibid., col. 722.
154. Ibid., col. 714–15.
155. Barritt and Carter (1962), 125.
156. *Fermanagh Herald*, 19 July 1952.
157. Farrell (1976), 204.
158. Barritt and Carter (1962), 30–1.
159. PRONI, CAB 9R/196/1, Death of Pope Pius XII, 10 Oct. 1958.
160. Barritt and Carter (1962), 31.
161. Whyte (1990), 31.
162. PRONI, CAB 9B/205/1; *Derry Journal*, 4 May 1951.
163. Barritt and Carter (1962), 77.
164. Ibid., 91–2.

Chapter 3 (p. 121–170)
1. O'Neill (1969), 48.
2. Ibid., 128–31.
3. Ibid., 124–5.
4. Ibid., 53.
5. Ibid., 51.
6. Ibid., 47–8.
7. Ibid., 56–7.
8. *Belfast Telegraph*, 16 Nov. 1965.
9. Ibid., 24 Nov. 1965.
10. Ibid., 23 Nov. 1965.
11. Farrell (1976), 232.
12. *Northern Ireland House of Commons Debates*, vol. 71, col. 413–14, 29 Jan. 1969.
13. PRONI, CAB 9R/196/1, Death of Pope John: Memorandum, 12 June 1963.
14. PRONI, CAB 9R/196/1, Prime Minister to Most Rev. William Conway.
15. *Northern Ireland House of Commons Debates*, vol. 71, col. 414–15, 29 Jan. 1969.
16. PRONI, HO 5/189.
17. Ibid.

18. Whyte (1983), 18–22.
19. Ibid., 8–10.
20. Ibid., 13.
21. PRONI, HO 5/189, Why Justice Can Not Be Done: The Douglas-Home Correspondence.
22. Ibid., Gregory to Longford, 18 Nov. 1964.
23. PRONI, HO 5/188, McCluskey to Thomas.
24. Ibid., Wilson to McCluskey, Sep. 1964.
25. PRONI, HO 5/191, Wilson to Carlwell, 14 Jan. 1965.
26. *CDU Newsletter*, no. 1 (Nov. 1966).
27. Purdy (1990), 116–17.
28. Ibid., 128.
29. *News Letter*, 5 June 1963.
30. *Disturbances in Northern Ireland* (1969), 118–19.
31. Rose (1971), 254–5.
32. Ibid., 300–1.
33. Ibid., 234–6.
34. Ibid., 193–6.
35. Ibid., 350–1.
36. Ibid., 363–4.
37. *Disturbances in Northern Ireland* (1969), 30–1.
38. *Irish News*, 26 Nov. 1968.
39. *Belfast Telegraph*, 18 Nov. 1968.
40. *Spotlight Ulster*, Jan. 1968.
41. *News Letter*, 6 Dec. 1968.
42. *Belfast Telegraph*, 16 Dec. 1968.
43. O'Neill (1969), 171–4.
44. Ibid., 140–6.
45. *News Letter*, 1 Jan. 1969.
46. *Belfast Telegraph*, 16 Dec. 1968.
47. *Daily Telegraph*, 27 Oct. 1969.
48. *Northern Ireland House of Commons Debates*, vol. 71, col. 443–6, 29 Jan. 1969.
49. Ibid., col. 412–20.
50. *Irish Times*, 1 Feb. 1969.
51. *Belfast Telegraph*, 18 Feb. 1969.
52. *Irish News*, 1 Aug. 1969.
53. Purdy (1990), 216–17.
54. *Disturbances in Northern Ireland* (1969), 91–2.
55. Ibid., 83–6.
56. Ibid., 92–3.
57. Ibid., 88–90.
58. Ibid., 64–5.
59. Faulkner (1978), 50–1.

60. Ibid., 47–8.
61. *Belfast Telegraph*, 5 Feb. 1969.
62. Ibid., 14 Feb. 1969.
63. Ibid., 15 Feb. 1969.
64. Ibid., 1 Feb. 1969.
65. *Protestant Telegraph*, 22 Feb. 1969.
66. Ibid.
67. Ibid., 9 May 1970.
68. Ibid., 11 July 1970.
69. Ibid., 28 June 1969.
70. Ibid., 25 Oct. 1969.
71. Ibid., 9 May 1970.
72. *Belfast Telegraph*, 14 Feb. 1969.
73. O'Neill (1972), 121.
74. O'Neill (1969), 200.
75. Gordon (1989), 161.
76. O'Neill (1972), 139.
77. *Violence and Civil Disturbances in Northern Ireland in 1969* (1972), vol. 1, 7–9.
78. Ibid., 88.
79. Ibid., 87.
80. Ibid., vol. 2, 44.
81. Ibid., vol. 1, 88.
82. Ibid., vol. 2, 36–7.
83. Ibid., 39.
84. Ibid., vol. 1, 15–17.
85. Ibid., 10–14.
86. Ibid., 11.
87. *A Record of Constructive Change* (1971), 13–14.
88. *Protestant Telegraph*, 30 Aug. 1969.
89. *Civil Rights News Service Bulletin*, no. 3 (21 Aug. 1969).
90. Ibid., no. 4 (22 Aug. 1969).

Chapter 4 (p. 171–234)
1. Mac Stiofáin (1974), 133–8.
2. *An Phoblacht*, Feb. 1970.
3. Ibid., Nov. 1970.
4. Ibid., July 1970.
5. Ibid., Mar. 1970.
6. Ibid., Apr. 1970.
7. Mac Stiofáin (1974), 145–6.
8. Ibid., 167.
9. Sunday Times Insight Team (1972), 205.
10. Bew and Gillespie (1993), 28–9.
11. Devlin (1993), 134.

12. Flackes and Elliott (1989), 206–7.
13. Ibid., 138.
14. *An Phoblacht*, July 1972.
15. Ibid., Sep. 1971.
16. Ibid.
17. Mac Stiofáin (1974), 209.
18. *Irish News*, 7 Feb. 1969, 45.
19. Ibid., 24 Jan. 1970.
20. *Irish Independent*, 22 Oct. 1969.
21. *Sunday Press*, 30 Aug. 1970.
22. *Irish News*, 2 Mar. 1970.
23. *Sunday News*, 11 Oct. 1970.
24. *Fortnight*, 5 Feb. 1971.
25. McAllister (1977), 39–40.
26. *Alliance Bulletin*, no. 4 (20 Oct. 1970).
27. *Alliance*, vol. 1, no. 3 (Apr. 1971).
28. *Belfast Telegraph*, 29 Aug. 1969.
29. *News Letter*, 24 Sep. 1969.
30. *Belfast Telegraph*, 21 Nov. 1969.
31. *News Letter*, 23 Apr. 1970.
32. Ibid., 14 Oct. 1969.
33. *Irish Times*, 17 Apr. 1970.
34. *Belfast News Letter*, 14 Nov. 1969.
35. Bew and Gillespie (1993), 26.
36. *Financial Times*, 12 Aug. 1970.
37. *News Letter*, 8 Apr. 1970.
38. *Irish Times*, 12 Aug. 1970.
39. *Belfast Telegraph*, 30 Sep. 1970.
40. *News Letter*, 22 Oct. 1970.
41. *Belfast Telegraph*, 1 Dec. 1970.
42. *News Letter*, 10 Apr. 1970.
43. *Guardian*, 7 Sep. 1970.
44. *Belfast Telegraph*, 21 Sep. 1970.
45. *Daily Mirror*, 30 Oct. 1970.
46. *Belfast Telegraph*, 25 Jan. 1971.
47. Kelly (1972), 13.
48. Faulkner (1978), 78.
49. Ibid., 80.
50. Ibid., 82–3.
51. Ibid., 92.
52. McAllister (1977), 88–9.
53. PRONI, D3816.
54. *The Future Development of the Parliament and Government of Northern Ireland* (1971).

55. McAllister (1977), 88–90.
56. Ibid., 91.
57. Ibid., 91–2.
58. Faulkner (1978), 108.
59. Devlin (1993), 155.
60. McAllister (1977), 93.
61. Faulkner (1978), 114–20.
62. Bew and Gillespie (1993), 36–7.
63. Ibid., 41.
64. Mac Stiofáin (1974), 192–3.
65. Ibid., 206–8.
66. McAllister (1977), 99–102.
67. Ibid., 104–6.
68. Ibid., 103–10.
69. *Sunday Times*, 7 Nov. 1971.
70. *SDLP News*, 5 Oct. 1972.
71. PRONI, D3816, 15 July 1971.
72. Ibid., 22 Jan. 1972.
73. Ibid., 1 Nov. 1971.
74. Ibid., 12 Nov. 1971.
75. Ibid., 14 Oct. 1971.
76. Ibid., 11 21 Oct. 1971.
77. *Ulster: the Facts*, vol. 2 (1972), no. 1.
78. PRONI, D3816/11, 3 Nov. 1971.
79. Ibid., 8 Oct. 1971.
80. Ibid., 8 Oct. 1972.
81. Ibid., 3 Mar. 1972.
82. Faulkner (1978), 133–4.
83. *UDA News*, vol. 1, no. 2.
84. Ibid., vol. 1, no. 1.
85. *Official UDA News*, vol. 1, no. 6.
86. Bruce (1992), 41–2.
87. *UDA News*, vol. 1, no. 5.
88. Bew and Gillespie (1993), 39.
89. *UDA News*, vol. 1, no. 10.
90. *Loyalist News*, 13 May 1972.
91. *Official UDA News*, vol. 1, no. 24.
92. Ibid., vol. 1, no. 16.
93. Bruce (1992), 52–5.
94. Bew and Gillespie (1993), 44–8.
95. *Campaign Newsletter*, no. 16 (23 Jan. 1972).
96. Hadfield (1989), 100–1.
97. Bew and Gillespie (1993), 46.
98. *News Letter*, 8 Nov. 1971.

99. *Guardian*, 4 Apr. 1972.
100. *United Ulsterman*, Sep. 1972.
101. *Loyalist News*, 19 Feb. 1972.
102. *Irish News*, 14 Oct. 1971.
103. *Unionist Review*, Apr. 1973.
104. Ibid., June 1973.
105. Mac Stiofáin (1974), 234.
106. Ibid., 281–2.
107. Bew and Gillespie (1993), 54–5.
108. Cunningham (1991), 67–8.
109. Flackes and Elliott (1989), 258.
110. Cunningham (1991), 110.
111. Ibid., 103.
112. *Irish Times*, 17 Aug. 1970.
113. *Sunday Press*, 1 Nov. 1970.
114. *Irish Times*, 2 Feb. 1971.
115. *The Future of Northern Ireland* (1972), 32–3.
116. Bew and Gillespie (1993), 60–1.
117. *Unionist Review*, May 1973.
118. Ibid., June 1973.
119. Ibid., May 1973.
120. Hadfield (1989), 104–10.
121. Faulkner (1978), 189.
122. Ibid., 193–6.
123. Bew and Gillespie (1993), 65.
124. *Northern Ireland Assembly Official Report*, vol. 2, col. 1835–6, 19 Mar. 1974.
125. Ibid., vol. 1, col. 430–1, 24 Oct. 1973.
126. Hadfield (1989), 113–14.
127. Faulkner (1978), 236–7.
128. Devlin (1975), 32.
129. *SDLP News*, 1 5 Oct. 197.
130. *Northern Ireland Assembly Official Report*, vol. 1, col. 1510, 14 Dec. 1973.
131. Ibid., col. 1965, 19 Dec. 1973.
132. Ibid., 14 Dec. 1973.
133. *Orange Standard*, June 1974.
134. Ibid., Feb. 1973.
135. Ibid., June 1973.
136. *Combat*, 8 Mar. 1974.
137. *UWC Journal*, vol. 1 (1975), no. 2.
138. Bew and Gillespie (1993), 83–9.
139. *Northern Ireland Constitutional Convention Debates*, 22 Sep. 1975, 537–40.
140. Ibid., UUUC Policy Position, 26 Aug. 1975, 587–8.

141. Ibid., annex C, Outline of SDLP Position, 609.
142. Ibid., annex B, Comments of SDLP on UUUC Policy Document dated 26 August 1975, 608.
143. Ibid., SDLP and Vanguard Proceeding, 6 Feb. 1976, 942–3.
144. Ibid., 1 Oct. 1975, 636–9.

Chapter 5 (p. 235–300)
1. Michael Connolly and Andrew Erridge, 'Central government in Northern Ireland' in Connolly and Loughlin (1990), 23–32.
2. Colin Knox, 'Local government in Northern Ireland: adoption or adaption?' in Connolly and Loughlin (1990), 35–8.
3. M. Connolly and S. Loughlin, 'Legislating for Northern Ireland at Westminster' in Connolly and Loughlin (1990), 66–7.
4. Richard Harrison, 'Industrial development in Northern Ireland: the Industrial Development Board' in Connolly and Loughlin (1990), 157–63.
5. Liam O'Dowd, 'Development or dependency?: state, economy and society in Northern Ireland' in Clancy, Drudy, Lynch and O'Dowd (1995), 153–4.
6. Ibid., 142–4.
7. Ibid., 135–7.
8. Whyte (1991), 55–6.
9. Ibid., 59.
10. Whyte, 61–4.
11. Boyle and Hadden (1994), 45–6.
12. Bew and Gillespie (1996), 94.
13. Ibid., 141.
14. Cormack and Osborne (1994), 67–76.
15. Boyle and Hadden (1994), 49–54.
16. O'Dowd, 152.
17. Boyle and Hadden (1994), 31.
18. Ibid., 55–7.
19. Anthony Gallagher, 'The approach of government: community relations and equity' in Dunn (1995), 32–4.
20. Boyle and Hadden (1994), 117.
21. Derick Wilson and Jerry Tyrrell, 'Institutions for conciliation and mediation' in Dunn (1995), 230–3.
22. Ibid., 241.
23. Alan Smith, 'Education and the conflict in Northern Ireland' in Dunn (1995), 172–3.
24. Smith and Robinson (1996), 13.
25. Robert Cormack and Robert Osborne, 'Education in Northern Ireland: the struggle for equality' in Clancy, Drudy, Lynch and O'Dowd (1995), 505–8.
26. John Sugden, 'Sport, community relations and community conflict in Northern Ireland' in Dunn (1995), 200–2.

27. Steve Bruce and Fiona Alderdice, 'Religious belief and behaviour' in Stringer and Robinson (1993), 5–10.
28. *Northern Ireland House of Commons Debates*, vol. 84, col. 199, 8 Feb. 1972.
29. *UWC Journal*, vol. 1 (1975).
30. Karen Trew, 'National identity' in Breen, Devine and Dowds (1996), 141–3.
31. Bryson and McCartney(1994), 49–55.
32. John Darby, 'Legitimate targets: a control on violence?' in Guelke (1994), 47.
33. Ryder (1991), 113.
34. Ibid., 249–50.
35. Andrew Hamilton and Linda Moore, 'Policing a divided society' in Dunn (1995), 191–2.
36. Urban (1992), 81.
37. Ibid., 242.
38. Ibid., 227–37.
39. Andrew Hamilton and Linda Moore, 'Policing a divided society' in Dunn (1995), 193.
40. Urban (1992), 187.
41. Ryder (1991), 134–5.
42. Adrian Guelke, 'Paramilitaries, republicans and loyalists' in Dunn (1995), 120.
43. Boyle and Hadden (1994), 47.
44. Ryder (1991), 123.
45. O'Malley (1983), 287.
46. O'Brien (1993).
47. *An Phoblacht*, June 1974.
48. Ibid.
49. O'Brien (1993), 170–1.
50. Bew and Gillespie (1993), 98–9.
51. Coogan (1970), 578–81.
52. Bruce (1994), 102.
53. O'Malley (1983), 328–31.
54. Bruce (1994), 102.
55. O'Malley (1983), 332–3.
56. Ibid., 266.
57. Ibid., 270.
58. Ryder (1991), 194.
59. O'Malley (1983), 268.
60. Bew and Gillespie (1993), 164–5.
61. Ibid., 170.
62. O'Malley (1983), 281–2.
63. Devlin (1975), 52–3.

64. *Fortnight*, Oct. 1984.
65. O'Malley (1983), 101.
66. Ibid., 101–3.
67. Bew and Gillespie (1993), 135–6.
68. *New Ireland Forum Report*, 26.
69. *New Ireland Forum Public Session*, 19 Jan. 1984, 22–34.
70. *New Ireland Forum Report*, 1984, 19–21.
71. Ibid., 31–8.
72. Ibid., 23.
73. Ibid., 25–6.
74. Ibid., 17.
75. Hadfield (1989), 179–80.
76. Ibid., 152–4.
77. *Northern Ireland Assembly Official Report*, Molyneaux and Paisley to Thatcher, 28 Aug. 1985, 149–50.
78. Ibid., Thatcher to Paisley, 13 Sep. 1985, 151–2.
79. Ibid., Molyneaux and Paisley to Thatcher, 30 Sep. 1985, 153–5.
80. Hadfield (1989), 192–8.
81. Bew and Gillespie (1993), 195.
82. Ibid., 198.
83. *Northern Ireland Assembly Official Report*, vol. 237, 33–42.
84. Ibid., vol. 237, 72–3.
85. O'Malley (1990b), 25.
86. Rowan (1995), 16.
87. O'Malley (1990), 18.
88. Ibid., 22.
89. Rowan (1995), 17.
90. Brooke-Mayhew Inter-Party Talks Papers: SDLP Necessary but Not Sufficient (paper submitted to Inter-Party Sub-Committee, 27 May 1992).
91. Ibid., Ulster Unionist Party: The Nature of the 'Blockade', 27 May 1992.
92. Ibid., Strand 2: Ulster Unionist Party submission, 7 July 1992.
93. Ibid., Political Talks: Common Principles, 5 May 1992.
94. Bew and Gillespie (1996), 29.
95. *Setting the Record Straight* (1995).
96. Ibid.
97. Adams (1995), 209.
98. *Setting the Record Straight*.
99. Adams (1995), 215.
100. *Joint Declaration* … (1993).
101. Adams (1995), 227.
102. Bew and Gillespie (1996), 63.
103. *Sunday Tribune*, 1 Oct. 1995.
104. Bew and Gillespie (1996), 63–5.

105. Ibid., 90.
106. Ibid., 123.
107. Bruce (1993).
108. Cusack and Taylor (1993), 24.
109. Rowan (1995), 71–2.
110. Dunn and Morgan (1994), 8–22.
111. Bruce (1994), 91.
112. Rowan (1995), 126.
113. *Frameworks for the Future* (1995).
114. Ibid., 93.
115. Ibid., 122.
116. Ibid., 134.
117. Ibid., 151–2.
118. Ibid., 118–19.
119. Ibid., 157.
120. Forum for Peace and Reconciliation (1995), 12–13.
121. Ibid., 35.
122. Adams (1995), 110–23.
123. Ibid., 231.
124. Ibid., 233.

Bibliography

1. OFFICIAL AND PRIVATE PAPERS

Cabinet Papers (PRONI)
Brian Faulkner Papers (PRONI)
Cahir Healy Papers (PRONI)
Home Office Papers (PRONI)
Brooke-Mayhew Inter-Party Talks Papers (private, 1991–92)
Setting the Record Straight (Sinn Féin-British Government Contacts, Belfast 1995)

2. PRINTED RECORDS

House of Commons Debates
House of Lords Debates
New Ireland Forum Public Submissions
New Ireland Forum Report
Northern Ireland Constitutional Convention Debates
Northern Ireland House of Commons Debates
Northern Ireland Assembly Debates, 1973–74
Northern Ireland Assembly Papers, 1982–86

Report of the Proceedings of the Irish Convention, 1918 (Cd. 9019), 1918
Disturbances in Northern Ireland: Report of the Committee Appointed by the Governor of Northern Ireland (Cmd. 532), Belfast 1969
A Commentary by the Government of Northern Ireland to Accompany the Cameron Report (Cmd. 534), Belfast 1969
Report of the Advisory Committee on the Police in Northern Ireland (Cmd. 535), Belfast 1969
A Record of Constructive Change (Cmd. 558), Belfast 1971
Report of the Enquiry into Allegations against the Security Forces of Physical Brutality in Northern Ireland Arising out of Events on 9 August 1971 (Cmnd. 4823), London 1971
The Future Development of the Parliament and Government of Northern Ireland: A Consultative Document (Cmd. 560), Belfast 1971
Report of the Tribunal Appointed to Inquire into the Events on Sunday, 30 January 1972, which Led to the Loss of Life in Connection with the Procession in Londonderry on That Day, London 1972
The Future of Northern Ireland: A Paper for Discussion, Belfast 1972
Violence and Civil Disturbances in Northern Ireland in 1969: Report of Tribunal of Inquiry (Cmd. 566), Belfast 1972
Report of a Committee to Consider, in the Context of Civil Liberties and Human Rights, Measures to Deal with Terrorism in Northern Ireland (Cmnd. 5847), London 1975

Joint Declaration by An Taoiseach, Mr Albert Reynolds TD, and the British Prime Minister, the Rt Hon. John Major MP, 15 December 1993, Dublin 1993
Frameworks for the Future (Cmnd. 2964), London 1995

3. Newspapers and Journals

Alliance (Belfast)
Alliance Bulletin (Belfast)
Belfast Telegraph
Campaign Newsletter (Belfast)
CDU Newsletter (London)
Civil Rights News Service Bulletin (Belfast)
Combat (Belfast)
Daily Mirror (London)
Daily Telegraph (London)
Derry Journal
Éire
Fermanagh Herald (Enniskillen)
Financial Times (London)
Fortnight (Belfast)
Guardian (London)
Irish Independent (Dublin)
Irish News (Belfast)
Irish Press (Dublin)
Irish Times (Dublin)
Loyalist News (Belfast)
News Letter (Belfast)
Northern Whig (Belfast)
Official UDA News (Belfast)
Orange Standard (Belfast)
An Phoblacht (Dublin and Belfast)
Protestant Telegraph (Belfast)
SDLP News (Belfast)
Spotlight Ulster (Belfast)
Sunday News (Belfast)
Sunday Press (Dublin)
Sunday Times (London)
Sunday Tribune (Dublin)
UDA News (Belfast)
Ulster: the Facts
Unionist Review (Belfast)
United Ulsterman (Belfast)
UWC Journal (Belfast)
Weekly Northern Whig (Belfast)
Weekly Westminster (London)

4. BOOKS, PAMPHLETS, AND THESES

Adams, Gerry, *The Politics of Irish Freedom*, Dublin 1986.

Adams, Gerry, *Free Ireland: Towards a Lasting Peace*, Dublin 1995.

Adamson, Ian, *The Identity of Ulster*, Belfast 1982.

Alter, Peter, *Nationalism*, London 1989.

Anderson, Don, *Fourteen May Days: The Inside Story of the Loyalist Strike of 1974*, Dublin 1994.

Arthur, Paul, *The People's Democracy, 1968–73*, Belfast 1974.

Arthur, Paul, *Government and Politics of Northern Ireland*, Harlow 1980.

Arthur, Paul, and Jeffrey, Keith, *Northern Ireland since 1968*, Oxford 1988.

Aughey, Arthur, *Under Siege: Ulster Unionism and the Anglo-Irish Agreement*, Belfast 1989.

Bardon, Jonathan, *A History of Ulster*, Belfast 1992.

Barritt, D., and Carter, Charles, *The Northern Ireland Problem: A Study in Group Relations*, Oxford 1962.

Barton, Brian, *Brookeborough: The Making of a Prime Minister*, Belfast 1988.

Barton, Brian, *Northern Ireland in the Second World War*, Belfast 1995.

Bell, Desmond, *Acts of Union: Youth Culture and Sectarianism in Northern Ireland*, London 1990.

Bell, J. Bowyer, *The Secret Army: The IRA, 1916–1979*, Dublin 1979.

Bell, J. Bowyer, *The Irish Troubles: A Generation of Violence, 1967–1992*, Dublin 1993.

Beresford, David, *Ten Men Dead: The Story of the 1981 Irish Hunger Strike*, London 1987.

Bew, Paul, Darwin, Kenneth, and Gillespie, Gordon, *Passion and Prejudice: Nationalist-Unionist Conflict in Ulster in the 1930s and the Foundation of the Irish Association*, Belfast 1993.

Bew, Paul, Gibbon, Peter, and Patterson, Henry, *Northern Ireland, 1921–1994: Political Forces and Social Classes*, London 1995.

Bew, Paul, and Gillespie, Gordon, *Northern Ireland: A Chronology of the Troubles, 1968–1993*, Dublin 1993.

Bew, Paul, and Gillespie, Gordon, *The Northern Ireland Peace Process, 1993–1996: A Chronology*, London 1996.

Birrell, Derek, and Murie, Alan, *Policy and Government in Northern Ireland: Lessons of Devolution*, Dublin 1980.

Bishop, Patrick, and Mallie, Eamon, *The Provisional IRA*, London 1987.

Bloomfield, Ken, *Stormont in Crisis: A Memoir*, Belfast 1994.

Bowman, John, *De Valera and the Ulster Question, 1917–1973*, London 1982.

Boyce, D. G., 'British Conservative opinion, the Ulster question and the partition of Ireland, 1912–1921', *Irish Historical Studies*, vol. 17 (1970), no. 65.

Boyce, D. G., *Nationalism in Ireland*, London 1982.

Boyce, D. G. (ed.), *The Revolution in Ireland, 1879–1923*, London 1988a.

Boyce, D. G., *The Irish Question and British Politics, 1868–1986*, London 1988b.

Boyce, D. G., *Nineteenth-Century Ireland: The Search for Stability*, Dublin 1991.

Boyce, D. G., Eccleshall, R., and Geoghegan, V. (eds.), *Political Thought in Ireland since the Seventeenth Century*, London 1993.

Boyce, D. G., and Stubbs, John, 'F. S. Oliver, Lord Shelbourne and federalism', *Journal of Imperial and Commonwealth History*, vol. 5 (1976).

Boyd, Andrew, *Brian Faulkner and the Crisis of Ulster Unionism*, Tralee 1972.

Boyle, Kevin, and Hadden, Tom, *Ireland: A Positive Proposal*, Harmondsworth 1985.

Boyle, Kevin, and Hadden, Tom, *Northern Ireland: The Choice*, London 1994.

Brady, Ciarán (ed.), *Worsted in the Game: Losers in Irish History*, Dublin 1989.

Breen, Richard, Devine, Paul, and Dowds, Lizanne (eds.), *Social Attitudes in Northern Ireland: The Fifth Report, 1995–1996*, Belfast 1996.

Brewer, John, with Magee, Kathleen, *Inside the RUC: Routine Policing in a Divided Society*, Oxford 1991.

Brooke, Peter, *Ulster Presbyterianism: The Historical Perspective, 1610–1970*, Dublin 1987.

Bruce, Steve, *God Save Ulster!: The Religion and Politics of Paisleyism*, Oxford 1986.

Bruce, Steve, *The Red Hand: Protestant Paramilitaries in Northern Ireland*, Oxford 1992.

Bruce, Steve, 'Loyalists in Northern Ireland: further thoughts on "pro-state terror"', *Terrorism and Political Violence*, vol. 5 (1993), no. 4, 262–3.

Bruce, Steve, *The Edge of the Union: The Ulster Loyalist Political Vision*, Oxford 1994.

Bryson, Lucy, and McCartney, Clem, *Clashing Symbols?: A Report on the Use of Flags, Anthems and Other National Symbols in Northern Ireland*, Belfast 1994.

Buckland, Patrick, *Irish Unionism, 1: The Anglo-Irish and the New Ireland, 1885–1923: A Documentary History*, Dublin 1973a.

Buckland, Patrick, *Irish Unionism, 2: Ulster Unionism and the Origins of Northern Ireland, 1886–1922*, Dublin 1973b.

Buckland, Patrick, *The Factory of Grievances: Devolved Government in Northern Ireland, 1921–39*, Dublin 1979.

Buckland, Patrick, *James Craig, Lord Craigavon*, Dublin 1980.

Buckland, Patrick, *A History of Northern Ireland*, Dublin 1981.

Budge, Ian, and O'Leary, Cornelius, *Belfast: Approach to Crisis: A Study of Belfast Politics, 1613–1970*, London 1973.

Burton, Frank, *The Politics of Legitimacy: Struggles in a Belfast Community*, London 1978.

Campbell, Brian, McKeown, Laurence, and O'Hagan, Felim (eds.), *Nor Meekly Serve My Time: The H-Block Struggle, 1976–1981*, Belfast 1994.

Campbell, Colm, *Emergency Law in Ireland, 1918–1925*, Oxford 1994.

Campbell, T., *Fifty Years of Ulster, 1890–1940*, Belfast 1941.

Cash, John, *Identity, Ideology and Conflict: The Structuration of Politics in Northern Ireland*, Cambridge 1996.

Cathcart, Rex, *The Most Contrary Region: The BBC in Northern Ireland, 1924–1984*, Belfast 1984.

Clancy, Patrick, Drudy, Sheelagh, Lynch, Kathleen, and O'Dowd, Liam (eds.), *Irish Society: Sociological Perspectives*, Dublin 1995.

Coldrey, B., *Faith and Fatherland: The Christian Brothers and the Development of Irish Nationalism, 1838–1921*, Dublin 1988.

Collins, Peter (ed.), *Nationalism and Unionism: Conflict in Ireland, 1885–1921*, Belfast 1994.

Connolly, Michael, *Politics and Policy Making in Northern Ireland*, London 1990.

Connolly, Michael, and Loughlin, S. (eds.), *Public Policy in Northern Ireland: Adoption or Adaption?*, Belfast and Coleraine 1990.

Coogan, Tim Pat, *The IRA*, London 1980.

Coogan, Tim Pat, *Michael Collins: A Biography*, London 1990.

Coogan, Tim Pat, *De Valera: Long Fellow, Long Shadow*, London 1993.

Coogan, Tim Pat, *The Troubles: Ireland's Ordeal, 1966–1995, and the Search for Peace*, London 1995.

Cormack, Robert, and Osborne, Robert (eds.), *Religion, Education and Employment: Aspects of Equal Opportunity in Northern Ireland*, Belfast 1983.

Cormack, Robert, and Osborne, Robert (eds.), *Discrimination and Public Policy in Northern Ireland*, Oxford 1991.

Cormack, Robert, and Osborne, Robert, *New Perspectives on the Northern Ireland Conflict*, Aldershot 1994.

Coulter, Colin, 'The character of unionism', *Irish Political Studies*, vol. 9 (1994), 1–24.

Crawford, Robert, *Loyal to King Billy: A Portrait of the Ulster Protestants*, Dublin 1987.

Crozier, Maurna (ed.), *Cultural Traditions in Northern Ireland: Varieties of Irishness*, Belfast 1989.

Crozier, Maurna (ed.), *Cultural Traditions in Northern Ireland: Varieties of Britishness*, Belfast 1990.

Crozier, Maurna (ed.), *Cultural Traditions in Northern Ireland: All Europeans Now?*, Belfast 1991.

Cunningham, Michael, *British Government Policy in Northern Ireland, 1969–89: Its Nature and Execution*, Manchester 1991.

Curran, Frank, *Derry: Countdown to Disaster*, Dublin 1986.

Cusack, Jim, and Taylor, Max, 'The resurgence of a terrorist organisation, part 1: the UDA: a case study', *Terrorism and Political Violence*, vol. 5 (1993), no. 3.

Daly, Cathal *The Price of Peace*, Belfast 1991.

Darby, John, *Northern Ireland: the Background to the Conflict*, Belfast 1983.

Darby, John, *Intimidation and the Control of Conflict*, Dublin 1986.

Davis, Richard, *Arthur Griffith and Non-Violent Sinn Féin*, Tralee 1974.

de Baróid, Ciarán, *Ballymurphy and the Irish War*, Dublin 1989.

Devlin, Bernadette, *The Price of My Soul*, London 1969.

Devlin, Paddy, *The Fall of the Northern Ireland Executive*, Belfast 1975.

Devlin, Paddy, *Straight Left: An Autobiography*, Belfast 1993.

Dudley Edwards, Ruth, *Patrick Pearse: The Triumph of Failure*, Dublin 1977.

Duggan, John P., *A History of the Irish Army*, Dublin 1991.

Dunlop, John, *A Precarious Belonging: Presbyterians and the Conflict in Ireland*, Belfast 1995.

Dunn, Séamus (ed.), *Facets of the Conflict in Northern Ireland*, London 1995.

Dunn, Séamus, and Hennessey, Thomas, 'Ireland' in Séamus Dunn and T. Fraser (eds.), *Europe and Ethnicity: World War I and Contemporary Ethnic Conflict*, London 1996.

Dunn, Séamus, and Morgan, Valerie, *Protestant Alienation in Northern Ireland: A Preliminary Survey*, Coleraine 1994.

Dwyer, T. Ryle, *Éamon de Valera*, Dublin 1980.

Eames, Robin, *Chains to be Broken: A Personal Reflection on Northern Ireland and its People*, London 1992.

English, Richard, and Walker, Graham, *Unionism in Modern Ireland: New Perspectives on Politics and Culture*, Dublin 1996.

Ervine, St John, *Craigavon: Ulsterman*, London 1949.

Eversley, David, *Religion and Employment in Northern Ireland*, London 1989.

Farrell, Brian, *The Founding of Dáil Éireann: Parliament and Nation-Building*, Dublin 1971.

Farrell, Michael, *Northern Ireland: The Orange State*, London 1976.

Farrell, Michael, *Arming the Protestants: The Formation of the Ulster Special Constabulary and the Royal Ulster Constabulary, 1920–27*, London 1983.

Faulkner, Brian, *Memoirs of a Statesman*, London 1978.

Fisk, Robert, *In Time of War: Ireland, Ulster and the Price of Neutrality*, London 1985.

FitzGerald, Garret, *All in a Life: An Autobiography*, Dublin 1991.

Flackes, W. D., and Elliott, Sydney, *Northern Ireland: A Political Directory, 1968–88*, Belfast 1989.

Follis, Brian, *A State Under Siege: The Establishment of Northern Ireland, 1920–1925*, Oxford 1995.

Forester, Margery, *Michael Collins: The Lost Leader*, London 1971.

Forum for Peace and Reconciliation, *Paths to a Political Settlement in Ireland: Policy Papers Submitted to the Forum for Peace and Reconciliation*, Belfast 1995.

Foster, R. F., *Modern Ireland, 1600–1972*, London 1988.

Fulton, John, *The Tragedy of Belief: Politics and Religion in Northern Ireland*, Oxford 1991.

Gailey, Andrew (ed.), *Crying in the Wilderness: Jack Sayers, a Liberal Editor in Ulster, 1939–69*, Belfast 1995.

Gallagher, Eric, and Worrall, Stanley, *Christians in Ulster, 1968–1980*, Oxford 1982.

Gallagher, Frank, *The Indivisible Island*, London 1957.

Gallagher, Tom, and O'Connell, James, *Contemporary Irish Studies*, Manchester 1983.

Galliher, John, and de Gregory, Jerry, *Violence in Northern Ireland: Understanding Protestant Perspectives*, Dublin 1985.

Garvin, Tom, *Nationalist Revolutionaries in Ireland, 1858–1928*, Oxford 1987.

Garvin, Tom, *The Evolution of Irish Nationalist Politics*, Dublin 1981.

Gearty, Conor, *Terror*, London 1991.

Gibbon, Peter, *The Origins of Ulster Unionism: The Formation of Popular Protestant Politics and Ideology in Nineteenth-Century Ireland*, Manchester 1975.

Gordon, David, *The O'Neill Years: Unionist Politics, 1963–1969*, Belfast 1989.

Guelke, Adrian, *Northern Ireland: The International Perspective*, Dublin 1988.

Guelke, Adrian (ed.), *New Perspectives on the Northern Ireland Conflict*, Aldershot 1994.

Gwynn, Dennis, *The Life of John Redmond*, London 1932.

Gwynn, Stephen, *The Last Years of John Redmond*, London 1919.

Hadfield, Brigid, *The Constitution of Northern Ireland*, Belfast 1989.

Hadfield, Brigid, *Northern Ireland: Politics and the Constitution*, Milton Keynes 1992.

Hamill, Desmond, *Pig in the Middle: The Army in Northern Ireland, 1969–1985*, London 1985.

Hand, Geoffrey, *Report of the Irish Boundary Commission, 1925*, Dublin 1969.

Harbinson, John, *The Ulster Unionist Party, 1882–1973: Its Development and Organisation*, Belfast 1973.

Harkness, David, *Northern Ireland since 1920*, Dublin 1983.

Harris, Mary, *The Catholic Church and the Foundation of the Northern Irish State*, Cork 1993.

Harris, Rosemary, *Prejudice and Tolerance in Ulster: A Study of Neighbours and Strangers in a Border Community*, Manchester 1972.

Hempton, David, and Hill, Myrtle, *Evangelical Protestantism in Ulster Society, 1740–1890*, London 1992.

Hennessey, Thomas, 'Ulster unionist territorial and national identities, 1886–1893: province, island, kingdom and empire', *Irish Political Studies*, vol. 8 (1993).

Heskin, Ken, *Northern Ireland: A Psychological Analysis*, Dublin 1980.

Hickey, John, *Religion and the Northern Ireland Problem*, Dublin 1984.

Hogan, Gerald, and Walker, Clive, *Political Violence and the Law in Ireland*, Manchester 1989.

Holland, Jack, and McDonald, Henry, *INLA: Deadly Divisions*, Dublin 1994.

Holt, E., *Protest in Arms: The Irish Troubles, 1916–1923*, London 1963.

Howell, David, *A Lost Left: Three Studies in Socialism and Nationalism*, Manchester 1986.

Hume, John, *Personal Views: Politics, Peace and Reconciliation in Ireland*, Dublin 1996.

Hutchinson, John, *The Dynamics of Cultural Nationalism: the Gaelic Revival and the Creation of the Irish Nation State*, London 1987.

Hyde, H. Montgomery, *Carson: The Life of Lord Carson of Duncairn*, London 1953.

Jackson, Alvin, *The Ulster Party: Irish Unionists in the House of Commons, 1884–1911*, Oxford 1989.

Jackson, Alvin, 'Unionist myths, 1912–1985', *Past and Present*, no. 136 (Aug. 1992), 164–85.

Jackson, Alvin, *Sir Edward Carson*, Dundalk 1993.

Jalland, Patricia, *The Liberals and Ireland: The Ulster Question in British Politics to 1914*, Brighton 1980.

Kee, Robert, *The Green Flag*, London 1972.

Keena, Colm, *A Biography of Gerry Adams*, Dublin 1990.

Kelly, Henry, *How Stormont Fell*, Dublin 1972.

Kendle, John, *Ireland and the Federal Solution: The Debate over the United Kingdom Constitution. 1870–1921*, Kingston 1989.

Kennedy, Dennis, *The Widening Gulf: Northern Attitudes to the Independent Irish State, 1919–1949*, Belfast 1988.

Kennedy-Pipe, Caroline, *The Origins of the Present Troubles in Northern Ireland*, Harlow 1997.

Keogh, Dermot, *Twentieth-Century Ireland: Nation and State*, Dublin 1994.

Laffan, Michael, *The Partition of Ireland, 1911–1925*, Dundalk 1983.

Lawlor, Sheila, *Britain and Ireland, 1914–23*, Dublin 1983.

Lawrence, R., *The Government of Northern Ireland*, Oxford 1965.

Lee, J. J., *Ireland, 1912–1985: Politics and Society*, Cambridge 1989.

Longford, Lord, and McHardy, Anne, *Ulster*, London 1981.

Longley, Edna, 'The Rising, the Somme and Irish memory' in Máirín Ní Dhonnchadha and Theo Dorgan (eds.), *Revising the Rising*, Derry 1991.

Loughlin, James, *Gladstone, Home Rule and the Ulster Question, 1882–93*, Dublin 1986.

Loughlin, James, *Ulster Unionism and British National Identity since 1885*, London 1995.

Lyons, F. S. L., *Ireland since the Famine*, London 1973.

McAllister, Ian, *The Northern Ireland Social Democratic and Labour Party: Political Opposition in a Divided Society*, London 1977.

McAuley, James, *The Politics of Identity: A Loyalist Community in Belfast*, Aldershot 1994.

McCabe, Ian, *A Diplomatic History of Ireland, 1948–49: The Republic, the Commonwealth and NATO*, Dublin 1991.

McCann, Éamonn, *War in an Irish Town*, London 1980.

McDowell, R. B., *The Irish Convention, 1917–18*, London 1970.

McElroy, Gerald, *The Catholic Church and the Northern Ireland Crisis, 1969–86*, Dublin 1991.

McGarry, John, and O'Leary, Brendan (eds.), *The Future of Northern Ireland*, Oxford 1990.

McGarry, John, and O'Leary, Brendan, *Explaining Northern Ireland: Broken Images*, Oxford 1995.

McGuire, Maria, *To Take Arms: A Year in the Provisional IRA*, London 1973.

McIntyre, Anthony, 'Modern Irish republicanism: the product of British state strategies', *Irish Political Studies*, vol. 10 (1995).

McKeown, Ciarán, *The Passion of Peace*, Belfast 1984.

McKeown, Michael, *The Greening of a Nationalist*, Lurgan 1986.

McMahon, Deirdre, *Republicans and Imperialists: Anglo-Irish Relations in the 1930s*, Yale 1984.

McNeill, Ronald, *Ulster's Stand for Union*, London 1922.

Mac Stiofáin, Seán, *Revolutionary in Ireland*, Farnborough 1974.

MacVeigh, Jeremiah, *Home Rule in a Nutshell*, London 1911.

Mallie, Eamon, and McKittrick, David, *The Fight for Peace: The Secret Story Behind the Irish Peace Process*, London 1996.

Mansergh, Nicholas, *The Unresolved Question: The Anglo-Irish Settlement and its Undoing, 1912–72*, Yale 1991.

Marjoribanks, Edward, and Colvin, Ian, *The Life of Lord Carson*, London 1932–34.

Miller, David, *Queen's Rebels: Ulster Loyalism in Historical Perspective*, Dublin 1978.

Moloney, Ed, and Pollak, Andy, *Paisley*, Dublin 1986.

Moxon-Browne, Edward, *Nation, Class and Creed in Northern Ireland*, Aldershot 1983.

Murphy, Brian, *Patrick Pearse and the Lost Republican Ideal*, Dublin 1991.

Murphy, Richard, 'Faction in the Conservative Party and the Home Rule Crisis, 1912–14', *History*, vol. 71 (1986) no. 232.

Murray, Dominic, *Worlds Apart: Segregated Schools in Northern Ireland*, Belfast 1985.

Murray, Raymond, *The SAS in Ireland*, Dublin 1990.

Nelson, Sarah, *Ulster's Uncertain Defenders: Loyalists and the Northern Ireland Conflict*, Belfast 1984.

O'Brien, Brendan, *The Long War: The IRA and Sinn Féin, 1985 to Today*, Dublin 1993.

O'Brien, William, *The Irish Revolution and How It Came About*, Dublin 1923.

O'Connor, Fionnuala, *In Search of a State: Catholics in Northern Ireland*, Belfast 1993.

O'Dowd, Liam, Rolston, Bill, and Tomlinson, Mike, *Northern Ireland: Between Civil Rights and Civil War*, London 1980.

O'Halloran, Clare, *Partition and the Limits of Irish Nationalism*, Dublin 1987.

O'Leary, Brendan, and McGarry, John, *The Politics of Antagonism: Understanding Northern Ireland*, London 1993.

O'Malley, Pádraig, *The Uncivil Wars: Ireland Today*, Belfast 1983.

O'Malley, Pádraig, *Biting at the Grave: The Irish Hunger Strikes and the Politics of Despair*, Belfast 1990a.

O'Malley, Pádraig, *Northern Ireland: Questions of Nuance*, 1990b.

O'Neill, Terence, *Ulster at the Crossroads*, London 1969.

O'Neill, Terence, *The Autobiography of Terence O'Neill, Prime Minister of Northern Ireland, 1963–1969*, London 1972.

Orr, Philip, *The Road to the Somme: Men of the Ulster Division Tell Their Story*, Belfast 1987.

Osmond, John, *The Divided Kingdom*, London 1988.

Patterson, Henry, *Class Conflict and Sectarianism: The Protestant Working Class and the Belfast Labour Movement, 1868–1920*, Belfast 1980.

Patterson, Henry, *The Politics of Illusion: Republicanism and Socialism in Modern Ireland*, London 1989.

Phoenix, Eamon, *Northern Nationalism: Nationalist Politics, Partition and the Catholic Minority in Northern Ireland, 1890–1940*, Belfast 1994b.

Phoenix, Eamon, 'Northern nationalists, Ulster unionists, and the development of partition, 1900–1921' in Collins, *Nationalism and Unionism*, 1994b, 109–10.

Pollak, Andy (ed.), *A Citizens' Inquiry: The Opsahl Report on Northern Ireland*, Dublin 1993.

Purdy, Ann Molyneaux: *The Long View*, Belfast 1989.

Purdy, Bob, *Politics in the Streets: The Origins of the Civil Rights Movement in Northern Ireland*, Belfast 1990.

Rea, Desmond (ed.), *Political Co-operation in Divided Societies: A Series of Papers Relevant to the Conflict in Northern Ireland*, Dublin 1982.

Roche, Patrick, and Barton, Brian (eds.), *The Northern Ireland Question: Myth and Reality*, Aldershot 1991.

Rolston, Bill (ed.), *The Media and Northern Ireland: Covering the Troubles*, London 1991.

Rose, Richard, *Governing Without Consensus: An Irish Perspective*, London 1971.

Rowan, Brian, *Behind the Lines: The Story of the IRA and Loyalist Ceasefires*, Belfast 1995.

Rowthorn, Bob, and Wayne, Naomi, *Northern Ireland: The Political Economy of Conflict*, Cambridge 1988.

Ruane, Joseph, and Todd, Jennifer, *The Dynamics of Conflict in Northern Ireland: Power, Conflict and Emancipation*, Cambridge 1996.

Ryder, Chris, *The RUC: A Force Under Fire*, London 1989.

Ryder, Chris, *The Ulster Defence Regiment: An Instrument of Peace?*, London 1991.

Shea, Patrick, *Voices and the Sound of Drums: An Irish Autobiography*, Belfast 1981.

Sinn Féin, *Colonial Home Rule: What It Means*, Dublin 1917.

Smith, Alan, and Robinson, Alan, *Education for Mutual Understanding: The Initial Statutory Years*, Coleraine 1996.

Smith, David, and Chambers, Gerald, *Inequality in Northern Ireland*, Oxford 1991.

Smith, M., *Fighting for Ireland: The Military Strategy of the Irish Republican Movement*, London 1995.

Smyth, Clifford, *Ian Paisley: Voice of Protestant Ulster*, Edinburgh 1987.

Stewart, A. T. Q., *The Ulster Crisis: Resistance to Home Rule, 1912–14*, London 1967.

Stewart, A. T. Q., *The Narrow Ground: The Roots of Conflict in Ulster*, London 1977.

Stewart, A. T. Q., *Edward Carson*, Dublin 1981.

Stringer, Peter, and Robinson, Gillian (eds.), *Social Attitudes in Northern Ireland*, Belfast 1991.

Stringer, Peter, and Robinson, Gillian (eds.), *Social Attitudes in Northern Ireland: The Second Report*, Belfast 1992.

Stringer, Peter, and Robinson, Gillian (eds.), *Social Attitudes in Northern Ireland: The Third Report, 1992–1993*, Belfast 1993.

Stubbs, John, 'Unionists and Ireland, 1914–1918', *Historical Journal*, vol. 4 (1990), no. 33.

Sunday Times Insight Team, *Ulster*, London 1972.

Teague, Paul (ed.), *Beyond the Rhe*   ¯ ˙ ics, the Economy and Social Policy in Northern Ireland, London 1987.

Thatcher, Margaret, *The Downing S*   ' ɔndon 1993.

Todd, Jennifer, 'Two traditions ir   ɔlitical culture', *Irish Political Studies*, vol. 5 (1990).

Tools, Kevin, *Rebel Hearts: Journeys ι*   ιs Soul, London 1995.

Townshend, Charles (ed.), *Consensus*   , Oxford 1983a.

Townshend, Charles, *Political Violen*   ιreland: Government and Resistance since 1848, Oxford 1983b.

Travers, Pauric, *Settlements and Divisions: Ireland, 1870–1922*, Dublin 1988.

Urban, Mark, *Big Boys' Rules: The Secret Struggle Against the IRA*, London 1992.

Walker, B., *Ulster Politics: the Formative Years, 1868–86*, Belfast 1989.

Walker, Graham, *The Politics of Frustration: Harry Midgley and the Failure of Labour in Northern Ireland*, Manchester 1985.

Walsh, Pat, *From Civil Rights to National War: Northern Ireland Catholic Politics, 1964–74*, Belfast 1989.

Walsh, Pat, *Irish Republicanism and Socialism: The Politics of the Movement, 1905 to 1994*, Belfast 1994.

Ward, Margaret, *Unmanageable Revolutionaries: Women and Irish Nationalism*, London 1983.

White, Barry, *John Hume: Statesman of the Troubles*, Belfast 1984.

Whyte, J., *Church and State in Modern Ireland, 1923–1979*, Dublin 1979.

Whyte, J., 'How much discrimination was there under the unionist regime, 1921–1968?' in Tom Gallagher and James O'Connell (eds.), *Contemporary Irish Studies*, Manchester 1983.

Whyte, John, *Interpreting Northern Ireland*, Oxford 1990.

Wichert, Sabine, *Northern Ireland since 1945*, Harlow 1991.

Wilson, Tom, *Ulster: Conflict and Consent*, Oxford 1989.

Wright, Frank, *Northern Ireland: A Comparative Analysis*, Dublin 1987.

Index